MILTON STUDIES

VIII

MILTON
STUDIES
VIII *Edited by*
James D. Simmonds

UNIVERSITY OF PITTSBURGH PRESS

MILTON STUDIES

is published annually by the University of Pittsburgh Press as a forum for
Milton scholarship and criticism. Articles submitted for publication may be
biographical; they may interpret some aspect of Milton's writings; or they
may define literary, intellectual, or historical contexts—by studying the work
of his contemporaries, the traditions which affected his thought and art, contemporary political and religious movements, his influence on other writers,
or the history of critical response to his work.

Manuscripts should be upwards of 3,000 words in length and should
conform to the *MLA Style Sheet*. Manuscripts and editorial correspondence
should be addressed to James D. Simmonds, Department of English, University
of Pittsburgh, Pittsburgh, Pa. 15260.

Milton Studies does not review books.

Within the United States, *Milton Studies* may be ordered from the University of Pittsburgh Press, Pittsburgh, Pa. 15260.

Overseas orders should be addressed to Feffer and Simons, Inc., 100 Park
Avenue, New York, N.Y. 10017, U.S.A.

Library of Congress Catalog Card Number 69-12335

ISBN 0-8229-3174-5 (Volume I) (out of print)

ISBN 0-8229-3194-x (Volume II)

ISBN 0-8229-3218-0 (Volume III)

ISBN 0-8229-3244-x (Volume IV)

ISBN 0-8229-3272-5 (Volume V)

ISBN 0-8229-3288-1 (Volume VI)

ISBN 0-8229-3305-5 (Volume VII)

ISBN 0-8229-3310-1 (Volume VIII)

US ISSN 0076-8820

Feffer & Simons, Inc., London

Manufactured in the United States of America

CONTENTS

MILTON STUDIES
VIII

MILTON AND THE ART OF LANDSCAPE

G. Stanley Koehler

Milton's description of Eden, which is on one level the English countryside, on another the ideal place of legend, is on still a third level an elaborately developed landscape in the informal style of the seventeenth century, including effects which the eighteenth century would label "picturesque." The ways in which Milton observed the theories of landscape design are seen in the general arrangement of the grounds; in the particulars of wall and prospect; in the handling of foliage and water; and in the consistent emphasis on mass and shade that is characteristic both of the baroque taste of the seventeenth century and of the picturesque taste of the eighteenth century, which Milton's example helped to determine. Still another dimension of the landscape experience, in Milton as in the Renaissance garden, is seen in the introduction of elements for moral and psychological, as opposed to purely aesthetic reasons. Milton's own concern to keep the garden in scale with its human occupants results in a consistent focus on the nuptial bower as the physical, narrative, and thematic center of the action. On a larger plane, the Garden of Eden is presented as the center of the cosmos itself. Through description that dwells on shade and moisture, trees and streams, Milton presents it as the ideal mean between those extremes of negation and fulfillment, destruction and perfection for which hell and heaven are the emblems.

MILTON'S DESCRIPTION of Eden, drawing as it does on so rich a tradition of classical, biblical, and medieval example, is the most fully developed in literature of the *locus amoenus*, or ideal place. It is our purpose to look closely at that description as a reflection of seventeenth- and eighteenth-century style in landscape, and at its moral and psychological implications as conveyed through the medium of landscape and garden. It will appear, in this discussion, that Milton's account of paradise played its part in the development of landscape

3

tradition, anticipating and no doubt helping in some degree to form that style of natural beauty which the eighteenth century would label the "picturesque."

In its simplest form, as recent criticism has been more and more aware, the Garden of Eden is an account of the English countryside as Milton knew it, with lawns and downs, grazing sheep, and ornamental trees, the scenery of Horton, Cambridge, and Chalfont St. Giles. At the other end of the scale is the elaborate artifact which drew on itself so much unfavorable attention from the criticism of two decades ago, a landscape raised by every means of art to the perfection thought worthy of God's handiwork and the epic genre, a heaven on earth in the most literal terms, with jeweled rivers and gilded fruit. Between these realms of reality and hyperbole is that middle region of improved nature to which Milton devoted his best efforts. On this level, Milton would seem to have furnished as good a model as Hogarth for the kind of effects so prized by garden authorities like Sir Uvedale Price or Humphry Repton. Both found in Milton's poetry their favorite instances of the picturesque, a style which in Price's three-volume treatise takes its place between classic beauty and the more romantic sublime, with an affective sphere somewhere between the calm serenity of the one and the restless energies of the other.[1] It is in this vein that Milton developed the descriptions of his maturer verse, perhaps under the influence of Italian scenery and landscape painting,[2] but partly too, no doubt, from that genuine feeling for darker nature which we associate with the next century. Given the scale on which Milton worked, the results often approach the sublime.

As for the moral and psychological element, it must be noted that in the seventeenth century the pastoral environment was not merely a refuge from city life, a source of agreeable moods or aesthetic pleasures. The effect of locale on an age that still had the emblematic habit of mind and could see any object as a symbol went beyond such things into questions we must regard as moral and philosophical, whether the setting at hand was a garden or a church. John Evelyn notes how gardens "influence the soule and spirits of man, and prepare them for discourse with good angells": "caves, grotts, mounts . . . do contribute to contemplative and philosophicall enthusiasme; how *elysium, antrum, nemus* . . . &c signifie all of them *rem sacrum et divinum.*"[3] It is not surprising, then, that the art of landscape should include a concern for moral matters. Milton's rejection of classical form in garden design may be quite as significant in its way as his opinions of monarchy and episcopacy are in theirs. In each instance the priority of nature and the individual is asserted over conventions imposed by art or society. The shaping of the garden, with Adam as the presiding spirit and Eve and the bower at its center, can thus tell us as much of Milton's attitude toward man as it does of his feeling for nature. Before looking at the "philosophical" aspects of Milton's garden, however, we will deal with the elements of terrain, water, and vegetation that compose its physical setting.

I

"Love of prospect seems . . . an inherent passion of the human mind," observes Humphry Repton.[4] Satisfying that passion is a major end of landscape design. The vogue of prospect in the landscape painting of the Commonwealth period itself is expressed by Henry Peacham in terms that again make Milton's description the ideal: "The most proper way is to make the nearest Hill highest and so to make the rest that are further off, to shoot away under that, that the Landskip may appear to be taken from the top of an Hill."[5] This view from an eminence, which Repton calls one of the most pleasing circumstances of natural landscape, is the kind of view that Adam and Eve are somehow afforded, despite the wall that rises above the surrounding treetops. Satan himself has such a view, rather more realistically, from his perch on the Tree of Life: "Beneath him with new wonder now he views / To all delight of human sense expos'd / In narrow room Nature's whole wealth" (*PL* IV, 205–07).[6] As "prospect" is part of our initial experience of Eden, so in the closing books we are given that ultimate panorama in which Adam surveys the regions of earth and all the events therein from a mount within the garden, a vista that brings all of human experience into range. Such views from an elevated viewpoint are more difficult to achieve in painting than in literature, as Price points out, although it is to painting that he would direct the gardener's eye for the secrets of picturesque effect. Milton's way of handling the process in poetry suggests some of the methods by which the longer view can be made to work on canvas, especially the use of a low sun at morning or evening to soften the light in which objects are seen, and increase the shadow to give a sense of repose and mystery. We should perhaps expect to have our first glimpse of Eden by morning light, but the narrative has it otherwise. Since Satan's address to the sun from Mt. Niphates comes just at noon and his ascent of the hill (compared later to Mount Amara, "A whole day's journey high") must take till late afternoon, what we see from Satan's vantage point in the Tree of Life is a landscape in relatively low light. The description sums up a completed day with its reference to morning sun, noontide bowers and supper fruits. The animals are "fill'd with pasture . . . Or Bedward ruminating," the sun declines, "the Stars that usher Evening" rise. The effect of pastoral scenery viewed in such a fading light is not without its implications. Milton has used the technique of his contemporary, Claude Lorraine, to give his landscape distance and repose with a touch of melancholy, not only here but in earlier poems like *Il Penseroso, Comus*, and *Lycidas*, where again a setting sun fixes both the moment and the mood.

The provision of a view is but one advantage of an elevated site in the eyes of the landscape architect. Besides improving the air and lending interest to the approach, such a situation enhances the seclusion proper to the pastoral retreat. For Eden, the journey of Satan through chaos and the created universe and finally up the "steep and savage Hill" provides the inaccessibility essential to our idea of a lost paradise:

> So on he fares, and to the border comes
> Of *Eden*, where delicious Paradise,
> Now nearer, Crowns with her enclosure green,
> As with a rural mound the champaign head
> Of a steep wilderness, whose hairy sides
> With thicket overgrown, grotesque and wild,
> Access deni'd.   (IV, 131–37)

We may note here a difficulty inherent in landscape design which Milton could not wholly evade in his poetry. It was the ideal of such design, as Repton points out, to combine antithetical effects of liberty and seclusion. While the former requires a sense of openness, with the kind of view we have seen, the latter implies some means of enclosure, by wall or foliage or both. These conflicting ends are sometimes resolved by means of topographical elevations and a lowering of the wall in appropriate places. Bacon, for example, in "Of Gardens," provides "at the end of both the side grounds . . . a mount of some pretty height, leaving the wall of the enclosure breast-high, to look abroad into the fields."[7] It is a compromise that does not suit an ideal garden already threatened by a hostile force. Milton leaves his wall intact but implies at the same time some surmounting elevation therein, crowning "As with a rural mound" the plateau of paradise (IV, 134–35). By this means, and the grander height from which Adam sees the panorama of the final books, Milton may have satisfied the requirements of prospect without loss of privacy. Yet a conflict remains between that sense of openness which Repton mentions and the marking of boundaries which convention required. The anomaly appears at the start when Satan, mounting the hill, notes before him "the verdurous wall of Paradise" which, as Milton oddly has it, "to our general Sire gave prospect large / Into his nether Empire neighboring round." Since it is hard to see how a wall could "give" a prospect, we may wonder what sort of enclosure is meant. "Verdurous wall" implies a combination of rock and trees, a cliff masked by foliage, perhaps. Such a wall would have one face, barring approach from outside without blocking the view from within, and preserving the air of liberty which is to Repton "the true portal of happiness": "That the boundary fence of a place should be concealed . . . is among the few general principles admitted in modern gardening. The mind feels a certain disgust under a sense of confinement in any situation, however beautiful."[8] This kind of invisible fence or "ha-ha" was a feature of country places intended to keep animals out, without interrupting a sweep of lawn. Something like this, on the grander scale of the epic, is suggested by the cliff face of mountain fastnesses like Mount Amara, which was one model for paradise. Though its image affects the description at this point and makes a convenient resolution to the problem, it is not really what Milton had in mind. Nor is it in all probability a simple hedge of foliage, though this has been suggested.[9] The reference to trees inside the garden as being higher than the wall makes sense only for a conventional sort of enclosure. The imagery of a sheepfold over which Satan leaps to light "sheer within" again suggests an ordinary wall, as may the word "paradise" itself. Though he is more concerned at this point with security, Milton's persistence in emphasizing the view in spite of the wall demonstrates his regard for at least the principles of landscape, however conflicting they may sometimes be. Having allowed Satan to overleap the wall for the sake of the plot, Milton resumes the charade of Eden's impregnability with an account of the eastern gate, three or four hundred lines later.

Here at last is the official approach to Eden, "winding with one ascent / Accessible from Earth." Milton's one chance to supply the kind of architectural detail upon which landscape in the grand manner must focus comes in his description of that gate: "a Rock / Of Alablaster, pil'd up to the Clouds, / Conspicuous far" (IV, 543–45). Adam's parting glimpse of this same gate in the moment of the expulsion represents the final image of the poem. There, as here in Book IV, the scene is completed with a *tableau vivant* of the angelic guard, restoring some sense of security to the lost garden.

The English criterion of landscape as improved nature, the principle of the *ferme ornée*, has its perfect illustration in the interior landscape of Eden. Milton's description of it is extremely general, leaving no single scene in our memory, and contingent on no particular or unusual feature: "A prospect of mere extent, if that extent be very great, has, without any striking features, a powerful effect on the mind. If to extent you add a richly wooded and cultivated country, with a varied boundary of hills and mountains; and to that again effects of water . . . it is enchantment."[10] It is just this sort of enchantment that Milton so successfully evokes:

> Thus was this place,
> A happy rural seat of various view:
> Groves whose rich Trees wept odorous Gums and Balm,
> Others whose fruit burnisht with Golden Rind
> Hung amiable, *Hesperian* Fables true,
> If true, here only, and of delicious taste. (IV, 246–51)

The heavier touches of art and myth in those rich trees, with their Hesperian fruit, frame a middle distance of almost pure English countryside.

> Betwixt them Lawns, or level Downs, and Flocks
> Grazing the tender herb, were interpos'd,
> Or palmy hillock, or the flow'ry lap
> Of some irriguous Valley spread her store. (IV, 252–55)

We note here now Milton resolved the issue of the boundaries. The plurals (lawns, downs, flocks), the alternatives ("or palmy hillock"), and the distancing generalization ("some irriguous Valley") suggest a region so broad that any notion of enclosure is forgotten.

Before leaving these preliminary matters, there is one other connection to be observed between the effects at which Milton is aiming and those broader principles of the landscape art which Repton catalogues, under sixteen headings, as "sources of pleasure in landscape gardening." Some of these, like "simplicity," "contrast," and "intricacy," are obvious or can be dealt with below as aspects of the picturesque. What Repton calls "congruity" and "appropriation," however, are so uniquely applicable to Eden as to bear special notice. "Congruity" represents for Repton our sense of a whole "adapted to the character, situation, and circumstances of the place and its possessor." It is this sense more than any other that Eden, as Milton describes the beauty and innocence of the garden and its occupants, is meant to give. Not only Eden, however, but the world itself is Adam's domain, and here the question of "appropriation" or extent of property enters; that is, "pleasure derived from the unity and continuity of unmixed property."[11] "Appropriation" thus returns us to the question of prospect and boundary: "As far as vision is concerned, taste, in Shenstone's language, 'appropriates all we see.' But (without any reference to actual property) a narrow line of partition is of itself a disagreeable object; and wherever it obtrudes upon the sight in such a form, necessarily destroys harmony of landscape."[12] We can appreciate in these terms Milton's embarrassment with the wall and the reason for that sleight of hand by which he disguises, confuses, and finally dismisses it to concentrate upon the expanded interior of Eden, which so successfully preserves the interests of "appropriation" and "congruity." The effect is typical of that "English" style in which the transition between garden and park is hidden, as it is between the park and that still more natural "wilderness" beyond it. The virtual disappearance of the wall in Eden has additional importance, lessening in some measure the force of the expulsion. As Michael suggests to Adam, concerned to find God in the world outside, "Thou know'st . . . all the Earth [is His] / Not this Rock only" (XI, 335–36). In the words of Horace Walpole, once man leaped that wall, he saw all nature as a garden. Having seen the importance of site and prospect to Milton's Eden, we may come to the details of that landscape, seen in relation to Renaissance design.

II

The conventions of formal landscape divide the terrain into three areas. First, at the center is a formal garden of walks and flower beds. Beyond this lies a park or open area of grass and trees usually called the English garden. Last is that wilder area just referred to where nature could be left to its own devices. Milton begins in effect with something like the central garden, treated in a way suitable to the subject, with an extreme of art if not of formality:

> to tell how, if Art could tell,
> How from that Sapphire Fount the crisped Brooks,
> Rolling on Orient Pearl and sands of Gold,
> With mazy error under pendant shades
> Ran Nectar, visiting each plant, and fed
> Flow'rs worthy of Paradise. (IV, 236-41)

Though the richness of the scene links it with the central, formal portion of the garden, the effect of artifice in it comes rather from the materials than from the form. In the following lines Milton dismisses the continental parterre, with its "Beds and curious Knots," the "nice art" of Le Nôtre, for the more generous art of God, which "Nature boon" pours forth

> profuse on Hill and Dale and Plain,
> Both where the morning Sun first warmly smote
> The open field, and where the unpierc't shade
> Imbrown'd the noontide Bow'rs. (IV, 243-46)

The second part of Milton's description gives the park and field of conventional design. In the lawns and level downs earlier noted we see again the familiar countryside of *L'Allegro*, so artless as to fall under the complaint of Sir William Chambers against English gardens which in his opinion "differ little from common fields": "The scenery of a Garden should differ as much from common nature as an heroic poem doth from a prose relation."[13] In the third stage which follows, however, nature or the art that conceals art does all that the eighteenth century could ask in the way of the picturesque. Description that begins like Spenser or Botticelli, with sapphire fount, crisped brooks, Orient pearl and sands of gold, goes off in quite a different direction. From the regularity, smoothness, and limited scale of the classically beautiful it moves toward the variety and intricacy to which Price attributes the pleasures of the picturesque. In this kind of effect, which Wölfflin calls "painterly," "a partial and uncertain concealment excites and nourishes curiosity."[14] Edges overlap or are hidden by foliage, deep shade, or running water. Such things can be seen in the opening description of the stream, with its "mazy error under pendant shades," but the climax of "playful wildness" comes in the account of the "other side" of Eden, with its caves, vines, steep slopes, and falling streams:

Another side, umbrageous Grots and Caves
Of cool recess, o'er which the mantling Vine
Lays forth her purple Grape, and gently creeps
Luxuriant.   (IV, 257-60)

The description shows the characteristic tendency of Milton's style toward mass, shade, and closure:

The Renaissance garden was light and open: according to Alberti the villa was to be surrounded by flowering meadows and a sunny open landscape. . . . In the Roman baroque garden there were few such open spaces. Dense masses of dark foliage replaced the sunny grove and the bright meadow . . . and bright colors changed to dark masses.[15]

It is such a change that we see in Milton, evident in his tendency to favor trees over flowers in natural description. The use of flowers as an aspect of landscape is a feature of the early poetry, as seen in the "meadows trim with daisies pied" of *L'Allegro*, the "bells and flowerets of a Thousand hues" in *Lycidas*. By the time he describes the creation in *Paradise Lost*, Milton no longer lists flowers as he does fish, birds, animals, insects, or trees. Despite his fondness for them, he does not seem to find flowers effective as part of a larger scene. Even the flower passage of *Lycidas* is not presented as part of the setting. Though we are reminded of the valleys and green turf in which they grew, empurpling the ground, what we see is cut flowers adorning a bier. Milton may share the feeling of Sir Uvedale Price that flowers do not sufficiently arouse the "curiosity" which is the object of the picturesque, and which comes from effects of concealment rather than decoration.

In such a preference for trees over flowers, the baroque effect is as important as the picturesque. In baroque garden architecture, as Wölfflin points out, "Everything had to be as large as possible . . . *'e sopra tutto non pecchino di stretto o angusto.'*"[16] The flower beds with their color and delicacy were accordingly banished from the park to be indulged in some *giardino segreto* at the center or off in a corner of the grounds. Thus, when it comes to landscape proper, Milton is content, as we have seen, with the briefest mention: flowers "worthy of paradise." The only extensive description is that of the bower: "Iris all hues, Roses, Jessamin" and so on (IV, 698). An alternative to the secret garden itself may be found in that shady bank to which the couple go after the Fall, to take their sensual pleasures: "Flow'rs were the Couch . . . Earth's freshest softest lap" (IX, 1039-

41). The later setting prolongs for a moment an air of innocence. Yet, as Adam is quick to see, the woods are a more fitting background for his guilt and introspection:

> O might I here
> In solitude live savage, in some glade
> Obscur'd, where highest Woods impenetrable
> To Star or Sun-light, spread thir umbrage broad,
> And brown as Evening   (IX, 1084–88)

What has been said of flowers is true of lawns. Indeed, the two are included in the objection against small effects in the baroque garden, "*lavori minuti di erbette e fiori.*"[17] Though lawns may be "insipid" in the paintings from which Price takes so many of his ideas, they work better in literary or real landscapes, as in the soft green *erbetta* of the Continental dream vision or the broad greensward of an English garden. Noting that "nothing is more pleasant to the eye than green grass kept finely shorn," Bacon assigns at least four acres to the "green" in his garden paradigm.[18] It is actually one function of such nibbling flocks as those in *L'Allegro* and *Lycidas* to provide those stretches of well-cropped grass to which the English are so partial, even in those areas that lie beyond the dressed portion of the grounds. As elements in a picturesque scene, however, such things need help from other quarters, and it is here that Price's emphasis on the heavier vegetation of trees is important. "Trees scattered on lawns lend interest . . . groves and dense coverts should clothe the knolls . . . dingles and dells may be made mysteriously intricate by filling them with dark woods and tangled thickets."[19] The last phrase, a quotation from Milton's Nativity ode, suggests again where Price looked for picturesque effects deriving from heavy foliage. For Milton as for Price, this means not only trees but an undergrowth of "shrubs and tangling bushes" like that which Satan encounters on his approach. Even the green expanses of field in Eden are given in a frame of trees: "Betwixt them [the groves] Lawns, or level Downs, and Flocks / Grazing the tender herb, were interpos'd" (IV, 252–53).

Though we have seen these effects anticipated in the Nativity ode, there is a general tendency in the earlier verse toward description of the sort one associates not with baroque but with Renaissance style, involving as it does a taste for color, detail, and order as opposed to light, shade, and mass. One sees the tendency in *L'Allegro* and

Il Penseroso, where objects in the middle distance are shown singly, in profile, and with sharp definition: hedgerow elms, a cottage chimney, two aged oaks, towers, and battlements. Though the imagery shifts to sound in *Il Penseroso*, as being possibly more suggestive to the imagination or more congenial to thought, there is still this same sharpness and singularity in the auditory images: the song of Philomel, the call of the bellman, and the sounds of cricket, bee, leaves, or rain. The most effective visual images, on the other hand, are those given in darkness: the moon through fleecy clouds, the midnight lamp and lonely tower. In accordance with this tendency, impressions of trees and shade are more limited and orderly than they are in Eden. It is not into dense woods that the poet retires but to "arched walks of twilight groves," or beneath some single monumental oak. In both poems, that is to say, there is a bent toward particularity and pattern. And yet, similar as they may be in this regard, there is also a difference between the two poems that points toward *Paradise Lost*. The visual images of *L'Allegro* are properly accompanied by details implying uninterrupted space: a light and open scene of lawns and fallows, sunlit meadows, wide rivers. The closed spaces of *Il Penseroso* that go with meditation imply also an auditory image not impeded by the barriers that block vision; in the thick woods, the song of the nightingale. If the poet does venture into the open, it is only at night, and by moonlight. The close and visible river of *L'Allegro* becomes more remote, an image evoked by sound heard in seclusion, "over some wide-water'd shore, / Swinging slow with sullen roar." The poem moves toward images of subdued light and enclosure: twilight groves, the cloister's pale, the hermit's mossy cell, all suiting the interest of the picturesque with their note of mystery and concealment. Such things anticipate the landscape of paradise. We have seen that the description of Eden follows just this pattern, from the lawns and fields of the opening section to grots and caves, from tender herb to mantling vine. It is for this reason that the wall of Eden, however illusory, is such an important element in the opening description, where the sense of closure is not otherwise provided. It soon disappears, its place taken as in *Il Penseroso* by dark retreats, the "shadows brown that *sylvan* loves."

The development from the particular to the general in Milton's descriptions, from hedgerow elm and single oak to forest, becomes more obvious in *Comus*. Here the feeling for larger masses of water so apparent in *Lycidas* begins to find its counterpart in woods, "The nodding horror of whose shady brows / Threats the forlorn and wand'ring Passenger" (38–39). The effect is more concerned with atmosphere than with scene, with psychological impressions and moods than with physical images. In fact, there is a tendency in *Paradise Lost* to lose the pictorial or specific in abstract generalizations like "Insuperable highth of loftiest shade," even where a more concrete image would seem appropriate. If ever there was an occasion for introducing that effect of which English landscape was so fond, the conspicuous single tree that is *ipse nemus*, a grove in itself, it is in *Paradise Lost*, with its legendary trees of Life and Knowledge. By the time of this poem, however, the tendency toward mass has won out; and these individual trees, symbolic as they may be, are still subordinated to the larger and more literal representation of woods, against which the Tree of Life itself can scarcely be made out, standing "all amid them," however "eminent." The Tree of Knowledge "fast by" offers even less of an image. It is referred to in Book IX simply as the Tree of Prohibition, more of an idea than an object, with little that we can visualize but its golden fruit.

The treatment of trees in Eden, though it is usually quite literal, is further generalized by Milton's practice of associating them with Adam's role in the garden, as flowers are associated with Eve's. This too reflects convention, for the disposition of grounds that separated the central garden with its flowers from the outlying park with its trees went along with a division of responsibility between the sexes. As John Evelyn observed at Swallowfield, flowers were considered the women's part rather then the men's: "My lady being so extraordinarily skill'd in the flowering part, and my Lord in diligence of planting."[20] When Eve suggests a specialization of this kind in Eden, it is the first step toward the Fall:

> Let us divide our labors, thou where choice
> Leads thee, or where most needs, whether to wind
> The Woodbine round this Arbor, or direct
> The clasping Ivy where to climb, while I
> In yonder Spring of Roses intermixt
> With Myrtle, find what to redress till Noon.   (IX, 214–19)

The association of Adam with trees is seen also in Eve's first glimpse of him, "fair . . . and tall, / Under a Platan" (IV, 477–78). Eve's involvement with flowers is more explicit. She wakes on flowers at her creation; her day's routine is timed to their opening and shutting, and her concern for the flowers that were her daily care is the most moving aspect of her exile: "O flowers,"

> That never will in other Climate grow,
> My early visitation, and my last
> At Ev'n, which I bred up with tender hand
> From the first op'ning bud, and gave ye Names,
> Who now shall rear ye to the Sun? (XI, 273–78)

Specialization like this would not divide the couple in Eden, where "park" and "garden" intermingle; the plots that lie distant from the bower still show "the hand of Eve"; and the spicy forest that is Adam's care is in full view from the bower (V, 298–300). What Eve suggests in dividing their labors is not, therefore, that they specialize, but that they part company, a suggestion more arbitrary for the joint tasks everywhere at hand. Satan is understandably surprised at finding Eve alone:

> He sought them both, but wish'd his hap might find
> *Eve* separate, he wish'd, but not with hope
> Of what so seldom chanc'd. (IX, 421–23)

The imminence of the Fall for both Adam and Eve is clear from their positions in the landscape, with the reversal of roles that it implies: Adam at home in the bower weaving the roses we link with Eve; Eve herself away in the orchard violating the tree that we associate with Adam. Her removal, in Satan's company, from that "sweet recess" to the fateful tree is a significant step, not simply a self-assertion or shift in roles, but an intrusion on divinity: "That ye should be as Gods." As fruit, the flower was no longer in Eve's sphere, but the fruit itself, changed to something like wine, as its intoxicating effect shows, is beyond the province of either.

We may note, as a final detail here, with what curious exactness Milton's image in *L'Allegro* of "Towers and Battlements . . . / Bosom'd high in tufted Trees" accords with the eighteenth-century view that saw rounded trees as being more effectively picturesque than pointed ones.[21] Gilpin and Repton both quote these very lines from *L'Allegro* to support a feeling that "the prevailing lines of Gothic buildings are best contrasted with round headed trees, or, as Milton calls them, tufted trees."[22] Whether or not Milton thought about such nice-

ties, battlements bosomed high in trees serve very well the visual
interests of the picturesque, at the same time that they reflect what
Repton calls the coeval antiquity of oaks and medieval towers.

To sum up, one feels in all Milton's descriptions the force of
Price's argument that "it is in the arrangement and management of
trees, that the great art of improvement consists":

Trees, detaching themselves at once from the surface, and rising boldly into
the air, have a more lively and immediate effect on the eye: they alone form
a canopy over us, and a varied frame to all other objects, which they admit,
exclude, and group with, almost at the will of the improver. . . . Their beauty
is complete and perfect in itself, while that of almost every other object requires their assistance.[23]

III

Eloquent as Sir Uvedale Price is on the subject of trees for picturesque effect, Gilpin is all but equally so on behalf of water, the management of which "has ever been considered as the highest achievement
of the improver's skill."[24] To Wölfflin's mind, "a villa without water is
unthinkable" in the baroque period: "it was the period's favorite element."[25] Not surprisingly, then, the style that preferred the shade and
mass of trees, i boschi grandi, to the color and detail of flower beds,
the salvatico to the garden, expressed itself also in the handling of
water in its various functional and decorative forms. Even Bacon,
for all his reservations about standing water ("pools mar all, and make
the garden unwholesome, and full of flies and frogs") concedes enough
to the universal taste to allow "a fair receipt of water, of some thirty
or forty foot square," but "without fish, slime, or mud."[26] In Chinese
gardens, as Chambers points out, water is not only a main source
of variety; it lends "gloom to the melancholy, gaiety to the pleasing,
sublimity to the great, and horror to the terrible."[27] All these effects
are observable in Milton's description. Milton's earliest poem, a paraphrase of Psalm cxiv, shows the Almighty's hand most powerfully
in images of water: the Red Sea thrown back, or water crushed from
rock. At age nineteen he concludes the poetic portion of the Vacation
Exercise by listing a dozen or more of the English rivers, suggesting
in so doing the great variety upon which he would draw in his future
verse. It is in Lycidas that the spell of water over Milton's imagination
is first seen in its full force, the sense of loss reaching its height in
a vision of drowning: "Ay me! Whilst thee the shores and sounding

Seas / Wash far away"; or even more, of submerging: "Where thou perhaps under the whelming tide / Visit'st the bottom of the monstrous world." Nothing more deeply stirs his feelings or his poetic impulse. The glassy, cool, translucent wave of the Severn is as good a sample of the "beautiful" as the sounding seas of *Lycidas* are of the sublime, or the myrtle-fringed streams of Eden of the picturesque.

Most of the effects in the garden are of the latter kind, though here again a distinction is to be made between descriptions covering all of Eden and those meant to give a more local sense of the garden. For streams as for trees the large picture comes first. "Southward through *Eden* went a River large": "And now divided into four main Streams, / Runs diverse, wand'ring many a famous Realm" (IV, 233–34). From this view connecting Eden with the larger world, Milton turns to the immediate scene, the sapphire fount with its crisped brooks watering the garden. An irrigation system suggests normally some rectangular pattern (cf. "four main Streams"), but Milton leaves nature to effect a more casual and pleasing disposition of the water, still "visiting each plant." Here for the last time in Milton are the waters *"bele et clere, et nete et pure"* of French dream vision, and those medieval and Renaissance renderings of ideal scenery that go from "The Pearl" and "The Court of Sapience" to *The Faerie Queene*. The image of crystal-clear water which was for Winckelmann the talisman of a pure classic taste did not satisfy the sensibilities of 1660. "Once the taste for massive forms was established, we no longer find in landscape painting the clear, transparent streams and pools of the . . . earlier Renaissance."[28] The difference is evident in Milton's description. The nectar stream is touched already with "mazy error," under pendant shades which darken and obscure it. The increasingly picturesque account which follows anticipates Price's prescription as aptly for water as for vegetation:

> meanwhile murmuring waters fall
> Down the slope hills, disperst, or in a Lake,
> That to the fringed Bank with Myrtle crown'd,
> Her crystal mirror holds, unite thir streams. (IV, 260–63)

Here are the effects so esteemed in the picturesque garden, the spreading and flowing that by movement lend "variety and animation," the gathering in "mirrors" that "freshen and soften by reflection," giving depth to shadows and adding transparency.[29] Such pools furnish a focus for observation and are in themselves an emblem of meditation, the "reflection" which gardens were designed to encourage.

The succession of still and running water that Price recommends for full picturesque effect is again illustrated in Eve's first waking moments. Like the speaker in a medieval dream vision, she wakes to find herself "reposed / Under a shade on flow'rs":

> Not distant far from thence a murmuring sound
> Of waters issu'd from a Cave and spread
> Into a liquid Plain, then stood unmov'd
> Pure as th' expanse of Heav'n.   (IV, 453–56)

Again a setting of dark enclosure is linked with one of bright openness by the stream:

> I thither went
> With unexperienc't thought, and laid me down
> On the green bank, to look into the clear
> Smooth Lake, that to me seem'd another Sky.   (IV, 456–59)

The clearness of the water, the ease with which Eve can see herself reflected "just opposite," and the expanse of sky suggest level ground, low banks, an open space, and a full stream. The effect has become a bit tame for the picturesque, yet something like this happens wherever the human figures enter. Though they lack society, Adam and Eve are no rustics. If the elegance of the pastoral tone reduces the picturesque effect at times, it is perhaps an insurance against crudeness. Note the arrangement where Adam and Eve sit sidelong on the soft downy bank, damasked with flowers, "and in the rind / Still as they thirsted scoop the brimming steam" (IV, 335–36), another bit of improved nature with its grassy edge and water close to the grass. Sir Uvedale Price himself found the "brimmed waves" of the Severn in *Comus* acceptable more as a compliment to the goddess than as a specimen of landscape. Such effects are normally enhanced by roughness, broken ground, rude stones, and so on, as a means of transcending the merely "beautiful," which Price again illustrates in terms that virtually describe the setting before us: a glade, gentle knolls, the smooth or fringed banks of a lake, a stream running on pure gravel. For Milton's purpose here, this smoother version of pastoral is better, suiting the innocence of Eve and the beauty of unfallen nature. When Eve is not in it, the picture darkens, the stream takes on the winding course natural to level ground, and preferred by the picturesque taste, whence the wanderings of the river in Eden, the "circuit wide" and "serpent error" of rivers drawing their train across the newly created earth in Book VII.

If water in these forms is a source of the beautiful or picturesque, falling water on the scale on which Milton describes it outside Eden approaches the sublime. Here again Milton reflects the baroque sensibility, which had a passion for the cascade. "The finest was the long *cascata* at the Villa Aldobrandini. The water appears high up at the top in an untamed, natural setting as a *fontanone rustico;* it falls straight down . . . gathers, falls . . . alternates again between falling and gathering in a pool.[30] Milton took advantage of the Creation to provide an extraordinary development of the motif, in the forming of earth from the womb of waters:

> So high as heav'd the tumid Hills, so low
> Down sunk a hollow bottom broad and deep,
> Capacious bed of Waters: thither they
> Hasted with glad precipitance
>
> . . . .
>   where way they found,
> If steep, with torrent rapture, if through Plain,
> Soft-ebbing.   (VII, 288-91, 298-300)

This passion for ebbing and falling waters is seen again in the enthusiasm of the next century for rivers poured from hilltops, with cascades in different directions "which, through various impediments, at last unite, and form one vast expanse of water."[31] The violence and accompanying noise of such displays are another baroque note, heard also in Milton's description of the waters at the Flood: "With clamor thence the rapid Currents drive / Towards the retreating Sea thir furious tide" (XI, 853-54). There is a notable range of scale and texture in these watery effects, from the vast seas of Creation or the Flood to the receding runnels of those flood waters receding "from standing lake to tripping ebb, that stole / With soft foot towards the deep" (XI, 847-48). It is remarkable too how sharply in focus the description remains, whatever the scale, in images of crisped brooks, washy ooze, and the "wrinkled face of deluge."

The most remarkable feature of the river of Eden, is the way it runs underground on its southward course, "ingulft" beneath the mountain, which becomes a kind of "garden mould," "high raised upon the current," through which the river is drawn in turn to water the garden, descending in the cascades we have seen to meet the "nether flood," "which from his darksome passage now appears" (IV, 225–32). In linking the dark caverns with the sunlit mountains, the stream becomes, according to Maud Bodkin, a double image for imaginative fear and divine bliss,[32] thus contributing to the psychological experience which, as we shall see, was an important aspect of landscape.

Even more impressive is that image of deep, still water that Milton equates with God's creative power, first seen in the Nativity ode, where "Birds of Calm sit brooding on the charmed wave," and again with stronger overtones of Genesis in the invocation to the Heavenly Muse in *Paradise Lost:*

> Thou from the first
> Wast present, and with mighty wings outspread
> Dove-like satst brooding on the vast Abyss
> And mad'st it pregnant.   (I, 19–22)

It is used once more in the scene of Creation, Chaos being for Milton simply another version of that whelming tide that had obsessed him since *Lycidas.* The hoary deep appeared as an ocean to Satan, as it does to the Son at the moment of Creation, an abyss "Outrageous as a Sea, dark, wasteful, wild, / Up from the bottom turn'd by furious winds / And surging waves" (VII, 212–14). On these turbid masses order is imposed in one gesture: "Silence, ye troubl'd waves, and thou Deep, peace" (VII, 216). The effect is true sublime, energy without the perturbations of the baroque, serenity without the stasis of the classically beautiful. For this effect the image from Genesis serves for the third time:

> on the wat'ry calm
> His brooding wings the Spirit of God outspread,
> And vital virtue infus'd, and vital warmth
> Throughout the fluid Mass.   (VII, 234–37)

It would appear that water in all its forms, falling and flowing, gathering or dispersed, or standing in pools and deeps is the key to Milton's landscapes, running through, over and beneath them, infusing physical life and bestowing not only richness but a large part of such unity as they possess.

IV

One other feature of conventional garden design to be noticed here is the bower or sheltered arbor. The nature of gardens in the formal pattern, designed for public spectacle and social ceremony, made some provision for intimacy essential. In the English garden too, with its openness and concealment of boundaries, some sort of retreat was needed, hedged off, sunken, or hidden away in a corner. Oriental gardens provided elegant pavilions where sensual pleasures could be enjoyed. The nuptial bower as Milton describes it is an elevated version of this convention:

> Here Love his golden shafts imploys, here lights
> His constant Lamp, and waves his purple wings,
> Reigns here and revels; not in the bought smile
> Of Harlots, loveless, joyless, unindear'd,
> Casual fruition, nor in Court Amours.   (IV, 763–67)

The passage ends with a picture of perfect pastoral love, a blissful seclusion amid flower petals and bird song: "These lull'd by Nightingales imbracing slept, / And on thir naked limbs the flow'ry roof / Show'r'd Roses, which the Morn repair'd."

Effective as it may be in this respect, the bower provides much more than a romantic setting for love, since it is in this bower rather than in any feature of the terrain that we find the narrative and thematic center of Eden itself. That this should be true says much about the composition of the garden and the meaning of events there. Though baroque landscape generally reduced the terrain to a preconceived plan, "the whole design . . . dominated by one all-embracing view, and the position and effect of every detail . . . determined by its relation to the whole,"[33] Nature in its first perfection is not open to such managing, and Milton made no such effort, content with an English countryside with such Continental features as grotto and bower. Since there is no evidence that Milton ever saw his entire picture in one frame, we must find its center not, as in landscape painting, in some dominant feature of architecture or topography, but in something so inconspicuous as the nuptial bower of Eve.

Milton's failure to use any of the more conventional motifs of myth as the emblematic center of the story is worth noting. The mountain of paradise itself is a case in point, since it would seem to us to be the world mountain of primitive myth, that great axis between earth and heaven which appeared in various forms, as mountain, tree, or ladder, its function being sometimes served also by a form of flight. Milton, however, is not a mythologist, nor is his steep and savage hill the link between earth and heaven. When we have reached its

top and gained the prospect it offers, it becomes the stage for purely
"historical" actions, the entry of Satan, the Fall, the descent of angels.
Yet even as reality this hill is not consistent, being at one point a
mountain slope hidden by trees, at another a rock of alabaster "conspicuous far." Once we have entered Eden, what appeared a craggy
cliff, as in the accounts of Purchas or Diodorus, is described as a
mass of organic material elevated upon the river, which is drawn
up through it to descend irrigating its sides in the way we have seen.
We end with the impression of a mountain topped by a plateau, setting
for a description so detailed that it develops an individual topography.
Book IV refers vaguely to "Hill and Dale and Plain," but in the last
two books Milton introduces two specific mountains. From one Adam
has his vision of history: "It was a Hill / Of Paradise the highest"
(XI, 377–78). Upon the other, angels alight to take possession of the
garden. When the "Visions of God" are done and Adam has come
down from the "top of Speculation," the cherubim also descend "from
the other Hill / To thir fixt Station" (XII, 626–27). It is not until the
closing lines that these two hills are ever seen in relation to each other,
and even then the occasion is more narrative than descriptive. Two
such mountains disposed about a central vale would make an ideal
setting for paradise, but there is no evidence that Milton meant this,
and in fact it takes a lapse of memory to keep one hill from impeding
the view from the other in Adam's vision of the world.

With this blurring of the mythical mountain, we are left with
the fountain of life and the trees of Life and Knowledge as the only
thematic centers, outside of the nuptial bower. The waters of life
that are conventionally central in medieval works like Lactantius' *De
Ave Phoenice* are basically symbolic in nature. Milton reserves his
symbols, including the river of life, for the scenery of heaven. The
rivers of Eden, though ideal, have purely worldly properties. Crystal
in purity, running nectar to water the flowers, "milky" where Eve
draws them for repast, there is no suggestion that they convey immortality in the unfallen garden. As for the trees of Life and Knowledge,
it would be natural to look for them as in Genesis "in the midst of
the Garden," probably together. Milton does place them beside each
other at first—"next to Life / Our Death the Tree of Knowledge grew
fast by" (IV, 220–21)—yet apparently not at the center. Perhaps in
order to prevent the note of prohibition from impairing the bliss,

or more likely for narrative convenience, to facilitate the separate temptation of Eve, Milton actually places the Tree of Knowledge at some distance from the bower. Eve's departure "to the groves" on the fatal morning obviously takes her out of Adam's sight, as she intended. Satan can see no sign of him though he views "far round," yet to arrive at the Tree she must be led still farther: "Beyond a row of Myrtles, on a Flat, / Fast by a Fountain, one small Thicket past / Of blowing Myrrh and Balm" (IX, 627–29). Thus do we reach at last the center of the original myth, with just a suggestion of the waters of life—"fast by a fountain"—and none at all by this time of the Tree of Life which grew beside it.

It is the bower, then, that we must take as the center, not simply by default of tree or stream, but again by specific indications from the narrative. In the angels' search for Satan, it is not the ones circling north or south through the area but those proceeding along the diameter who discover him whispering at the ear of Eve asleep in the bower. It is a curiously precise way of locating things, supported by what we see of the bower as center of life in the garden, where the two sleep and pray, take their noon repast, and entertain their angel guests, the scene of their nuptials celebrated with heavenly choirs. Both for its location and its structure, "of firm and fragrant leaf," Eve's bower suggests not only the *"giardino segreto,"* the Oriental pavilion, the pergolas and summer houses of medieval gardens, but the bowers that have such strong erotic overtones in narrative verse from Poliziano and Petrarch to Spenser. To put this at the center rather than the Tree of Knowledge, for example, shifts the emphasis from knowledge and death to love.

In our first view of Adam and Eve in "naked majesty," these overtones are clear, however innocent, in the disheveled tresses of Eve, her "sweet reluctant amorous delay": "Nor those mysterious parts were then conceal'd, / Then was not guilty shame" (IV, 312–13). When the leering Satan has departed, we see the bower as a setting for connubial love combining the sensual with the spiritual: "Hail wedded Love, mysterious Law, true source / Of human offspring, sole propriety / In Paradise of all things common else" (IV, 750–52). Since, as these lines suggest, it is an experience given to man alone, not only is the bower in which it is accomplished central, it is that "holiest place" in which *caritas* is realized: "Here Love his golden shafts imploys, here lights / His constant Lamp, and waves his purple wings" (IV, 763–64). On these sacred precincts none of the creatures will venture, only the heavenly choirs that sing the wedding hymn. Such a connubial love, consummated under divine auspices in a setting chosen by the sovereign planter at the heart of the garden, is in strong contrast with the lustful love indulged after the Fall: at noon, still in the vicinity of the tree, on a shady bank "Thick overhead with verdant roof imbowr'd," and with a couch of flowers. It is almost a bower, yet sex in such a place, without the centrality and spiritual air of the true bower, is a wholly different thing, "of their mutual guilt the Seal." They wake "as from unrest," and "bare of all their virtue." But it is not only in this way, as the setting for so ideal a relationship, that the bower comes into perspective. It is the focus too of that larger cosmos in which the action goes on, the object of visitors from heaven and hell, the scene of Eve's first temptation, the point which they avoid in their shame for the shade of woods and to which they are called again for judgment. It is the place to which they return of their own will to offer repentance and receive "Strength added from above, new hope to spring / Out of despair" (XI, 138–39). At the end it is the aspect of the garden that Eve most laments: "Thee lastly nuptial Bower, by mee adorn'd . . . from thee / How shall I part" (XI, 280–82). Adam, too, sees it as the point from which their exile begins. The meaning of the bower, blissful rest in a place chosen by God, is implied in the closing lines: "The World was all before them, where to choose / Thir place of rest, and Providence thir guide" (XII, 646–47). What the bower has stressed from the beginning, the mutual nature of their lot, whether wandering or at rest, is seen again in the last two lines of *Paradise Lost*. The opening image of Adam and Eve passing "hand in hand, alone . . . to thir blissful Bower" (IV, 689–90), an image that was reversed on the morning of the Fall— "from her Husband's hand her hand / Soft she withdrew" (IX, 385–86)—is restored in the concluding image as they take their way from that central bower: "They hand in hand with wand'ring steps and slow, / Through *Eden* took thir solitary way" (XII, 648–49). With such imagery it is not hard to argue a romantic interpretation of the Fall. The arrangement of the landscape and the degree to which both setting and action are oriented on the bower make Adam's feelings for Eve the expression of genuine love, rather than the irrational passion for which Raphael takes them. We may be encouraged to look not only to the expository statements of God in Book III but to the scenery and the poetry of Book VIII for the message of *Paradise Lost*, which, if we take the cue from landscape, has as much to do with human love as with divine proscription.

v

We have looked now at the elements of landscape important to theorists of the picturesque and the baroque, as they are incorporated by Milton into his picture of Eden: an elevated site with a view, within which the fields and flowers, lawns and trees, stream and bower are disposed to ensure the pleasures of beauty, seclusion, rest—and love. We have not done justice to the seventeenth-century garden, however, if we confine our attention to the terrain as a source only of mood and atmosphere. The Renaissance view of gardens saw them as furnishing a much wider range of experience. Beyond aesthetic effect, which combined with landscape the resources of painting, sculpture, architecture, and even music, were other dimensions, reaching in one direction into physical therapy and the wholesome influences of environment, and in the other into the kind of content we expect of philosophy, psychology, and literature. We must look into this aspect of the garden experience and the way it is represented in *Paradise Lost*.

One of the customary functions of landscape, in eras no less fond of the sensational than our own, was the registering of some sort of shock upon the sensibilities of the onlooker. In the eighteenth century, indeed, gardens were to become more and more a medium for such experience. Burke's emphasis on terror as the key to the sublime indicates the degree to which both physical sensation and psychological effect had entered into the aesthetic experience. Just this side of the romantic sensibility is seen in the theory that considers the "pleasing," nature at its most familiar and attractive, as less desirable than the "terrible"—effects that derive from her wilder and gloomier aspect— or the "surprising," wherein the marvelous or supernatural is added to provide a shock of novelty beyond the ordinary.

The difference between the terrible and the surprising, though not always clear, is based on the distinction between the real and the supernatural in nature itself. To deal first with the terrible: some-

thing of this somber effect, short of terror, is at least suggested in
the shadowy grots and caves of Eden. The darker pastoral is seen
to much better effect in the wilderness setting of Christ's meditation
in *Paradise Regained*: "on every side . . . / A pathless Desert, dusk
with horrid shades" (I, 295–96), a scene not unlike Eden, that includes
wild beasts:

> they at his sight grew mild,
> Nor sleeping him nor waking harm'd, his walk
> The fiery Serpent fled, and noxious Worm;
> The Lion and fierce Tiger glar'd aloof.   (*PR* I, 310–13)

The introduction of such creatures here is interesting. Their momentary
recovery of innocence or innocuousness serves to suggest Eden, but
the zoological garden was a feature of romantic landscape: "Noble
spirits contented not themselves with trees, but by . . . all variety
of animals they made their gardens the epitome of the earth."[34] The
presence of animals in the heart of Eden reflects, of course, the ideal
nature of the place: "About them frisking play'd / All Beasts of th'
Earth, since wild, and of all chase / In Wood or Wilderness, Forest
or Den" (IV, 340–42). The innocence and beauty of nature before the
Fall evokes eighteenth-century notions of the nobility of things in their
natural state, yet even here the shock effect desired in such landscapes
is not entirely missing. Our knowledge of beasts "since wild" adds
novelty and even fear at seeing them so close, an apprehension which
Adam feels after the Fall. "Beast now with Beast gan war, and Fowl
with Fowl / . . . nor stood much in awe / Of man, but fled him, or
with count'nance grim / Glar'd on him passing" (X, 710–14). Though
short of terror, the incipient fear adds to the psychological dimension
which completes the landscape, as does the change of atmosphere
to damps and dreadful glooms, and the growing sense of cosmic forces
at work in Eden.[35]

The category of the "surprising" is closely related to that of the
"terrible" in a setting like Eden, where the line between the natural
and supernatural is so frequently crossed. Effects achieved in ordinary
gardens by mock earthquakes, sinister or unreal creatures like snakes
or furies, and the introduction of eerie music and echoes can be given
on a larger scale and without the impression of deceit in paradise,
where monsters like Sin and Death appear, and Satan himself takes
on a variety of forms as bird, serpent, or mist. Such things are seen

in the storm summoned by Satan in *Paradise Regained*, which proceeds from lightning and thunder to effects quite beyond nature—"terrors, voices, prodigies":

> nor yet stay'd the terror there.
> Infernal Ghosts, and Hellish Furies, round
> Environ'd thee, some howl'd, some yell'd, some shriek'd,
> Some bent at thee thir fiery darts, while thou
> Satt'st unappall'd. (*PR* IV, 421-25)

Sound effects were a standard item in baroque water displays: lion fights with spurts of water to imitate the snarls, jets like shells exploding, centaurs blowing horns. In addition, "watery jokes played a large role in contemporary illustrations and no garden is represented without a few figures taken unawares by jets of water."[36] To be unsettled by practical jokes and assaults on the imagination is part of the expectation, but Christ contemns both the false portents and the physical discomforts: "Mee worse than wet thou find'st not."

These extraneous effects are not always merely diverting; they may be employed in connection with the moral instruction which was one purpose of a garden. In Oriental as in European gardens, sculpture encouraged contemplation of antiquity,[37] and in formal gardens like those of the Villa Aldobrandini a kind of *teatro* was the scene of dramatic presentations and tableaux meant for pleasure and edification. Milton anticipates the function in his opening description, with its trees ascending "Shade above shade, a woody Theatre / . . . Of stateliest view" (IV, 141-42). In the final books of *Paradise Lost* the results of the Fall make a vivid series of tableaux beheld by Adam from the mountain top, from the pantomime of Cain and Abel through all the consequences of that "violent stroke": fire, flood, famine, disease. "Immediately a place / Before his eyes appear'd, sad, noisome, dark, / A Lazar-house it seem'd" (XI, 477-79). The horror show is followed by other exhibits: age and the melancholy effects of lust, war, and sin. Even when Adam's power to take in the spectacle fails, and vision yields to narrative, Milton tends to forget the distinction. At all events the episodes in these two final books, with their lessons from both Testaments, are obviously intended as part of the psychological experience of Eden, edifying as well as sensational. At the end of this account, both visual and narrative, the mood is suddenly lightened, dismay giving place to assurance with the prospect of redemption.

At the same time the mood in which one confronts the landscape of the larger world shifts also, but from hope to misgiving. The greater world beyond stands to Eden as the "wilderness" to a formal garden. The historical and geographical pageant which discovers that world is both impressive and sobering, the excitement of the Renaissance before the possibilities of discovery being tempered by the weariness of fallen man, and perhaps too by the poet's own blindness and disillusion. Clearly the pastoral will not work on such a scale. In terms of landscape, the larger world is quite literally what it was in Genesis, a place in which man must take both ease and responsibility. For the older Milton, then, paradise is envisioned finally as a refuge from such concerns. The bliss that is to be recovered in a garden is not so much in its "liberty" as in its security and repose. In terms still faintly evoking the conventions of Renaissance landscape, long wandered man will be led back "Through the world's wilderness . . . / Safe to eternal Paradise of rest" (XII, 313–14).

Though such thoughts are grander than those ordinarily induced in gardens, and their content much more specific, the pastoral setting has always been the proper place in which to entertain them, gardens being virtually emblems for the contemplative life. The association of gardens with monasteries made their care a ready equivalent for the tending of the soul, and *contemptus mundi* the moral posture most natural to the scene. With heavier woods the mood deepens; the sprightly thoughts of l'Allegro's daytime musings become the broodings of il Penseroso in twilight groves. For Milton, only the cloister itself could compete for this purpose with that peaceful hermitage of the forest, the "Mossy Cell" where he could sit "and rightly spell . . . / Till old experience do attain / To something like Prophetic strain" (*Pens.*, 170–74). Scenes of wilder nature, with thick or twisted trees and rocky crags, were the background for spiritual crises in landscape painting. We have noted Satan's tortured monologues as a poetic example, set as they are just before and after the account of the approach to paradise, "With thicket overgrown, grotesque and wild." Adam's inner torment after the Fall is similarly reflected in the scenery, including in this case the hostility of animals:

> these were from without
> The growing miseries, which *Adam* saw
> Already in part, though hid in gloomiest shade,
> To sorrow abandon'd, but worse felt within.   (X, 714–17)

The convention is echoed a final time in *Paradise Regained*, when Christ pursues his holy meditations in the "bordering Desert wild . . . with dark shades and rocks environ'd round" (I, 193–94).

The contemplative turn of mind so natural in gardens, where growth and decay bring thoughts of time and mortality, explains the prevalence in formal landscape of sundials and mottoes, ruins, and other evidence of the temporal. The inclination to such things is present also in Eden. Even before the Fall, the idea of death occurs in Adam and Eve's first mention of the fruit—"So near grows Death to Life"— and their one labor, to check the "wanton growth," "tending to wild," is linked with time, "till younger hands assist us." But time has already entered the garden with Satan. Reduced in stature, an emblem of heaven's first loss, he colors our original view of Eden with a sense of change. From the moment of the Fall, the day declines: "Earth felt the wound, and Nature from her seat / Sighing through all her Works gave signs of woe, / That all was lost" (IX, 782–84). The difference is seen in the changed life of Eden, where an untimely indulgence more appropriate to night displaces the noon repast, and "mutual accusation" and "fruitless hours" replace the afternoon's repose. Already in Book X the odor of decay draws Sin and Death earthward, and the larger human consequences become clear in the *tableau vivant* unfolded to Adam in Books XI and XII, a vision of disease and the many shapes of death.

Shock effects aside, the conventional view of gardens saw them not only as a vantage point for a vision of history but also as a refuge in which the thought of time might be softened. To this end the gardens of the Renaissance were designed to include also objects of art, not for their aesthetic value only, but as representing that ideal realm outside time which Eden in its first state had represented. Insofar as the picturesque style prefers the natural, or the art that conceals art, we will find in paradise only those artistic touches that mark the work of God, as sovereign planter. As we have seen, the terrain is not an organized composition in the baroque manner. When it is likened to a "woody Theatre of stateliest view," a phrase evoking a Greek amphitheater or its natural equivalent, we have not yet entered the garden. Inside, of course, there is no possibility of architecture as the center for a composition, as Pandemonium in hell, or the towers of heaven, or the throned pavilion of Chaos serve to focus their respective landscapes. We are left again with the bower as both thematic

and artistic center of the garden. Not only its location, but its design
and construction are attributed to the divine Architect, thus further
justifying the attention Milton gives it. Where Satan's Pandemonium
is classical, with pillars and frieze, and the architecture of heaven
Gothic with its towers and battlements, there is a Byzantine touch
in the highly wrought mosaic of flowers in the roof, sides, and floor
of the bower:

> underfoot the Violet,
> Crocus, and Hyacinth with rich inlay
> Broider'd the ground, more color'd than with stone
> Of costliest Emblem.   (IV, 700–03)

To the artifice of God is added the handiwork of Eve, decking the
nuptial bed with flowers. Such a relationship between man and his
Creator, God creating, man adorning and maintaining that Creation,
helps to keep the environment from overwhelming its occupants. It
also helps that Milton avoids the overriding symmetry among natural
objects that Pope ridiculed, as he avoids that "square" garden of which
Marvell complained, the "dead and standing pool of air" of "The
Mower against Gardens": "'Tis all enforced, the fountain and the grot,
/ While the sweet fields do lie forgot" (31–32). The walks in Eden,
though "bordered and overarched with leaves," make no concession
to that architectural style of the earlier eighteenth century that made
of gardens a "roofless building of leaves." For Eden, as for the picturesque, the only acceptable art is that which prunes the bushes to
their natural shapes, at the same time encouraging their growth. Eve
notes to Adam this paradox of things grown luxurious by restraint.
It is her call for more efficient labors in this line that leads to their
separation and fall:

> what we by day
> Lop overgrown, or prune, or prop, or bind,
> One night or two with wanton growth derides
> Tending to wild.   (IX, 209–12)

While there is no architecture in Eden, not even landscape architecture, no formal garden or topiary, the visible evidence of art is
not necessarily absent. Sculpture itself could add nothing more statu-
esque than Adam and Eve, in their nakedness: "in thir looks Divine
/ The image of thir glorious Maker shone" (IV, 291–92). From Michelangelo we go, in the next line, to emblem books, with their ideal

qualities: "Truth, Wisdom, Sanctitude severe and pure." To all of this Satan responds as to a work of art, aware not only of its beauty but of the skill and presence of the Creator: "so lively shines / In them Divine resemblance, and such grace / The hand that form'd them on thir shape hath pour'd" (IV, 363-65). Nothing could show Milton's humanism better than this image of mankind as God's sculpture. When the couple move, at a pace proper to garden paths, their progress brings them to a fountain side for a modest *fête champêtre:*

> to thir Supper Fruits they fell,
> Nectarine Fruits which the compliant boughs
> Yielded them, side-long as they sat recline
> On the soft downy Bank damaskt with flow'rs.   (IV, 331-34)

The subject is better suited to painting than to sculpture, especially in the niceties of color and detail in the last line. It seems a quieter version of Titian's *Bacchanal* with the addition of sportive beasts, and overtones of Giorgione's *Tempest*, itself "an enchanted idyl, a dream of pastoral beauty soon to be swept away."[38] Milton's scene is lighter than Titian's and more sensuous: "nor endearing smiles / Wanted, nor youthful dalliance" (IV, 337-38), as Eve

> with eyes
> Of conjugal attraction unreprov'd,
> And meek surrender, half imbracing lean'd
> On our first Father, half her swelling Breast
> Naked met his under the flowing Gold
> Of her loose tresses hid.   (IV, 492-97)

But this scene too has its darker elements, not satyrs as in Titian, nor a storm in the background as in Giorgione, but Satan's jealous presence threatening an even more ideal realm. Another "portrait" of this sort with the same attention to composition and the disposition of the figure is given when Adam wakes Eve in Book V: "hee on his side / Leaning half-rais'd, with looks of cordial Love / Hung over her enamor'd" (V, 11-13). For erotic subject and pastoral setting it is another *Venus and Adonis*, with the roles of the sexes significantly changed.[39]

Natural as it may be, then, the garden does claim some tangible benefits from art as well. What results at times is a reality so heavily stylized as to be unfamiliar in detail, however recognizable the background. The effect is seen in natural objects in the vegetable gold

that weighs the "compliant boughs," and in the way living figures
are enlarged and slowed in their movement to become figures in a
tableau. In Milton, the grandest spectacles are reserved for heaven
and hell, the state processions and military reviews presented in so
uniform a way that we can hardly tell the standards and gonfalons
of heaven, "Ten thousand Ensigns high advanc't," from the imperial
ensign of hell with its "Seraphic Arms and Trophies." It is for such
ceremonies that the grounds of a Fontainebleau or Versailles were
designed. Milton's inclination to elevate the human tempts him into
similar things, even in Eden. At the entrance where angels guard the
gate we see "Heroic Games," by "the unarmed Youth of Heaven."
In the center of things, in the bower or perhaps ranged in the clouds
above it, there is the chorus of angels singing the Hymenaean. At
the end there is a final spectacle: "from the other Hill / To thir fixt
Station, all in bright array / The Cherubim descended" (XII, 626–28).
With this occupation of its open spaces by a military force, the pastoral
of Eden is ended. Yet note how the simile that follows this account
of the angels' descent returns us from the ideal or ceremonial to that
level of reality on which man must live after the Fall:

> as Ev'ning Mist
> Ris'n from a River o'er the marish glides,
> And gathers ground fast at the Laborer's Heel
> Homeward returning.   (XII, 629–32)

It is this procedure, avoiding sustained formality, recurring always
to a real landscape, that keeps the human element from being lost
in the sublime. With art so disguised or deferring to nature, we have
the impression which Pliny so esteemed, of gardens as a world made
to human measure, an effect equally typical of Renaissance design
at its best. The test of Milton's humanism, and of the success with
which he has designed the garden as a setting for man, comes when
Adam walks forth to greet his godlike guest, "without more train
/ Accompanied than with his own complete / Perfections; in himself
was all his state" (V, 351–53). Nakedness is a state that Milton specifically reserves for man. Raphael is completely shadowed in his six
wings; Michael comes "as Man clad to meet Man." The impression
of a dignity inherent in man's nature, not derived from costume, is
extended to include Eve ministering naked, crowning their flowing
cups with pleasant liquors, a sight to enamor the sons of God.

What Milton has done to make man the center of the garden is paralleled on a grand scale by his achievement in making paradise the center of not only the created world but the universe. From a garden focused on a bower we have had a panorama of the surrounding world as well. To appreciate Eden as Milton gives it we must now see it also in that larger setting that goes from the flux of Chaos at one extreme to the stasis of hell or heaven at the other. The created world, as we shall see, becomes an ideal middle where order is given to anarchy without the elimination of freedom or possibility. In this paradigm of living order conveyed in pastoral terms, not heaven but earth is the appropriate antithesis to hell. We begin to see both heaven and hell, in fact, as exercises in the antipastoral. We may finish our discussion of Milton's garden by looking at it in this larger context which, along with hell and heaven, includes Chaos and the created world.

VI

Milton's descriptions of hell and heaven are best understood as landscapes done without benefit of vegetation. The emphasis falls not on extremes of dark or light—visible darkness, or brightness that blinds—but on an effect of abstraction or barrenness, the absence of significant detail. The description of heaven is presented in such terms that the mind is more engaged than the eye, contemplating generality in the form of courts and streets, hills and plains. We confront the lake and plain of hell in a similar way, with that meditative bent with which we stare at space or fire. In expressions like "sights of woe" or "regions of sorrow," the first element ("sights," "regions") is abstract and general; the second ("woe," "sorrow") more affective than visual. Thus a phrase like "doleful shade" will differ in more than mood from its counterpart on earth. In so recognizable a place as Eden, the shade comes from visible trees, not the mere absence of light. Insofar as the terrain of hell is visible at all, a "dreary Plain, forlorn and wild, / The seat of desolation" (I, 180–81), it is like earth at a stage of Genesis, "desert and bare" before the vegetable creation; or even more like the elements of Chaos but separated to hot and cold, wet and dry, smitten with the petrific mace of Death. In pursuing these implications Milton produces two regions of hell, in the second of which, not often noted, the elements are as tightly linked with cold as they were in the first with fire. Looking at this other hell reveals interesting associations with Eden.

To begin with, the four rivers of hell, taken from Greek myth, are also counterparts of the rivers of Eden. Where the nourishing streams of paradise flow out to water the earth, the rivers of hell bear their flood of hate, sorrow, lamentation, and rage into an image of stagnation and death in the burning lake. To darkness, barrenness, and the antithesis of hot and cold we may add another contrast with Eden in the silence of the place. Not only bird song but the murmuring streams of Eden are missing. A fifth stream, Lethe, with its slowness and stillness, renders ominous a feature of landscape which in Eden is musical, scenic, and useful. What lies beyond is even more pertinent. For the exploring angels, their venture is not a progress down familiar paths but a search for rest in a world that summarizes the most forbidding aspects of landscape: "O'er many a Frozen, many a Fiery Alp, / Rocks, Caves, Lakes, Fens, Bogs, Dens, and shades of Death" (II, 620-21). This episode, which anticipates the situation of Adam and Eve at their expulsion, comes to a climax with a development of that last phrase: "A Universe of death, which God by curse / Created evil, for evil only good, / Where all life dies" (II 622-24). Except for the emblematic suggestion of a landscape of hot and cold, the moral element is slow to appear. Questions of good and evil come up only in this neglected account of a hell of ice, when Milton, with the inconsistency which frees him from his preconceptions, gives up the notion of a universe of death, dreadful enough, for the more terrifying vision of a place "Where all life dies, death lives, and Nature breeds, / Perverse, all monstrous, all prodigious things." It is Chaos and hell combined, life and death, energy and disorder realizing together their worst capabilities, a nightmare vision of life as cancer, lacking control—"growth" in the worst sense. With this judgment, moral and aesthetic, on the nature of hell and evil as things "abominable, inutterable," past the power of the classical imagination, it is clear that the passage is not an episode but a central statement pointing to the landscapes of heaven, earth and Chaos, not simply for contrast but as alternatives.

The relation of hell to heaven in terms of pastoral is especially interesting. Antithetic though they are, the inertness of hell and the perfection of heaven seem to be simply two forms of stasis to which

the formless flux of Chaos offers an opposite extreme, and the blend-
ing of time and timelessness, growth and perfection in the Garden
a kind of mean. The apt symbol for the power that does not change,
yet causes change, is of course light, emblem of energy and order.
The poetic celebration of the bright effluence in Book III and elsewhere
leaves nothing to be desired as poetry. It is the documenting of its
qualities of brightness and order that inhibits imagination. Other than
lyric invocation there is no way the symbol can be extended but through
narrative and description, tending to allegory, as in those spectacular
ceremonies for which the scenery of heaven seems designed. (It is
interesting to note that the grounds of Versailles were completed by
Le Nôtre in the year *Paradise Lost* was published). Perhaps Milton's
enthusiasm for such things is less aesthetic than moral. In any case
their analogy is not to be found in Eden, which mirrors heaven so
much less than Raphael says, but in hell, or that first fiery region
of it which Milton envisions, as he does heaven, less as a world than
as a kingdom, a setting for ceremony on the grand scale—"Ten thousand
Banners . . . with Orient Colors waving." Noting a flourish or two
like this in the garden, an epic touch which impairs the atmosphere
there, we become again aware how much the pastoral is, as Frank
Kermode suggests, an urban product.[40] Milton's background as a native
of London, and culturally of Alexandria, makes such moments inevitable, but his experience under the Restoration and his antipathy to
Gallic manners would assure a resolution toward the pastoral. It is
unfortunate for heaven that as kingdom and even more as celestial
city it must take on so much of the urban role, in this respect sharing
the note that makes Pandemonium, that other center of sophistica-
tion, so strongly suggest the papal city.

As has been said, it is through the presence or absence of trees
that the rural or urban setting can be most easily conveyed. In hell,
there is only the fleeting allegorical grove that springs up to mock
the fallen angels with its forbidden fruit. In heaven, one feels the
force of Milton's youthful comment on Cambridge as niggardly of
shade, yet here the pastoral is not only nominal but symbolic—Trees
of Life, living streams, and immortal amaranth. Any natural detail
beyond this comes from narrative: the shaggy hills hurled in battle,
bowers from which the angels are summoned to hear God's judgment,
and the plants that "adorn" the ground where Satan digs for nitre,

"adorn" suggesting the merely decorative planting of formal landscape. Only Satan seems aware of a living force in heaven below the "bright surface" of its ethereal mold, a surface which seems frozen like the continent of hell.

Between hell and heaven, the vast expanse of Chaos offers what is in effect another alternative. From the theoretical point of view, Milton's picture of Chaos might seem, to an eighteenth-century land-scape artist, the reduction to absurdity of principles which produced the picturesque, just as the taste of Le Nôtre would find elements of Chaos in so natural a garden as Eden. In Milton's hands, conversely, Chaos offers to Satan its glimpses of the sublime, "the womb of Nature and perhaps her Grave": "Unless th' Almighty Maker them ordain / His dark materials to create more Worlds" (II, 915–16). The elements at war in this region, "hot, cold, moist, and dry," struggling under the eye of Chaos and Chance, are the materials of creation upon which the Son sets forth his golden compasses in Book VII: "This be thy just Circumference, O World." The implication of a perfect abstract form suits the geometry of the heavens, but God's formal landscape ceases with the Creation of the world. For this Milton is content to separate the warring elements, conglobing "like things to like" out of the "fluid Mass," and giving to each its proper place and function. The part that water plays in the garden must reflect this image of it as the womb of nature:

> The Earth was form'd, but in the Womb as yet
> Of Waters, Embryon immature involv'd,
> Appear'd not: over all the face of Earth
> Main Ocean flow'd, not idle, but with warm
> Prolific humor soft'ning all her Globe,
> Fermented the great Mother to conceive,
> Satiate with genial moisture.   (VII, 276–82)

The conceit of God as landscape architect fashioning a world for man's use and pleasure raises the art to epic levels:

> Be gather'd now ye Waters under Heav'n
> Into one place, and let dry Land appear.
> Immediately the Mountains huge appear
> Emergent, and thir broad bare backs upheave
> Into the Clouds.   (VII, 283–87)

Half of the account is devoted to the waters, in detail that we have seen; after which, in even greater detail, the gardener's art is applied:

> Earth, till then
> Desert and bare, unsightly, unadorn'd,
> Brought forth the tender Grass, whose verdure clad
> Her Universal Face with pleasant green.　　　(VII, 313-16)

It is a celebration of vegetation in every form—herbs and flowers of all colors and scents, vine and gourd, reed, shrub, and bush; and last "the stately Trees" to crown the hills and border the rivers:

> That Earth now
> Seem'd like to Heav'n, a seat where Gods might dwell,
> Or wander with delight, and love to haunt
> Her sacred shades.　　　(VII, 328-31)

Having been given dominion in a world so much more to Milton's taste than heaven itself, man is brought thence into its most delicious grove: "this Garden planted with the Trees of God." At this point in Book VII, and in the larger context we have gained from the preceding books, we can appreciate the charm of Eden as Milton gives it, the potential of Chaos made real, the breeding energies of hell so graphically portrayed in Book II put under control. The result is nature at its ideal best, yet still nature. The art of God which in heaven produces so smothering a formality and such limited variation here takes on a more generous spontaneity, the symptom of which is water and vegetation, not only as decorations for a landscape but as emblems, of a sort, for the values Milton most wished to advance. Distorted into images of flame, water helps to define through paradox the negative qualities of hell. In Chaos, that "ocean," it is the emblem of flux. In Eden, however, it is seen in its natural form as a sign of that infinite potential which the perfection of heaven, expressed through light and order, reduces to symbols and abstractions. Most significantly, though, water is, as we have seen, the matrix out of which the ordered possibilities of the created world emerge. As one of two essentials for the inception of life, its presence under, within, and throughout the garden acquires a symbolic dimension more effective because it is so real, so familiar, and so attractive in all its forms, as fountain or spring, subterranean stream or hillside cascade.

If moisture is one of the conditions of creation, darkness is, for poetic purposes, the other. Milton may celebrate the idea of light as a sign of the divine and human mind, but it is in darkness that he works his own creative acts. The dense vegetation that testifies to the life forces at work in the garden comes to the light out of the depth of earth, as earth itself from the abyss. Fittingly, the trees that most impressively typify that life in the pastoral scene provide too the shade or dark seclusion which is for Milton the most congenial setting for his art and thought. We find the perfect type of that setting, a combination of water and shade, very soon in Milton's poetry, in that "close covert by some Brook" to which Il Penseroso repairs, hidden from day's garish eye, to receive the vision and to hear the music. Whatever form that setting might take in later years, from the twilight groves of *Il Penseroso* to the wilderness of *Paradise Regained,* the profundities of mind or spirit were generally equated with shade. For Milton, as for Samson or Tiresias, blindness is but the reflection of an inner light.

We see then that Milton's inclination to effects that are called painterly, picturesque, or baroque, according to the mode in which the inclination to deal with darker matters of substance declared itself, or the degree to which it was indulged, comes from motives too serious to be laid to taste alone. If we are moved by such effects, it is because they meet some need deeper than is to be answered by art, unless by art we mean something more like religion. By the end of Book XII, the Garden of Eden has become the vehicle of much that Milton has to say of human life as a harmony of order and freedom, stability and growth, obedience and will. There is thus a link between the epic poet justifying God's ways to man and the picturesque gardener interpreting God's nature in human perspective. Poem and garden both are efforts to mediate between the divine intention and our human ability to respond. The result is a poem as complex and coherent, in style and content, as the garden which is its emblem, or that larger landscape through which so many of its meanings are expressed.

University of Massachusetts, Amherst

NOTES

1. Sir Uvedale Price, *On the Picturesque, as compared with the Sublime and the Beautiful, and, on the use of Studying Pictures for the purpose of improving real landscape* (London, 1810), vol. I, p. 43; vol. III, pp. 73, 79–86, 149–63.

2. See Hannah D. Demaray, "Milton's 'Perfect' Paradise and the Landscapes of Italy," *Milton Quarterly,* VIII, 2 (May 1974), 33–41.

3. In Sir William Temple, *Upon the Gardens of Epicurus, or of Gardening in the Year 1685, Works* (New York, 1968), p. 253.

4. "Letter to Uvedale Price, Esq.," in *An Enquiry into the Changes of Taste in Landscape Gardening. To which are added, some Observations on its Theory and Practice, Including a Defence of the Art* (London, 1806), p. 154.

5. In Henry Ogden and Margaret S. Ogden, *English Taste in Landscape in the Seventeenth Century* (Ann Arbor, 1955), p. 63.

6. The edition quoted throughout this essay is *John Milton, Complete Poems and Major Prose*, ed. Merritt Y. Hughes (New York, 1957).

7. Francis Bacon, *Essays*, ed. Ernest Rhys, Everyman's Library (New York, 1911), p. 142.

8. Repton, *Enquiry*, p. 56; and *Observations on the Theory and Practice of Landscape Gardening, Including some remarks on Grecian and Gothic Architecture* (London, 1803), p. 80.

9. See Roy Daniells, "A Happy Rural Seat of Various View," in *"Paradise Lost," A Tercentenary Tribute*, ed. B. Rajan (Toronto, 1969), p. 4; and Charlotte Otten, "'My Native Element': Milton's Paradise and English Gardens," in *Milton Studies*, V, ed. James D. Simmonds (Pittsburgh, 1973), p. 255.

10. Price, *On the Picturesque*, vol. III, pp. 128–29.

11. Repton, *Enquiry*, pp. 165–66.

12. George Mason, *An Essay on Design in Gardening* (London, 1768), in William S. Gilpin, *Practical Hints upon Landscape Gardening, with some Remarks on Domestic Architecture* (London, 1832), pp. 77–78.

13. *A Dissertation on Oriental Gardening* (London, 1773), pp. iv, 21.

14. Price, *On the Picturesque*, vol. I, p. 22.

15. Heinrich Wölfflin, *Renaissance and Baroque* (Ithaca, 1967), p. 152.

16. Ibid., p. 151.

17. Ibid.

18. *Essays*, p. 139.

19. *On the Picturesque* (1794 ed.), p. 206.

20. *The Diary of John Evelyn*, ed. E. S. deBeer (Oxford, 1955), vol. IV, p. 481. See also on this point Temple, *Upon the Gardens of Epicurus*, p. 44.

21. Gilpin, *Practical Hints upon Landscape Gardening*, p. 50. Price, too, points out the advantage to the picturesque of trees like the oak in providing for a more varied outline than such cone-shaped trees as the larch, whose conspicuous pointed tops will make an entire countryside bristle (*On the Picturesque*, 1810 ed., vol. I, pp. 269–70).

22. Repton, *Enquiry*, p. 79.

23. *On the Picturesque* (1810 ed.), vol. I, p. 259.

24. *Practical Hints upon Landscape Gardening*, p. 151.

25. *Renaissance and Baroque*, p. 154.

26. *Essays*, p. 140.

27. *Oriental Gardening*, p. 69.

28. Wölfflin, *Renaissance and Baroque*, p. 154.

29. Price, *On the Picturesque*, (1810 ed.), vol. I, p. 298.

30. Wölfflin, *Renaissance and Baroque*, pp. 157–58.

31. Chambers, *Dissertation on Oriental Gardening*, p. 83.

32. *Archetypal Patterns in Poetry* (New York, 1958), p. 110.

33. Wölfflin, *Renaissance and Baroque*, p. 150.

34. Sir Thomas Browne, "The Garden of Cyrus," in Temple, *Upon the Gardens*

of Epicurus, p. 91. See also Evelyn's comments on the "forest" of St. Germain, "which
. . . being very large is stor'd with deare, wild boares, wolves, and other wild game"
(Temple, p. 210).

35. Such things, of course, go considerably beyond the picturesque. Price quotes
Milton's descriptions of Eve, Adam, and Satan to suggest the means by which one
moves along the line leading from the beautiful through the picturesque to the sublime.
To the beauty of Eve, her "softness . . . and sweet attractive Grace" is added, for
the picturesque, an air "less winning soft, less amiably mild" than Eve had beheld
in herself—reflected, significantly enough, in the clear, still pool that is in itself a type
of classical beauty. For the sublime, one needs the additional dimensions available
in Satan, whose faded but still terrible glory Milton likens to that of the sun in eclipse,
that sheds "disastrous twilight" on "half the Nations" (I, 597–98). The note of terror
essential to the sublime is reinforced, as Price notes in citing this passage, by developing the public dimensions of the reference: "and with fear of change / Perplexes
Monarchs" (*PL* I, 598–99). See *On the Picturesque* (1810 ed.), vol. I, pp. 89, 97–98.

36. Wölfflin, *Renaissance and Baroque*, pp. 158–59.

37. Chambers, *Dissertation on Oriental Gardening*, p. 19.

38. H. W. Janson, *History of Art: A Survey of the Major Visual Arts from the
Dawn of History to the Present Day* (New York, 1967), p. 372.

39. For comment and additional references on the subject of Milton's landscape
and the landscape painting of Giorgione, Titian, Claude Lorraine, and Poussin, see
John R. Knott, Jr., *Milton's Pastoral Vision* (Chicago, 1971), pp. 49–50.

40. *English Pastoral Poetry from the Beginnings to Marvell* (London, 1952), p.
14.

POET-PRIEST: VOCATIONAL TENSION IN MILTON'S EARLY DEVELOPMENT

John Spencer Hill

Milton's decision to become a poet, like that to become a minister, was taken early; and the vocational streams issuing from these twin and complementary resolves run parallel until at least 1637, when he composed *Lycidas*. Neither *Sonnet VII* nor the "Letter to a Friend" (1633) will support a case for Milton's abandoning a priestly, and embracing a poetic, career in 1632; similarly, although the unsettling events of 1637 drove Milton to a reassessment of his plan to take holy orders, the available evidence suggests that he did not take this step in 1637. The combination of his Italian experience and events in England (principally the promulgation of the Laudian *Canons* of 1640) finally led Milton to the belief that he had been "Church-outed by the Prelats." The most striking vocational feature of the pre-1639 poetry is its reiterated protestation of unpreparedness; after his Italian trip, however, Milton has a firm sense of poetic direction and purpose, and his recognition that poetry is an extension of the ministerial function resolves any vocational tension between poetry and the pulpit, for Milton believes himself to be a national poet-priest who will serve as God's spokesman and interpreter through poetry.

MILTON'S DECISION to become a poet is frequently assumed to have been intimately connected with his resolve to abandon a career in the church. A. S. P. Woodhouse, for instance, puts the moment of choice in 1632, on the threshold of Milton's retirement to Hammersmith, and locates the central statement of his resolve in *Sonnet VII*; John T. Shawcross, on the other hand, believes the decision between poetry and the pulpit to have been deferred until the autumn of 1637.[1] Despite their differences, both of these readers suggest that Milton's determination to serve God through poetry either involved

41

or was determined by his decision to forgo holy orders. According
to this view, Milton is seen as standing at a fork in the vocational
road, where the choice of one career necessarily implies the rejection
of the other. Although the evidence is meager and often unfortunately
vague, there are compelling reasons for believing that no necessary
correlation existed in Milton's experience between the decision to become a poet and the decision to abandon a career in the church.
Indeed, once the notion of a vocational tension and its corollary of
an enforced choice is discarded, a revaluation of the evidence leads
to significant conclusions about Milton's early development.

There can be little doubt that Milton went up to Cambridge in
1625 to prepare himself for admittance into the brotherhood of Puritan
preachers who were then working for further reform within the ecclesiastical establishment.[2] It is equally clear from *At a Vacation Exercise*
(1628) that at about this same time or shortly thereafter he began
to harbor serious poetic aspirations. There is no conflict here. Numerous
contemporary clerics wrote poetry and had gained reputations in both
employments: Giles and Phineas Fletcher, John Donne, and George
Herbert, to mention only four of the more prominent figures. Moreover, although an early allegiance to Ovid and the classical elegists
influenced much of his verse in the Cambridge period, Milton was
nonetheless confirmed early in the belief that literature was an important extension of the ministerial function; as he was to put it later,
poetic ability is "of power beside the office of a pulpit, to imbreed
and cherish in a great people the seeds of vertu, and publick civility."[3]
It was to this same conviction that he appealed in writing, shortly
before he left the university, that "a single house-hold, even a single
individual, endowed with the gifts of Art and Wisdom, may often
prove to be a great gift of God, and sufficient to lead a whole state
to righteousness."[4]

In *The Reason of Church-Government*, Milton asserts with some
acerbity that he was "Church-outed by the Prelats." The phrase argues
that the decision, the final and irrevocable decision, to reject a ministerial calling was one forced upon him by events and not one to
which he was driven by his preference for poetry. However, there
is absolutely nothing in Milton's writings from 1626 to 1637 (when
he wrote *Lycidas*) to suggest that before this latter date there was
any serious rift between his views and those of the church. Moreover,

the program of studies undertaken at Hammersmith and Horton, heavily larded as it was with patristic and historical writings, was as much suited to a cleric in training as to an aspiring epic poet. It is clear, of course, that Milton also wanted to be a poet; and there is no reason to assume that the studious retirement of 1632–1637 was not designed to serve the dual purposes of ministerial and poetic preparation. I cannot accept the argument that Milton's decision to become a poet was deferred until the autumn of 1637. The decision to become a poet, like that to become a minister of the Word, was taken early; and the vocational streams issuing from these twin resolves run parallel and are of equal strength until at least 1637. The final decision to abandon a clerical vocation, however, a step considered perhaps as early as the summer of 1637, was not taken until Milton was "Church-outed by the Prelats" in 1640. Although it is certainly possible to distinguish between a formal career in the church and a literary vocation to act as poet and defender of the church, it is unlikely that Milton would have considered such a distinction necessary before 1640 when, believing himself forced out of holy orders by the bishops, he determined to raise his left hand against the Laudian Episcopate.

I. "A Person Separate to God": The Ministerial Vocation

In December 1629, some eight months after the composition of the delightfully "pagan" *Elegy V* ("*In adventum veris*"), the first stage of Milton's literary apprenticeship came to an end and he imposed, for the first time, a sense of direction on his poetic career. Henceforth, he asserted in *Elegy VI*, he would dedicate his poetic talent to the service of God, and he offered the Nativity ode as the first pledge of that resolve.[5] However, as Woodhouse has demonstrated, Milton more than once relapsed, in 1630–1631, into those secular and erotic veins he had determined, in December 1629, to eschew.[6] Thus, "vastly important as is the experience recorded in the *Nativity Ode*, it is not final. It does not turn Milton into the religious poet whom we know. It requires for its completion another experience."[7] And Woodhouse locates the record of that completing experience in *Sonnet VII*:

I think that the decision which Milton finally reached in respect of his poetry, and the religious experience from which the decision sprang, turned on a larger axis than the rejection of the elegaic and the erotic [in *Elegy VI*]. This becomes clear if *Sonnet 7, How soon hath Time* . . . is given its proper place

as the record of an experience just as definite and far more decisive than
that of the *Nativity Ode* and *Elegy VI*. For it is impossible to escape the
conclusion that there is some fading of the experience recorded in the latter
poems and some relapse from the position which they attain. . . . On the
threshold of the Horton period Milton's act of self-dedication required to
be renewed, as it was in *Sonnet 7*. From the determination there taken, to
live and write hereafter "As ever in my great Taskmaster's eye," there is no
retreat: it leaves its mark on the whole of Milton's subsequent career. . . .
[Thus,] if the December of 1629 sees a first decision and resolve, that of
1632 sees its final and irrevocable confirmation.[8]

Since the appearance of Woodhouse's paper in 1943, no one has doubted
the importance of *Sonnet VII*; however, a number of readers (and
I propose to join them) have stopped short of ascribing to the sonnet
the finality which Woodhouse sees in the experience it records and
have been unable to accept the inferences about Milton's poetic career
which he affirms the sonnet to contain.

    From the evidence of the sonnet and the "Letter to a Friend"
(1633), Woodhouse draws two conclusions: (1) shortly after his arrival
at Horton, Milton rededicated himself to God's services (a renewal
of the original dedication of 1629) and resolved to become a religious
poet, and (2) his decision to become a poet necessitated his rejecting
a clerical career. Both the sonnet and the letter are too inconclusive,
however, to bear the weight of either assertion.

    Sonnet VII, which antedates the letter by some months, merits
citation in full:

> How soon hath Time the suttle theef of youth,
> Stoln on his wing my three and twentith yeer!
> My hasting dayes flie on with full career,
> But my late spring no bud or blossom shew'th.
> Perhaps my semblance might deceive the truth,
> That I to manhood am arriv'd so near,
> And inward ripenes doth much less appear,
> That som more timely-happy spirits indu'th.
> Yet be it less or more, or soon or slow,
> It shall be still in strictest measure eev'n,
> To that same lot, however mean, or high,
> Toward which Time leads me, and the will of Heav'n;
>   All is, if I have grace to use it so,
>   As ever in my great task-Masters eye.

That the sonnet enshrines an act of conscious self-dedication to God's
service is beyond dispute. But to precisely what "service" does the

dedication apply? Milton does not say. He laments that he, unlike many young men of comparable age, has not attained the "inward ripenes" (intellectual and spiritual maturity) necessary for the career (notice the pun on "career" in line 3) he proposes to follow. However, the uncertainty and insecurity of the octave give way in the sestet to assurance and security: he is in God's hands. He senses himself led toward an *unspecified* "lot" which, "however mean, or high" (again inconclusive), has been determined for him by Providence and in which he will be confirmed by time (the "suttle theef" of his youth is now the precondition of his vocational preparedness) and the "will of Heav'n," if only God will grant him the grace to conform to his destiny. As Shawcross (whose reading of this poem is similar to my own) has pointed out, "God's prescience, though certain, does not necessitate occurrence; that depends upon man's moral responsibility."[9] Endowed with reason and the power of moral choice, Milton, like the Adams of *Areopagitica* and *Paradise Lost,* is an instrument fit and sufficient to stand, but also free to fall. Having dedicated his life to God's service, Milton prays for the grace to follow the divine will by which he feels himself led and which is made known to him through the promptings of his own will. But he does not say that the inward urgings of divine Providence are directing him toward poetry. Indeed, if there is in the sonnet a conflict between God's will and Milton's (and I do not believe that there is), or if the poem marks the resolution of a tension between a poetic and a clerical calling (and this is certainly possible), then it would seem that he is asking for the grace to obey the divine will by accepting, not a poetic vocation, but rather his original dedication at the hands of his parents to God's ministry. But this position too is untenable, for *Sonnet VII* (unlike *Elegy VI*) rejects nothing; Milton makes no decision except to follow the promptings of God's will. And might not the divine will sanction both poetry and preaching, especially since, for Milton, literature ought to be treated as an extension of the ministerial function? There is no contradiction, either overt or implied, between these two occupations.

How, then, ought we to interpret the experience recorded in *Sonnet VII?* I think the answer is straightforward: Milton is dedicating himself and his labors to God's service as he had done in 1629; however, here, on the threshold of his retirement at Hammersmith to prepare himself for his life's work, he vows that there will be no backsliding,

as there was after the resolve of 1629, into Arcades or the realms
of Flora and old Pan. After 1632, Milton is a dedicated spirit both
in thought and deed. And, since the original vow of 1629 had been
broken in poetry rather than in anything directly related to his training
for the ministry, it is fitting that the renewed dedication of *Sonnet
VII* should be applied most specifically to poetry. The poem is an
act of submission and acceptance rather than one of rejection, and,
as such, it is (as Woodhouse rightly notes) perhaps the most important
milestone in Milton's spiritual life, for it marks the completion of his
conversion experience as this was understood by contemporary Puritans. Under the impulse of the divine hand and with the satisfaction
of having taken the first firm step in his spiritual renovation (the remak-
ing of himself, with the aid of grace, in the image of his Maker),
Milton settled in at Hammersmith to complete the process of his regeneration and to prepare himself both intellectually and spiritually
to serve God from the pulpit and through his poetry.

Such a reading of *Sonnet VII* is further supported by the "Letter
to a Friend" written in 1633 to an unknown correspondent in order
"to give you account . . . of this my tardie moving; according to
the praecept of my conscience, wch I firmly trust is not wthout
god."[10] Milton justifies his "study-leave" at Hammersmith and his decision to delay taking holy orders on the grounds that he is not prepared,
either in learning or spiritual accomplishments, to take this final step:

Lastly this Love of Learning as it is ye pursuit of somthing good, it would
sooner follow the more excellent & supreme good knowne & praesented and
so be quickly diverted from the emptie & fantastick chase of shadows &
notions to the solid good flowing from due & tymely obedience to that comand
in the gospell set out by the terrible seasing of him that hid the talent. it
is more probable therfore that not the endlesse delight of speculation but
this very consideration of that great comandment does not presse forward
as soone as may be to underg[o] but keeps off wth a sacred reverence &
religious advisement how best to undergoe[,] not taking thought of beeing
late so it give advantage to be more fit, for those that were latest lost nothing
when the maister of the vinyard came to give each one his hire.[11]

There is nothing here to indicate that Milton is studying to be a poet
rather than a clergyman, and conversely, there is no reason for assuming that the words do not apply to his poetic as well as his ministerial
vocation. But, immediately after the sentences cited above, he goes
on to make it tolerably plain that he is thinking primarily of his calling

to the ministry. He excuses the length of this justification of his tardy moving and need for studious retirement by observing wittily that, "heere I am come to a streame head copious enough to disburden it selfe like Nilus at seven mouthes into an ocean, but then I should also run into a reciprocall contradiction of ebbing & flowing at once & doe that wch I excuse myself for not doing[,] preach & not preach."[12] Does this statement mean, as many critics have assumed it does, that Milton has decided against the ministry and yet here finds himself doing that which he has determined to abandon by "preaching" to his friend? Surely not; for the meaning of the sentence is clear and unequivocal, and may be paraphrased thus: I have just told you that I am not ready to become a preacher; yet, in the very act of making this assertion, I have belied myself by preaching to you! And, at the conclusion of the letter, Milton makes the quality of this "preaching" to his friend the justification of his retirement to Hammersmith for study and preparation for the ministry:

this therfore alone may be a sufficient reason for me to keepe me as I am least having thus tired you singly, I should deale worse wth a whole congregation, & spoyle all the patience of a Parish. for I my selfe doe not only see my owne tediousnesse but now grow offended wth it that has hindered [me] thus long from comīng to the last & best period of my letter.[13]

The earliest record of Milton's dissatisfaction with the ecclesiastical establishment comes in 1637, in the passionate and violent indictment of the prelatical church in *Lycidas*. There, in lines 108–31, is found a thunderous denunciation of the Laudian church, delivered by St. Peter, keeper of the keys of heaven and himself the first bishop:

> Last came, and last did go.
> The Pilot of the *Galilean* lake,
> Two massy Keyes he bore of metals twain,
> (The Golden opes, the Iron shuts amain)
> He shook his Miter'd locks, and stern bespake,
> How well could I have spar'd for thee young swain,
> Anow of such as for their bellies sake,
> Creep and intrude, and climb into the fold?
> Of other care they little reck'ning make,
> Then how to scramble at the shearers feast,
> And shove away the worthy bidden guest.
> Blind mouthes! that scarce themselves know how to hold
> A Sheep-hook, or have learn'd ought els the least
> That to the faithful Herdmans art belongs!

What recks it them? What need they? They are sped;
And when they list, their lean and flashy songs
Grate on their scrannel Pipes of wretched straw,
The hungry Sheep look up, and are not fed,
But swoln with wind, and the rank mist they draw,
Rot inwardly, and foul contagion spread:
Besides what the grim Woolf with privy paw
Daily devours apace, and nothing sed,
But that two-handed engine at the door,
Stands ready to smite once, and smite no more.

Both Edward King, the ostensible subject of the poem, and Milton had planned to enter the ministry, and both were poets. King's premature death brought forcefully home to Milton the possibility that he, too, might not survive to accomplish all that he hoped, especially in poetry. But the elegy is not concerned, as the lines quoted demonstrate clearly, with poetry and poetic aspirations alone. From the lament for Lycidas as the poet-shepherd, Milton turns to a consideration of Lycidas as the priest-shepherd, where (in Arthur Barker's words) "the frustration of a sincere shepherd in a corrupt church, is resolved by St. Peter's reference to the 'two-handed engine' of divine retribution."[14]

That Milton was very greatly dissatisfied with the prelatical church when he wrote *Lycidas* is beyond dispute. With the exception possibly of Chaucer and Langland, there is scarcely a more bitter indictment of the clergy in English literature than in these lines of Milton's. But do lines 108–31 of *Lycidas* imply a disillusionment so complete, a resentment so deep-rooted, that he determined to abandon his plans to enter the church? Did the events of 1637—the oppressive parochial visitations of Archibishop Laud (begun in 1633 and pursued with unremitted zeal until 1637), the dismissal from their charges of numerous Puritan clerics who had deviated from the prescribed form of worship, the imprisonment (January 1637) of John Lilburne for his involvement in the printing and distributing of forbidden books like the *Letany of John Bastwick*, the heavy punishment inflicted on Burton, Prynne, and Bastwick for their antiprelatical writings (June 1637), and so forth— did these events, the immediate causes of the indictment of the Laudian church in *Lycidas*, bring home to Milton his alienation from the church in such a way that he gave up further thought of a clerical vocation? It is possible that they did; and Shawcross has argued persuasively that "sometime during the summer of 1637 Milton decided against a church career and, by the beginning of autumn, in favor of a poetic one."[15]

I do not, however, believe this to have been the case. There are compelling reasons for assuming that the final decision to give up a career in the church was not made until 1640. It seems certain that the rejection of a clerical vocation was not a step which Milton took either lightly or hastily; the decision, when it was finally and irrevocably made, was the climax of a long process of self-examination. Milton was never one to abandon any of his plans or hopes easily. Through all the vicissitudes of civil war and the Interregnum (right up to the eve of the Restoration, when all hope was lost), he was to give most of his energy and all of his eyesight to the cause of liberty and the establishment of the English New Jerusalem. It is hardly conceivable that such a man would abandon his plans to enter the priesthood until he was certain that there was no possibility, from a position within the church itself, of redressing prelatical evils and effecting ecclesiastical reformation. Milton was not, by nature, a Satanic rebel seeking to overthrow a cause from without by proclaiming his *non serviam* and resorting to subversion and insurrection to achieve his ends. Rather, he sought always, as long as it remained possible to do so, to work for change and reformation within the framework of constituted authority; on more than one occasion over the course of his career, he had just cause to view himself in the role of an Abdiel, that "Servant of God" who was "Among the faithless, faithful only hee" (*PL* V, 897), and whose steadfastness in the face of rebellion the blind poet was to cause the Almighty to praise in the words:

> Servant of God, well done, well hast thou fought
> The better fight, who single hast maintain'd
> Against revolted multitudes the Cause
> Of Truth, in word mightier than they in Arms;
> And for the testimony of Truth hast borne
> Universal reproach, far worse to bear
> Than violence: for this was all thy care
> To stand approv'd in sight of God, though Worlds
> Judg'd thee perverse.   (VI, 29–37)

Given Milton's firmness of conviction and Abdiel-like character, the indictment of the clergy in *Lycidas* seems insufficient evidence to prove that he abandoned a ministerial calling *within the church* in 1637.

If, as Shawcross argues, the decision between the pulpit and poetry
was taken in 1637, then we might reasonably expect two things: (1)
increased poetic activity, and (2) further denunciations of the Laudian
primacy and the corrupted clergy. Yet neither of these things happens.
Leaving the first point aside for the moment, let me concentrate on
the second. What does Milton have to say about the priestly office
and his own plans for the ministry? Before the writing of *Lycidas*,
he has nothing whatever to say on the subject aside from the facetious
remarks in the "Letter to a Friend" of 1633, a letter which, incidentally,
Shawcross erroneously assigns to 1637.[16] After the writing of *Lycidas*,
no mention is made of the ministry, either in prose or verse, until
the composition of the antiprelatical tracts in 1641–1642. In other words,
the anticlerical outburst in *Lycidas* is an isolated instance, and, moreover, it is general in its application, for it is the critics rather than
the poet himself who have imposed a vocational significance upon
the lines. That Milton was greatly dissatisfied with the church as it
then was, is obvious; that he was led to a fundamental revaluation
of his plan to take orders by the unsettling ecclesiastical events of
1637 is almost certain; but that he had determined to abandon the
priesthood is neither implied in nor susceptible of induction from
the lines of *Lycidas*. Indeed, the imminence of a purgation of ecclesiastical evil, of divine retribution in the form of the "two-handed engine"
(whatever that may be) which stands ready "at the door," makes
it plain that Milton expected the church in which he proposed to
serve to become, shortly, a reformed and regenerate one; certainly,
the image of the "two-handed engine" has more of hope than of despair in it, more to suggest a reason for embracing than for abandoning
the church. We may conjecture that Milton, pursuing his private studies
in seclusion at Hammersmith and later at Horton, venturing forth to
London from the "obscurity and cramped quarters"[17] of his father's
country estate only occasionally, "either to purchase books or to become
acquainted with some new discovery in mathematics or music,"[18] was
informed of, but not affected either seriously or immediately by, the
deep religious divisions and the emotional contagion bred by those
issues which were sweeping London at the time.[19] In the two letters
of 1637 to Diodati, he spoke only of his studies, from which he permitted
"scarcely anything to distract me."[20] The estate at Horton was sufficiently isolated and Milton sufficiently occupied with his present studies

and his future plans (poetry, the ministry, and the projected Continental tour) that he remained relatively untouched, in a way that residence in the heart of London would scarcely have allowed, by events that few could have foreseen would erupt in the divisive convulsions soon to rend church and state. The significance of the condemnation of the Laudian church in *Lycidas* is that, for the first time, Milton consciously and with determination aligns himself with the Puritan faction. Such an allegiance has, of course, been implicit all along, as (for instance) in his choice of "Puritan" Cambridge over "Anglican" Oxford; but, despite temperamental affinities which made the decision inevitable, *Lycidas* is the first public statement of his position in religion. And, while it is true that other Protestant poets, notably Spenser, had attacked the false shepherds of the church, the denunciation of the clergy in *Lycidas* is far from a literary convention; it implies, however vaguely and imprecisely, a "declaration" of religious allegiance. At the same time, however, it must be remembered that this indictment of the clergy and the episcopal institution does not necessarily preclude a plan to work for reform, as many Puritans were then doing, from a position within the Church of England. Like the experience which led, in 1629, to the act of self-dedication to God's service, the dedication to the Puritan cause required time to mature.[21] And, as the decision of 1629 was reaffirmed three years later in *Sonnet VII* and the original resolve made firm and final, so the determination of 1637 (toward which he had been moving, possibly for some time, but had not articulated until *Lycidas*) was not completed until it was reconfirmed and made more rigid in 1641–1642, when a pledge to the Presbyterian cause achieved fruition in the antiprelatical tracts.

Let me pause for a moment over a critical problem. Milton and his critics often approach his career from different directions. Milton lived his life forward, from one day to the next; he tested his responses and forged his convictions on the anvil of experience. The critic, on the other hand, who almost inevitably comes to Milton through *Paradise Lost* and the later poems, stands at the end of a long career, looking back. Since Milton was not free from hopes and aspirations, and since we of three centuries later can often see him moving toward goals and decisions of which he was himself probably ignorant until the moment of choice, retrospect is an invaluable critical advantage. But the danger is that the critic may ascribe the hindsight of his own vantage point to prescience in the poet. The catalogue of heroic subjects in the *Vacation Exercise* no doubt seems more important to us than it was to Milton, for we know that he will write *Paradise Lost* and, in 1628, he did not. Similarly, Milton was always a Puritan, but there is nothing before 1637 to indicate that he felt, deeply and personally, the tension between Puritan and Anglican, and there is nothing before at least 1639 (when news from England cut short his Italian trip) to suggest that his Puritanism was militant enough to cause him to become involved in a personal way in ecclesiastical controversy. The anti-Anglican outburst in *Lycidas* is, then, more of a "position paper" than a religious manifesto whose claims would issue in immediate action.

In *The Reason of Church-Government* (1642), in the *only* passage in all of his writings where he speaks *directly* of his own (by then abandoned) plan to enter the church, Milton explains and justifies his reasons for rejecting a clerical vocation:

But were it the meanest under-service, if God by his Secretary conscience injoin it, it were sad for me if I should draw back, for me especially, now when all men offer their aid to help ease and lighten the difficult labours of the Church, to whose service by the intentions of my parents and friends I was destin'd of a child, and in mine own resolutions, till comming to some maturity of yeers and perceaving what tyranny had invaded the Church, that he who would take Orders must subscribe slave, and take an oath withall, which unlesse he took with a conscience that would retch, he must either strait perjure, or split his faith, I thought it better to preferre a blamelesse silence before the sacred office of speaking bought, and begun with servitude and forswearing. Howsoever thus Church-outed by the Prelats, hence may appear the right I have to meddle in these matters, as before, the necessity and constraint appear'd.[22]

Milton is qualified, then, to meddle in the controversy over prelacy because he was destined from childhood to the service of the church and because he had himself planned and intended to follow a church career. But when did he decide against such a course? Too many readers have sought the answer in the phrase, "till comming to some maturity of years," which is so vague and chronologically ill defined that it can yield no conclusions. The solution of *when* he rejected a church career is implicit in the response to the question, *Why* did he not enter the church? The decision was, he tells us, forced upon him (he did not leave willingly: he was "Church-outed") by prelatical tyranny, and especially by an oath in which that tyranny manifested itself most oppressively. The oath to which Milton refers, as Ralph A. Haug suggests,[23] is almost certainly the obnoxious "Et Cetera Oath" in the Laudian *Constitutions and Canons Ecclesiastical*, promulgated in 1640. Milton had already subscribed at Cambridge to the oath in the canons of 1604; and it was likely that the oath of the 1604 canons was soon forgotten when the new oath, "which was a burning issue in 1641,"[24] was forced upon the Puritans in 1640. In any case, the "Et Cetera" oath would have given Milton firmer ground than the oath of 1604 for feeling that he was "Church-outed by the Prelats" because he would not perjure himself or split his faith.

The chronology that I am suggesting, then, is this. During his retirement at Horton, Milton's dissatisfaction with the Laudian church and his appreciation of the rift between his position and that of the Anglican establishment became sufficiently acute for him to denounce ecclesiastical evil in the anticlerical passage in *Lycidas*. And this poem, as Arthur Barker observes, "performed a cathartic function for the poet himself, was indeed the very process through which a balanced calm was brought out of emotional disquiet."[25] But, like the choice between God and Apollo in 1629, the experience of 1637, while extremely important, was not final; and so Milton continued his studies and left for Italy, perhaps thinking the issues at home (from which he had largely been isolated at Hammersmith and Horton) would resolve themselves in time. In Catholic Italy, the young Protestant, who "had determined within myself that in those parts I would not indeed begin a conversation about religion, but if questioned about my faith would hide nothing, whatever the consequences,"[26] must have been made aware, in a way scarcely possible from the books at Horton or the association with men who shared his own religious convictions, of the ideological gulf between Catholic and Protestant; and he must, at the same time, have come to appreciate, both doctrinally and emotionally, the forceful charge that Laud was moving the English church toward Papism. His doubts about a clerical career can only have been heightened by his contact with Catholicism in Italy. Certainly, his Puritan convictions were given ample opportunity for pointed development and entrenchment, and he seems to have become more vocal in his views as time passed, for he wrote of his return trip to Rome: "What I was, if any man inquired, I concealed

from no one. For almost two months, in the very strong-hold of the
Pope, if anyone attacked the orthodox religion, I openly, as before,
defended it."[27] Such head-on confrontations over theology must have
taught Milton much about himself and his faith; they must also have
sharpened the felt distinctions, not only between Protestantism and
Catholicism where differences were obvious, but between Puritanism
and Laud's Anglicanism.

It was probably the first Bishops' War (March 1639) which caused
Milton to cancel a projected visit to Sicily and Greece: "the sad tidings
of civil war from England summoned me back. For I thought it base
that I should travel abroad at my ease for the cultivation of my mind,
while my fellow-citizens at home were fighting for their liberty."[28]
But he did not hurry home; and these sentences from the *Defensio
Secunda* have more than once been derided because of the leisurely
pace at which he answered the summons of his countrymen fighting
for their liberty. However, the sentences need little justification, for
they occur in a passage where he is making a polemical point and
defending his personal integrity against the charges of his adversary.
Moreover, we may suspect that the fifteen years separating the *Defensio
Secunda* from the return to England, years employed with unremitted
zeal in the defense of liberty (ecclesiastical, domestic, and political)
have led the respondent to overstate the cause as it then affected
him. And finally, the Bishop's War was preeminently a political struggle
between Charles and Parliament, and Milton had shown little interest
in politics up to that time; he no doubt felt that he had little to contribute
but had best return home (arriving in August or September, 1639)
in case he could be of help.

Back in England, he took quarters in St. Bride's Churchyard, near
Fleet Street, "and there, blissfully enough, devoted myself to my interrupted studies, willingly leaving the outcome of these events [the second
Bishops' War (August-September 1640) and its aftermath], first of all
to God, and then to those whom the people had entrusted with this
office."[29] In other words, he kept out of the political arena and resumed
the program of studies begun at Hammersmith; he also, although he
does not mention it in the *Defensio Secunda*, undertook the education
of his nephews, Edward and John Phillips, at this time. With the
promulgation of the canons of 1640, Milton took the decisive step
he had no doubt long considered: he gave up all thought of a clerical

career. It was perhaps this decision which led him to move into the larger house in Aldersgate Street and to increase the number of his students; if he were not to be a preacher, then he could be a school-master.

It is not known why Milton decided to enter the controversy over episcopacy; but, whether on his own initiative or at the invitation of the Smectymnuans (one of whom was Thomas Young, Milton's former tutor), he first raised his left hand against the prelates in *A Postscript*, which was appended to the Smectymnuan's *Answer to a Booke Entituled, An Humble Remonstrance* (March 1641). And in the five pamphlets which Milton published between May 1641 and April 1642, references to the vocation of the ministry are relatively frequent. The break with the Anglican establishment is complete; he argues for a Presbyterian settlement and, like Puritans throughout the century, he asserts that it is the inward call of God and not the cere-mony of ordination that makes a man a chosen vessel of the Word.[30] Combined with the facts that Milton had not spoken (except in *Lycidas*) of clerical vocation before 1641 and that, after 1642, he did not mention the subject again until his discussion of clerical calling in *De Doctrina Christiana* and his attack on tithing and hireling clerics in *The Likeliest Means* (1659), the frequent references to ministerial calling in the anti-prelatical tracts suggest that the topic was much in his thoughts and that the decision to reject a church career had been a recent one.

II. "Growing my Wings and Practising Flight": The Poetic Vocation

Perhaps the most striking feature of the early poetry, from a vocational standpoint, is its reiterated protestation of unpreparedness, coupled with its strong sense of hope for what may be done in the future when the poetic aspirations of youth have been realized. In a very real sense, the vocational emphasis of every serious poem Milton wrote from 1629 to 1637 may be said to have been summed up in the relaxed and picturesque conclusion of *Il Penseroso*:

> But let my due feet never fail,
> To walk the studious Cloysters pale,
> And love the high embowed Roof,
> With antick Pillars massy proof,
> And storied Windows richly dight,

Casting a dimm religious light.
There let the pealing Organ blow,
To the full voic'd Quire below,
In Service high, and Anthems cleer,
As may with sweetnes, through mine ear,
Dissolve me into extasies,
And bring all Heav'n before mine eyes.
And may at last my weary age
Find out the peacefull hermitage,
The Hairy Gown and Mossy Cell,
Where I may sit and rightly spell,
Of every Star that Heav'n doth shew,
And every Herb that sips the dew;
Till old experience do attain
To somthing like Prophetic strain.   (155–74)

As a poet, Milton has a very clear idea of where he is going; but he also knows that he has a long way to go before he arrives. Like Bunyan's pilgrim, he sees the goal in the distance but is aware that the road leading to it is winding and arduous. The passage is composed of three sentences, each beginning with a verb in the subjunctive mood; and these verbs control the tone of the lines. The search for the "Prophetic strain," the poet's goal, is conditioned by "old experience" which, as D. C. Allen observes, is the end result of an educating process where common, intellectual, and poetic experience are met and re-experienced over and over again.[31] In other words, Milton's poetic aspirations and plans are tempered by the recognition that experience, of which he has little, is the precondition of achievement. This same sense of hope and unpreparedness pervades, as I have already argued, the poetic response of *Sonnet VII;* and in another poem, probably written about the same time, Milton enlarges on the prophetic and visionary nature of the poetry he hopes to write:

Blest pair of *Sirens*, pledges of Heav'ns joy,
Sphear-born harmonious Sisters, Voice, and Vers,
Wed your divine sounds
            .   .   .   .

And to our high-rais'd phantasie present,
That undisturbed Song of pure concent,
Ay sung before the saphire-colour'd throne
To him that sits theron
            .   .   .   .

> That we on Earth with undiscording voice
> May rightly answer that melodious noise
> As once we did, till disproportion'd sin
> Jarr'd against natures chime, and with harsh din
> Broke the fair musick that all creatures made
> To their great Lord.   (*At a Solemn Musick*, 1–3, 5–8, 17–22)

The "Prophetic strain" of *Il Penseroso* is here an "undisturbed Song of pure concent." The voice of the sacred poet on earth must imitate and be in tune with the universal harmony of heaven, from which harmony man has been cut off by sin. The poet's function, therefore, is to reeducate fallen man by teaching him to hear again the harmony of heaven and to know God aright. But the poet who aspires to such a high goal first requires visionary experience (grace) and all the experience of truth with which life and learning (nature) can provide him. And in the prayer for enlightenment at the end of *At a Solemn Musick*, Milton was no doubt thinking primarily of himself, as the future scribe of that "Song of pure concent":

> O may we soon again renew that Song,
> And keep in tune with Heav'n, till God ere long
> To his celestial consort us unite,
> To live with him, and sing in endless morn of light.   (25–28)

But Milton in 1632 did not feel himself prepared, either artistically or spiritually, to be the instrument through which such prophetic strains of pure consent, such echoes of heavenly harmony and obedience, might find utterance.

In terms of poetic productivity, the Hammersmith and Horton years (1632–1638), rising in the twin peaks of *Comus* and *Lycidas*, were most certainly fruitful. But there is in the poetry of those years no indication that Milton had come to think of himself as a mature poet. (If the experience recorded in *Sonnet VII* were of as profound a significance to him poetically as it was spiritually, it has left no mark upon the poetry itself.) The same declarations of present unreadiness but of hopes for the future which characterize the pre-1632 verse also pervade the poems of the Hammersmith-Horton period. Thus, *Comus*, composed and performed in 1634, was not published until 1637; and then it was Henry Lawes, not Milton himself, who arranged for the printing of the masque. In the epistle dedicatory, addressed to Viscount Brackley, Lawes describes the poet's reticence and the

circumstances leading to publication: "Although not openly acknowl-
edg'd by the Author, yet it is a legitimate off-spring, so lovely, and
so much desired, that the often Copying of it hath tir'd my Pen to
give my severall friends satisfaction, and brought me to a necessity
of producing it to the publike view."[32] And on the title page, Milton
himself added the motto, taken from Virgil's second eclogue, "Eheu,
qui volui misero mihi! floribus astrum / Perditus" (58–59), meaning,
"Alas! what have I wished upon myself, unhappy man; I have let
the south wind in upon my flowers."[33] The significance of the motto
has been variously interpreted, but one aspect of its meaning is certain:
even after submitting the masque to extensive revision before allowing
publication, Milton was reluctant to permit its being sent forth into
the light of day.

Although Milton has left no explanation of why, despite his doubts
and hesitation, he allowed Lawes to publish *Comus*, I suspect that
his reasons were not dissimilar to those of Keats who, in sending his
Endymion to press, invited his reader to judge more the attempt than
the result and to expect more in the future than the present had succeeded in producing: "It is just that this youngster should die away:
a sad thought for me, if I had not some hope that while it is dwindling
I may be plotting and fitting myself for verses fit to live."[34] As Keats
in 1818 was fitting himself for "verses fit to live," so Milton in 1637,
as we know from a letter of that year to Diodati, was contemplating
"an immortality of fame" and preparing himself to compose works
that later generations would not willingly let perish: "You ask what
I am thinking of? So help me God, an immortality of fame. What
am I doing? Growing my wings and practising flight. But my Pegasus
still raises himself on very tender wings."[35] In spite of the bantering
good humor of earlier parts of this letter, there is no reason to doubt
Milton's sincerity here. *Practising flight* is the dominant vocational note
of the early poetry—poetry which shows us a young man learning
his craft, experimenting with various subjects and poetic forms and
meters, growing stronger and more self-assured with each successive
effort. He knows himself to have a poetic calling; and he has already
delineated his exalted conception of the religious poet he aspires to
become: not only a divinely inspired teacher, but also an instrument
of regeneration whose mimetic re-creations of celestial harmony constitute a mode of continuing revelation, by means of which God manifests

his will to errant humanity. However, while his achievements to date give good cause for believing that the longed-for "immortality of fame" will indeed be realized in due course, Milton is well aware also that he has much still to learn, both about himself and about poetry. But his assurance, he knows, is well founded: he has been called to serve as God's poet-priest; and all is, if he has grace to use it so, as ever in his great Taskmaster's eye.

The protestation of unpreparedness and the reluctance to commit himself to print before due season, implied in the bibliographical history of *Comus*, is made explicit in the opening lines of *Lycidas* (where the first words, "Yet once more," refer perhaps to the recently published masque):

> Yet once more, O ye Laurels, and once more
> Ye Myrtles brown, with Ivy never-sear,
> I com to pluck your Berries harsh and crude,
> And with forc'd fingers rude,
> Shatter your leaves before the mellowing year.
> Bitter constraint, and sad occasion dear,
> Compels me to disturb your season due:
> For *Lycidas* is dead. (1–8)

The primary reference in these lines is not to Edward King but rather to Milton himself; the passage is a forceful and unequivocal assertion of his own artistic immaturity and unripeness. The "sad occasion" of King's death has constrained him to gather prematurely and "with forced fingers rude" the plants symbolic of the poet's garland.

At the end of the poem, the note of unreadiness is heard again; but now it is coupled, in a union familiar from the poetry of 1629–1633, with the promise of future achievement. In line 185, the poet reenters his poem as an "uncouth Swain," rude but full of promise, who

> touch'd the tender stops of various Quills,
> With eager thought warbling his *Dorick* lay:
> And now the Sun had stretch'd out all the hills,
> And now was dropt into the Western bay;
> At last he rose, and twitch'd his Mantle blew:
> To morrow to fresh Woods, and Pastures new. (188–93)

In striking contrast to the hesitancy and reluctance of the prelude, it is with "eager thought" that the poet here fingers the responsive, yet still frail ("tender") stops of his pastoral pipe. The composition of the monody has given him additional experience and additional confidence. Like the day dying in the western bay, the long period of experimentation and preparation is drawing also to a close. Pulling around his shoulders his bardic mantle of blue—the color symbolic of hope—he rises confidently to greet the new dawn of poetic promise, when he will don the singing robes of God's fully fledged bard. (In view of Milton's conception of the religious poet's sacerdotal function, "Mantle blew" may be thought to allude to the divine instructions given for Aaron's priestly vestments in Exodus xxviii, 31: "And thou shalt make the robe of the ephod all of blue.") But the "fresh Woods, and Pastures new" of poetic achievement lie still in the future ("To morrow"), albeit the proximate future. *Lycidas*, then, rather than being the first product of that new dawning, is but its harbinger.

The evidence of *Ad Patrem* is extremely difficult to assess, and this for two reasons: (1) we have no idea what occasioned the composition of the poem and the defense of his poetic talent and inclinations contained therein, and (2) it is impossible to date the poem with any certainty at all. A variety of dates—1632, 1634, and 1637–1638—have been proposed for *Ad Patrem,* and the difficulty arises because each dating has been skillfully and persuasively defended. However, it strikes me that, while each of the suggested dates is certainly *possible,* the 1632 dating is the *least likely* to be correct.[36] The case for 1634 is not so easily dismissed and is much more attractive; W. R. Parker has recently asserted the claims of 1634 in a most convincing manner:

The poem nowhere states or suggests, nor is there elsewhere any evidence, that the father's dislike of poetry had been expressed before or was of long standing. On the contrary, Milton argues that his whole careful education, and his father's agreement to the Hammersmith period of additional study, had been, in effect, an endorsement of literary activity. Something, therefore, had happened to arouse the old man's antagonism to the Muses. Can we doubt that it was the composition of the masque? There is one fact in the poet's biography which puts the matter almost beyond dispute—a fact truly inexplicable if the conflict expressed in *Ad Patrem* does not apply to *Comus.* The masque was written in 1634; and during 1635, 1636, and the first ten months of 1637 Milton *wrote no more poetry.* Instead he was studying, at his father's expense—at his father's wish. In *Ad Patrem,* as in the 1633 letter to an unknown friend, Milton's future career as a clergyman is assumed throughout. The matter is not mentioned because it is taken for granted between the poet and his father, and the poem is not at all concerned with it. Indeed, the poem is not a plea that Milton be allowed to undertake a career as a poet; he speaks, instead, of his youthful verses as his amusement and pastime (line 115), and concedes that they have been trivial (4). He asks only that his father should not despise and condemn this pleasant avocation. *Ad Patrem* is an argument that poetry is congenial to Milton's (unstated) life work, and he cleverly thanks his parent for not forcing him into business or law, where poetry would be uncongenial. It is clearly implied that his father thinks he is preparing his son for *something*—and obviously not for poetry.[37]

The argument is compelling, and Parker is almost certainly correct in his interpretation of what the poem is saying about a poetic avocation (as opposed to poetry as a full-time career). However, it strikes me that the central contention (the composition of *Comus*) supporting a 1634 dating for *Ad Patrem* may more reasonably be used to assert the claims of a date in late 1637 or early 1638.

Two important points militate against Parker's view. First, it is strange that Milton should justify his Muse to his father and then (as Parker himself notes) silence that Muse for nearly three years; one might more legitimately expect the defense of poetry in *Ad Patrem* to have been followed by literary activity than to have introduced almost three years of silence. And second, Milton's father would more likely have been disturbed by the publication than by the composition of *Comus*. It was to the advantage of young men preparing to enter the church, as John Donne and George Herbert both knew, to cultivate connections with the nobility, for often such acquaintances could lead to pastoral appointments. Thus, the decision to write a masque (and a masque on chastity, at that) for the private entertainment of the Bridgewater family would hardly have been cause for alarm on the part of Milton's father. The decision to publish the masque, on the other hand, to make *Comus* public and thereby to gain a reputation as a poet, might well have upset a man who had destined his son for the ministry; the danger of publication was that it might lead the young poet to consider a career, not in the church, but rather in poetry; and besides, the *publication* of the masque could have no direct effect on the obtaining of a pastoral charge.

In favor of a 1637–1638 dating for *Ad Patrem* are the following points. First, it was probably not until 1637 that Milton began to entertain serious doubts about a clerical vocation; as Shawcross observes, "That his interest in the church as a career was waning had not impressed him until the despotic, oppressive events of 1637 obtruded themselves upon his consciousness."[38] His son's growing uneasiness

about the church could hardly have passed unnoticed by the elder
Milton. Second, Milton's waning interest in the church corresponded
to a deepening interest in poetry. That this was so is attested (1)
by the fact that he published not only *Comus* in 1637 but *Lycidas*
in early 1638 as well (his only other published work was the sonnet
On Shakespear, which appeared in 1632), and (2) by his hopes for
fame and reputation as given utterance in *Lycidas* and the letter of
1637 to Diodati. Third, shortly after justifying his poetic endeavors
to his father, Milton left for the Continent in the spring of 1638. The
trip was preeminently motivated by his interest in literature, a fact
made clear by his extended visit to Florence and his activities in the
learned academies of that city, his visit to the Vatican library and
his presence at a musical entertainment at the Barberini palace, his
visit to the home of John Baptista Manso, the friend and patron of
Tasso, and finally his intention of passing over to Sicily and Greece,
the homelands of Theocritus and of Homer, Euripides, and Plato.
Since, however, Milton's father gave his son permission to undertake
the Continental journey,[39] it would seem clear that the family tensions
alluded to in *Ad Patrem* had been resolved before Milton's departure.
To summarize, then: some time between the composition of *Lycidas*
(November 1637) and the start of the Continental journey (late April
or early May, 1638), the poet justified his Muse to his father, who
had (we may assume) expressed alarm at his son's waning interest
in the ministry and waxing delight in poetry, by writing *Ad Patrem*.
One could, after all, devote oneself to both endeavors (poetry and
God's word) with success and without contradiction, even as the elder
Milton had combined the composition of music with the trade of
the scrivener. It is not, therefore, to be wondered at that "we pursue
kindred art and related interests" (*Ad Patrem*, 63).

The rousing motions of *Lycidas*, the premonitions of a new and
exciting period in his poetic development, gave rise, not to an increase
in poetic activity, but to a literary voyage (in a sense a pilgrimage)
to Italy, with the further intention of visiting Sicily and Greece. The
importance of the Italian journey, as it affected Milton's self-dedication
to the Muse, can scarcely be overstressed, for the Italian experience
confirmed his belief in his poetic abilities and imposed new dimensions
and new directions on his aspirations. His own account in *The Reason
of Church-Government* is important in understanding the vocational
significance of the experience.

I must say therefore that after I had from my first yeeres by the ceaselesse diligence and care of my father, whom God recompence, bin exercis'd to the tongues, and some sciences, as my age would suffer, by sundry masters and teachers both at home and at schools, it was found that whether ought was impos'd me by them that had the overlooking, or betak'n prosing or versing, but chiefly this latter, the stile by certain vital signes it had, was likely to live. But much latelier in the privat Academies of *Italy*, whither I was favor'd to resort, perceiving that some trifles which I had in memory, compos'd at under twenty or thereabout (for manner is that every one must give some proof of his wit and reading there) met with acceptance above what was lookt for, and other things which I had shifted in scarsity of books and conveniences to patch up amongst them, were received with written Encomiums, which the Italian is not forward to bestow on men of this side the Alps, I began thus farre to assent both to them and divers of my friends here at home, and not lesse to an inward prompting which now grew daily upon me, that by labour and intent study (which I take to be my portion in this life) joyn'd with the strong propensity of nature, I might perhaps leave something so written to aftertimes, as they should not willingly let it die. These thoughts at once possest me, and these other. That if I were certain to write as men by Leases, for three lives and downward, there ought not regard be sooner had, then to Gods glory by the honour and instruction of my country. For which cause, . . . I apply'd my selfe to that resolution . . . to be an interpreter & relater of the best and sagest things among mine own citizens throughout this Iland in the mother dialect.[40]

When he penned this account of his dedication to the Muse in 1642, Milton clearly felt that the Italian experience had been a catalyst in bringing together the many elements which, united, confirmed him in the belief of his aptitude and talent. He remembered, of course, his debt to the efforts of his father and his early training at the hands of tutors like Thomas Young and in the schools, but it was (he says) preeminently the warm reception of his poetic gifts by the intellectual and artistic elite of Italy (coupled with the "inward prompting" of God which increased almost daily after the return from Italy), which led him to acknowledge and act upon the praise of friends at home (Alexander Gill, for instance) and his own natural inclination for poetic creativity. It was Italy which convinced him that he might "perhaps leave something so written to aftertimes, as they should not willingly let it die." But as the Italian experience taught him that he was destined to be a poet, that he was "certain to write," and that his writings would survive him and live in future ages ("as men buy Leases, for three lives and downward"), it also taught him that, after the example of Tasso and Ariosto, he should bend his efforts toward instructing

his countrymen in their native language. England might be honored
in Latin, but she could be instructed only in English; and thus Milton,
as he expressed it in the *Epitaphium Damonis* (1640?), resolved to
abandon international, in favor of domestic, fame:

One man may not do all things, one man may not hope all things; for me
there will be a sufficiently ample reward, a sufficiently great glory (though
I then be unknown to fame forever and altogether without repute in the
outside world), if only fair-haired Ouse shall read me and he who drinks
of Alan and eddying Humber and all the woods of Trent; and if above all
the rest my own Thames and dark-metaled Tamar, and the Orkneyes, whose
waves are at the end of the world, shall commit my verse to memory. (*The
Student's Milton*, p. 108)

From the determination here taken, "to be an interpreter & relater
of the best and sagest things among mine own Citizens throughout
this Iland in the mother dialect," Milton did not retreat or waver
until a decade later when Salmasius forced him to defend his nation,
in Latin, in the international forum.

Thus, the Italian journey confirmed Milton in two important beliefs:
(1) he was destined to be a poet, and (2) he would employ his talents
in instructing his countrymen in virtue and righteousness. Toward
achieving these ends, he began planning in earnest a poem that would
be "doctrinal and exemplary" to his nation and, between 1640 and
1642, recorded in the *Cambridge Manuscript* a list of about a hundred
possible subjects for plays from the Bible and from British history;
moreover, in both *Mansus* and the *Epitaphium Damonis*, he spoke
of his plan to compose an Arthuriad. But it is only after the visit
to Italy that the hopes and premonitions of poetic destiny (hopes
felt all the way from the *Vacation Exercise* of 1628 to *Lycidas* of
1637), are permitted to issue in concrete planning. Milton returned
from the Continent assured of his poetic talent and imbued with a
firm sense of artistic direction. With the promulgation of the Laudian
Canons of 1640 and the subsequent determination to abandon a career
in the church, he began in earnest preparations for a poetical vocation;
however, before embarking on such a career, much "labour and intent
study" were necessary, and so, while preparing his Pegasus for flight,
he solved the immediate economic problem (that of earning a living)
by opening a private school and taking in pupils, beginning with his
nephews, John and Edward Phillips. The effect of the Italian expe-

rience, therefore, on Milton's decision to become a "professional" poet is comparable to the spiritual resolve (the culmination of his conversion experience) in *Sonnet VII* to dedicate himself to God's service.

But the poetic plans of 1640 were soon interrupted by his entry into the controversy over episcopacy. The pamphlets of 1641–1642, far from being (as some readers have argued) an unfortunate setback to Milton's poetic plans, are in actuality the fulfillment (in prose rather than poetry, as he had originally planned) of his decision to serve God and work for his glory, "by the honour and instruction of my country." And, important as Italy was to his poetic aspirations, it was only the experience of ecclesiastical controversy that turned Milton into the religious poet whom we know. *Paradise Lost* and the last poems of 1671 could almost (political events aside) have been composed any time after 1642; before that date, no such poetry would have been possible. The antiprelatical tracts are the final step in Milton's developing view of himself as God's poet, for in these early pamphlets he learned what it was to be the Lord's spokesman, the prophet of his will for reformation in the church; they are the school in which he first was taught to justify God's ways to men. And, as Tillyard has observed, Milton in these pamphlets more than once "attaches his poetical ambitions to the imagined religious and political rebirth of his country."[41]

The decision to fight for the establishment of the English New Jerusalem and the experience of *active* service in God's cause are the final stages in Milton's developing view of his own poetic role. Although for many years he would be the prose prophet of national liberty and reformation, it is clear from the first of the antiepiscopal pamphlets that, when God's will for England has been realized (and that will be in the proximate future), Milton aspires to be the poet of that new age:

Then amidst the *Hymns*, and *Halleluiahs* of *Saints* some one may perhaps bee heard offering at high *strains* in new and lofty *Measures* to sing and celebrate thy *divine Mercies*, and *marvelous Judgements* in this Land throughout all Ages; whereby this great and Warlike Nation instructed and inur'd to the fervent and continuall practice of *Truth* and *Righteousnesse*, and casting farre from her the *rags* of her old *vices* may presse on hard to that *high* and *happy* emulation to be found the *soberest*, *wisest*, and *most Christian People* at that day when thou the Eternall and shortly-expected King shall open the Clouds to judge the severall Kingdomes of the World.[42]

The "Prophetic strain" for which he had longed ten years earlier in *Il Penseroso* is here, in contrast to the unspecified and vague hopes of the early poem, centered on a definite theme: the praise of divine mercy and justice for the special favor shown to England and the exhortation to his countrymen to live in virtue and righteousness in preparation for the Second Coming and the Last Judgment. Thus, Milton's private vocation as poet is but the extension of his public role as the prose prophet of reformation; his poetic calling is both defined by and subsumed into the national mission of bringing reformation to the world. A similar view of poetic destiny is found in *Animadversions upon the Remonstrant's Defence* (July 1641):

When Thou hast settl'd peace in the Church, and righteous judgement in the Kingdome, then shall all Thy Saints address their voyces of joy, and triumph to thee, standing on the shoare of that red Sea into which our enemies had almost driven us. And he that now for haste snatches up a plain ungarnish't thanke-offering to thee, which could not bee deferr'd in regard of thy so many great deliverances wrought for us one upon another, may then perhaps take up a Harp, and sing thee an elaborate Song to Generations.[43]

Milton has every expectation that the "ungarnish't thanke-offering," the product of his left hand, will soon be replaced by that "elaborate Song to Generations" which will mark him as the poet of the new age, the praiser of God's mercies to England.

Perhaps the most famous statement of the poetic function and of his own aspirations in all of Milton's writings is that in the Preface to Book Two of *The Reason of Church-Government*. In this preface, Milton declares himself to be a serious national poet and sets down both his poetic creed and the types of poetry he proposes to write. From a vocational standpoint, however, what is most interesting is that he stresses the ministerial function of poetry. Poetry is, he says, a priesthood in its own right, and the ability to compose the epic, tragedy, or ode is "the inspired guift of God rarely bestow'd, but yet to some (though most abuse) in every Nation: and is of power beside the office of a pulpit, to imbreed and cherish in a great people the seeds of vertu, and publick civility, to allay the perturbations of the mind, and set the affections in right tune, to celebrate in glorious and lofty Hymns the throne and equipage of Gods Almightinesse, and what he works, and what he suffers to be wrought with high providence in his Church."[44] It is no accident that, having defined the sacredness of the poetic office, he concludes the preface by telling his readers that he has been "Church-outed by the Prelats." The man who aspires to be the poet-priest of his nation has not so much rejected a calling into the church (except as Laud would define such a calling) as he has broadened the notion of clerical vocation to include the call to serve as God's spokesman and interpreter through poetry. Thus, the tension between the ministry and poetry was finally resolved, not by a categorical rejection of one of the alternatives, but rather by the recognition that the functions and aims of the two offices overlap. It was this discovery, felt as early as *Prolusion VII* but not finally confirmed until his active participation in the ecclesiastical dispute of 1641–1642, which led Milton to embrace a literary vocation, at first in prose, but always looking forward to that time when he would be England's poet-priest and compose a poem "doctrinal and exemplary" to his nation.

University of Western Australia

NOTES

All quotations from Milton's poetry are from *The Student's Milton*, ed. F. A. Patterson (New York, 1933). Quotations from the prose works are from *Complete Prose Works of John Milton*, ed. D. M. Wolfe et al., 8 vols. (New Haven, 1953–); this edition is cited in the notes below as YP.

1. Woodhouse, "Notes on Milton's Early Development," *UTQ*, XIII (1942–43), 66–101; a revised (but substantially unaltered) version of this paper appears as chap. 2 in *The Heavenly Muse: A Preface to Milton*, ed. H. R. MacCallum (Toronto, 1972), pp. 15–54. Shawcross, "Milton's Decision to Become a Poet," *MLQ*, XXIV (1963), 21–30.

2. See William Haller, *The Rise of Puritanism* (New York, 1957), pp. 288–322.

3. *The Reason of Church-Government*, YP, I, p. 816.

4. *Prolusion VII*, YP, I, p. 292.

5. The importance of the Nativity ode in terms of Milton's spiritual autobiography and understanding of his poetic vocation was first pointed out by Arthur Barker, "The Pattern of Milton's *Nativity Ode*," *UTQ*, X (1941), 167–81.

6. "Notes on Milton's Early Development," pp. 77–78. Woodhouse's argument relies quite heavily on the dating of the Italian sonnets, which he places confidently in 1630 and treats as examples of Milton's reversion to secular and amatory verse after the resolve of December 1629 to write only sacred poetry. The dating of these sonnets is more problematical than Woodhouse believed (see the summary in *Milton's Sonnets*, ed. E. A. J. Honigmann [New York, 1966], pp. 76–81). Recent criticism has placed the Italian sonnets in either 1629 (that is, before the resolve taken in *Elegy VI* and the Nativity ode) or 1638 (well after both the resolve of late 1629 and the rededication

in *Sonnet VII*); a 1630 dating of these sonnets is, however, reasserted by J. E. Shaw
and A. B. Giamatti in *A Variorum Commentary on the Poems of John Milton* (New
York, 1970-), vol. I, p. 367. In any event, Woodhouse's argument is still valid even
without the evidence of the Italian poems, for Milton wrote much nonreligious verse
in 1630-1631: for instance, the jocular epitaphs on Hobson, *On Shakespear,* and (almost
certainly) *L'Allegro* and *Il Penseroso.*

7. Woodhouse, "Notes on Milton's Early Development," p. 77.

8. Ibid., p. 67.

9. "Milton's Decision to Become a Poet," p. 25.

10. YP, I, p. 319.

11. Ibid., p. 320.

12. Ibid.

13. Ibid., pp. 320-21.

14. "The Pattern of Milton's *Nativity Ode,*" p. 172.

15. "Milton's Decision to Become a Poet," p. 30.

16. The letter, preserved in two drafts in the *Trinity MS,* is undated; however,
W. R. Parker long ago proved beyond any reasonable doubt that the letter belongs
to early 1633 and that it may have been written to Thomas Young, Milton's former
tutor, himself a clergyman. See Parker's "Some Problems in the Chronology of Milton's
Early Poems," *RES,* XI (1935), 276-83, and also his note, "Milton's Unknown Friend,"
Times Literary Supplement (May 16, 1936), 420.

17. Letter 8 (1637), to Diodati, YP, I, p. 327.

18. *Defensio Secunda,* YP, IV, pt. 1, p. 614.

19. There was a great deal of excitement in London in the spring and summer
of 1637. The mutilations in June of Prynne, Bastwick, and Burton, for instance, were
executed in public and attracted much attention. D. M. Wolfe writes that "when Burton
was taken from the Fleet to be imprisoned at Lancaster Castle, it was estimated that
a hundred thousand people lined the streets to acclaim the earless hero" (YP, I, p. 44).

20. Letter 7 (1637), to Diodati, YP, I, p. 323.

21. One aspect of Milton's developing and changing religious views seems clear
enough: the Puritan who wrote *Lycidas* in 1637 is not identical with the convinced
Presbyterian of the antiprelatical pamphlets (1641-1642). No committed Presbyterian
sympathizer would have exposed ecclesiastical evils through the mouth of St. Peter,
the first bishop.

22. YP, I, pp. 822-23.

23. Ibid., p. 823, n. 161. The oath itself is reproduced ibid., pp. 990-91.

24. Ibid., p. 823, n. 161.

25. "The Pattern of Milton's *Nativity Ode,*" p. 171.

26. *Defensio Secunda,* YP, IV, pt. 1, p. 619.

27. Ibid.

28. Ibid.

29. Ibid., p. 621.

30. See YP, I, pp. 537, 715, 721, 755, and 843.

31. *The Harmonious Vision: Studies in Milton's Poetry* (Baltimore, 1954), pp.
22-23.

32. *The Student's Milton,* p. 44. W. R. Parker is rationalizing in saying that Lawes
"had to explain (using a familiar formula) that it was 'not openly acknowledged by
the Author'" (*Milton: A Biography,* 2 vols. [Oxford, 1968], vol. I, p. 142). Formula
or no formula, it was Lawes, not Milton, who arranged for the publication of *Comus.*
That fact makes Milton's reticence an inescapable conclusion.

33. The destructiveness of the South Wind (Auster) had earlier been mentioned by Milton in *Elegy IV* (1627): "Bisque novo terram sparsisti Chlori senilem / Gramine, bisque tuas abstulit Auster opes" (35–36) ("And twice, Chloris, thou hadst scattered fresh grass over the aged earth, and twice had Auster carried off thy riches" [*The Student's Milton*, p. 88]).

34. Keats, *Poetical Works*, ed., H. W. Garrod (Oxford, 1966), p. 54.

35. Letter 8 (1637), to Diodati, YP, I, p. 327.

36. The case for 1632 has recently been reargued by Douglas Bush, "The Date of Milton's *Ad Patrem*," *MP*, LXI (1964), 204–08. The defense of this date is usually made heavily dependent upon the assumption (which I have taken pains to discredit) that Milton, as *Sonnet VII* and the "Letter to a Friend" of 1633 are alleged to show, had determined against a clerical career and in favor of a poetic one by late 1632, and that *Ad Patrem*, being a defense of his choice of a poetic career, is further evidence of this decision. There are, however, other arguments for a 1632 dating, and for these I refer the reader to Bush's article. See also the summary of dating evidence for *Ad Patrem* in Bush, *A Variorum Commentary on the Poems of John Milton*, vol. I, pp. 232–40.

37. *Milton: A Biography*, vol. I, p. 126.

38. "Milton's Decision to Become a Poet," p. 26.

39. "I became desirous, my mother having died, of seeing foreign parts, especially Italy, and with my father's consent I set forth, accompanied by a single attendant" (*Defensio Secunda*, YP, IV, pt. 1, p. 614).

40. YP, I, pp. 808–12.

41. E. M. W. Tillyard, *Milton* (1930; reprint ed., London, 1966), p. 101.

42. YP, I, p. 616.

43. Ibid., pp. 706–07.

44. Ibid., pp. 816–17.

THE CIVIC HERO IN MILTON'S PROSE

Annabel Patterson

The heroic metaphors and allusions in Milton's prose have received little attention in their own right, having been subordinated to study of either his early epic plans or his mature rejection of classical epic. But following Milton's heroic language from pamphlet to pamphlet one finds a coherent and partly self-contained pattern. In wrestling with the problematical role of the intellectual in times of crisis, and in trying to define that role as heroic, Milton created a linguistic and metaphoric synthesis of action and contemplation which differs from the passive fortitude of the great poems. Its affinities are with Ciccro's definition of the orator, and with Aristotle's *Nicomachean Ethics* at the point where they lead into the *Politics*, rather than with the Book of Job; and its emphasis is on the hero as public benefactor. Developed in part to justify his decision to enter the church reform debates, Milton's synthesis is held defensively in the divorce pamphlets, actively in the *Areopagitica*; set aside for political expediency in the regicide pamphlets, it is triumphantly restated in the *Second Defence*; and finally, in the *Pro Se Defensio*, Milton found it crumble in his hands. When Milton dropped out of politics, his civic heroism had become impossible to maintain, not only because of the Restoration, but because, as his language reveals, his confidence in his own impartiality and unselfishness had been destroyed.

I⊤ has become customary to see Milton's prose, whether deftly or clumsily left-handed, as part of the explanation for his movement from a projected Arthuriad to the achieved poems of the better fortitude. Whether that movement is explained as disillusionment with national politics,[1] with the Arthurian legends themselves,[2] or recognition that the written defense of the English people itself constituted a national epic, thereby satisfying the earlier ambition,[3] it has been critical practice to ransack the prose for comments about or allusions to epic or romantic heroism in support of such theories, not all of which can be held simultaneously. The heroic language has been connected backward with the epic ambitions revealed in the *Vacation Exercise, Elegy VI,* and *Mansus,* and forward to the explicit rejections of a military and chivalric ethos in the late poems; and criticism has charted through the prose various patterns of transition from one to the other.

What has not been done, or not done systematically, is an analysis of the heroic allusions of the pamphlets in their own right. Are we wise to assume that all such allusions merely reflect the tensions of postponing a great poem? Or that they do not have a coherence of their own which, if not independent of the poetry at either end, would still be intellectually valid without it? Following Milton's heroic language from pamphlet to pamphlet has led me to give negative answers to these questions and to propose instead a positive finding which avoids the contradictions among the theories mentioned above. In the prose, Milton develops a modification of the heroic ethos which differs substantially from the passive fortitude of the mature poems. Let us call it, although the term will never be entirely adequate, civic fortitude. In wrestling with the problematical role of the intellectual in time of crisis, and in trying to define that role as heroic, Milton adopted his own synthesis of active and contemplative, public and private, fortitude and prudence, which sanctioned much of the egocentricity for which active or military fortitude was disesteemed. Unlike the tradition of passive fortitude which, thanks to Steadman, Lewalski, and others,[4] we now so thoroughly understand, this modification of fortitude is not religious in orientation, although its causes include the politics of religion; its affinities are with Cicero's definition of the orator, and with Aristotle's *Nicomachean Ethics* at the point where they lead into the *Politics,* rather than with the Book of Job; and its emphasis is on the hero as public benefactor, whose egoism is justified by the event rather than in spite of it. When Milton dropped out of politics, this version of heroism had become intellectually impossible for him to maintain, not only because the efforts of twenty years had gone to waste in the Restoration, but because, as his language clearly reveals, his confidence in his own unselfishness and impartiality had been destroyed.

To say that Milton adopted his own synthesis is not, of course, to imply that he was independent of earlier intellectual movements toward synthesis, of which we can identify three major forms. To begin with, the formulation of such a compromise in terms of an educational ideal for princes and governors had long before reached commonplace status through such exempla as Alexander's dependence on the bedside reading of Homer. The effective use of both military skill and book learning, symbolized by the relationship between hand and head, sword and pen, passes into Milton's own pamphlet on education via humanist educational theory. The proposition that a well-schooled man should be fitted to perform "all the offices both private and publike of peace and war" is not, however, so much a synthesis of opposites as an aggregate of complementary skills.

More genuinely synthetic was the Ciceronian ideal of the orator as political figure and legislator by persuasion, an ideal which was extrapolated by the Italian civic humanists of the late Trecento and Quattrocento in Florence, and connected with contemporary arguments for the survival of republicanism and civil liberties. Despite the often startling similarities in thinking between Milton and the Italian civic humanists, one cannot be sure that he read the *Della Vita Civile* of Salutati's pupil, Matteo Palmieri, or the *Dialogues* of Bruni based on Cicero's *De Oratore;*[5] but we can be certain that he had read the *De Oratore* itself, with its opening lament for the personal burden of political activism balanced by its totally convincing praise of the orator as public benefactor, legislator and civilizer (I, viii, 31–34). This application of learning to the active life through the political effectiveness of rhetoric provides a genuinely synthetic solution to the action-contemplation dichotomy, and the orator is thereby defined as uniquely qualified to mediate *between* the two *genera vitae.* In addition, Cicero anticipates one of Milton's literary strategies for synthesis, by using military metaphors to describe his profession. In distinguishing between classroom and real political rhetoric, he describes how "at last our Oratory must be conducted out of this sheltered training-ground at home, right into action, into the dust and uproar, into the camp and fighting-line of public debate," ("Educenda deinde dictio est ex hac domestica exercitatione et umbratili medium in agmen, in pulverem, in clamorem, in castra, atque in aciem forensem" [I, xxxiv, 157]).[6]

By using this metaphorical language, Cicero provides us with a link between his professional synthesis and the third major tradition of fusion, which evolves within the development of epic poetry and commentaries upon it. The fusion of military valor and intelligence, in the forms of Achilles and Odysseus, into a single heroic virtue or figure had been attempted by poets and commentators from Virgil onward, and, as E. R. Curtius points out, there are passages in the *Iliad* to indicate that Homer himself held "that strength and intelligence in equipoise (VII, 288; II, 202; IX, 53) represent the optimum in warrior virtue."[7] Curtius traces the *fortitudo-sapientia topos* from Fulgentius' commentary on the opening lines of the *Aeneid* through Isidore of Seville, Statius, Dictys, and Dares, and into the Renaissance, where it merges with the arms and letters *topos*. In epic poetry itself, one method of synthesis is by the comrade or cooperative formula (which leads into allegory) by which, in the *Chanson de Roland*, Roland's and Oliver's differences are merged in their common cause and common end, while Charlemagne is left to carry the burden of both values; the fusion which the paratactic formula ("Rolland est proz, e Oliver est sage" [1093]) cannot or will not achieve linguistically is achieved dramatically. Alternatively there are attempts at fusion which are metaphorical only, and which achieve their end by deliberately blurring the boundaries of the antithesis. George Chapman, for example, in the preface to his translation of the *Odyssey*, distinguishes between Homer's two epic propositions only to blend them:

The first word of his *Iliads* is . . . wrath; the first word of his *Odysses* . . . Man—contracting in either word his each worke's Proposition. In one, Predominant Perturbation; in the other, overruling Wisedome; in one, the Bodies' fervour and fashion of outward Fortitude to all possible height of Heroicall Action; in the other, the Mind's inward, constant and unconquerd Empire.

The military and imperial metaphors of the last phrase have already made one subject as it were the image of the other, before Chapman declares that *all* epic poetry is composed of a body, or narrative fiction, and a soul, or allegorical interpretation. This melting of dichotomies into each other supports Chapman's insinuated value judgment that the *Odyssey* is a more complete poem than the *Iliad*, having for its subject "the information or fashion of an absolute man."[8]

This view of the *Iliad* as an active narrative and the *Odyssey* as a contemplative one, with the *Aeneid* as a combination of the two, is explained somewhat differently by Torquato Tasso in his Allegory to the *Gerusalemme Liberata* (1581); an "active" action is one which is publicly motivated, and performed in public, while a contemplative action is personally motivated, and performed by a solitary figure. Thus, "Aeneas is seen to be accompanied, when he fighteth, or doth other civil Acts, but when he goeth to Hell and the Elysian fields, he leaves his Followers, accompanied only with his most faithfull Friend Achates, who never departed from his side." The same numerical distinction operates at the allegorical level:

> Moreover the Operation of the Understanding speculative, which is the Working of one only Power is commodiously figured unto us by the Action of one alone; but the Operation political, which proceedeth together from the other Powers of the Mind (which are as Citizens united in one Common Wealth) cannot so commodiously be shadowed by Action, wherein many together, and to one End working, do not concur.[9]

In other words, an epic poem can have active and contemplative structures at *both* the literal and allegorical levels; while at the same time the relationship between literal and allegorical levels is that between physical action and intellectual process. This already baffling chiasmus becomes even more confusing when Tasso starts to interpret his own poem. Thus the Christian army "signifieth Man, compounded of Soul and Body"; the joint endeavor of the "diverse Princes" represents the cooperation of the "Powers of the Mind" in achieving civic happiness; and "all the Actions of the politic Man, Godfrey . . . stands for Understanding."[10] The constant movement of these dichotomous terms between levels of meaning may well be intended to produce a synthesis; the final effect, however, is of intellectual smudging.

Nevertheless, we can with some certainty include Tasso among those whose theories influenced Milton, with the Allegory to the *Gerusalemme* among texts he must have read. Moreover, Tasso's juggling of dichotomies, however unsatisfactory, is a useful introduction to the range of linguistic and metaphorical strategies Milton uses to manipulate epic tradition in the prose and reshape it in his own image.

Of the three types of synthesis, then, all of which he uses to some extent, Milton's is most closely related to that which grows out of epic tradition; but what makes it peculiarly his own is the personal bias, the driving need in pamphlet after pamphlet to explain the relation between public statement and personal "digression," between results and motives. His synthesis evolves in the form of a mixed heroic persona for *himself*. Developed in part to account for his decision to enter the church reform debates, it is held defensively in the divorce pamphlets, actively in the *Areopagitica;* set aside for political expediency in the regicide pamphlets, it is restated with unmistakable triumph in the *Second Defence;* and finally, in the *Pro Se Defensio,* Milton found it crumble in his hands. The method of this paper will simply be to demonstrate this pattern by following Milton's language of heroism from pamphlet to pamphlet. The interpretation of this language will necessarily be subjective to the extent that all rhetorical and stylistic analysis is subjective; objectivity will be provided by the historical context of the pamphlets, and the way in which their larger arguments support the linguistic evidence.

As Tillyard has shown,[11] prior to the prose period there is evidence that different kinds of heroic precedent were being weighed in Milton's mind as he contemplated his vocation—the Homeric, the chivalric, a hint of the Herculean, and the combination of all three already achieved by Ariosto, Tasso, and Spenser. From Milton's comments in the verse letter to Mansus and the *Epitaphium Damonis,* Tillyard concludes that "Milton's long-projected *Arthuriad* was to be a patriotic poem of vast range, beginning with the Trojans in Britain, dealing with British history up to the defeat of the Spanish Armada, and having Arthur as the hero."[12] More important than its scope, for the present argument, is the fact that the sketch provided in the two Latin poems is clearly of a synthetic work in the Virgilian tradition. Onto a base of Arthurian material in its nationalistic or semihistorical form is to be grafted an Iliadic war between two nations which will "shatter the Saxon phalanxes under the British Mars," and an Odyssean or Virgilian voyage, "the story of the Trojan ships in the Rutupian sea . . . and of the Armorican settlers who came at last under British law."[13] For whatever reasons Milton put this poem aside, it is clear that the same synthetic imagination is at work when he turns to the other medium and begins to create metaphors for the struggle, not between Saxon and British but between Puritan and bishop.

In *Of Reformation* (1641), Milton has chosen to present that conflict in a mixture of images from chivalry and from the Apocalypse. Such a mixture had, of course, already been adapted by Spenser to the problems of an embattled national church, and, like Spenser's Book of Holiness, Milton's first pamphlet is characterized by clear oppositions and sharp antitheses. The opponents of Reformation, in seeking to defend the status quo by recourse to the Fathers, are characterized as seeking "the dark, the bushie, the tangled Forrest" instead of the "plain field of the Scriptures."[14] The suggestion of Spenser's Wood of Error, first hazard for the Red Crosse Knight and Truth, is reinforced by Milton's image of medieval Catholicism, "the huge overshadowing traine of Error which had almost swept all the Starres out of the Firmament of the Church," when the "bright and blissfull Reformation . . . strook through the black and settled Night of Ignorance" (YP, I, p. 524).

Milton has no difficulty in identifying an impersonal champion for this cause. It is the nation-as-hero, with the king at the head. His concern, however, is to convert the metaphors of chivalric conflict to the vision of an apocalyptic peace, and to the actual political situation between England and Scotland. He asks impatiently "how it should come to passe that England (having had this grace and honour from God to bee the first that should set up a Standard for the recovery of lost Truth, and blow the first Evangelick Trumpet to the Nations . . . should now be last" (YP, I, p. 525). But the standard of truth and the trumpet of war are in fact invoked paradoxically, since the action to which England is being urged involves a denial of militarism. The pamphlet praises the *refusal* of Parliament to wage war with Scotland over the prayer book, and their unwillingness to "ingage the *un*attainted Honour of English Knighthood, to *un*furle the streaming Red Crosse, or to reare the horrid Standard of those fatall guly Dragons for so *un*worthy a purpose" (YP, I, p. 597; italics added). It is this nonaction which will become "the Praise and the Heroick Song of all Posterity" (YP, I, pp. 596–97). Milton is here returning to a technique which he had used to effect in the Nativity ode, the negative invocation of images of war to define the seven-year Augustan peace: ("*No* War, or Battles sound / Was heard the World around . . . The hooked Chariot stood / *Un*stain'd with hostile blood, / The Trumpet spake *not* to the armed throng"; italics added).

The transformation of these heroic metaphors to the service of an apocalyptic peace is achieved essentially by paradox and negative syntax. Though full of energy, these techniques beg the question of how this intellectual crusade shall operate in practice; and it is in this context that we first hear of "someone" who "may perhaps bee heard offering . . . in new and lofty *Measures* to sing and celebrate thy *divine Mercies,* and *marvelous Judgements* in this Land throughout all *AGES;* whereby this great and Warlike Nation instructed . . . shalt put an end to all Earthly *Tyrannies*" (YP, I, p. 616). The nation-as-hero needs advice, a counselor figure, a head to direct its hand, even when that hand is only metaphorically engaged; and it takes no ingenuity to discover the identity of this poetic counselor. This third-person figure of the future conditional is the first phase of Milton's development of a heroic persona for himself. Its limitation by person and tense may, as Joan Webber suggests, be "partly convention, partly unsureness,"[15] but the sense in which it is either cannot be determined until we can compare with it other and later forms of Milton's prose "self."

In *Animadversions* (July 1641)[16] Milton comes forward in defense of the Smectymnuans, as the Answerer of the Remonstrant. He has already discovered the uncomfortable fact that defense of others soon involves one in self-defense, and the Answerer is forearmed in the preface by a series of careful distinctions between justifiable and un-justifiable violence in speech: "Wee all know," says Milton

> that in private and personall injuries, yea in publique sufferings for the cause of Christ, his rule and example teaches us . . . not to answer the reviler in his language though never so much provok't. Yet in the detecting, and convincing of any notorious enimie to truth and his Countries peace . . . it will be nothing disagreeing from Christian meeknesse to handle such a one in a rougher accent . . . especially, seeing they which thus offend against the soules of their brethren, do it with delight to their great gaine, ease, and advancement in this world, but they that seeke to discover and oppose their false trade of deceiving, do it *not without* a sad and unwilling anger, *not without* many hazards, but *without* all private and personall spleene, and *without* any thought of earthly reward. (YP, I, pp. 662–63; italics added)

The heroic allusions are here extremely subdued ("a notorious enimie to truth," "not without many hazards") because Milton knows himself to be facing the dilemma of Spenser's Red Crosse Knight himself: to what extent does *any* participation in the wars of truth deny the claims of "Christian meeknesse?" And what happens to the contemplative who takes up, even metaphorically, the world's weapons? His solution is, firstly, to distinguish between the "cause of Christ" as such, which indeed requires passive fortitude, and the cause of "his Countries peace" which provides a *civic* justification for engagement; secondly, to distinguish between private and public injuries, between "private and personall spleene" and public zeal; and thirdly, to justify the public engagement of the contemplative in controversy on the grounds that such engagements bring danger but no rewards. This is therefore the first of Milton's definitions of the civic hero, he who without public office is called by instinct and intellectual capacity to speak his mind in the public service. This fusion of public and private is achieved by juggling the terms so that we feel a compromise emerging between them, rather than by the simple paradoxes and inversions of *Of Reformation;* and the complexity of the solution by which the charge of egoism is refuted depends on the series of interlocking negatives: "not without a sad and unwilling anger, not without many hazards, but without all private and personall spleene, and without any thought of earthly reward." The first pair of clauses could apply to an Achillean Answerer; the second two deny any such possibility.

This interpretation of the preface is reinforced later in *Animadversions* when, as part of his argument against the desire of the clergy for temporal power, Milton defines "a man" who chooses not to be a member of Parliament, because his unofficial and unpaid advice has more legislative force than Parliamentary speeches:

Would he tugge for a Barony to sit and vote in Parliament, knowing that no man can take from him the gift of wisedome, and sound doctrine which leaves him free, though not to be a member, yet a teacher, and perswader of the Parliament? and in all wise apprehensions the perswasive power in man to win others to goodnesse by instruction is greater, and more divine, then the compulsive power to restraine men from being evill by terrour of the Law; and therefore Christ left *Moses* to be the Law-giver, but himselfe came down amongst us to bee a teacher. (YP, I, pp. 721-22)

This definition of the "true Pastor," although it claims to be a generalized model, is almost certainly a form of self-portrait, not only because Milton has already developed the concept of an inward and personal ordination, but because as he wrote it, in the context of pastoral unworldliness, he was working with the tenth book of Aristotle's *Nicomachean Ethics.* The distinction he makes between persuasive and compulsive power derives from this chapter, as Milton himself tells us later in the *Doctrine and Discipline of Divorce.*[17] Since Aristotle plans this chapter as a bridge to the *Politics,* he is less sanguine about the efficacy of persuasion on the public at large than is Milton himself. But the subject is introduced in the context of praise of the contemplative life, which is said to exceed the pursuits of war and politics in value because of its "self-sufficiency, leisuredness, such freedom from fatigue as is possible for man" (*Ethics*, X, vii, 7), and because it is not dependent on worldly goods (X, viii, 4–12): "For . . . it is possible to perform noble deeds even without being ruler of land and sea; one can do virtuous acts with quite moderate resources. They may be clearly observed in experience; private citizens do not seem to be less but more given to doing virtuous actions than princes and potentates."[18] This Aristotelian authority for both the freedom and the force of the private teacher becomes increasingly important for Milton as he successively defines and justifies his own role in the Puritan Revolution; and it becomes clear that he transfers the teacher's freedom from political pressures to the transitional figure of the orator, who uses the materials of learning to change the laws of the land.

The Reason of Church Government, the "well-temper'd discourse" which follows so gratefully after the unpleasantries of *Animadversions*, is clearly an attempt to put into practice Milton's conception of persuasive law, as its own preface points out. To the authority of Plato in the *Laws* is added that of Moses, now accommodated to the contemplative ideal by regarding Genesis as a persuasive preface to the Old Testament judicial and ceremonial rules, a sort of divine *captatio benevolentiae*. The pamphlet is famous, of course, for the account it gives of Milton's generic theory at this stage of his career, and the evidence of a still unsettled choice between the three highest genres—epic, tragedy, and hymn. But, from his liberal use of heroic allusion, one might be justified in assuming that epic is closest to his imagination. The heroic protagonist is now more clearly divided. At times it is "a right pious, right honest, and right hardy nation" (YP, I, p. 797), which Milton urges onward to speedy reform of church government, in terms still highly reminiscent of the first book of the *Faerie Queene*. Since "the reforming of a Church . . . is never brought to effect without the fierce encounter of truth and falsehood together," Milton sees the development of schisms as the necessary "splinters and shares of so violent a jousting" (YP, I, p. 796). He urges the nation-as-hero, under the figure of St. George, to tackle the Dragon of prelaty:

And if our Princes and Knights will imitate the fame of that old champion, as by their order of Knighthood solemnly taken, they vow, farre be it that they should uphold and side with this English Dragon; but rather to doe as indeed their oath binds them, they should make it their Knightly adventure to pursue & vanquish this mighty sailewing'd monster. (YP, I, p. 857)

Even his reference to the impetus of shame as a motive for heroic action, though taken from the *Iliad* (VI, 440–46), is phrased in language which belongs to the chivalric romance: "Hence we may read in the Iliad where *Hector* being wisht to retire from the battel, many of his forces being routed, makes answer that he durst not for shame, lest the Trojan Knights and Dames should think he did ignobly" (YP, I, pp. 840–41).

But in the second chapter there also appears a different kind of hero. Again we hear of a mysterious "one" who will guide the nation in the "perpetuall stumble of conjecture and disturbance in this our darke voyage" with "the card and compasse of Discipline" (YP, I, 753). This counselor figure is now revealed by the use of metaphor to be distantly related to Odysseus, but to an Odysseus who is much more than half of the Homeric system of values. In order to function as counselor to the heroic nation, and to discover the discipline which God has intended, such a "one" must be "a true knower of himselfe, and himselfe in whom contemplation and practice, wit, prudence, fortitude, and eloquence must be rarely met, both to comprehend the hidden causes of things, and span in his thoughts all the various effects that passion or complexion can worke in mans nature; and hereto must his hand be at defiance with gaine, and his heart in all vertues heroick" (YP, I, p. 753). The editor of the Yale edition of the prose accepts Tillyard's view that this is a portrait of "the ideal Renaissance statesman" and refers it forward to the concept of the man in *Of Education* who would "perform justly, skillfuly and magnanimously all the offices both private and publike of peace and war." However, in its emphasis on eloquence, on philosophical and psychological insight, and on freedom from "gaine," this definition would seem more relevant to Milton's growing definition of the orator than to the active statesman. It is worth noticing that *Of Education* concludes with a statement reminding us of Milton's view of himself as a teacher, and a significant metaphor for the difficulty of his task: "I believe that this is not a bow for every man to shoot in that counts himself a teacher; but will require sinews almost equall to those which Homer gave Ulysses" (YP, II, p. 415). The emphasis on the bow of Odysseus as the supreme test of heroic strength is another way of activating the contemplative through metaphor, and of reminding his readers that Odysseus can be seen as a composite figure of both prudence and fortitude, brains and brawn—as Chapman put it, "an absolute man."

However, *The Reason of Church Government* introduces still a third version of a heroic protagonist. In Book II, the trumpet, which will blow "a dolorous or a jarring blast," is now in the hands of a reluctant prophet. Speaking in the first person, he would much prefer "to be silent, as *Jeremiah* did, because of the reproach and derision he met with daily" (YP, I, p. 803), but he is forced to speak out in the church's defense or bear in anticipation the accusation of cowardice, the shame of misused opportunities for thought. It is this "I" who introduces the personal "digression" about his literary intentions which has absorbed most of the interest of today's readers and critics. This persona also identifies himself through metaphor as an unwilling hero of a journey into experience. The very outline of his literary plans is designed to show his audience how lacking he is in personal ambition, or the "self-pleasing humor of vain glory" (YP, I, p. 806), to show how unwilling he is to

leave a calme and pleasing solitarynes . . . to imbark in a troubl'd sea of noises and hoars disputes, put from beholding the bright countenance of truth in the quiet and still air of delightfull studies to come into the dim reflexion of hollow antiquities . . . and there be fain to club quotations with men whose learning and beleif lies in marginal stuffings . . . what pleasure or profoundnesse can be in this, or what honour to deal against such adversaries. (YP, I, pp. 821–22)

In other words, the first-person speaker describes his actual attempt at public counsel as an unplanned version of the "darke voyage" which is to test the knowledge and discretion of the absolute "one." But here his tone is so negative, so expectant of criticism, so conditional of fulfillment and apologetic for both precociousness and delay, that it forms a striking contrast with the ideal synthesis defined in the second chapter. It appears that Milton's "I" is the man of the present, who must face the paradox that heroic action is necessary but inevitably impure; his "one" or "a man" is the Milton of the future, who remains an ideal hypothesis.[19]

In the *Apology for Smectymnuus* (1642), Milton further develops the theory of *Animadversions,* that aggressive defense in the cause of an impersonal truth is not really aggressive at all. The difference is now that defense has really become self-defense, and he is "put unwillingly to molest the publick view with the vindication of a private name" (YP, I, p. 870). Consequently it is an appropriately objective strategy to enlist autobiography and confession on the Puritan side; the "digression" on his own intellectual growth is "as it were in skirmish to change the compact order, and instead of outward actions to bring inmost thoughts into front" (YP, I, p. 888). In the "digression" itself, he defends his reading of chivalric romances as a necessary stage in his intellectual and moral growth, a stage on the way to a fully Platonic or Pauline chastity, and in so doing he clarifies the mental connection between the civic hero and the chivalric metaphors of the prose:

> I betook me among those lofty Fables and Romances, which recount in solemne canto's the deeds of Knighthood founded by our victorious Kings; & from hence had in renowne all over Christendome. . . . From whence even then I learnt what a noble vertue chastity sure must be, to the defence of which so many worthies by such a deare adventure of themselves had sworne. And if I found in the story afterward any of them by word or deed breaking that oath, I judg'd it the same fault of the Poet, as that which is attributed to *Homer*, to have written undecent things of the gods. Only this my mind gave me that every free and gentle spirit without that oath ought to be borne a Knight, nor needed to expect the guilt spurre, or the laying of a sword upon his shoulder to stirre him up both by his counsell, and his arme to secure and protect the weaknesse of any attempted chastity. (YP, I, pp. 890–91).

Milton's defense of the romances here is important, as has been noted, both for its difference from the attitudes of *Paradise Lost* and *Paradise Regained* and for its ability to penetrate past the humanist or Puritan perception of "manslaughter and bold bawdrie" to the essential quality of romance—its ability to posit an ideal while failing to illustrate it.[20] But even more interesting is the articulation of an inward chivalry to match his concept of an inward ministry. In *Animadversions* Milton had observed, "As for Ordination, what is it, but the laying on of hands, an outward signe or symbol of admission? It creates nothing, it conferres nothing; it is the inward calling of God that makes a Minister" (YP, I, p. 715). So here "every free and gentle spirit" may dub himself knight without "the laying of a sword upon his shoulder," provided he lives in the spirit of the chivalric ideal. Moreover, the peculiar insertion of the prudence-fortitude *topos* ("both by his counsell and his arme") in this context suggests strongly that Milton's persona is now true knight as well as true pastor, and that both metaphors are subsumed in the civic heroism of the orator.

The antiprelatical pamphlets, then, have set in motion a series of interlocking antitheses which have themselves created a composite heroic persona. The divorce pamphlets both build on this persona and qualify it. This was no simple issue of attack and defense. The distinction between public and private motives must have been harder for Milton to handle here, knowing as he did what personal hurts lay behind the bitter language of *Doctrine and Discipline of Divorce,* and having to argue in a public forum for the removal of divorce from the public jurisdiction. The nature of the biblical texts involved meant also that Milton had to demote Christ as an authority on the subject and elevate Moses; perhaps for this reason the third-person heroic persona, who hopes to solve the problem of the divorce laws, now sounds respectably like Moses leading the people of Israel out of Egypt into the promised land:

He therefore that by adventuring shall be so happy as with successe to ease & set free the minds of ingenuous and apprehensive men from this needlesse thraldome . . . he that can but lend us the clue that windes out this labyrinth of servitude to such a reasonable and expedient liberty as this, deserves to be reck'n'd among the publick benefactors of civill and humane life; above the inventors of wine and oyle. (YP, II, pp. 239–40)

This placing of his ideal persona so firmly among the "publick benefactors" may or may not be caused by a sense of uneasiness about the ambiguity of his motives in *Doctrine and Discipline.* It certainly makes a striking contrast with the gloomy recognition, in the preface to *Martin Bucer,* that his efforts have not been gratefully received, and that if he is to salvage for himself the consciousness of heroic quest, it must be in the figure of the hero as solitary outcast: "I resolv'd at length to put off into this wild and calumnious world. For God, it seems, intended to prove me, whether I durst alone take up a rightful cause against a world of disesteem, & found I durst" (YP, II, p. 434).[21]

Apart from a brief hope that the diseased hold of canon law over the mind will be cut by "som heroick magistrate, whose mind equall to his high office dares lead him both to know and to do" (YP, II, p. 600), Milton does not use heroic allusion in *Tetrachordon*

(March 1635). The organization of four major scriptural texts into one harmonious argument, as compared to the often shockingly confessional tone of *Doctrine*, was achieved smoothly, not to say mechanically, and the result is neither aggressive, defensive, nor exploratory. The same, however, cannot be said about *Colasterion* (March 1645), "the place or instrument of punishment," about which Milton seems to have felt rather bad, since it is full of signs of defiance and self-doubt and was not reprinted during his lifetime. Taking as his rubric the disputed advice of Proverbs xxvi, 5, "Answer a Fool according to his folly," Milton returns to the satiric tone and weapons of *Animadversions* and the *Apology for Smectymnuus;* but the pamphlet ends with an elaborate apology for his tactics, presented through modifications of his own heroic role. In the first place, he has been forced by circumstances to adopt a new heroic prototype and replaces the Homeric and chivalric with the Herculean, because "*Hercules* had the labour once impos'd upon him to carry dung out of the *Augean* stable" (YP, II, p. 756). Secondly, he apologizes for having to discard his own theory of a tragic or heroical satire as developed in the *Apology* and blames the clergy and licensers for sending against him only a mock-heroic adversary:

And what defence can properly bee us'd in such a despicable encounter as this, but either the flap or the spurn? If they can afford mee none but a ridiculous adversary, the blame belongs not to mee, though the whole Dispute bee strew'd and scatter'd with ridiculous . . . hee shall bee my *Batrachomuamachia.* (YP, II, p. 757)

And thirdly, he offers a challenge to anyone willing to meet him in "fair argument"; such an honorable adversary, Milton concludes, "shall confess that to doe so is my choice, and to have don thus was my chance," thus identifying the widening gap between the ideal orator and the real.

The Herculean prototype is to make a significant comeback in the regicide pamphlets; in between comes *Areopagitica*, which is central to Milton's definition of the heroism of oratory and the nature of its victories. The championship of Truth has become much more complicated since Milton wrote the first antiprelatical pamphlets, and he has developed a Ciceronian consciousness of the "dust and heat" of the conflict; nor, we may suppose, was he particularly proud of his efforts on behalf of the Presbyterians, now revealed as the new

forcers of conscience. The result is a strategic retreat from the figure
of the Red Crosse Knight to that of Spenser's Guyon, himself modeled
on Odysseus, who looks before he leaps and resists more challenges
than he accepts. No other figure of Spenser's so pertinently analyzes
the interaction of active and passive, or so triumphantly embodies
(at least as invigorated by Milton's prose rhythms) the principle of
not doing in the active metaphors of battle and quest. This famous
passage, so often quoted, can still be a source of new perceptions,
if we observe how much of its achievement depends on the linguistic
synthesis of battle and race:[22]

I can*not* praise a fugitive and cloister'd vertue, *un*exercis'd & *un*breath'd,
that *never* sallies out and sees her adversary, but slinks out of the race, where
that immortall garland is to be run for, *not without* dust and heat. (YP, II,
p. 515; italics added)

The syntax recalls the "not without" strategy of the preface to *Animadversions;* but the heroic metaphors, no longer subdued, have taken
on a new energy from the ambiguity of the contest.

Moreover, when toward the end of *Areopagitica* Milton moves
away from the issue of temperance and back to the heroic definition
of the act in which he himself is employed, the third-person persona
reappears in a very mixed metaphor indeed:

When a man hath bin labouring the hardest labour in the deep minds of
knowledge, hath furnisht out his findings in all their equipage, drawn forth
his reasons as it were a battell raung'd, scatter'd and defeated all objections
in his way, calls out his adversary into the plain, offers him the advantage
of wind and sun,

he will either find himself, Milton says, like a chivalric challenger
on a "narrow bridge of licensing" which, in effect, prevents his opinions
from passing from the private sphere to the public, or he will, in
arguing for freedom, be forced to admit that Truth, though not absolutely Protean, may yet "have more shapes than one" (YP, II, pp.
562–63). Although Milton's military metaphor here owes something
to the influence of William Walwyn's *Compassionate Samaritane*, the
extraordinary fluidity of the passage is his own; and the Protean character of the allusive process is both Milton's best argument against
the licenser and his own admission that no one can successfully bind
Truth to his own side.[23]

Areopagitica would seem to mark a point of stasis in Milton's development of a heroic ethos. Its greater stylistic certainty in part derives from a greater linguistic ambiguity. In the regicide pamphlets, however, Milton is forced to depart from creative uncertainty, whether presented as the equipoise of Temperance or the fluidity of Truth. England was in effect on trial before Europe, and the death of a king was in no sense one of "all that rank of things indifferent, wherein Truth may be on this side, or on that" (YP, II, p. 563). The *Tenure of Kings and Magistrates* (1649 and 1650) therefore asserts the "fortitude and Heroick vertue" of the Independents and army leaders responsible for bringing Charles to trial and execution. In fact, his use of the term "fortitude" indicates how this pamphlet stands midway between the approved metaphorical militancy of the church reform pamphlets and the pacificism of *Paradise Lost* and *Paradise Regained*. His conditional praise of the proregicide group, "the Parlament and Military Councel," provides a new composite hero to replace the nation, which has become too divided to be addressed simply. The "matchless deeds" of this new composite hero are distinguished from past heroism, which "in the persuance of fame and forren dominion, spent it self vaingloriously abroad"; and from their example future generations "may learn *a better fortitude,* to dare execute highest Justice on them that shall by force of Armes endeavour the oppressing and bereaving of Religion and thir liberty at home" (YP, III, pp. 237–38; italics added). In this return to the praise of unqualified fortitude, Milton deals heavily in the force of "masculine" abstractions like "Justice," "Victory" and the sword of God, which he weighs against "feminine" abstractions like mercy and pity. And the treatise, though at base a systematic attack on the main Presbyterian arguments against both deposition and regicide, written *after* these events have occurred, presents itself in the image of hortatory rhetoric prior to battle. The Herculean prototype is reintroduced briefly, not now in connection with anything sordid, but as the spokesman for the conviction of the Greeks and Romans, that it is "not only lawfull, but a glorious and Heroic deed . . . to kill an infamous Tyrant" (YP, III, pp. 212–13); and there are allusions to the trial of Mary, Queen of Scots, Charles' grandmother, which serve, among other things, to recall the tone and emphasis of Spenser's Book of Justice, which takes that trial as the heart of the argument between rigor and lenity, Justice and Mercy.[24]

This politic harshness was to take new impetus from a strange literary event. When in 1649 Milton published his response to the *Eikon Basilike*, supposedly written by Charles himself "in his solitudes and sufferings," he found himself facing an image very different from the tyrant posited in the *Tenure*. He now had to face up to the problem of discrediting the contemplative ideal itself. The iconographical title page presented Charles kneeling, with the Latin motto *Vota dabunt quae bella negarunt*, "What he could not compass by war he would achieve by his devotions," and Charles had also identified himself with gentle suffering by professing readiness to "wear a Crown of Thorns with our Saviour." Milton's response is to tackle this retrospectively pacifist position head-on. Accordingly he avoids the issue of martyrdom by positing the king as still alive, and challenging him to single combat: "I shall make no scruple to take up (for it seems to be the challenge both of him and all his party) to take up this Gauntlet, though a Kings, in the behalf of Libertie, and the Commonwealth" (YP, III, p. 338). And he shrewdly devalues the pacifism of the *Eikon* by observing that it is merely a pose designed to rationalize defeat. The king, once captured, may have been left with only prayers and tears as weapons against his persecutors, but "were they Praiers and Teares that were listed at *York*, muster'd on *Heworth* Moore, and laid Seige to *Hull* for the guard of his Person?" (YP, III, p. 452).[25]

But Milton's most effective strategy was the notorious use of Pamela's Prayer. In *Areopagitica* he had obliquely defended Sir Philip Sidney's *Arcadia*, along with Jorge de Montemayor's *Diana Innamorada*, as part of the mixed literary experience which reason needs for its exercise, and as the thinking man's version of country ballads and other uncensorable pastimes (YP, II, pp. 524-25). But now, in Charles' plagiarism from *Arcadia*, Milton perceived a unique opportunity to embarrass the Presbyterians, by associating the king's ultimate pieties with a "pagan" fiction, and the "polluted orts and refuse of *Arcadia's* and *Romances*." Chance made him an offer he could not refuse; and the result is an emphatic rejection of the chivalric tales he had defended, and from which he had drawn the metaphors for his own political heroism.

For he certainly whose mind could serve him to seek a Christian prayer out of a Pagan Legend, and assume it for his own, might gather up the rest God knows from whence; one perhaps out of the French *Astraea*, another out of the Spanish *Diana; Amadis* and *Palmerin* could hardly scape him . . . so long as such sweet *rapsodies* of Heathenism and Knighterrantry could yeild him prayers. How dishonourable then, and how unworthy of a Christian King were these ignoble shifts to seem holy and to get a Saintship among the ignorant and wretched people. (YP, III, pp. 366–67)

This passage was in fact added to the edition of 1650 to generalize Milton's attack on the romances and to discredit the king further by associating him not only with the English *Arcadia*, but also with the French and Spanish romances, and by extension with their disreputable Roman Catholic cultures. Consequently, when Milton returns to the subject of his own heroism, he provides for himself a strictly biblical prototype, the figure of Zorobabel (1 Esdras, chaps. iii–iv), and restates the relationship between contemplation and action in terms of Zorobabel's judgment in the court of Darius. In fact, he revises it and expands it to suit the attack on the contemplative poses of the *Eikon:*

I shall pronounce my sentence somewhat different from *Zorobabel;* and shall defend, that either Truth and Justice are all one, for Truth is but justice in our knowledge, and Justice is but Truth in our practice . . . or els, if there be any odds, that Justice, though not stronger than truth, yet by her office is to put forth and exhibit more strength in the affairs of mankind. For Truth is properly no more than Contemplation; and her utmost efficiency is but teaching: but Justice in her very essence is all strength and activity. . . . And if by sentence thus writt'n it were my happiness to set free the minds of English men from longing to returne poorly under that Captivity of Kings, from which the strength and supreme Sword of Justice hath deliverd them, I shall have don a work not much inferior to that of *Zorobabel:* who by well praising and extolling the force of Truth, in that contemplative strength conquer'd *Darius.* (YP, III, pp. 583–85)

Milton has thus been forced by circumstances to deny his own fusion of action and contemplation, and to accept for the time being the sword as the emblem of justice (figurative language which is only just below the surface of the literal) instead of the metaphor for truth (figurative language which goes through the looking glass of paradox and reappears in a different world). The result is reminiscent of Spenser's Legend of Justice, already implicit in the *Tenure*, and here confirmed by Milton's wish for "a man of iron, such as *Talus*, by our poet *Spencer* is fain'd to be the page of Justice, who with his iron flaile could doe all this, and expeditiously" (YP, III, p. 391).

The preface to the *Defence of the People of England* (1651) restates Milton's confidence in his own heroic synthesis, now that the need for the iron flail is receding into the past. Itself a work of epic proportions, it opens with an invocation establishing God as his muse and the recognition of the epic scope of his task: "To treat worthily of all these great events, and to compose a memorial which every nation and every age may perhaps read." The leaders of the republic have called upon the civic hero, the orator, "to furnish the deeds they so gloriously performed under God's guidance with a defence against jealous slanders (a duty second in importance to theirs alone, and one in which the sword and implements of war are of no avail, but which requires other weapons" (YP, IV, pt. 1, p. 305). However, this redefinition of civic as distinct from active fortitude is a good deal nobler than the defense itself; the heroic persona does not appear; and the "other weapons" which Milton uses include the occasional satiric and even frivolous use of heroic allusion.[26]

The *Second Defence* is, from a literary point of view, far more interesting in its deliberate mixture of tones and its containment of insult and satire in a reassuring rhetorical framework of exordium and peroration. Whether the form of an oration gave Milton greater confidence in himself and his subject, or whether greater confidence in himself and his subject allowed him to return to that form, the modes of praise and blame have not been so masterfully unified in his prose before.[27] From his opening praise of the Republic, Milton modulates into "self-esteem, grounded on just and right" as he claims for himself a peculiar share in the English epic:

For I did not avoid the toils and dangers of military service without rendering to my fellow-citizens another kind of service that was much more useful and no less perilous. . . . Having from early youth been especially devoted to the liberal arts, with greater strength of mind than of body, I exchanged the toils of war, in which any stout trooper might outdo me, for those labors which I better understood. . . . And so I concluded that if God wished those men to achieve such noble deeds, He also wished that there were other men by whom these deeds, once done, might be worthily praised and extolled, and that truth defended by arms be also defended by reason—the only defense truly appropriate to man. Hence it is that while I admire the heroes victorious in battle, I nevertheless do not complain about my own role. (YP, IV, pp. 552–53)

This masterful restatement of the synthesis, reinforced by its absorption of the Herculean concept of "labors," shows Milton satisfied that he is once again clearly on the side of Truth; and this further allows him to see himself as an Odyssean traveler returning home after his multifarious experiences, bringing with him the "renewed cultivation of freedom and civic life":

> I seem now to have embarked on a journey and to be surveying from on high far-flung regions and territories across the sea, faces numberless and unknown. . . . Now, surrounded by such great throngs, from the Pillars of Hercules all the way to the farthest boundaries of Father Liber, I seem to be leading home again everywhere in the world, after a vast space of time, Liberty herself. (YP, IV, pt. 1, pp. 554–55)

The punning reference to Bacchus as Liber, and the claim to have benefited humanity as much or more than Bacchus or Ceres, who bestowed viniculture and agriculture on the world, implies a euhemeristic approach to the deification of public benefactors and connects with the statement in the *Doctrine and Discipline of Divorce* that he who "by adventuring" shall resolve the contradictions of divorce law "shall deserve to be reck'n'd among the publick benefactors of civill and humane life; above the inventors of wine and oyle" (YP, III, p. 240). His confidence of public benefaction in turns flows into a retrospective view of his conflict with Salmasius as a chivalric episode, despite the radical discourtesy of its polemic: "When he with insults was attacking us and our battle array, and our leaders looked first of all to me, I met him in single combat and plunged into his reviling throat this pen, the weapon of his own choice" (YP, IV, pt. 1, p. 556). Furthermore, the ultimate proof of Milton's unselfishness and impersonality lies in his blindness, which allows him to make a brilliant modification of the Achillean choice between death and honor:

> I thought that two lots had now been set before me by a certain command of fate: the one, blindness, the other, duty. Either I must necessarily endure the loss of my eyes, or I must abandon my most solemn duty. And there came into my mind those two fates which, the son of Thetis relates, his mother brought back from Delphi. (YP, IV, pt. 1, p. 588)

This striking accommodation of Achillean to civic fortitude receives one more strange and touching addition. Returning to the post-Homerican contest between Ajax and Odysseus for the arms of Achilles (which he had alluded to briefly in the first *Defence*), as an example of how one turns to one's enemies for an impartial judgment of one's greatness as a fighter, Milton reflects upon the debased and partial judgment of Alexander More. And he adds:

Yet, my fine fellow, I shall without difficulty circumvent you. For although
I should like to be Ulysses—should like, that is, to have deserved as well
as possible of my country—yet I do not covet the arms of Achilles. I do
not seek to bear before me heaven painted on a shield, for others, not myself
to see in battle, while I carry on my shoulders a burden, not painted, but
real, for myself, and not for others to perceive. (YP, IV, pp. 595–96)

The burden Milton carries is not explained here; but it may be deduced
from the aggregate of all his heroic self-identifications—the burden
of isolation, the strain of adventure in unpathed areas of debate, the
sense of precious time going by, the loss of sight, and perhaps worse
of all, the burden of calumny, of insult given and received. The shield
of civic fortitude, therefore, is the conviction that "all the insults that
are hurled . . . are suffered for the sake of the state, not for myself"
(YP, IV, p. 596). We may possibly see in this moment of unaccustomed
pathos the beginning of a movement from intellectual civic fortitude
to the meeker passive fortitude of the mature poems.

It is this conviction which integrates the digression on his own
career as a pamphleteer; defense of his own reputation is legitimately
part of the nation's defense. Milton makes it clear that he does regard
this account as part of the praise/blame structure of the oration; and
"praise of his own integrity" is followed by praise of the careers of
Bradshaw, the active lawyer and judge, and Cromwell, the active
statesman and soldier, each of whom has clearly fulfilled in fact and
in public the roles which Milton had dreamed of achieving as the
private orator.

This is particularly true of Cromwell, on whom Milton bestows
all the virtues of the ideal figure which he has been so long defining.
Cromwell exemplifies the perfect blend of military fortitude and moral
prudence, moving from "private citizen" known for his religious devotion, to "counsellor" as member of Parliament for Huntingdon, to
the command of an army, and "deeds [which] require the grand scope
of a true history, a second battlefield, so to speak, on which they
may be recounted, and a space for narrative equal to the deeds themselves" (YP, IV, pt. 1, pp. 667–68); at the same time he too is eligible
for the metaphoric fusion of outer and inner fortitude, since "he was
a soldier well-versed in self-knowledge, and whatever enemy lay within
—vain hopes, fears, desires—he had either previously destroyed within
himself or had long since reduced to subjection. Commander first

over himself, victor over himself, he had learned to achieve over himself the most effective triumph" (YP, IV, pt. 1, pp. 667–68). When we recall the description of the ideal orator in *The Reason of Church Government*, the "one" who must be "a true knower of himselfe, and himselfe in whom contemplation and practise, wit, prudence, fortitude, and eloquence must be rarely met, both to comprehend the hidden causes of things, and span in his thoughts all the various effects that passion or complexion can worke in a man's nature" (YP, I, p. 753), we can see clearly why the defense of Cromwell was so closely related, as Milton admits, to defense of himself. Not only have they been "deeply involved in the same slanderous accusations" (YP, IV, p. 666), but Cromwell is living proof that the synthesis Milton wanted for himself can exist. The result of the vicarious justification comes with startling effect at the very end of the *Second Defence*, when the "one" who has been missing from all pamphlets since *Areopagitica* returns in a prophetic statement of mixed warning and reassurance. Though it may seem to posterity

that a mighty harvest of glory was at hand, together with the opportunity for doing the greatest deeds, but that to this opportunity men were wanting. Yet there was not wanting one who could rightly counsel, encourage, and inspire, who could honor both the noble deeds and doers illustrious with praises that will never die. (YP, IV, pp. 685–86)

Milton claims here that he has redeemed the "pledge" that he made in *The Reason of Church Government* (YP, I, pp. 820–21) and has written a national epic with the English nation, momentarily personified in Cromwell, as hero.

Although his perception that the pledge has been fulfilled is partly a rationalization for the postponement, perhaps forever, of his verse epic, it is not entirely a rationalization. There is, after all, at least one kind of epic which changes direction as it goes along and is not necessarily fully planned from the start; that is Spenser's version of the romantic epic. The extent to which one can use analogy to prove a point is severely limited; nevertheless it is clear that Milton *is* thinking of the *Faerie Queene* as his prose develops. There really is a transference, and an appropriate transference, of images associated with the Red Crosse Knight into Milton's antiprelatical pamphlets; Guyon's appearance in *Areopagitica* in defense of intellectual temperance needs no comment; the champion of justice in the regicide pamphlets explicit-

ly wishes for a Talus to do his harsh work for him; and Milton's
total hero remains the sum of all the virtues, like the Arthur of the
Letter to Raleigh, an ideal statement in the prophetic background
of the work, while the real knight struggles forward on his quest
for truth or grapples in single combat with its enemies. The point
is, I think, that the tension between active and contemplative heroism
had been suggestively if not fully analyzed by Spenser; and Milton's
retention of the chivalric metaphors for his own experience, even after
his politic rejection of some of the romances in *Eikonoklastes,* is quite
possibly an important qualification to what is usually assumed. His
loyalty to the heroic genres—epic, romance, and romantic epic—sur-
vives throughout the prose because they provide a generic language
for the definition of several fundamental problems: what is the role
of the intellectual in a time of crisis? What is the relationship between
politics and literature? What relevance has a man's private life to
his public utterances? Or, to put the same question more poignantly,
when, if ever, does a man's personality, the influence of his "hopes,
fears, desires," invalidate or corrupt positions taken publicly which
are yet valid by public standards of debate? These are the questions
with which Milton's prose is concerned; and, if one of the criteria
for applying generic terms be, as it should be, evidence that the author
has consciously and comprehensively invoked a generic tradition, that
evidence has, I think, been presented here. Milton wrote over twenty
years a romantic epic in prose, with himself as the primary hero of
all the books.

But clearly one cannot stop at the end of the *Second Defence,*
although critics who relate the prose to the subject of *Paradise Lost*
tend to do so. What follows the *Second Defence* is at least as much
to the point. In the *Pro Se Defensio* (1655) Milton is more uncomfortable and less sure of his synthesis than ever before. He had lost confidence in Alexander More's authorship of the *Regii Sanguinis Clamor,*
and his anxiety had caused him to spend two years collecting evidence
about More's scandalous liaisons. He had been accused in the *Fides
Publica* of two faults totally irreconcilable with his view of himself:
firstly, that he was primarily motivated by self-interest in the *Second
Defence:*

For, indeed, Christian that you are, you pursue private injuries fiercely and
with an implacable spirit; this is the chief part of the thing; the people is

a mere appendage. . . . Not without justice is that called *A Second Defence of the People* which your own defence of yourself, prepared with far greater solicitude, perpetually surpasses. (YP, IV, pt. 2, p. 1160)

Secondly, he was accused of having deliberately published the *Second Defence* at a time when it was potentially destructive to international peace, since More was involved with the presentation to the Dutch of the terms of the 1654 treaty. The *Fides Publica* cites as evidence a letter from the Dutch ambassador, William Nieuport, describing himself as "grieved exceedingly that after the most violent spirits among the Naval Militia had acquiesced in the peace, this man, who professes to be a man of letters and learning . . . should be unwilling at our request to show such a little moderation" (YP, IV, pt. 2, p. 1101). This goes far beyond the standard polemical attack on one's opponent's style as lacking in moderation and modesty, and there is, I think, little doubt that Milton had a guilty conscience when he began the *Pro Se Defensio*, and an even guiltier one when he completed it, or at least completed the first part.

The pamphlet begins with a highly self-conscious emphasis on the solitariness of his task, reminiscent of the lone quester in the preface to *Martin Bucer*, but with much more rhetorical emphasis on the first person. He claims to have foreseen that the current of feeling against the regicides would fall on him "almost alone" ("in me prope unum"), and that when European protest against the nation died down, it would remain focused upon him:

Against you, then, the fury and violence of the enemy have left off their raging; for *me*, as it appears, *for me alone*, it remains to fight the rest of this war. . . . Those desperate men, our own citizens as well as foreigners, the more meddlesome they are in the affairs of others, the more churlish and corrupt they are, the more they fly *at me*, who am busy only with my own duty; *against me* they direct their venom and their darts. (YP, IV, pt. 2, pp. 698–99; italics added)

There are rhythms here which, even in translation, anticipate what Broadbent calls the "central ploce" of *Paradise Lost*, by which first the Son, then Adam, and finally Eve accept responsibility and lay themselves open to divine wrath: "first and last / On mee, mee only . . . all the blame lights due."[28] The difference is that Milton's "*in me*" (repeated four times in the first paragraph of *Pro Se Defensio*) is not self-accusative, and hence not redeeming.

Milton's defense of his own scurrility is the same argument from decorum which he had developed in the earlier satirical pamphlets; he is, moreover, on strong ground when he accuses More of being "severe in words, obscene in deeds" (YP, IV, pt. 2, p. 744). But he is much harder pressed on the issue of egoism and his characteristic method of personalizing all issues. In that "former defence, to which [he] was called by public order and private injury" he could claim application to the "common cause," his country's cause and his own having been officially linked (YP, IV, pt. 2, p. 794). But the very title of the present work indicates that this is no longer so; and the title of More's pamphlet, *Fides Publica*, raises in an acute form the whole dilemma of the personal reputations of public figures. As a result, Milton spends a great deal of time in the *Pro Se Defensio* juggling the terms "public" and "private" and is eventually forced to face the issue directly. "I confess," he says,

> that public testimony is indeed a great ornament to virtue, just as I think it is far from being a firm and certain proof . . . it is, to be sure, evident that the private manners of private men, and especially their vices, are very rarely brought to the gravest ears, which are occupied with so many various matters. And those who seek public testimony, as well as those who give it, are alike the good and the bad; indeed, evil men, decked out in the false cloak of probity, seek it more often than good men. To the extent that any man is virtuous, so stands he less in need of extrinsic testimony; for a good man, content with himself, does nothing to make himself known. If he needs commendation, he has always with him that virtue which is the best commender; if defence—and, of a truth, he will be attacked not infrequently with envious detractions and slanders—he surrounds himself with his own integrity and the invincible knowledge of righteous deeds, by which, as if by the strongest bulwark and garrison, he both receives the vain attacks of vicious men and frustrates their spears. (YP, IV, pt. 2, p. 791)

Such a statement, at this stage in his career, could not have been written without self-consciousness of its double application; and it is shortly followed by what is virtually an admission that Milton's prose has been conditioned by the habits of mind derived from his rhetorical training. Praise and blame, he says, are so closely allied that "whoever vituperates another bears at one and the same time the burden and the odium of two very serious things: of accusing another and thinking well of himself"; consequently most writers prefer the hypocritical blandness of praise. It requires real courage to put into practice the fully antithetical structure of classroom rhetoric, and "when it is needful to our country, when the Commonwealth requires it, casting exercise-shafts aside, now to venture into the sun, and dust, and field of battle, now to exert real brawn, bandish real arms, seek a real enemy."[29] The noble echoes of *De Oratore* and *Areopagitica* are disturbingly undermined by the implications of "hostem petere" ("to seek out the enemy"), and the suspicion, raised for the first time, that Milton has sought occasion for wrath because he wished to make some practical use of an otherwise "imaginary eloquence."

But the really conclusive sign of Milton's self-doubts about this form of exercise appear in the final paragraph of *Pro Se Defensio*, where everything he has done to More is held up for our evaluation. There is none of the resonant confidence of the heroic persona; no prophetic mention of "one" who will use his rhetorical training to create some absolutely memorable work; but rather an extremely conditional and diffident statement, in which even that which might be positively construed is expressed in negative terms:

My principle . . . is . . . that *if* as a youth in that literary leisure I then had I [*sic*] profited aught either from the instructions of the learned or from my own lucubrations, I would, in proportion to my poor abilities, employ all this to the advantage of life and the human race, *if* I could range so far. And *if* sometimes from private enmities public transgressions are wont to be censured and oft corrected, and *if* I have now, impelled by all possible reasons, prosecuted in a most just vituperation not merely my personal enemy, but the common enemy of almost all mankind . . . *whether* I have done this with that success which I ought, . . . I do indeed hope (for why should I distrust?) that herein I have discharged an office *neither dis*pleasing to God, *uns*alutary to the church, *nor un*useful to the state. (YP, IV, pt. 2, p. 796; italics added)

"Cur enim diffidam?" This must be the closest Milton ever came to admitting error. It is also the last intonation of the voice of the civic hero. The heroic persona does not reappear. In *Of Civil Power in Ecclesiastical Causes* (1659), *Means to Remove Hirelings* (1659), and the *Ready and Easy Way to Establish a Free Commonwealth* (1660), though Milton speaks in the first person and with dignity, there is no trace of isolationism or personal pride. Milton speaks "among many others in this common concernment," for he has learned that "in these matters, wherein every Christian hath his free suffrage," it is "*no way misbecoming Christian meeknes* to offer freely, without disparagement to the wisest, such advice as God shall incline him and inable him to propound."[30] And along with this new humility, the speaker now completely dependent on divine prompting, there goes a revision of his past achievement into the passive voice:

Nor was the heroic cause *un*successfully defended to all Christendom against the tongue of a famous and thought invicible adversarie; *nor* the constancie and fortitude that so nobly vindicated our liberty . . . *un*praised or *un*celebrated in a written monument, likely to outlive detraction.[31]

Although these are not the fully positive negatives of passive fortitude "unsung," they are much less confessional and self-assertive than those which conclude *Pro Se Defensio*. And in a pamphlet which argues so forcibly against the authority of a "single person" and for the "joint providence and counsel of many industrious equals" in a free commonwealth, it is tempting to see additional evidence that Milton has finally thought through the egocentric predicament and discovered that the composite heroic persona is no protection. He may, in other words, have abandoned civic in favor of passive fortitude *before* the Restoration, and for private rather than public reasons.

York University, Toronto

NOTES

1. E. M. W. Tillyard, *The Miltonic Setting Past and Present* (Cambridge and New York, 1938), pp. 168–201.

2. Roberta Brinkley (in *Arthurian Legend in the Seventeenth Century* [Baltimore, 1932], pp. 126–41) suggests that the British myth had become embarrassingly associated with the Royalists, while George Williamson ("Milton the Anti-Romantic," *MP*, LX [1962], 13–21, reprinted in his *Milton and Others* [Chicago and London, 1965]) argues that Milton rejected the Arthurian legends because of their "extra-marital 'defilement'" of his 'casta' theme."

3. Herbert Grierson, *Milton and Wordsworth* (Cambridge, 1937), pp. 72–73.

4. John M. Steadman (*Milton's Epic Characters* [Chapel Hill, N.C., 1959] and *Milton and the Renaissance Hero* [Oxford, 1967]) analyzes Milton's critique of both the Achillean and the Odyssean types of heroism in the major poems, and Barbara Lewalski (*Milton's Brief Epic* [Providence, 1966]), concentrates on the development of biblical minor epics prior to Milton and the development of the Jobean hero. Burton O. Kurth (*Milton and Christian Heroism* [Hamden, Conn., 1966]) also correlates Milton's modification of biblical heroism to biblical poems in England. See also James Holly Hanford, "Milton and the Art of War," *SP*, XVIII (1921), 232–66, which establishes that Milton had more than a literary familiarity with military language and suggests

that his textbook knowledge of military theory may have contributed to "his reflection on the nature and sources of fortitude."

5. For an analysis of the writings of Salutati, Bruni, Palmieri, and others, and their relation to the concept of Florence as an isolated stronghold of liberty in the face of Visconti's territorial imperative, see Hans Baron, *The Crisis of the Early Italian Renaissance: Civic Humanism and Republican Liberty* (Princeton, 1966). A more philosophical and less political approach to the same movement is presented by Eugenio Garin, *L'Umanesimo Italiano: Filosofia e vita civile nel Rinascimento* (Bari, 1952) and *La cultura Filosofica del Rinascimento Italiano* (Florence, 1962). The influence of Cicero is specifically emphasized in Baron's earlier article, "Cicero and the Roman Civic Spirit in the Middle Ages and the Early Renaissance," *Bulletin of the John Rylands Library,* XXII (1938), pp. 72-97; see also August Buck's chapter on "Matteo Palmieri als Repräsentant des Florentiner Bürgerhumanismus" in *Die Humanistische Tradition in der Romania* (Berlin and Zurich, 1968), pp. 253-70; Eugene Rice, *The Renaissance Idea of Wisdom* (Cambridge, Mass., 1958); and Walter Ullmann, "The Rebirth of the Citizen on the Eve of the Renaissance Period," in *Aspects of the Renaissance,* ed. Archibald Lewis (Austin, Texas, 1967), pp. 5-25.

6. Cicero, *De Oratore,* tr. E. W. Sutton and H. Rackham, Loeb edition (London, 1942). See also J. A. Wittreich's brief article on "Milton's Idea of the Orator," *Milton Quarterly,* VI (1972), 38-40, which points out the iconography of synthesis on the title page of the *First Defence,* but which puts more emphasis on Milton's desecularization of the oratorical ideal than seems to me to be justified by the subject of the prose.

7. *European Literature in the Latin Middle Ages,* tr. Willard R. Trask (New York, 1953), p. 171.

8. *Chapman's Homer,* ed. Allardyce Nicoll (Princeton, 1956), vol. II, pp. 4-5.

9. Torquato Tasso, *Jerusalem Delivered,* tr. Edward Fairfax, ed. Henry Morley (London, 1890), pp. 436-37. The Allegory was added to the *Gerusalemme* in 1575.

10. In *Il Forno, o della Nobiltà* (in Tasso, *Opere* [Pisa, 1821-32], vol. VIII, pp. 94-95), there are signs of a different attempt at compromise, related to the Ciceronian ideal. This dialogue, on the nature of noble conduct, combines metaphoric fusion—prudence "considers the customs and passions in some way as its subject . . . rather as if it were a captain of soldiers",—with more rational qualifications. One of the speakers points out that prudence, like fortitude, is practical as well as speculative and "has regard to the benefit of the state no less than the other virtue"; the other suggests that there may really be two sorts of fortitude, one military and the other civic: "So Cicero believed; and he believed that the civic is not worthy of less honour." C. P. Brand (*Torquato Tasso* [Cambridge, 1965], p. 180) states that *Il Forno* was "first written in 1578, had by 1586 been through several phases of revision and was never published with Tasso's approval." We know that Milton had read at least one of Tasso's dialogues, since he refers, in his verse letter to Mansus, to the dialogue on friendship named after Mansus.

11. *The Miltonic Setting,* pp. 168-92.

12. Ibid., p. 191.

13. *Complete Poems and Major Prose,* ed. M. Y. Hughes (New York, 1957), pp. 130-37.

14. *Complete Prose Works,* ed. Don M. Wolfe et al. (New Haven, 1953-), vol. I, p. 569, hereafter cited as YP. I have omitted the italicization of the original where it would conflict with that necessary for linguistic analysis.

15. *The Eloquent "I": Style and Self in Seventeenth-Century Prose* (Madison, Wis., 1968), p. 190.

16. There are no heroic allusions in *Of Prelatical Episcopacy*.

17. YP, II, p. 346: "Which made Aristotle in the 10th of his *Ethicks* to *Nicomachus* aim at a kind of division of law into private or perswasive, and publick or compulsive."

18. Aristotle, *Nicomachean Ethics*, tr. H. Rackham, Loeb edition (London, 1926).

19. It should now be apparent in what respects my reading differs from that of Joan Webber, who in *The Eloquent "I"*, pp. 196-97, gives a religious explanation for Milton's alternation between personal and impersonal syntax: "Despite the impartial devices, the first person is stifled in neither poetry nor prose. . . . The combination . . . of the present, eagerly assertive first person with the persistent, almost awkward avoidance of it is a way of imitating that conformity between God's will and man's that for Milton was so central a theme."

20. Barbara Lewalski, in "Milton: Revaluation of Romance," a paper delivered to the MLA Convention in December 1969, pointed out the analogy between Spenser's defense of the romances and Sidney's defense of the golden world of poetry; George Williamson ("Milton the Anti-Romantic," 16-17) reads this passage more as an apology for the romances than a defense, a preliminary of their rejection on the grounds of unchastity.

21. It is important, however, not to overstress the bad publicity received by the *Doctrine*. See the corrective comments of William Haller in *Liberty and Reformation in the Puritan Revolution* (New York, 1955), p. 179:

No-one, however, let alone any learned divine, paid any explicit attention to Milton's tract in public and in print until it had been out about a year, and then the preachers merely girded at it in the pulpit and finally . . . egged the stationers to take action against it. The continuing burden of Milton's complaint was, not unjustifiably, that all the "sound argument and reason" he had offered had been "put off, either by an undervaluing silence, or the maisterly censure of a rayling word or two in the Pulpit."

22. For this reason I cannot accept Sirluck's simple resolution of the textual crux (YP, II, p. 515, n. 102) in favor of "the true warfaring Christian" instead of "wayfaring." *Both* meanings are present in the passage.

23. This fluidity of allusion is also, of course, characteristic of Milton's epic similes in the first two books of *Paradise Lost*, where the purpose is partly to have us experience the uncertainties of fallen vision.

24. This is particularly true of the final paragraphs of the pamphlet, which recall the king's "Grandmother at her death" and contrast the "moodie" consciences which have been softened by the king's rhetoric to the "constancie and solid firmness of any wise Man"; so Spenser's Book V, ix, contrasts the waverings of Arthur at the trial of Duessa (Mary Queen of Scots) with the response of Artegall, who "with constant firme intent, / Or zeale of Iustice was against her bent."

25. John Steadman, in *Milton and the Renaissance Hero*, p. 46, also sees *Eikonoklastes* as anticipating the critique of false prudence in *Paradise Lost* and *Paradise Regained* and cites: "*What providence deny'd to force*, he though it *might grant* to fraud, which he stiles *Prudence*. But Providence was not couzen'd with disguises, neither outward nor inward" (YP, III, p. 545).

26. Salmasius is compared to the Ajax of Sophocles, who went mad when Odysseus put on the armor of Achilles (YP, IV, p. 324); he is demoted below even the mock-heroic by having a "voice so foul and quavering that surely its trumpeting could never have moved even Homer's mice to fight the frogs" (YP, IV, pt. 1, p. 323); and he is "not a Eurylochus but an Elpenor, a foul Circean beast" (YP, IV, pt. 1, p. 518).

27. Compare the merely rhetorical modulations from one to the other in the *Apology for Smectymnuus* (YP, I, pp. 922, 928).

28. *PL*, X, 831–33; 935; III, 236. See J. B. Broadbent, *Some Graver Subject* (London, 1960), pp. 151–52.

29. YP, IV, pt. 2, p. 795. I have taken the liberty of correcting the translation in one significant place, where the Latin reads not "the burden and odium of two very different things" but "duarum in uno tempore *gravissimarum* rerum onus atque invidiam sustinet." (Latin texts are available in *The Prose Works of John Milton*, ed. Robert Fletcher [London, 1834], p. 754.)

30. It is unfortunately necessary to change editions here, since the last volumes of the Yale edition of the prose are not yet available. See, therefore, *Works of John Milton*, ed. F. A. Patterson et al. (New York, 1931–38), vol. VI, pp. 44, 47; italics added.

31. Ibid., p. 116; italics added.

MILTON AND
THE MARPRELATE TRADITION

James Egan

The decorum of seventeenth-century controversy demanded that Milton reply in kind to opponents who had ridiculed the positions he championed in his prose tracts. In the Marprelate tradition he found the appropriate weapon. Milton's *Animadversions* (1641) and *Colasterion* (1645) display not only a variety of characteristics identified with the Marprelate genre, but also several Miltonic innovations in that genre. The *Animadversions* is structured, in Marprelate fashion, as a mock debate. Verbal ploys with moral overtones, mock logic, and a distinctive rhetorical persona find numerous analogues in the Marprelate tradition. However, the apocalyptic imagery of the *Animadversions* and its occasional stylistic majesty are uniquely Miltonic. Because Milton's intent in the *Animadversions* is satiric, he spares no pains in castigating the evil of Bishop Hall. Unlike the *Animadversions*, *Colasterion* exploits the comic possibilities of the Marprelate idiom. Milton uses Marprelate's rhetorical tricks, in addition to reiterated images and comic "scenes" of his own, to caricature his opponent as a mere scullion unfit for serious debate. The reader is called upon to share in the measure of comic delight Milton derives from rendering a fool an object of ridicule.

I

MILTONISTS HAVE long preferred to equate the totality of Milton's prose work during the 1640s with the lofty grandeur of *Areopagitica* and *The Reason of Church-Government*, documents which elevate him above the cacophony of sectarian squabbling. Yet when he embarked upon the "troubl'd sea of noises and hoars disputes" Milton was prepared to scorn as well as to eulogize, for he recognized that one who sought to reform Reformation might well have occasion to "Answer a Fool according to his folly." In the *Animadversions* and

Colasterion that occasion presented itself, and Milton responded by launching the verbal fusillades of pamphlet warfare. Milton's "flyting" owes much to the satiric strategies of an earlier English pamphleteer, the renowned Martin Marprelate. In wielding the weaponry of Marprelate to chastise antagonists who had belittled the cause he championed, Milton left a distinctive imprint upon a rich polemic genre.

The Puritan struggle against prelacy which Milton entered in 1641 had been waged intermittently since the days of Elizabeth. During the sixteenth century the most illustrious Puritan combatant was the pseudonymous Martin Marprelate, who lampooned the episcopal hierarchy in a series of tracts issued between 1588 and 1589.[1] The rhetorical importance of Marprelate derives not from the doctrinal commonplaces he echoed, but from the devastating polemic mode he devised to express them. Marprelate satire is organized around the framing device of a dialogue between the persona and his satiric target: Martin cites at random passages from his antagonist's text and uses them as the basis for a rebuttal.[2] He forges a satiric fiction by quoting the opponent without regard for the context of his remarks, thereby distorting the literal sense of the passage enough to engender a fictive context which empowers the satirist to reveal unsuspected "meanings" in the opponent's words. From the dialogue framework emerges the illusion of an oral debate or, more precisely, an interrogation, a conscious parody of the debate process.[3] Martin sustains the illusion by constantly addressing his foe and by appealing to an "audience" presumably consisting of his readers.

Martin's debate strategem permits him to dissect the prelates' arguments while denying them the opportunity for refutation. The energetic zaniness of Marprelate's dialogue should not, however, prompt the assumption that his antics are merely a means of delineating his victims as vacuous fools. Underlying Marprelate's quarrel with episcopacy are profound moral issues which render prelatical chicanery grotesque and monstrous, not humorous. Because episcopal ineptitude impedes the advancement of the Reformation, the laughter evoked by Martin is contemptuous and scornful instead of carefree. Marprelate's premise that his "mirth" was a "covert / wherin I would bring the truth into light" (*HAW*, p. 14) leads one to deduce that he seeks not only to expose prelatical evil, but also to call attention to the wisdom of the Puritan position.

Often Martin's wit takes the shape of verbal equivocation. In *Hay any worke* he twits Bishop Thomas Cooper about the fact that the printer had blotted out an embarrassing admission in Cooper's *Admonition to the People of England* (1589): "Here you see that if this *patch* T.C. had not used two *patches* to cover his *patcherie* / the bishops would have accounted him to be as very a *patch* as Deane John" (*HAW*, p. 38; italics added).[4] Martin's punning hints at malicious motives behind Cooper's bungling: Cooper is a conniving sophist bent on concealing the truth. Marprelate's talent extends to coining names for the bishops. The title page of *The Epistle* designates John Bridges, Dean of Sarum, as "doctor of Divillitie," and Martin later apostrophizes him as "[your] grace of Cant." Here equivocation brings about a satiric redefinition in morally suggestive terms: Bridges' titles are "devilish" or "canting," icons of the deception the Dean practices. Throughout the Marprelate tracts the polemicist's word play illuminates the ironic disparity between the bishops' ideal roles as spiritual leaders and their actual identities as self-serving hypocrites.

An equally potent weapon in Marprelate's arsenal is logic. Martin relishes a form of mock logic ("mimic sophistry") akin to the *reductio ad absurdum*, whereby he demolishes episcopal assertions by extracting ridiculous conclusions from them.[5] Analogical rebuttal supplements "mimic sophistry." In *Hay any worke*, "Reverend T. C." submits: "Though bishops should offende as Noah did in drunkenness / yet good children should cover their fathers falts" (*HAW*, p. 33), and "Reverend Martin" replies: "But me thinks brother T. C. you defend the bishops but evil favoredly in these pointes. For you doe / as though a thiefe shoulde saye to a true man / I must needs have thy purse / thou must beare with me / it is my nature / I must needes playe the thiefe" (*HAW*, pp. 33–34). As Martin's treatment of Cooper above indicates, specimens of the argument *ad hominem* likewise appear in the Marprelate tracts. If logic fails him, Marprelate turns to sarcasm and invective. Occasionally, he sees fit to sneer at his adversary, "Now good your grace you shall have small gaynes in medling with Margrete Lawson I can tell you" (*Epist.*, p. 10), or to taunt him, "Deny this if you dare" (*HAW*, p. 19). Abandoning indirection, Martin often rails at the bishops bitterly, in harsh, colloquial language: "we have so many swine . . . / as theeves / murtherers / . . . cormorants / . . . so many covetous popish Bp. in our ministery" (*Epist.*, p. 33).

Lest the reader become so caught up in the persona's rapid shift-
ing from punning to excoriation that he ignore the Puritan ideals of
church government advocated by the satirist, Martin takes pains to
declare those ideals directly. When he does so, his style is uncompromis-
ingly plain. Usually such declarations clarify points of Scripture, perhaps suggesting that Martin's plain dealing aims to emulate the lucidity
of the Word. Homely statements of doctrine comprise a phase of
Marprelate's rhetorical appeal, an appeal dependent upon what I shall
term an "aggregate persona." Straightforward presentation of the Puritan position fosters a moral rapport with the reader by assuring him
of the persona's integrity and reliance upon scriptural authority. Invective and sarcasm bolster that rapport because they convey feelings,
presumably shared by many readers, of disgust and righteous anger
toward the abuses spawned by prelacy. Martin's rustic wit, which
lays bare prelatical sophistry, embraces the wisdom most respected
by a considerable part of his audience and verifies that one whose
station in life is simple need not be ignorant, but rather finds himself
in closer accord with scriptural directives than the sophisticated clergy-
men are. The aggregate persona—a man of sincerity, righteous anger,
and caustic sarcasm—defines a type of response which the reader
must make toward prelacy: mocking laughter, disgust, and, consequently, acceptance of Puritan principles.

That the Marprelate tracts approximate an allegorical encounter
between good and evil forces is suggested by Marprelate's delineation
of the moral chasm separating Puritanism and episcopacy. The intense
polarization of moral qualities has a structural counterpart in the dialogue mechanism: Martin and the bishops, standard-bearers of truth
and falsehood, debate the theological alternatives available to the
reader in the present crisis. The satirist's rhetorical denial of episcopal
arguments adumbrates a practice—denial of episcopacy—to be imi-
tated by the reader should he wish to attain salvation. C. L. Barber's
observation that Marprelate's opponents sometimes identified his
pranks with those of the summer lord of holiday festivity offers an
analogue to Martin's strategies.[6] Just as the Lord of Misrule in the
May games defies and vanquishes his enemies, the "plot" of Marprelate
satire consists of a series of allegorical vanquishings of the adversary's
position.

In the seventeenth century the influence of Marprelate was pronounced enough to inspire a satiric tradition. Crusading for various

theological and political movements, Martin's successors adapted unchanged some of his ploys to new polemic contexts and modified or abandoned others.[7] Imagery, used infrequently by Marprelate, became a favorite resource of his disciples. The imagistic groupings of the anonymous *Vox Borealis* (1641)[8] are resplendently colloquial, while those of John Taylor's *Nashe's Ghost* (1644)[9] are predominantly classical. Moreover, the allegorical dimensions of Marprelate satire underwent amplification. Richard Overton's *Araignment of Mr. Persecution* (1645), a parable depicting Presbyterian oppression of the Independents, focuses upon the emblematic antagonism between the righteous Independents and their depraved tormentors.[10] Overton heightens the dramatic immediacy of the arraignment by assigning appropriate, morally relevant names to the "characters" taking part. Speaking against Persecution are "Gospel," "Light-of-nature" and "Liberty-of-Conscience"; taking the stand in his defense are Sir Symon Synod, who urges the inclusion of Satan among the jurors, and Sir John Presbyter. The most significant transformation affected the Marprelate persona. Martin had commonly posed as a buffoon, but in *The Rehearsal Transpros'd* (1672), Andrew Marvell dons the role of the witty, detached, ironic manipulator, intent upon shouting out the absurdities of the Anglican Samuel Parker's contentions.[11] Unlike Marprelate, who had portrayed the bishops as symbols of infamous corruption, Marvell conceives of Parker as a drooling fanatic unworthy of serious rebuttal because he is incapable of coherent thought. Rather, Parker is a simpleton upon whom Marvell's wit may be practiced, and Marvell adapts the stratagems of Marprelate polemic to that end. As he adroitly demonstrates the comic improbability of Parker's case, Marvell's tone is patronizing, his allusions urbane.

Marprelate's imitators, then, drew upon a wide range of satiric tactics. During the five-year period when Milton wrote the *Animadversions* and *Colasterion*, Martinists were extremely active. *Vox Borealis*, the opening Marprelate round of the 1640s, was fired in October or November of 1640,[12] early enough to have attracted Milton's attention before he composed the *Animadversions*. In 1642, a reprint of Martin's own *Hay any worke*[13] was issued from an unknown source, and another reprint, *The Character of a Puritan*, ventured forth in 1643.[14] John Taylor's *Nashe's Ghost* can be dated at some time in 1644.[15] The protracted pamphlet warfare of the decade would surely have acquainted Milton with the aforementioned tracts.[16]

He found in the Marprelate tradition a bludgeon ready-made for foes who had resorted to satiric rebuttals of his positions. Milton's mastery of the Marprelate idiom shows his awareness of its versatility as a means of argument. Marprelate polemic evolved between 1588 and 1672 from a medium for denouncing Satanic wickedness, in Marprelate's hands, to an ingenious gesture of contempt toward a clownish adversary, for Andrew Marvell. Just as the Marprelate mode progressed from satire to comedy, Milton's design in the *Animadversions* is satiric, while *Colasterion* is an exercise in the comic.[17]

II

The *Animadversions*, Milton's reply to Bishop Joseph Hall's *Defence of the Humble Remonstrance*, appeared in July 1641.[18] In his *Defence*, Hall had occasionally hurled invective-ridden tirades at the Presbyterians, arousing the ire of the antiprelatical camp. Having explained his stand on episcopacy with dignity in *Of Reformation* and *Of Prelatical Episcopacy*, Milton now chose to answer scorn with scorn. When he attacked the prelates decades earlier, Marprelate had availed himself of denunciation and laughter, claiming that his "mirth" was a "covert / wherin I would bring the truth into light." Milton's proposal is similar: he insists that the present situation calls for the satirist to elicit "anger and laughter." This "veine of laughing," he continues, "hath oft-times a strong and sinewy force in teaching and confuting." "Indignation and scorne" are the surest remedies for those who would attempt the "cheat of soules." Milton's reason for evoking scorn and laughter is to unmask Hall as an "enimie to truth" resolved upon leading astray the unwary Christian. The preface to the *Animadversions* characterizes the bishop imagistically as a type of devilish deception, a wily enemy poised to ambush the Christian with "counterfeit principles," one who substitutes "Sophistry" for disputation. Milton's polemic strategy acts as an antidote to such trickery by permitting the reader to "see . . . Sophistry taken short at the first false bound" (YP, I, p. 664). His rhetorical vanquishing of Hall, like Marprelate's demolition of Bridges and Cooper, constitutes an allegorical "plot" in which the "truth" of the Reformation will be "vindicated."

Disdaining serious disputation with Hall, Milton structures the *Animadversions* to resemble a Martinist mock debate between the "Remonstrant" and the Miltonic persona.[19] Milton marches through

Hall's *Defence* section by section, placing quotes or paraphrases into the mouth of the Remonstrant, and then providing an "Answer." When Milton quotes Hall out of context or paraphrases passages so that they seem ludicrous or "sophistical," he transforms the dialogue format into a satiric fiction. Milton maintains the illusion of a dialogue by quoting frequently from his opponent's text questions which lend themselves to snide rejoinders.[20] As did Marprelate, Milton pulls the reader into the debate by directing numerous remarks to him.

Within this satiric framework, Milton gives free reign to his verbal ingenuity. In Marprelate fashion, he provokes grim laughter at his victim through complex word play. Like Marprelate's, Milton's quibbling is rooted in theological issues, and his wit lays bare prelatical corruption. Milton moves to the attack in the opening lines of the *Animadversions:*

Remonstrant. My single *Remonstrance* is encountred with a plurall *Adversary.*
Answere. Did not your single Remonstrance bring along with it a hot sent of your more than singular affection to spirituall pluralities, your singleness would be lesse suspected with all good Christians then it is. (YP, I, pp. 664-65)

Hall may have intended "plurall *Adversary*" as a slap at the "protean 'many' of Puritan error."[21] Milton counters by equivocating "plurall" to intimate the Puritan charge of multiple livings held by the Anglican clergy.[22] In the passage cited, Hall played into Milton's hands. However, Milton need not have waited for an obvious occasion because he was always ready to invoke satiric inflation to twist the Remonstrant's meaning against him:

Remon. It is no little advantage to our cause, and piety, that our Liturgy is taught to speak severall languages for use and example.
Answ. The language of *Ashdod* is one of them, and that makes so many English-men have such a smattering of their *Philistian* Mother. (YP, I, p. 680)

By adding an "example" of one of the languages to which Hall presumably alluded, thereby linking the prelates with the Philistines, Milton "amplifies" Hall's boast. Many of the bishop's assertions took the form of curt aphorisms, offering Milton ample opportunity for mimicry. Hall's taut question, "No seduced persons reclaim'd," inspires this retort: "More reclaimed persons seduc'd" (YP, I, p. 731). The tactic of reassembling Hall's word order into an aphorism of his own enables Milton to calculate the effect of prelacy more accurately.

Milton's polemical repertoire includes Martinist "mimic sophistry," a species of *refutatio* which often brings into play a critique of the component parts and operation of an opponent's syllogism:

Remon.   Episcopall government is cry'd down abroad by either weak or factious persons.
Answ.   Choose whether you will have this proposition prov'd . . . to be ridiculous, or sophisticall . . . this axiom Episcopall Government is cry'd downe abroad by either weake or factious persons, is as much as to say, they that cry downe Episcopacy abroad are either weak or factious persons . . . this axiom contains a distribution . . . and . . . a distribution in which any part is wanting, or abundant, is faulty, and fallacious. If therfore distributing by the adjuncts of faction, and weaknes the persons that decry *Episcopacy*, you made your distribution imperfect for the nonce, you cannot but be guilty of fraud intended toward the honourable Court, to whom you wrote. If you had rather vindicate your honesty, and suffer in your want of Art, you cannot condemne them . . . that attributed to you more skill then you had, thinking you had beene able to have made a distribution . . . and so take againe either your manifest lesing, or manifest ignorance. (YP, I, p. 694)

As he does here, Hall had sometimes objected that accusations against episcopacy betokened moral flaws in the accusers rather than sound reasoning. With polemic derring-do, Milton flings in the Remonstrant's face the "faulty" logic responsible for this conclusion. In Marprelate fashion, Milton applies an assortment of analogical rebuttals, many of which gain additional strength from the satiric associations they call to mind. To the Remonstrant's complaint that "Any thing serves against Episcopacy," Milton replies: "See the frowardnes of this man, he would perswade us that . . . Bishopdom hath bin unquestionable through all ages. . . . The *Pope* may as well boast his ungainsaid authority to them that will beleive that all his contradictors were either irreligious, or heretical" (YP, I, pp. 673–74). His analogy brands Hall as pompous, arrogant, determined to deny the evidence of corruption in order to retain power. Evident as well in the *Animadversions* is *ad hominem* argument, a maneuver equally effective in indicting Hall and in striking out at all prelates and episcopacy itself through the medium of Hall's assertions.

Matching Martin's swiftness and dexterity, often within the compass of a few brief paragraphs, Milton races back and forth between punning and mock logic, and then on to the biting sarcasm and caustic denunciation integral to Marprelate satire. He may lavish "praise" upon some of the Remonstrant's eminent qualities, derisively "agree" with him, or merely snicker:

Remon.   No one Clergie in the whole Christian world yeelds so many eminent schollers . . . grave, holy and accomplish'd Divines as this Church of *England* doth.
Answ. Ha, ha, ha. (YP, I, p. 726)

Like Marprelate, Milton harangues his opponent in abrasively colloquial language: "Wee know where the shoo wrings you, you fret, and are gall'd at the quick (YP, I, p. 668). In this excerpt verbs connote the violent contortion and discomfort dramatized by grating consonants.

Marprelate announced rhetorically the ideal response of the humble reader to the theological controversy at hand, and Milton does the same. Unlike Marprelate, however, Milton specifically affiliates himself with the Puritan layman, the better to emphasize that his own reactions of laughter and contempt toward Hall constitute the type of answer to prelacy that the layman should make. Finally, Milton not only enunciates the Presbyterian stance in a direct, forcible manner, but repeatedly explores the implications of that stance. By so doing, he confirms Presbyterianism as a viable form of church government available to the reader after he has rejected prelacy. Yet the *Animadversions* differs from the Marprelate tracts insofar as those portions wherein Milton articulates the ideals of the Reformation are usually distinguished by a rhetorically elaborate high style.[23] In Milton's plea for divine aid to advance the Reformation, the style takes on apocalyptic overtones:

Let us all goe every true protested Brittaine . . . and render thanks to God the Father of light . . . and to his son *CHRIST* our Lord. . . . For he . . . hath yet ever had this Iland under the speciall indulgent eye of his providence . . . he knockt once and twice and came againe, opening our drousie eyelids leasurely by that glimmering light which *Wicklef*, and his followers dispers't. . . . Every one can say that now certainly thou hast visited this land . . . in a time when men had thought that thou wast gone up from us to the farthest end of the Heavens, and hadst left to doe marvelously among the sons of these last Ages. (YP, I, pp. 704–06)

With its vision of the providential forces guiding human affairs, Milton's prayer unites temporal and eternal, present and future, the reforming of Reformation with the piety and zeal of Puritanism. The cadenced, resonant high style sanctifies the virtues Milton consistently attributes to the layman, intimating that the prayer's purpose is to establish those virtues as characteristic of all true believers in Reformation. When celebrating Puritan spiritual yearning, Milton relies upon a distinct persona, analogous to Marprelate's, which appeals to the moral ardor of the reader; but the Miltonic high style lends to the persona, and hence to Puritan values, a dignity absent from Marprelate.

Following his model, Milton outlines a prototype of positive response to the theological controversies under debate, and he intensifies that response by contrasting it to the manifold evils of episcopacy. But Milton's extensive concentration upon the moral chasm between the attitudes of his persona and the maliciousness of prelacy represents a major enlargement of the framework of Marprelate satire. A reiterated juxtaposition of truth and falsehood includes the ideal minister as the Puritans envisioned him and the corrupt prelates whom they detested. To vivify this antithesis Milton chooses an allegorical fable, a tactic used to advantage in Overton's trial of Mr. Persecution:

A certaine man . . . had a faire Garden, and kept therein an honest . . . servant . . . to sow all wholsome herbs, and delightfull flowers. . . . now, when the time was come that he [the servant] should . . . looke to his tender slips, and pluck up the weeds that hinder'd their growth, he . . . makes account to doe what was needfull in his garden, and who . . . should know better than he how the dayes work was to be spent? Yet . . . there comes another strange Gardener that never knew the soyle . . . and yet challenges as his right the binding or unbinding of every flower . . . both in that, and all other Gardens thereabout. (YP, I, pp. 716–17)

A paragon of the humble pastor whose daily contact with his flock renders him uniquely competent to care for them, the "honest servant" must contend with an upstart who insolently attempts to usurp his duties. In the tale lies compelling evidence of the intolerable demands made by the established church. The "strange Gardener" is magnified into a symbol of the greedy prelates Milton had been castigating, and, when measured against the "honest servant" who upholds Puritan ideals of the ministry, the vileness of prelacy looms large.

Imagery and allusion, however, remain Milton's most forceful means of underlining the archetypal enmity of righteousness and iniquity. Although Martinists in the 1640s were fond of imagery, Milton's detailed apocalyptic patterns lack precedent in the tradition. Configurations derived from the book of Revelation set the apocalyptic tenor.

Milton links the Anglican liturgy with the Whore of Babylon ("And indeede our *Liturgie* hath run up and downe the world like an English gallopping Nun, proffering her selfe"), plays upon the Puritan identification of the Anglican Church with Antichrist, and warns that the spiritual contamination traceable to prelacy is prefigured in Revelation: "all *England* knowes they [the prelates] have been to this Iland not wood, but wormewood, that have infected the third part of our waters, like that Apostate starre in the Revelation; that many soules have di'd of their bitternesse" (YP, I, pp. 717–18). Allusions to Spenser's *Faerie Queene* complete the delineation of Hall and his cohorts as Satanic archetypes. Milton's account of Hall's style likens it to a "fashionably dressed"[24] woman, reminiscent of Spenser's Duessa: "The peremptory Analysis that you call it, I beleeve will be so hardy as once more to unpinne your spruce fastidious oratory, to rumple her laces, her frizzles, and her bobins" (YP, I, pp. 670–71). Duessa's gaudy garments and Hall's rhetoric both distract the reader from the malignant corruption lurking beneath.[25]

Archetypal image clusters, of which the most common is light, also transfigure the spiritual values Milton eulogizes and demonstrate how far he has taken Marprelate devices. Not only does Milton urge the reader to open his eyes to the "light of grace," but he describes God as the "Father of light" and the Reformation as "that glimmering light which *Wicklef*, and his followers dispers't." Apocalyptic import is attached to the light imagery by references to Revelation, especially Milton's mentioning of God "that hast the seven starres in thy right hand."[26] Heavenly light is the perfect foil for the hellish "darknesse" of episcopal tyranny.

As did Marprelate, Milton formulated a type of response to the theological controversy his satire revolved around, a response designed to thwart episcopal efforts at hindering the Reformation; but he made this response much more emphatic than had his predecessor. Chiefly through allegorical parables and imagery which highlight the polarities of truth and falsehood, Milton depicts the struggle between Puritanism and prelacy as an emblematic encounter between good and evil necessitating the participation of each warfaring Christian. The Miltonic persona wages rhetorically, voicing the appropriate moral reactions of indignation and zeal, the battle Christians must wage spiritually if they are to reform Reformation.

Milton was again provoked to counterattack after an anonymous pamphleteer had blasted *The Doctrine and Discipline of Divorce* with *An Answer to a Book, Intituled, The Doctrine and Discipline of Divorce* in November 1644. To those who sincerely demanded justification of his views on divorce, Milton offered a scholarly discourse, *Tetrachordon,* and he aimed a Martinist salvo, *Colasterion,* at the scullion who had mocked him. In rebutting *An Answer,* Milton took issue with a gross distortion of his argument in *Doctrine and Discipline.* The divorce tract had exalted the spiritual dimensions of marriage instead of the physical. In Milton's words, one chooses a mate partially "against all the sorrows and casualties of this life to have an intimate and speaking help" (YP, II, p. 251). The principal end of wedlock is not carnal satisfaction, but rather "the cherfull help that may be in mariage toward sanctity of life" (YP, II, p. 269). Most importantly, a blighted union stunts an individual's moral growth, so that "his whole duty of serving God must needs be . . . tainted with a . . . dejection of spirit wherein, God has no delight" (YP, II, p. 259). That the Answerer misunderstands Milton's hierarchy of marital values is apparent from his warning against the unlimited license which permission to divorce would grant to libertines.[27] He derides Milton's proposal that one ought to make "trial" of a spouse before the ceremony by implying that Milton intends only sexual trial. Milton's sensitive observation that "it is a lesse breach of wedlock to part with wise and quiet consent betimes, then still to . . . profane that mystery of joy . . . with a polluting sadnes" (YP, II, p. 258) meets with a sneer: "Mystery of joy, what language is this? is mariage now a Sacrament signifying joy? this I never heard of before" (*An Answer,* p. 36). The cumulative effect of *An Answer* is to vulgarize and trivialize the nonphysical components of marriage.

The Answerer's impudence earned the witty punishment meted out by *Colasterion.* Although Milton does not preface the tract with a précis of his rhetorical strategy, he recapitulates at the conclusion by saying: Let the reader not "guess by the handling, which meritoriously hath bin bestowd on this object of contempt and laughter, that I account it any displeasure don mee to bee contradicted in Print" (YP, II, p. 758). Milton has directed scorn and laughter at his foe as he had at Hall. Yet the polemic rationale of *Colasterion* differs from that of the *Animadversions,* for scorn and laughter are not now legitimated primarily by their usefulness in alerting the reader to spiritual pitfalls. On the contrary, the chastisement of the Answerer is self-justifying, whether it uncovers evil or not. In *Colasterion*, Milton, exploiting the comic potential of the Marprelate mode, derives a full measure of delight from rendering the Answerer an object of merriment. While the reader will surely see affirmed the integrity of Milton's posture on divorce, he will share as well in the comic *reductio* Milton presents.

Milton structures *Colasterion* as a mock debate, advancing through *An Answer* and quoting the passages most suitable for jest. Following the precedent set in the *Animadversions*, Milton sustains the illusion of a dialogue by addressing his opponent as though he were actually present and by "conversing" with the reader, the implied spectator at the disputation. Above all, Milton seeks to characterize his antagonist as an ignoble dolt unworthy to participate in serious discussion and deserving of dismissal as a comically ineffectual dullard. Essential to the tract is an ironic situation: even though the Answerer's intellectual shortcomings would seem to deny him the privilege of voicing an opinion on divorce, he has chattered inanely on the subject. That particular irony relates *Colasterion* to Marvell's *Rehearsal Transpros'd,* which built upon the assumption that Samuel Parker was a drooling fanatic unfit for debate. Milton trumpets the irony of his adversary's ineptitude with several image patterns, exposing him as a simpleton whose brutishness, small-mindedness, and impertinence are the exact antitheses of the reverence and wide-ranging acumen needed to evaluate the delicate matter of divorce.

Milton's caricature of his enemy as a scullion from the lower echelons of society is at the farthest extreme from the allegorical, mythic portraiture of Hall in the *Animadversions*. *An Answer*, Milton insinuates, was certainly not the product of a cunning, seductive mind like Hall's. Since the author of *An Answer* chose anonymity, Milton "names" him: "I am sure none will guess him lower, then an actual Servingman" (YP, II, p. 726). Through repetition Milton expands his conjecture into a comic genealogy for the Answerer; when it serves his purpose Milton need only allude to the pamphleteer's base "ancestry" to evoke laughter.

Lawyer images furnish additional information about the nameless controversialist.[28] As Milton notes, he "argues from the practice of Canon Law, which the Book hee would confute, utterly rejects" (YP,

II, p. 725). Milton's derisive jibe about the lawyer's familiarity with the fabled trickeries of popish canon law finds confirmation, ironically, in the Answerer's efforts to flaunt his knowledge by reciting from numerous legal codes, canon law among them. For instance, he had listed several cases involving the question of tenure, none of which bears upon Milton's thesis;[29] despite the Answerer's research, he has missed the point. Even more ludicrous is the fact that the precedents he discovers do not bear to any significant degree upon his own thesis. Yet the Answerer's scholarly catalogues are in character, for they advertise not only his ignorance of legal affairs, but also his pompous, pedantic preoccupation with minutiae, the letter of the law instead of its spirit. Awkward, amateurish fumbling with logic is still another measure of the lawyer's incompetence, and Milton's "mimic sophistry" publicizes that fumbling. At every opportunity, Milton parodies the legalist's logic, demonstrating that the Answerer can neither formulate propositions correctly nor interpret Milton's arguments accurately. Milton chides: "like a right cunning and sturdy Logician, he denies my Argument not mattering whether in the *major* or *minor*: and saith, *there are many Laws made for good, and yet that good is not attain'd, through the defaults of the party, but a greater inconvenience follows.* But I reply that this Answer builds upon a shallow foundation, and most unjustly supposes every one in default, who seeks divorce from the most injurious wedloc" (YP, II, p. 755). The "shallow foundation" upon which the Answerer grounds his charge verifies our suspicion that bungling barristers cannot be expected to reason expertly. In the *Animadversions,* Milton had painstakingly alerted his audience to the insidious half-truths of Hall's sophistry, but he is satisfied in *Colasterion* to parade his victim's inaccuracies before the amused reader.

Since the Answerer delights in brandishing his crudity and tactlessness, Milton justly designates him as a "Pork" with whom Milton refuses to "dispute Philosophy." The swine image reappears when Milton questions whether his foe's doctrine came "out of som School, or som stie" (YP, II, p. 739) and wonders "what should a man say more to a snout in this pickle" (YP, II, p. 747). Swine imagery stigmatizes the Answerer as the epitome of bad-mannered coarseness, leading the reader to conclude that a "Pork" ought to meddle in utterly mundane affairs because his insuperable churlishness can only contaminate the issue to which he has addressed himself.

Repeatedly Milton enlarges individual images into miniature comic scenes reflective of the Answerer's foolishness. The Miltonic narrator of these episodes approaches the witty ironist of Marvell's *Rehearsal Transpros'd* in his dramatization of an adversary's follies for the entertainment of the reader. Several scenes catch the Answerer in the act of preparing his own text or of examining Milton's. Milton muses:

> But what will become now of the busines I know not; for the man is suddenly takn with a lunacy of Law, and speaks revelations out of the *Atturneys Academy*. . . . But now his fit of Law past, yet hardly come to himself, hee maintains, that if Mariage bee void . . . *there needs no legal proceeding to part it*. (YP, II, pp. 741–42)

His vignette reduces to the absurd the legal marginalia of the Answerer by implying that he was mentally unsound when he inserted them. Equating fanaticism with the process of composition, moreover, undercuts even the Answerer's most cogent points. The "Serving-man" allusion animates another preposterous scene:

> Finally, hee windes up his Text with much doubt and trepidation; for it may bee his trenchers were not scrap't, and that which never yet afforded corn of savour to his noddle, the Salt-seller was not rubb'd: and therefore in this hast . . . he runs to the black jack, fills his flagon, spreds the table, and servs up dinner. (YP, II, p. 746)

At the instant that the Answerer degenerates into a careless tavern lackey sloppily attending to his duties, the intellectual activity involved in his pamphlet suffers a proportionate, humiliating shrinkage. Comic incidents of this sort metamorphose the Answerer into an ironic hero whose antics heap ridicule upon him; it remains for Milton merely to remind the reader of the unflagging enthusiasm with which a fool engineers his own downfall.

Even though Milton subjects his enemy to a blistering verbal banter resembling that of the *Animadversions*, equivocation is modified according to *Colasterion*'s comic intentions. Puns in the earlier pamphlet assailed the spiritual values symbolized by Hall, but now Milton's wit takes a more personal direction, singling out the abundant inadequacies of the Answerer himself, a man representative of no value except folly. Here Milton deftly parries the Answerer's pretentious footnoting of the "*twelfth Councel of Toledo*" on a point of law: "But all this craft avails him not; for seeing they [the *Councel*] allow no cause of divorce but fornication, what do these keen Doctors heer but cut him over the sinews with thir Toledo's" (YP, II, p. 735).

Imagistic parody and the double-entendre often yield to scorching sarcasm, the most vehement expression of Milton's contempt for the Answerer. Milton may propose condescending corrections ("that place in St. Paul commands nothing, as *that book* at large affirm'd, though you overskipt it"), or "salute" the loutish pamphleteer, once as an "acute Rabbie" for his inexact recitation of legal precedent, and later as "our doubty adversary" who so eagerly contributes to his own undoing. Having pilloried the Answerer skillfully, Milton properly treats him to the Martinist jeering he deserves. Finally, to a greater extent than in the *Animadversions*, Milton indulges in direct invective, denigrating his target as a "doult . . . as obtuse . . . as any mallet," and as an "incogitant woodcock." "Doult," "woodcock," and other disdainful titles effect a satiric redefinition consistent with Milton's imagistic portraiture. Predictably, much of this invective appears as coarse, rasping, colloquial taunts which surround the unfortunate polemicist with the vulgar and barbaric to which he is most accustomed.

Caricature and ridicule reduce the Answerer to an object of derision whom Milton declines to dignify with a sustained rebuttal. In the *Animadversions*, Milton had carefully articulated Presbyterian attitudes, whereas in *Colasterion* he usually rests content simply with bidding the reader to consult *Doctrine and Discipline* or Scripture itself on the divorce question. Citation of the self-evident verities of Scripture constitutes a refusal to justify or even to explain one's case for the benefit of a fool. Milton does not ennoble his doctrines by presenting them in an apocalyptic high style, because doing so would be tantamount to ennobling the nonsensical protestations of a prattler. Milton's assault on the Answerer advocates a type of response insofar as it implies that one ought to disregard irrelevant pamphlets and depend upon Scripture for a verdict on the controversy. Yet Milton's rhetorical identity in *Colasterion* is not shaped by his association with values specific and theological. Rather, his earnest desire to clarify the recommendations set down in *Doctrine and Discipline* sanctions the application of chastisement to dispense with nuisances such as *An Answer*. Nor is *Colasterion* an emblematic struggle between prelacy and truth epic in its import. Because he conceives of the Answerer's objections as ludicrous rather than persuasive, farcical instead of malevolent, Milton eliminates from the tract the elaborate allegorical contrasts between good and evil so dominant in the *Animadversions.* *Colasterion* signifies Milton's refinement of the Marprelate style into a mere gesture of contempt toward the folly of an unworthy foe, into a performance in wit whose comic catharsis is both public and personal in its effect.

To answer controversialists who had vilified his cause or his person, Milton utilized a mode of polemic rebuttal which had flourished since Elizabethan times. Reliance upon the mock debate stratagem and a multitude of Martinist-inspired verbal and logical ploys marks the *Animadversions* and *Colasterion* as specimens of a distinct genre of pamphlet literature. Although the Marprelate tradition provided a versatile satiric paradigm for Milton, the polemic success he enjoyed derives as much from innovation as from imitation. In the *Animadversions,* Milton took aim at the lofty viciousness, the "public evil"[30] of Bishop Hall, accentuating through an apocalyptic high style and imagistic polarities an archetypal antagonism between prelacy and truth which Martin had only outlined. With *Colasterion* Milton anticipated Andrew Marvell in realizing the comic possibilities of the Marprelate idiom. Comic scenes narrated with detachment and wit transformed Milton's antagonist into a doltish buffoon. Milton found, in short, that whether a fool be excoriated as a monster of iniquity or be deftly caricatured as an inept scullion, he could be made to pay dearly for his folly.[31]

The University of Akron

NOTES

1. A chronology of Marprelate's pamphlets and episcopal replies to them has been established by William Pierce, *An Historical Introduction to the Marprelate Tracts* (London, 1908), pp. 322–32. Pierce also summarizes (pp. 255–73) the theological issues important to Marprelate. My analysis will center upon Martin's *The Epistle* and *Hay any worke for Cooper,* hereafter abbreviated as *Epist.* and *HAW.* Page citations will be from *The Marprelate Tracts,* facsimile ed. (Yorkshire, 1967).

2. Marprelate's dialogue is also examined by Raymond A. Anselment ("Andrew Marvell's *The Rehearsal Transpros'd:* A Study in Renaissance Satire" [Ph.D. diss., Rochester, 1965], p. 50) and by Travis L. Summersgill ("The Influence of the Marprelate Controversy upon the Style of Thomas Nashe," *SP,* XLVIII [1951], 150).

3. Raymond A. Anselment, "Rhetoric and the Dramatic Satire of Martin Marpre-

late," *SEL*, X (1970), 112–17. In *HAW* (pp. 30–36), "Reverend Martin" and "Reverend T.C." engage in such a debate.

4. In the original text of the *Admonition*, Cooper had admitted that the Apostles and the primitive church practiced the Presbyterian "discipline." His damaging concession, "I will not deny it," was "pasted over" when the *Admonition* appeared in print. See Donald J. McGinn, *John Penry and the Marprelate Controversy* (New Brunswick, N.J., 1966), p. 176.

5. Anselment, "Andrew Marvell's *The Rehearsal Transpos'd*," pp. 68–72. An example may be found on p. 22 of *HAW*: "All Churches . . . have their imperfections."

6. *Shakespeare's Festive Comedy* (Cleveland, 1963), p. 55.

7. Imitators of the legendary Elizabethan sought the maximum benefit available from claiming to be his descendants; Martin's name is frequently dropped in their pamphlets, especially in those of Richard Overton. Yet the literary relationship between Marprelate and his "followers" is a loose, often nominal one: there is little verbatim continuation of Marprelate's techniques in the seventeenth century. For the most part, Martin's "kin" saw his polemic format as a paradigm which they felt free to modify, with the result that the differences between their satiric formulae and his invariably outweigh the similarities.

8. *Vox Borealis, Or The Northerne Discoverie. By Way of Dialogue, between Jamie and Willie* (London, 1641). Authored by *MARGERY MAR-PRELAT*, the tract is a dialogue between two rustics critical of Charles I and episcopacy. See also Anselment, "Andrew Marvell's *The Rehearsal Transpos'd*," pp. 127–30.

9. *Crop-Eare Curried, or, Tom Nash His Ghost*, in *Works of John Taylor the Water Poet Not Included in the Folio Volume of 1630*, ed. Spenser Society, 2d ed. (1873; reprint ed., New York, 1967), vol. II. Like Thomas Nashe, Taylor, a Royalist sympathizer, turned Martinist tricks against the Puritans, in this case William Prynne.

10. In *Tracts on Liberty in the Puritan Revolution 1638-1647*, ed. William Haller (New York, 1933), vol. III.

11. Marvell parodied several of Parker's inflammatory tracts, particularly *A Discourse of Ecclesiastical Politie* (1670) and *A Defence and Continuation of the Ecclesiastical Politie* (1671).

12. Don M. Wolfe, "Unsigned Pamphlets of Richard Overton: 1641-1649," *Huntington Library Quarterly*, XXI (1958), 178.

13. Anselment, "Andrew Marvell's *The Rehearsal Transpos'd*," p. 131.

14. The pamphlet was originally titled *A Dialogue Wherin is Plainly Laide Open, The Tyrannicall Dealing of L. Bishopps Against Gods Children*. It was recently edited by Joy Lee Belknap King (Ph.D. diss., Rutgers, 1968). King argues that *A Dialogue* was written by Marprelate himself, probably in 1590. With a few minor exceptions, the 1643 reprint is identical to the 1590 original.

15. Taylor's claim that he wrote the pamphlet in October 1643 suggests a likely publication date within the next few months. 1644 is the date given on the title page.

16. Milton's contact with the Leveller Richard Overton may have provided him with more information about the Marprelate tradition. That Milton knew Overton has been asserted by Don M. Wolfe ("Lilburne's Note on Milton," *MLN*, LVI [1941], 360–63) and by Denis Saurat (*Milton: Man and Thinker* [New York, 1925], pp. 310–22). The acquaintance of the two pamphleteers may have begun as early as 1641. Overton, operator of a London print shop, wrote five Mar-Priest satires against the Westminster Assembly in 1645-1646. Milton could have seen Overton's *Araignment of Mr. Persecution*, published on April 8, 1645 (shortly after *Colasterion*), in manuscript. If, as Wolfe

theorizes ("Unsigned Pamphlets of Richard Overton," p. 178), Overton penned *Vox Borealis*, Milton may have gained early access to this tract as well. Finally, Overton's fondness for Marprelate renders it likely that the two reprinted pamphlets mentioned above might have been the products of his press.

17. My subsequent argument follows the generic distinctions between Miltonic satire and comedy formulated by Irene Samuel in "Milton on Comedy and Satire," *Huntington Library Quarterly*, XXXV (1972), 107–30. She concludes that Milton "accepts comedy as the proper genre for folly, satire for eminent evil. . . . Comedy properly takes as its target the *humiles* and uses a language suitable to them in their private follies; satire selects the loftier vicious and adjusts itself to their public evil" (pp. 126–27). More precise descriptions of the *Animadversions* and *Colasterion* might be, respectively, satirical-comic and comic-satirical: clearly each tract contains elements of both comedy and satire. Milton's conception of his adversary's identity, his estimate of the strength of the adversary's case, and his subsequent polemic treatment of that adversary are the criteria I have relied upon to determine whether each tract is predominantly satirical or comic.

18. *Animadversions upon the Remonstrants Defence against Smectymnuus*, ed. Rudolph Kirk, in *Complete Prose Works of John Milton*, ed. Don M. Wolfe et al. (New Haven, 1953-), vol. I, p. 653, hereafter cited as YP. Hall's *Defence* was issued on April 12, 1641 (YP, I, p. 653). As Kirk observes (YP, I, p. 667, n. 16), Milton also responds several times to Hall's *Humble Remonstrance* (1640).

19. In YP, I, p. 654, Kirk concludes that Milton uses the "method of quotation and reply" left over from the Admonition Controversy of 1570–1572. See also Everett H. Emerson, ed., "The Anti-Prelatical Tracts, 1641-1642," in *The Prose of John Milton*, ed. J. Max Patrick (New York, 1967), pp. 32–33. Neither Kirk nor Emerson, however, connects the *Animadversions* with the Marprelate tradition.

20. See, for example, YP, I, p. 691: "Tell me . . . evill."

21. YP, I, p. 664, n. 2.

22. Ibid.

23. Its rhythmic cadences, abundant tropes and schemes, and Ciceronian sentence structure liken the style to the oratorical *genus grande* discussed by Cicero in *Orator* and by Quintillian in the *Institutio Oratoria*. Milton's frame of reference in passages written in this style is, however, explicitly Christian and frequently apocalyptic.

24. YP, I, pp. 670–71, n. 30.

25. For other Spenserian allusions, see YP, I, pp. 674, 719.

26. Revelation i, 16 (YP, I, p. 706, n. 25).

27. *An Answer to a Book, Intituled, The Doctrine and Discipline of Divorce . . . ,* in William Riley Parker, *Milton's Contemporary Reputation*, 2d ed. (1940; reprint ed., New York, 1971), p. 8. Subsequent references will be to this edition.

28. Cf. Diane Parkin Speer, " 'Freedom of Speech': Milton's View of Polemic and His Polemical Works" (Ph.D. diss., Iowa, 1970), pp. 107–24. Speer studies the servant and lawyer images as part of the negative rhetorical ethos Milton creates for the Answerer.

29. YP, II, p. 756, n. 150.

30. Samuel, "Milton on Comedy and Satire," p. 127.

31. A grant from the University of Akron Faculty Research Committee was instrumental in the preparation of this article.

BRIGHT PILGRIMAGE:
WILLIAM BLAKE'S DESIGNS FOR
L'ALLEGRO AND *IL PENSEROSO*

Stephen C. Behrendt

Blake's twelve illustrations for *L'Allegro* and *Il Penseroso* constitute a vigorous critical interpretation of Milton's twin lyrics. Completed after Blake had made most of his other Milton illustrations, this set of designs is the first to depict Milton extensively and presents Blake's judgment both of the poems and of the poet. Blake visually associates the poet of *L'Allegro* with the material, physical world of experience and with the inferior, conventionalized poetry of the merely average versifier. He associates the poet of *Il Penseroso* with the imaginatively superior world of higher innocence and directly with the poetic genius of Milton. The designs for *Il Penseroso* develop Blake's assessment of Milton's ascent into this higher state, the apotheosis of which appears in the prophetic Milton of the final design. Blake reveals the vast difference between the "young poet" and Milton most clearly in his depictions of each poet's dream, each of which reflects the individual poet's mental and physical state, the former conventional and restricted, the latter imaginatively free.

IN AN age of great attention to critical perspectives on Milton's poetry, remarkably little notice has been given to one of the most outstanding bodies of Milton criticism we have: William Blake's illustrations. Blake's illustrations have seldom been considered in terms of literary criticism because of the reluctance of modern criticism to recognize visual statements as criticism along with verbal statements. Yet Ralph Cohen has demonstrated that in the eighteenth century illustration was one form of a recognized and often utilized type of literary criticism he calls "by-product" criticism, which included critical commentary in the form of parodies, imitations, and illustrations.[1] It is in this

tradition of critical illustration—this spirit of vigorous interpretive statement—that we must place Blake's illustrations.

We may most easily approach Blake's visual criticism of Milton
by studying his designs for *L'Allegro* and *Il Penseroso*, five of which
are reproduced here. In these designs, Blake discusses John Milton
both as poet and as man. Just as Milton distinguishes in his twin lyrics
between the secular, Bacchian poet and the visionary bard—a distinction initiated in *Elegy VI*—so does Blake in his designs distinguish
between that secular, inferior poet and the prophetic bard Milton.
In the creation of his designs, Blake invokes both the literal context
of Milton's own text and the additional context of previous illustrations
of the two poems. Blake wishes to return us, by the visual medium
of his designs, to a correct reading of Milton's text, a meaning that
had gradually been obscured by the less perceptive artists who had
repeatedly compromised and sacrificed Milton's vision in their own
misguided illustrations. Hence we must see Blake's designs as corrective
criticism as well as interpretive criticism, applied both to Milton's
poems and to the tradition of their illustration.

Discussion of Blake's designs for *L'Allegro* and *Il Penseroso* has
been scant. The only substantial discussions have been those by Edward J. Rose and John E. Grant.[2] But Rose's approach is thematic
and, ultimately, erroneous, suggesting that Blake's designs culminate
in a vision of an old Milton in a "living grave," left with only memories
of the past, a definite misreading.[3] Grant's study, though more extensive, is primarily descriptive and tells us not nearly enough about
what we should make of Blake's assessment of Milton and his poetry,
and nothing about Blake's designs in relation to previous illustrations.

What neither Rose nor Grant emphasizes is the degree to which
we must understand that Blake's Milton illustrations constitute the dynamic encounter of one revolutionary artist with another. Both artists
confronted the artistic and intellectual traditions they inherited with
a view toward extracting what was of use to them in the exterioriza-
tion of their respective visions and abandoning the rest. Both refused
to allow their visions to be shaped totally by tradition, choosing instead
to be themselves shapers of vision. Thus Blake is not enslaved by
Milton's text, nor are his designs mere visualizations of that text. Rather,
they constitute "a passionate concentration of original thinking on the

"Mirth"

subject prescribed, resulting in the development of an unsuspected point of view, a new aspect."[4] Blake's method, as Joseph A. Wittreich, Jr., has pointed out, involves a critical process by which he "lifts us to his own level of perception, abstracts the 'spiritual essence' of the poem, and lays bare its metaphorical and mythic structures in designs that probe the central issues of Milton's art and resolve those issues in interpretations to which Milton's critics still are strangers."[5] They are, finally, "something to be understood in their own right and, once understood, to be used as a gloss on the poem they adorn; they are pictorial criticisms that greatly increase the intelligibility of Milton's poetry."[6]

Blake's designs for *L'Allegro* and *Il Penseroso*, done in 1816, may best be evaluated in relation to the tradition of anecdotal portraiture that customarily depicted Milton himself in some scene of biographical, historical, or artistic significance.[7] Blake's designs combine anecdotal significance with textual interpretation for the purpose of delineating those excellences he understood Milton to possess, those which raised him beyond the level of the average versifier to that of the visionary prophet. Whereas in his epic *Milton*, Blake exposes Milton's nude "spiritual form," in these designs he portrays Milton's "natural life in which we see his spiritual life."[8] This spiritual life proves to be associated with Milton's aesthetic life as well.

Blake's designs are based upon a concept of progress: Milton's genius develops in proportion to the imaginative progress he undergoes in the course of the *Il Penseroso* designs. Blake treats *L'Allegro* as a general portrait of the "typical" secular poet—the poet engaged in mundane experiences, whose slight though attractive productions please for perhaps a generation or so among "polite society" and then disappear forever. Blake reads *Il Penseroso* as a portrait of Milton, the true poet who progresses in imaginative insight in turning to the larger concerns of the epic and tragic modes and thereby creating a poetry that outlasts its competitors. Blake's critical commentary culminates in the triumphal final design of the *Il Penseroso* series ("Milton, Old Age"),[9] but that design's significance only emerges fully in the light of the two crucial dream illustrations, "The Youthful Poet's Dream" (*L'Allegro*, plate 6) and "Mysterious Dream" (*Il Penseroso*, plate 5).

Don Cameron Allen identified this controlling element of progress when he noted that

"Melancholy"

the revolution of the earth presents at each degree of its rotation a new grada-
tion by which the poet rises toward a comprehension of his created end,
towards the "everlasting companionship" with "holy minds and intelligences."
"L'Allegro" describes the lower level of each degree; "Il Penseroso" the higher.
By a continual mounting of the slopes of the intellect from common experience,
to intellectual experience, to religious inspiration, the poet trusts to arrive
at the supreme poetic gratification.[10]

This is the sort of progress Blake delineates in his designs; his visual
discussion of the two types of poet moving through time and experience
culminates, finally, in the clear critical assessment of Milton's achievement represented by the final design. Milton's progress, it turns out,
results from his correct response to the dynamic tension between the
contrary states he experiences, states that are not precise opposites
but are, rather, "contraries" in the Blakean sense. "Without Contraries
is no progression," Blake says in *The Marriage of Heaven and Hell*.[11]
In his own poetry it is the opposition of contraries—desire and reason,
the eternal and the finite, Innocence and Experience—that generates
progress. The individual progresses only in proportion to his exposure
to and participation in these states. To progress steadily is to move
ever nearer the vision of the prophetic bard—a movement Blake discerned clearly in Milton's poetic development.

A correct reading of Blake's designs requires that we view them
consecutively, in corresponding pairs, and "in unison" in a general
overview. For while Blake clearly follows Milton's bipartite structure,
he also recognizes the unity of vision controlling the poems as well
as the critical comparison implicit in that unified view. The following
discussion attempts to maintain this difficult perspective in analyzing
the designs.

Among early illustrators of Milton's works, the figures of Mirth
and Melancholy became standard subjects for depiction. Often these
were the only illustrations published with the poems.[12] Occasionally,
as in the case of a separate painting, the two principals were brought
together in a single illustration that often incorporated recognizable
historical figures or situations as well.[13] Still other illustrators chose
to depict "the poet"—sometimes identified as Milton, sometimes left
generalized—in some attitude of pensiveness or inspiration.[14] Blake
probably knew many, if not all, of these earlier illustrations from
his three years' proximity to the large library of William Hayley, editor
and biographer of Milton and Blake's patron from 1800 to 1803. Thus

"The Youthful Poet's Dream"

his departure from the tradition of illustration that had grown up about these poems is of particular interest, for it tells us much about the nature of the corrective Blake applies to both the poetry and its illustrator-commentators.

Blake's primary rebellion is directed against those who had taken liberties with Milton's text. By their addition of un-Miltonic topicality to their designs, previous illustrators had tended both to simplify and to historicize the poems. Blake refuses to allow this tendency toward historicization to enter into his own designs; hence he mythologizes the poems by returning to them their original Miltonic dimension. We must recognize that Blake does not illustrate by inserting new material not present in the text; rather he reveals what is already implicit there by stripping away the obscuring veils of narrative detail. Blake operates by interpreting, often correcting, Milton's vision rather than simply substituting his own under the guise of "illustration." In so doing, he necessarily rejects much of the illustrative tradition he had inherited.

Blake introduces an abundance of contrasting visual imagery into the two designs he titles simply "Mirth" and "Melancholy" and whose entire atmospheres are enormously different. Each design depicts all the figures Milton mentions, but Blake also captures in the designs the emotional and psychological tones of each poem. "Mirth" is a warm, active, strikingly open scene, alive with energetic figures. Mirth herself is the very embodiment of active participation, her left hand raised in some sort of participatory gesture. "Melancholy" presents a marked contrast; it is cool, restrained, and closed, with trees hemming in the figures. Melancholy herself provides the contrary to Mirth's attitude of exuberant participation, her hands expressing her attitude of reservation and withdrawal, perhaps even of aversion. She looks up, not forward like Mirth, at the bright figure of the Cherub Contemplation. She steps forward on her left foot, unlike Mirth, whose right foot is forward.

These two designs are significantly related to the frontispieces to Blake's own *Songs of Innocence and of Experience*. The frontispieces depict situations resembling those in "Mirth" and "Melancholy," but with an interesting reversal. The figure looking skyward at a cherub on a cloud, stepping forward on his left foot from a closed scene, is the shepherd of Innocence. In contrast, the shepherd of Experience,

"Mysterious Dream"

who is in physical contact with the cherub figure above him, steps forward on his right foot, eyes forward, from an open scene. Blake apparently invokes an intentional visual parallel here, with the surprise twist of aligning Mirth with Experience and Melancholy with Innocence, an alignment which the dream illustrations also bear out. The surprise twist proves to be more predictable than surprising, though. Blake had characterized the world of Experience as that of finite life: a mutable, materialistic world. It is with the trappings of this world that Mirth and her companions—and the poet of L'Allegro—are involved. In the contrary world of Innocence (or, more accurately in the long run, the higher, "organized" Innocence), the connection between man and eternity is understood to be closer. In this world we find the withdrawn, restrained figures of Melancholy and her companions—and their poet who ultimately gets beyond their imaginative capabilities—apparently involved in the contemplation of something literally above and beyond them.

In addition to the watercolor design, Blake made two engraved versions of "Mirth."[15] The earlier engraving follows the basic conception of the watercolor fairly closely, although there are some alterations in the details. The later engraved version is more significantly altered. Blake's use of shading makes this version much "harder"; the softness of the previous states is replaced by near gaudiness. Mirth herself is drastically altered. She is more coarsely earthy and embodies a sexuality not suggested in the other designs. All the principal figures are literally "fleshed out."

Blake also adds an inscription to this second engraved state: "Solomon says Vanity of Vanity all is Vanity & What can be Foolisher than This" (E, p. 667). Grant correctly interprets this inscription as a touch of irony on Blake's part.[16] Such an ascetic pronouncement can only be made by one grown weary of life. Unlike the Puritan moralist, Blake recognized that the world of Mirth and her companions is not wholly to be damned, regardless of its ties with Experience. "Mirth," in all its versions, depicts a "State": one of the contrary states of the human soul; the other is embodied in "Melancholy." Despite all their individual limitations, both states are absolutely essential. Each has its damning and redeeming aspects, but it is only through the interaction of the two states within the imaginative consciousness of

"Milton, Old Age"

the individual that progress can take place, for "Without Contraries is no progression."

The engraved versions of "Mirth" most succinctly illustrate Blake's evaluation of the ascetic Puritan ethic he felt Milton had succumbed to for a significant portion of his life. Blake says, in effect, that Milton's orthodox pronouncements concerning sensual enjoyment are finally as foolish as those of Solomon. That Blake's meaning is more explicit in the engravings follows logically from their isolation as separate engravings, apart from any series. Yet the same meaning is implicit already in the watercolor design for the series, where it exists in a less ironic atmosphere and is elucidated through its interaction with the other designs in the series.

Each series presents, in its second design ("The Lark" and "The Wandering Moon"), a night scene, each presided over by a dominant figure. In "The Lark," the lark announces a "new day" as he rises above the startled Urizenic figure of Old Night, Dawn and her four horses, and the awakening figure of Earth.

Blake says of "The Wandering Moon" that the Moon is "terrified as one led astray in the midst of her path thro' heaven" (E, p. 665). He thus encourages us to draw the parallel with Milton, seeing him also as a wanderer led astray from his path of innate poetic genius by the restrictive, reason-oriented world of rational learning symbolized by his academic garb and the spire of Cambridge, visible at the center of the design and pointing to "the Moon." Blake begins here to set up the visual progression by which he shows Milton ultimately to have overcome the restrictions of reason and orthodoxy in fulfilling his poetic potential and completing his "bright pilgrimage of sixty years" (E, p. 109; *Milton*, plate 15, l. 52). The source of light in "The Wandering Moon" is the moon, not a natural sun figure or even a symbolic one like the lark in "The Lark." The moon is the light of the material world of Generation which Milton himself must gradually transcend. By the final design (*Il Penseroso*, plate 6) Milton himself, in his prophetic state, provides the illumination.

The third and fourth designs of each series further advance Blake's association of *L'Allegro* with Experience and *Il Penseroso* with higher Innocence.[17] "The Sun at His Eastern Gate" (*L'Allegro*, plate 3) focuses upon the sun (to which Milton gives only four lines) rather than upon the pastoral scene Blake miniaturizes at the bottom of the design (to

which Milton devotes eighteen lines). The presence of the herald angels
in this design, along with both the winged figures at the upper left
who pour out the contents of cups and the three figures beneath the
central figure's right arm who ascend bearing urns or pots, suggests
the world of Generation-Experience in a state approaching the Day
of Judgment.[18]

These suggestions are carried over into the equally vibrant "A
Sunshine Holiday" (*L'Allegro*, plate 4). The two large, distressed figures
at the center are embodiments of age and world-weariness; the city
in the female's lap suggests, perhaps, the barrenness (possibly sexual)
of man's worldly social realm. Of greater importance is the figure
directly beneath this couple who drinks from a cup or chalice while
resting on an overturned urn from which a stream flows. Located
at almost the exact center of the design, this figure epitomizes the
whole cycle of existence in Experience, participating to the fullest
in the world of Generation, draining the symbolic cup while at the
same moment the waters of life drain away.[19]

To reinforce his meaning, Blake adds his own emphatic device
to the design. The large face in the tree at the right gazes at the
entire assembly of figures at the bottom. The group at the left, dancing
airily about on tiptoe, contrasts markedly with that on the right, all
the figures of which are more heavily drawn and are posed with feet
planted firmly on the ground. The group at the left appear to be
all about the same age, resembling Mirth and her companions, while
that at the right comprises an all-inclusive age grouping, from infant
to aged man. This second group represents the full spectrum of physical age in the generated world. The face in the trees gazes at all,
but his gaze falls particularly upon the "May pole" group. The figure's
right hand is raised with the index finger clearly indicating the reclining
drinker. This subtle but definite pointing is Blake's way of emphasizing
the transitory nature of the events portrayed and of locating the scene
in the generated universe of Experience. The repetition of the herald
angels and offering-bearers again suggests a cyclic completion, under-
scoring the probability, indicated initially by the drinking figure, that
man is to be included in this natural gesture of completion.

While both these designs present aspects of the sun of the material,
physical world, "The Spirit of Plato" (*Il Penseroso*, plate 3) presents
an alternative "sun." Now the illumination comes not from the natural

sun but from the questionable (for Blake) sun of Platonic vision. In a sense, Milton is still "astray" here in a scene lit by a different source of light from that in *Il Penseroso*, plate 2. "The Spirit of Plato" continues to advance Blake's association of *Il Penseroso* with the progression into higher Innocence. The *L'Allegro* designs are essentially stationary in time, with all the scenes representing a roughly equivalent condition of Experience. The *Il Penseroso* designs, on the other hand, illustrate Milton undergoing a clear progression from wanderer "led astray," through stages of ever decreasing reliance upon reason-oriented perception (as in *Il Penseroso*, plate 3), to aged visionary prophet, free at last. We note that even in "The Spirit of Plato" Blake indicates that Milton is beginning to reshape convention to suit his own needs, for careful examination of the three spheres above Milton's head reveals that all three contain foreshadowings of details of *Paradise Lost*.

Milton's continuing progress is evidenced in "The Sun in His Wrath" (*Il Penseroso*, plate 4) by the fact that he is being led by Melancholy into the groves and away from the sun. Here the sun is again more the natural sun of the physical, material world, the "light of common day" that Wordsworth as well has perceived as detrimental to imaginative vision. Already established as a figure associated with higher Innocence, Melancholy is a fit guide for Milton.

Of further significance is the fact that all the figures in this design, with the exception of Milton and Melancholy, are looking up in the direction of the sun's origin. The orientation of Milton and Melancholy is quite clearly elsewhere. Since Blake takes pains to point out that the figures in the trees are Spirits "under the domination of Insects raised by the sun's heat" (E, p. 666), it seems certain he is ascribing the sun and all that here falls under its influence to the material world of Generation-Experience. This emphasizes the importance of Milton's avoidance of the sun, under Melancholy's guidance. Appropriately, this design shows Melancholy with a halo, the first Blake has depicted since "Melancholy" (*Il Penseroso*, plate 1). This detail further indicates progress and suggests the superiority of the mental state embodied in Melancholy to the rest of the environment.

"The Goblin" (*L'Allegro*, plate 5) is perhaps best explained by seeing it simply as a depiction of the perverse spirits at large in the world of Experience. Goblins, ghosts, pinching fairies, people led about in the woods—these are indications of the nature of the state to which Queen Mab belongs and which manifests itself to man in the form

of needless superstitious terror and mental anguish.[20] That this design
has no direct counterpart in *Il Penseroso* is explained by the relationship
of the two dream illustrations and "Milton, Old Age" (*Il Penseroso*,
plate 6), which necessarily has no counterpart.

In a letter to the Rev. John Trusler dated August 23, 1799, Blake
explains his conception of imaginative perception:

> This World Is a World of imagination & Vision. I see Every thing I paint
> In This World, but Every body does not see alike. . . . Some See Nature
> all Ridicule & Deformity, & by these I shall not regulate my proportions;
> and Some Scarce see Nature at all. But to the Eyes of the Man of Imagination,
> Nature is Imagination itself. As a man is, So he Sees. As the Eye is formed,
> such are its Powers. You certainly Mistake, when you say that the Visions
> of Fancy are not to be found in This World. To Me This World is all One
> continued Vision of Fancy or Imagination.[21]

To the man of imagination all life is inspiration. Such a man sees
nature with the "fourfold vision." Blake's letter substantiates the concept
brought out in the dream illustrations: the mind of the true poet is
continually alert to inspiration, even when that alertness is concealed
by the outward physical act of sleep. With this concept in mind we
may look at the dream illustrations.

"The Youthful Poet's Dream" portrays, in deceptively simple pastoral terms, the young poet asleep on a river bank, dreaming of a
festive wedding, the sphere of his dream framed by the figures of
Jonson (on the left) and Shakespeare. As in "Mirth," the scene is an
open one, framed by a pair of trees which do not hinder the viewer's
depth perception. The sun sets at the left; the poet's head lies to
the right. The poet appears to write in the blank volume, working
even as he sleeps. His left hand is raised in a gesture of acknowledgment. The young poet's body positioning is strongly reminiscent of
that of Mirth: the hand gesture is the same, and if we rotate his body
(or the whole design) forty-five degrees counterclockwise we find
the poses are almost identical. Thus Blake presents his interpretation
of the concept he detected in Milton's poem, that the poet's dreams
necessarily reflect his own taste and indeed his whole state. Since
the young poet conjures up the vision of Mirth, it is only natural that
she should resemble him. After all, "As a man is, So he Sees."

The very configuration of the dream, neatly packaged in the sphere,
suggests an orderly, convention-laden dream. The figures of Jonson
with his book and Shakespeare with his pipe tend to "identify" the

conventions, and their presence on either side of the sphere physically restricts the dream sphere's boundaries, preventing any expansion.

The setting sun establishes a contrast with the dream sphere. The immense natural sun of the earlier design (*L'Allegro*, plate 3) is now totally outshone by the far greater sun of poetic genius. Yet for all its apparent immensity, this poetic genius is still limited by its own conventionality, just as it is physically limited by the clear line Blake has inscribed around the sphere and by the squeeze exerted by the figures of Jonson and Shakespeare. In this design Blake suggests the drawbacks of such limitations of poetic vision, even when that limitation can be attributed to the relative youth of the poet (a point subtly emphasized by Blake's use of the adjective in his title for the design).

By his visual delineation in "The Youthful Poet's Dream," Blake argues that such conventional, formal patterning of imagination or poetic genius must necessarily be exclusive of much that is important. Hence, six figures at the bottom of the design are excluded from the sphere of the poet's dream.[22] They probably include the Three Fates, hovering over the "haunted stream" and associated elsewhere with the world of Generation-Experience.[23] This reading suggests that the river might be that of Life Finite, the Fates being the supernatural powers governing physical life. Finally, the embracing couple suggests a sensual, physical aspect of life that is significantly absent from the dream sphere.

All the figures at the bottom, then, suggest the atmosphere of Generation-Experience. They are involved in the material world from which the young poet effects a temporary escape by means of his dream. But his dream is ultimately exposed as imitative and derivative; consequently, it is exclusive and incomplete. "Without Contraries is no progression," Blake has told us. Past and potential future are, in one sense, contraries that should yield, at least figuratively, the present, in which progress should take place. Yet "The Youthful Poet's Dream" illustrates the preservation of—and reversion into—the past of poetic convention; progress in the present is thus necessarily sacrificed to the demands of poetic conservatism.

The counterpart design is "Mysterious Dream" (*Il Penseroso*, plate 5). Blake does not mention Milton by name in his notes to "The Youthful Poet's Dream," but here he does: "Milton sleeping on a bank. Sleep descending with a Strange Mysterious Dream upon his Wings of Scrolls & Nets & Webs unfolded by Spirits in the Air & in the Brook around Milton are Six Spirits or Fairies hovering on the air with Instruments of Music" (E, p. 666). Like "Melancholy," this scene is basically closed, with heavy trees forming a near background to the scene. Instead of sunset, Blake illustrates dawn, when "the Sun begins to fling / His flaring beams" (*Il Penseroso*, 131–32). Milton is posed with his head to the opposite side of the design from that of the youthful poet, and he is without halo. His clothing is still gray like Melancholy's. His hands are inactive, folded across his thighs. Once again the poet is in visual parallel with the principal figure of the initial design, Milton here reflecting Melancholy's passive restraint.

Like its counterpart, "Mysterious Dream" focuses less upon its poet than upon the representation of his inspiration. Milton's dream is not at all the neat, orderly rendering of convention shown in "The Youthful Poet's Dream." Rather, it is pure, unorganized "direct" inspiration, free of the Urizenic fetters of convention. The "Strange Mysterious Dream" is precisely that, coming as it does in sleep. Milton's mind, alert even in sleep, encounters the vision directly and makes no visible effort to sort out the inspiration by pigeonholing the ideas. Instead, the inspiring muse is granted full freedom, and the poet's mind absorbs the entire experience from largest forms to minute particulars. Blake speaks of this type of response as it relates to his own work: "I hope that none of my Designs will be destitute of Infinite Particulars which will present themselves to the Contemplator. And tho' I call them Mine, I know that they are not Mine, being of the same opinion with Milton when he says That the Muse visits his Slumbers & awakes & governs his Song when Morn purples the East" (K, p. 28). So, too, is Milton depicted here in his sleep of poetic inspiration. Although it is dawn, he has been awake all night, and he now begs to be shielded from "Day's garish eye" (in a very real sense, the "light of common day"). So he sleeps. Consequently, the dominant figure in the design is Sleep, or, more correctly, the inspiration conveyed in sleep, portrayed as "a vast spirit descending from heaven, with the 'strange, mysterious dream' upon his enormous pinions. The mystery of course must remain a mystery still; but Blake speaks of it as a process of unveiling."[24]

Here, finally, is essentially the same process of unveiling Blake deals with in *Milton*, the process by which the *implicit* is made *explicit* by a stripping away of the obscuring veils of restrictive orthodoxy.

This "process of unveiling" describes the mental operation both Blake and Milton, as revolutionary poet-prophets, were capable of performing automatically. Their heightened consciousnesses simply "saw" those things that were already implicit—though hidden from lesser minds— in the universe. By virtue of the process of unveiling that their minds completed automatically, they were able to confront pure visionary inspiration uncorrupted by the emasculating influence of convention. Such is the point of "Mysterious Dream," which pictures not the dream of the average versifier but that of one capable of "fourfold vision"— that of a Milton or a Blake.

Just what is the nature of Milton's dream? Sleep's halo and his "angelic" characteristics suggest the divinity of inspiration, or poetic genius. His influence appears to be as supernatural as his appearance. The images suggested in this design are far more intense, far less conventional, than those suggested in "The Youthful Poet's Dream." Here now are figures of epic potential, in keeping with the tenor of Milton's poem. In Allen's words, "The dream of 'L'Allegro' is slighter in substance, common in poetic experience, and it leads to the sham reality of the theatre and the 'wanton heed' and 'giddy cunning' of Lydian music. The dream of 'Il Penseroso' is of a far higher order, a 'strange mysterious dream' which is succeeded by a mysterious music."[25]

In "Mysterious Dream" all physical ages are captured in the timeless instant of the dream. Significantly, the dream is not set off, as the previous dream had been, by any physical devices such as sphere or line. This dream totally surrounds and engulfs Milton; it is eternity contained in an instant. Milton is thoroughly relaxed and makes no attempt to write down his dream (Blake has eliminated the book). Rather, he gives himself over entirely to the experience. In short, Blake depicts Milton here on the verge of attaining his full capabilities as true poet. He is withdrawn from the material world (having followed the guidance of Melancholy) and is involved, through his dream, with the sublime.

The second dream is not easily explained by man's ordinary experience. It represents a state in which the balance between the contraries of reason and desire (or fancy, in this case) shifts momentarily. Milton has Adam speak of this moment:

> But know that in the Soul
> Are many lesser Faculties that serve
> Reason as chief; among these Fancy next
> Her office holds; of all external things,
> Which the five watchful Senses represent,
> She forms Imaginations, Aery shapes,
> Which Reason joining or disjoining, frames
> All what we affirm or what deny, and call
> Our knowledge or opinion; then retires
> Into her private Cell when Nature rests.
> Oft in her absence mimic Fancy wakes
> To imitate her; but misjoining shapes,
> Wild work produces oft, and most in dreams,
> Ill matching words and deeds long past or late.
>
> (*PL* V, 100–13)

Disjoint and chaotic as such a mental state may seem to Adam, it has its value for the mind that can deal adequately with it, for as Denis Saurat says, "Blake wants Desire to be free from the control of Reason. Reason follows Desire, is enlarged and transformed in the process, and transfigured into what Blake calls Imagination, or the Poetic Genius."[26] Even if in his waking moments Milton may sometimes have compromised his genius by allowing reason to rule inordinately, the fact remains that his visions did occur. It is the occurrence of these visions and Milton's instinctive, automatic receptivity to them that Blake emphasizes in the designs for *Il Penseroso* as the vital element in Milton's achievement of the "prophetic strain." Even the details of Sleep's wings reinforce the suggestion of Milton's developing prophetic vision: there is no escaping the suggestion there of eyes, of that vision that characterizes the true poet-prophet in the tradition of the Book of Ezekiel.

Finally, Milton is surrounded here by the miniaturized forms of his "sixfold emanation"—the six figures with "Instruments of Music" that Blake depicts elsewhere at moments of imminent triumph (as in plate 18 of *Milton*, as Milton overcomes his Satanic-Urizenic "spectre"). They, too, share in the redemptive act of this scene. Their presence here is an indication, grounded perhaps more in *Milton* than in *Il Penseroso*, of one personal aspect of Milton's redemption.[27]

The final design for *Il Penseroso*, "Milton, Old Age," has no counterpart in *L'Allegro*. It is the apotheosis of both sets of designs, the epitome

of Blake's emphatic critical assessment. It depicts the resolution of
the conflict of contrary states delineated in the first eleven designs.
Here at last Milton achieves his transcendence, bursting forth now
in prophetic strain, eyes heavenward. His eyes are opened now through
visionary insight, and the transcendence of his physical blindness signals a corresponding triumph over his imaginative blindness. His book
reappears in this design, lying open beside the poet. However, Milton
makes no attempt to write in it. It is Blake's Urizenic figures, finally,
not his prophets, who are writers of books. The restrictive Puritan
Milton might write in this scene, but not the awakened prophet Milton
who follows the precedent of Blake's own prophetic bards by singing
his vision—the more immediate, spontaneous creative act—rather than
attempting to commit that vision directly to paper. The poet, like
his vision, is totally unfettered. The candle burns beside him, but
its light is outshone by the "light" of Milton in his visionary state,
just as in "The Youthful Poet's Dream" the light of even that poet's
limited poetic vision had dwarfed the light of the natural sun. Here
the figure of Milton provides most of the illumination for the design.
The figures at the bottom of the design may be seen as further manifesta-
tions of the material world of Generation-Experience that the visionary
Milton transcends.[28] His very posture indicates that he is oblivious
to their presence.

   That this final design *is* without counterpart makes it doubly clear
that Blake intended his reader to see it as the culmination not just
of the *Il Penseroso* series but of the entire series of twelve designs
as well. Rose says of its place in the full series:

It is possible to read the twelve designs for *L'Allegro* and *Il Penseroso* in
terms of the metaphor of twelve visionary months in the year-life of Milton.
The twelfth "December" design portraying the aged Milton under the sky
of the winter solstice should be contrasted with the sixth "June" design of
the summer solstice in which the youthful Milton sees the real sun—the 'more
bright Sun of Imagination.' . . . The design ["Milton, Old Age"] looks forward
to rebirth and to the eternal day-year of the perfect summer life. Blake, the
visionary, sees beyond the cycle of the vegetable world, for once Milton anni-
hilates his selfhood, as he does in *Milton*, he overcomes Death and the winter-
life of Generation.[29]

But Rose's conclusion is not really correct, as a final look at the designs
makes clear. In the first place, Milton is not depicted in "Milton, Old

Age," nor has Blake given any verbal indication to that effect. The *L'Allegro* poet is not, in Blake's view, a Milton but rather a conservative secular poet of limited abilities and restricted vision. Blake's whole point in the *Il Penseroso* designs involves the delineation of the true nature of Milton's poetic superiority. The poet of *Il Penseroso* is Milton—specifically identified now by Blake in his notes for five of the six designs—the revolutionary bard of divine inspiration and prophetic vision. The Milton of "Milton, Old Age" is not the sad figure Rose posits, an old poet whose mental province is only "memories and the past" and whose "mossy cell underground is a kind of 'sepulchre' of himself, a 'living grave.' "[30] To focus on such details, to draw such conclusions, is to pay attention only to exterior detail and to miss the "interiority" of the state Blake wishes us to recognize in Milton. "Milton, Old Age" presents not the end of a cycle, not a winter. Rose would have us draw optimism from the external fact that spring follows winter; if our astronomy is correct we assume Milton is on the verge of rebirth. Blake's point, however, is that in "Milton, Old Age" Milton *is* reborn, *is* regenerated; his visionary insight makes it spring in winter's despite. This is the miracle of Milton's poetic genius, a miracle of visionary insight exemplified in *Paradise Regained* and celebrated in Blake's designs for that epic as well as those for *Il Penseroso*. Its essence lies in the progression undergone by Milton, the conscious development, based on continual intellectual and aesthetic choices, of his poetic genius out of the fetters of tradition and into the fourfold vision of the bard.

The sense of movement, of progression, in Blake's designs for *L'Allegro* and *Il Penseroso* is unmistakable. From the gay, unconcerned worldliness of *L'Allegro*, maintained in comparative stasis throughout the designs, to the sublime prophetic state Milton attains at the conclusion of *Il Penseroso* is a process of gradual ascent. Blake's designs form a visual commentary both on Milton's poems and on the nature of poetry in general, based on suggestions he discerned in those poems. He captures not only the values and spirits of the contrary states and their interaction, but also their effects on the poets who are exposed to those states, who live and work within them. The relationship of *L'Allegro* with Experience and *Il Penseroso* with higher Innocence that Blake implies initially proves, finally, to be far more complex than a simple one-to-one correspondence. *L'Allegro* begins and ends

in the materialistic world of Generation-Experience, with its lesser
entertainments, while in *Il Penseroso* the poet matures both physically
and imaginatively until he progresses beyond his original reason-
restricted world into a higher state, becoming in the process not just
a *poet*, but a *Milton*. That this is the case establishes a final critical
point. The visionary state clearly may exist in the midst of the world
of Experience. The imaginative superiority of a poet-prophet such
as Milton or Blake allows him to transcend Experience by projecting
his own inner mental state, externalizing it to create an entire environment of higher, organized Innocence. Thus "As a man is, So he Sees"
proves ultimately to be a shrewd psychological observation on Blake's
part.

"Milton, Old Age," then, is the culmination of Blake's visual criticism in these designs of the poems and their author. This final design
testifies to the degree to which Blake considers Milton to have passed
the ultimate test of his genius. Significantly, that test is essentially
a temptation: the temptation to settle into the comfortable mediocrity
of the conventional. Milton is enabled to pass the test by his unique
ability to utilize every aspect of his poetic genius to unite the contrary
states without becoming enslaved by either. Yet it is inestimably to
Blake's own credit that he himself emerges from the designs not as
a slave to Milton but as his own man and a critic of the greatest
sensitivity and importance.

University of Wisconsin, Madison

NOTES

The illustrations in this essay are reproduced from Adrian Van Sinderen's *Blake:
The Mystic Genius*, published by Syracuse University Press in 1949. They are reprinted
by permission of the trustees under the will of Adrian Van Sinderen.

1. *The Art of Discrimination: Thomson's "The Seasons" and the Language of Criticism* (London, 1964). See p. 2.

2. Rose, "Blake's Illustrations for *Paradise Lost, L'Allegro* and *Il Penseroso*: A
Thematic Reading," *Hartford Studies in Literature*, II (1970), 40–67. Grant, "Blake's
Designs for *L'Allegro* and *Il Penseroso*," *Blake Newsletter*, IV (1971), 117–34, and
V (1971–72), 190–202. The designs are reproduced in black and white and accompany
each of these articles. They are also reproduced in color by Adrian Van Sinderen
in *Blake: The Mystic Genius* (Syracuse, 1949).

After this essay was completed, Anne Kostelanetz Mellor's study, *Blake's Human Form Divine* (Berkeley, 1974), appeared in print. Mellor errs in her discussion of these designs (see especially pp. 270-85) in her suggestion that Blake chooses the orientation of vision represented in *L'Allegro* over that of *Il Penseroso*. Incorrectly associating the general exuberance of the former with Blake's world of Innocence, Mellor regards the youthful poet of *L'Allegro*, plate 6, as the "joyful, truly visionary poet, the contemplative poet, a man like Blair or Young or Milton" (p. 277), a curious grouping. Yet she does correctly perceive that the aged Milton of *Il Penseroso*, plate 6, is represented as having achieved a rebirth of poetic imagination. Mellor sees, though, no sense of Milton's progress in the second through fifth designs, asserting that as late as the fifth design the poet is totally immersed in the "retiring, secretive life" of Satanic error, his dream controlled by "the oppressive, law-giving Jehovah-Urizen who floats above Milton's head, hands raised in a gesture of prohibition" (pp. 282-83). To ignore the progress Blake shows Milton making in these middle designs is to suggest that the awakened visionary state of the final design is abruptly realized. Quite the opposite is true, however; Milton's prophetic vision is an acquired one, the result of a clear process of imaginative progress.

3. Rose, "Blake's Illustrations," p. 65.

4. Irene Langridge, *William Blake: A Study of His Life and Art Work* (London, 1904), p. 136.

5. "William Blake: Illustrator-Interpreter of *Paradise Regained*," in *Calm of Mind: Tercentenary Essays on "Paradise Regained" and "Samson Agonistes" in Honor of John S. Diekhoff*, ed. Joseph A. Wittreich, Jr. (Cleveland, 1971), p. 96.

6. Ibid., p. 104.

7. See Marcia Pointon, *Milton and English Art* (Toronto, 1964), pp. 251-54.

8. Rose, "Blake's Illustrations," p. 61.

9. In this discussion I adopt the titles attributed to Blake's own hand by Chauncey Brewster Tinker in "Blake: Dreams of Milton," *Art News*, XLIX (1950), 22. See also David V. Erdman, ed., *The Poetry and Prose of William Blake*, rev. ed. (Garden City, N.Y., 1970), pp. 663-66.

10. *The Harmonious Vision: Studies in Milton's Poetry* (Baltimore, 1954), p. 17. See also Leslie Brisman, *Milton's Poetry of Choice and Its Romantic Heirs* (Ithaca, 1973), pp. 9-25.

11. Erdman, *The Poetry and Prose of William Blake*, p. 34, *Marriage of Heaven and Hell*, plate 3. Subsequent references to the Erdman text are incorporated into the text of this study and noted as "E."

12. Most of the illustrations previous to Blake's were ultimately less than perfectly faithful to the original conception of Milton's poems. We should note the predominance of topicality and "compliment" in the illustrations by Francis Hayman (1752), George Romney (1770), Alexander Runciman (1773), Robert Smirke (ca. 1780), Richard Westall (1794-1797), and Stephen Rigaud (1801).

13. See George Romney, for instance, whose painting is reproduced in Pointon, *Milton and English Art*, p. 122. The contrary natures of Mirth and Melancholy are emphasized by their close juxtaposition.

14. Typical of this basically anecdotal portraiture is Francis Hayman's illustration, "The Poet by the Pool," dating from 1750 to 1753 (reproduced in Pointon, *Milton and English Art*, p. 56). Pointon sees this design as a precursor of romantic depiction in its emphasis on the mood of poetic self-awareness associated with melancholy, death, and the emotional complex glorified by the "graveyard school" of poets. Hay-

man's design concentrates on visually evoking the mood he wishes to associate with Milton's pensive study, but this evocation is accomplished at the sacrifice of a good deal of fidelity to Milton's text. Such designs are clearly not to be seen as Milton criticism but as imaginative statements by the illustrator that merely assume the figure of Milton and some *sense* of the poetry itself as their point of departure.

15. These are reproduced in Grant, "Blake's Designs," pp. 192–93.

16. Ibid., pp. 201–02.

17. Rose holds that the opposite relationship is true, but his argument fails to consider the concept of progression with which Blake is working in the designs ("Blake's Illustrations," p. 62).

18. Blake uses these same visual symbols elsewhere, most notably in the Arlington Court Painting, to suggest aspects of the world of Generation.

19. Grant believes this figure is enjoying a "regenerative dram" ("Blake's Designs," p. 124) but says nothing of the stream which flows away from her. In fact, Grant sees this entire design as a scene of resurrection, "one of the happiest visions in Blake" (p. 122). To arrive at such a conclusion is to misread by "unbalancing" the very clear balance Blake establishes between the joyous dancers and the pensive observers. We are expected to perceive the dichotomy and, with Blake's help, to recognize its implications.

20. One should recall the folklorish grotesques of Fuseli's designs based upon hints in this same episode of the poem. See, for instance, "Friar Puck" or "The Lubbar Fiend" (both reproduced in Pointon, *Milton and English Art*, p. 130).

21. *The Letters of William Blake*, ed. Geoffrey Keynes (Cambridge, Mass., 1968), p. 30. Subsequent references are incorporated into the text and listed as "K."

22. Rose contends wrongly that Milton is appearing in his own dream ("Blake's Illustrations," p. 65). Pointon would also have us believe that the youthful poet is Milton (*Milton and English Art*, p. 166). Both these views are inconsistent, Rose's because the figure is *outside* the dream sphere and hence cannot be a part of that dream, and Pointon's because Blake does not depict Milton so prominently in *L'Allegro* but reserves him for *Il Penseroso*. If we are to see Milton *at all* in this design (and Blake does not mention him), we might most properly look to the figure at the extreme lower left, hurrying out of the scene, arms thrown up in agitation, on the far side of the stream. This might conceivably be the Miltonic (or the Blakean) poet who simply cannot bear to be in this cramped, conventional environment.

23. Rose has decided that these three are clearly identifiable as Milton's three wives ("Blake's Illustrations," p. 65). But he neglects the problem of the identity of the *fourth* female figure, in the embrace of the man on the near shore. Rose identifies the man as Milton appearing in his own dream; even if such an identification *were* possible, there would still remain the problem of one woman too many for Rose's biographical reading.

24. Grant sees in the serpentine line extending up Sleep's wings and through the central sphere a scene of redemptive activity, with all the figures along this line and Sleep's wings being transitional figures in the regenerative process ("Blake's Designs," pp. 132–34). We need to bear in mind, though, that the regeneration is occurring within Milton's poetic consciousness—his imagination. We should probably question Grant's contention that Milton is sleeping near the river of death (unless we wish to qualify it as the river of *imaginative* death, a tenuous identification), with the figures being drawn from its waters into redemption by the "suction" of Sleep's right wing (pp. 132–34). The point is that Milton is receiving pure, imaginatively regenerative

vision in sleep; his sleep prevents his reasoning intellect from conventionalizing that vision or imposing upon it any of the strictures of orthodoxy.

25. *Harmonious Vision*, p. 21.

26. Denis Saurat, *Blake and Milton* (London, 1935), p. 59.

27. Northrop Frye, "Notes for a Commentary on *Milton*," in *The Divine Vision: Studies in the Poetry and Art of William Blake*, ed. Vivian de Sola Pinto (London, 1957), p. 104; Grant, "Blake's Designs," p. 132.

28. Rose suggests unconvincingly that these figures depict Milton's three wives, from right to left, Mary Powell, Katharine Woodcock, and Elizabeth Minshull, respectively ("Blake's Illustrations," p. 65). Rose's reading, though perhaps tenable, is weakened by the fact that it tends once again to force Blake's design into too narrow, and too overtly biographical, a context.

29. Ibid.

30. Ibid.

THE THEME OF PURIFICATION
IN MILTON'S *SONNET XXIII*

Dixon Fiske

The controversy over the dating, subject, and meaning of Milton's *Sonnet XXIII* can be resolved in the context of Milton's ideas of purification. Purification is a major theme in the sonnet, and the key to Milton's use of it is to be found in the background of the sonnet's second simile. Milton's allusion there to the rites of purification under the old law is part of a thematic pattern in which the poet progressively refers to pagan, Jewish, and Christian images of purification. The progression of these images of the dead wife returning in a dream dramatizes a purification of the dreamer's love. But the love cannot be wholly purified in this world, as suggested by the veil on the wife's face and the dreamer's inevitable awakening into darkness. This interpretation supports the traditional belief that the sonnet is to be dated after the death of Milton's second wife, Katherine Woodcock.

IN THE controversy initiated by William R. Parker over the dating and meaning of Milton's *Sonnet XXIII*, most scholars seek the solution by seeking to discover and describe the precise personal circumstances behind the poem.[1] In it Milton tells of his dead wife, his "late espoused saint," as she returned to him in a dream. For these scholars, then, explaining (and so dating) the poem means explaining how the pathetic facts of Milton's loss gave rise to the psychological process of wish fulfillment and disappointment that the poem supposedly represents. But of course these facts are anything but explicit in the sonnet. The poem's three elaborate similes seem to have broken adrift from the reality that they are expected to mark.

Parker especially singles out the second simile, in which the saint returns: "as whom washt from spot of child-bed taint, / Purification in the old Law did save."[2] The reference to the "child-bed taint" seems inevitably to suggest that the saint died directly or indirectly as a result of childbirth, but the significance of the simile's remaining details has proven much more obscure. The attempt has been for the most part to explain these as Milton's references to the circumstances surrounding the death of one of two possible wives. Parker and his supporters argue that the poem is about the first. Fitzroy Pyle and his supporters argue that it is about the second. Milton's second wife, Katherine Woodcock, had traditionally been thought the subject, but Parker points out that she died on February 3, 1658, "of a consumption," according to Milton's granddaughter, Elizabeth Foster.[3] Parker argues that Milton must be referring to his first wife, Mary Powell, who died about three days after bearing a daughter on May 2, 1652. But Katherine, too, had given birth to a daughter on October 19, 1657, some three and a half months before her death. So Pyle argues that Katherine's late death does not rule her out, because the strain of childbirth must have seemed the cause and indeed probably in fact hastened the action of the "consumption" of which she died. Conclusions about this matter affect, and are affected by, the question of whether Milton's later references to the saint's veiled face and to his "fancied sight" are meant to suggest his blindness. For the poet wed Mary before he was blind, and he would have remembered her features, but he married Katherine afterwards, and he could not have.

Leo Spitzer makes a vigorous attempt at a different sort of explanation.[4] He urges that the preoccupation with Milton's marriages reflects a bias toward romantic, expressive theories of art and ignores the more classical, impersonal aims that Milton would have had as a Renaissance poet. For Spitzer "the main theme and the only problem of the sonnet is not the problem of Milton's blindness (nor that of the death of his wife), but the generally human problem of the Ideal in our world" (p. 22). He sees a dramatic crescendo of the sonnet's three similes (the pagan, lines 1–4, the Jewish, lines 5–6, and the Christian, lines 7–8). As the dreamer views his saint in the progressively truer context of each religion, he perceives the ideal which she represents in a clearer and clearer light—only to be thrust back into the darkness of earthly life in the last two lines. Milton transforms his dead wife into the *donna angelicata* of Dante and Petrarch, veiled and unattainable finally, except in heaven.

Yet Spitzer has not been very persuasive, mostly, it seems, because at times he too vigorously rejects the pathetic and the personal elements that move so many readers today. Thomas Wheeler, for example, finds Spitzer unconvincing "because the poem obviously does refer to historical fact,"[5] by which he means the reference to the "child-bed taint." He thinks that the poem is primarily about "the almost insufferable loss of a beloved woman" (p. 513), though he does agree with Spitzer that Milton idealizes her at least to the extent of making her an ideal wife. Merritt Hughes, in his widely used edition, also protests that Spitzer "would dispose of the poignant reference to the poet's blindness as an irrelevant indulgence of self-pity by Milton,"[6] though Spitzer actually accepts the "motif of the poet's blindness as a second meaning added onto the first" (p. 22). And Spitzer does think that the poem "should be apperceived *half-concretely*" (p. 23).

Discussion nearly always returns to the specific problem that Parker originally discovered. Spitzer does not resolve it, nor has anyone else since, as Parker insists in his recent biography of Milton.[7] Within the tripartite development that Spitzer describes in the sonnet's similes, we may understand why Milton would compare his idealized saint to a woman saved under the old law. But if Milton is not being *wholly* and intrusively concrete, why should he refer to such a particular aspect of the law—the ceremonial purification from "child-bed taint" prescribed in Leviticus, chapter xii? And if he is being concrete, to which wife is he referring? The questions remain unanswered in Wheeler's article and in another by Martin Mueller that depends rather heavily upon Spitzer's interpretation.[8] One of the latest commentators on the sonnet, J. H. Huntley, even holds the question unanswerable. He argues that the full meaning of the second simile must be irrecoverably private and the poem in consequence "a partial failure."[9]

Now I believe that I can present a fully satisfactory explanation for Milton's second simile by relating it to one of the sonnet's dominant and neglected themes, the theme of purification. To do so it is necessary to consider the general Renaissance "ideal" somewhat less than Spitzer, and to consider somewhat more how the particular ideal of purification was received and adapted by the relentlessly combative intellect of John Milton. We need not conclude, however, that the sonnet is *mainly* about purification and not mainly about personal loss. We must only conclude, I think, that Milton is not as specific about the facts of his loss as Parker and others have thought. But it surely does not represent a bias toward romantic theory to suppose that Milton's loss is reflected as truly in the sonnet as are the ideas through which he seeks to comprehend the loss.

The theme of purification is implicit in the first simile on Alcestis, as I will show, but it emerges explicitly in the second and after the third, where the saint appears to the dreamer "vested all in white, pure as her mind." There she unavoidably recalls the purified state of the saints in Revelation vii, 14, who "have washed their robes, and made them white in the blood of the Lamb." The second simile, I think, is the key to the poem thematically, rather than biographically, as Parker maintains. Yet a thematic interpretation both resolves the difficulties that Parker raises and allows us to accept the traditional belief that Katherine is Milton's subject. The evidence assuredly does not suggest that the simile is irrecoverably private and so reason for the poem's "partial failure," for Milton is alluding to matters that he and his contemporaries had under vigorous discussion. The simile fits brilliantly into the pattern of ideas and images that Milton carefully develops throughout the sonnet.

Let us more closely examine the exact difficulties that Parker finds in the simile of the saint who returns "as whom . . . / Purification in the old Law did save." Parker assumes that Milton's "as" must mean "as though," obviously because a simile must involve some hypothetical likeness, but actual difference. His conclusion is that the comparison must turn upon the actual number of days that a specific wife did or did not survive after childbirth.[10] Leviticus, chapter xii, prescribes sixty-six days for purification. Katherine survived much longer than that, so Milton is telling us that Mary returned "as though" she had lived out her days of purification and been saved from the perils of childbirth. Parker adds that when Milton made the allusion to Leviticus, he was probably thinking of the Christian equivalent of the Jewish ceremony, the "churching of women," and was "remembering that his wife had not lived long enough even for this ceremony of thanksgiving."[11]

The number of days of purification is also important in Pyle's interpretation. Noting that Katherine died a day after the Virgin's Feast of Purification (Candlemas), he argues that Milton is comparing Katherine to her. Thus both Katherine and the Virgin survived the days of their purification, but Katherine's survival was only specious. Katherine returns like the Virgin, "as though" she had been actually saved by purification in the old law, instead of dying only a few weeks after the days of purification had passed.[12]

But if Milton intended his simile to turn upon such matters as these, it is very odd that in the poem he is not more specific about the details of his wife's death and identity. We should certainly expect him to point more directly than he does to the days of purification prescribed in Leviticus, or to the Virgin's story. Instead, his words draw attention to no more than the idea of a mother's saving purification *under the old law*. Is it not more reasonable to suppose that the simile turns upon this idea? The hypothetical likeness and actual difference are much more probably between a mother purified and saved under the old law and one who could not be. Milton's wife returned "as though" she had lived, been purified, and been saved under the old law—when of course she had not, first and foremost because she lived under the new law of Christ.

Moreover, Parker, Pyle, and their followers seem to base their arguments upon a false understanding of how Milton means that purification could "save" under the old law. They clearly believe that it might have saved Milton's saint from physical death, or that somehow in the dream he might have entertained that fancy. But from the first simile, the poet describes his saint returning as though she were saved, not from the threat, but from the actuality of physical death. She is like Alcestis, whom Hercules rescued from death *after* she had died in the place of her husband. In the third simile she is like a saved soul in heaven, an association that is continued in the following description of her costume, as I have noted. The context overwhelmingly suggests that Milton intends that the reader of the second simile will remember the role that the ancient Jewish ceremonies played in salvation under the old law.

Milton shared with his contemporaries a lively interest in the question of how those ceremonies and their Christian counterparts functioned under both dispensations. He naturally accepted the standard Christian belief that the new law abrogated the old. He fervently embraced the Puritan corollary that worship under the new law was contaminated by the remnants of the old ceremonies in the liturgy of the Church of England. In many of his controversial tracts he argues that the surviving ceremonies are in fact an obstacle instead of an aid to spiritual purification.

In *The Reason of Church-Government,* for example, he argues that they encourage men to put their faith in the letter and not the spirit, in outward instead of inward things, confounding "the purity of doctrin which is the wisdom of God." In *Of Reformation* he tells us that they cause men to backslide "into the Jewish beggery, of old cast rudiments, and stumble forward another way into the new-vomited Paganisme of sensuall Idolatry, attributing purity, or impurity, to things indifferent, that they might bring the inward acts of the *Spirit* to the outward, and customary ey-Services of the body, as if they could make God earthly, and fleshly, because they could not make themselves *heavenly,* and *Spirituall.*"

In *An Apology* he particularly attacks the churching of women. He ridicules the thanksgiving verse (Psalm cxxi, 6) prescribed for it in the Book of Common Prayer, deploring the "impertinences" of "those thanks in the womans Churching for her delivery from Sunburning and Moonblasting, as if she had bin travailing not in her bed, but in the deserts of *Arabia.*" Only a little later he condemns "those purifyings and offrings at the Altar" as a "pollution and disturbance to the Gospell it selfe."[13]

It is hard to believe that Milton would have found the specified days of purification so dramatically significant as Parker and Pyle suppose. What was significant was that the old law and any ceremony connected with it were wholly antiquated, irrelevant to Christian worship and to Christian salvation.

Milton did not believe that spiritual purification and salvation were achieved through the mere, rigid observance of ceremony, even before the old law was abrogated. The real function of the old law and its ceremonies was ironically symbolic. Though God required the Hebrews to cleanse their bodies, Milton says in *De Doctrina,* he was actually reminding them of the impossibility of likewise purifying their souls: "The Mosaic law was a written code consisting of many precepts, intended for the Israelites alone, with a promise of life to such as should keep them, and a curse on such as should be disobedient; to the end that they, being led thereby to an acknowledgement of the depravity of mankind, and consequently of their own, might have recourse to the righteousness of the promised Savior."[14] Though, like Lady Macbeth, they might wash their hands, only God through his Son could remove the stain of their sin.

Spiritual purification, Milton believed, occurs as Christ develops faith and zeal for good works to the point where man is cleansed and restored to innocence. He "purifies only such as are zealous of good works, that is believers; for no works are good, unless done in faith. . . . none are purified except their wills be consenting, and they have faith."[15] The only difference under the old law was that the zeal for good works had to include the zeal for performing the works of the ceremonial law: "Under the law, those who trusted in God were justified by faith indeed, but not without the works of the law."[16]

What Milton found significant in the ceremonies of the old law was not their formal elements, such as the number of days of purification, but their implications in a Christian context. And, to use Michael's words in *Paradise Lost*, those "shadowy expiations" implied man's "natural pravity," as well as his need for true purification through Christ.[17] From this point of view, possibly no ceremony suggests the originality of sin so well as that of the purification of women. Milton makes no direct comment on the implications of this particular ceremony in his writings, but since Calvin agrees exactly with Milton's general understanding of the old law,[18] we can accept Calvin's succinct interpretation of the ceremony. By it, Calvin says, God does not mean that the Hebrew mother was physically polluted. Her pollution, like all mankind's, was rather spiritual and extended to her child. The ceremony, Calvin says, openly refutes the error of the Pelagians, who denied the principle of original sin that the ceremony teaches: "Voluit igitur hoc ritu Deus veterem populum docere, cunctos homines maledictos nasci, et corruptionem haereditariam secum afferre, quae matres ipsas polluat" ("So with this ceremony God wished to teach the ancient people that all men are born cursed and carry with them the hereditary corruption that pollutes the mothers themselves").[19]

In comparing his saintly wife to a mother purified under the old law, then, Milton is implying much more than has been supposed. He undoubtedly wishes to suggest the immediate and literal cause of his wife's death, but he wishes at least as much to link it with its ultimate, metaphysical cause, to link it with one of the special consequences of that act for women: the difficulty and danger of

childbirth (see Genesis iii, 17). He accomplishes the linkage by referring
to the ceremony that has special relevance to his wife as mother,
but that, like all of the law before the coming of Christ, was meant
for the faithful to observe as a lesson on man's fallen state. His point
is that his wife observed the lesson of the old law, if not its rites.
Like a mother who observed the lesson (as well as the rites) of the
old law, she must be saved. With only apparent redundancy, he emphasizes the purity that is the condition of her salvation. She is not just
"washt from . . . child-bed taint." She is "washt from spot of child-
bed taint." That is, like a faithful mother under the old law, she has
been spiritually purified of the general "taint" of original sin whose
particular "spot" she had inherited and transmitted in the "child-bed."

The great opening simile of the sonnet presents a pagan image
of the same theme, though the implications are appropriately more
hidden and recondite:

> Methought I saw my late espoused Saint
> Brought to me like *Alcestis* from the grave,
> When *Jove's* great Son to her glad Husband gave,
> Rescu'd from death by force though pale and faint.

Readers are always referred to Euripides' *Alcestis*, because the details
of the simile vividly recall it, but we should consider how Milton
would have been led to interpret the myth behind the play. Christian
mythographers had consistently looked on the Alcestis myth as an
allegory of the salvation of the soul by means of virtue and grace.
In addition, of course, many of them understood her rescuer, Hercules,
to be a pagan type of Christ,[20] an association that Milton also makes
in the climactic simile of *Paradise Regained* (IV, 563–68). But in the
special perspective of Renaissance neo-Platonism, the rescue of Alcestis
occurs for the same reason nearly that the mother was purified under
the old law—because she achieved the equivalent of zeal, a divine,
purifying love of God (not her husband!) without which no one can
survive death.

The neo-Platonists tended to view most pagan myths in which
a god might love, abduct, or grant immortality to a mortal as mysterious
allegories of the human ability to defy death and achieve union with
the immortal Idea through love for it.[21] In a discussion of these myths
Pico cites the example of Alcestis. She loved perfectly, he says. Her
love was so divorced from worldly things, she so loved the Idea and

so wanted to unite herself with it, that she was willing to die in order to penetrate the fleshly barrier between her spirit and the Idea. And in being willing to die for love, Pico says, Alcestis won the grace of the gods and was spiritually regenerated: "Però Alceste perfetta-mente amò, che all' amato andare volse per morte, e morendo per amore fu per la grazia delli Dei a vita restituita, cioè regenerata in vita, non per corporale ma per spirituale regenerazione" ("But Al-cestis loved perfectly; she turned to go to the beloved through death, and in dying through love she was restored to life by the grace of the gods—that is, regenerated into life, not through corporal but through spiritual regeneration"). Alcestis' love is comparable to the love that resulted in the translation of Abraham, Isaac, Moses, Aaron, and Mary.[22] Valeriano, discussing the same kind of love, brings out its Christian manifestation even more clearly by citing the example of Paul's yearn-ing "to be dissolved and be with Christ."[23]

We are now in a position to support and refine Spitzer's description of the sonnet's "tripartite *crescendo*." The progression of similes repre-sents not just a progression toward the general Christian ideal, as Spitzer suggests, but a progression toward the more specifically Miltonic and Puritan ideal of purifying Christian zeal. The progression drama-tizes a purification of the speaker's own love. As the saint approaches, changing from a "pale and faint" image to an intensely bright presence about to embrace him, his perception of what she must be is cleansed of the impurities of the pagan and Jewish types, and he sees her, almost, in the full light of Christian truth. The pattern is not unusual in Milton's poetry, corresponding to what D. C. Allen calls the "descent to light," a descent that is simultaneously an ascent from the letter and the flesh to the spirit.[24] We must know and accept the Christian truth already, naturally, or the implications of the pagan and Jewish types will escape us, a necessity to which Milton alerts us in his first line by referring to his "saint." We are enjoined to view his coming allusions to Alcestis and purification in the old law in the Christian context of the last simile.

The impurities of the types are their literal and carnal elements. The first simile exhibits the most. Like Alcestis' husband, Admetus, the dreamer rejoices at the apparent restoration of an earthly marriage, believing that he is about to regain physical possession of his wife after she has been physically rescued. The husband is possessive, "glad"

to have had her rescued "by force," though such force is at odds
with the love allegorically implied. Indeed, Milton thought that force
in a religion necessarily signals its low place on the scale of spiritual
development.[25] We are meant to recognize that Alcestis is a figure of
purifying love, but to the speaker the figure must be alleogrically as
well as literally "pale and faint," just as in *Paradise Lost* the pagan
muse Urania is a figure of divine inspiration, but in herself "an empty
dream" (VII, 39).

The second simile emphasizes purification, but purification under
the old law. The law is superior to force, but we are to recall its
demand for rigid obedience to rigid and outwardly meaningless ceremony. In *Considerations Touching the Likeliest Means*, Milton points
out that the old law too was partly a matter of force, since it required
all those living under it to obey it as a civil matter "according to
the letter, willingly or unwillingly."[26] Though the law is superior to
myth, neither the sin, nor the faith and zeal that removed it under
the old law are explicit.

In the last simile and what follows, Milton explicitly associates
his wife's salvation with the new law of love and with the Christian
freedom of the purified:

> such, as yet once more I trust to have
> Full sight of her in Heaven without restraint,
> Came vested all in white, pure as her mind:
> Her face was veil'd, yet to my fancied sight
> Love, sweetness, goodness, in her person shin'd
> So clear, as in no face with more delight.

For the first time he seems to understand that the satisfaction of his
love must really depend upon a change in his own state rather than
in hers. He must achieve her condition rather than having her impossibly
returned to him in his. Thus he speaks not of powers rescuing her,
as in the previous two similes, but of his "trust" (an aspect of love)
in obtaining heaven and seeing her as only the purified can—freely,
"without restraint." And now he recognizes and appreciates the spiritual
state represented by the saint's white garments, "pure as her mind."
Without a hint of the force and possessiveness apparent in the first
simile, or of the legalism in the second, the dreaming poet is delighted
at merely seeing his saint's moral qualities shining forth, "Love, sweet-
ness, goodness." She bends to embrace him of her own free will.

But Milton's spiritual perception in the dream has a limitation set to it, as his third simile already suggests. Though he says there that he trusts to see his saint "once more" as he sees her now in the dream, what follows makes clear that only in heaven will he have "full sight" of her "without restraint." Even in the dream he cannot enjoy the full freedom of Christian liberty. He has certainly transcended his earlier perceptions and succeeded in viewing his wife in terms of the new law of love that calls for purification of the inward man. But in this life the inward man cannot escape the limitations of the outward man and be entirely purified. In the dream and in life, Milton's sight must remain obstructed. As a veil of allegory conceals the spiritual implications of the first two similes except to a Christian vision, so a veil conceals the full vision of purity except to the saints in heaven. His wife's saintly face is thus "veil'd" in the dream.

Since Parker's difficulties have, I think, been resolved, all the probabilities suggest that Katherine Woodcock is the original of Milton's saint.[27] So the veil is undoubtedly a pathetic symbol of the blindness that prevented Milton from dreaming of the face of the wife whom he never saw. Nor is it fortuitous certainly that the veil figures implicitly in all three of the similes. Parker and Edward Le Comte very justly explain the veil's presence by pointing out that Alcestis returns veiled in Euripides' play, that the mother traditionally wore a veil at her churching, and that the saints are often represented wearing veils.[28] But it is not at all inconsistent to suppose that the veil also has the major thematic significance that I have outlined. Just as Milton must have expected us to recognize the veil as a symbol of his physical blindness, so also he must have expected us to recognize it as a symbol of a corresponding and inevitable spiritual blindness. Just as he must have expected us to admire the appropriateness of the veil to all three similes, so also he must have expected us to admire how well the veil comments thematically upon the dreamer's yearning to enjoy, not the sight of the saint's person, but finally a heavenly vision of her purity. We know that that kind of vision most concerned Milton, as his Christianity enjoined. He proclaimed nothing more consistently about his blindness than that he held it morally trivial by comparison with the gain or loss of spiritual sight.

Milton is certainly levying on the long history of the veil as a symbol of the fleshly, earthly restraint upon spiritual sight. Spitzer argues this point well, but we may expand upon it, perhaps more persuasively. Milton had ample literary precedent for the veil symbolism in Dante, Petrarch, and Spenser,[29] but the symbolism almost certainly has its origin in an amalgam of two familiar passages in Paul. In the first (2 Corinthians iii, 13–18), Paul explains that Moses wore a veil after returning with the law as a symbol of the onlookers' spiritual blindness: "Moses . . . put a vail over his face, that the children of Israel could not steadfastly look to the end of that which is abolished: . . . their minds were blinded." Here the veil represents the particular ignorance of the Jews under the old law: the "vail upon their heart" will be taken away when they turn to the new law, where "there is liberty." But in describing this Christian liberty, Paul also suggests the limitations of even the Christian's vision in this world. Christians, he says, behold "as in a glass the glory of the Lord." In the second passage (1 Corinthians xiii, 12), dealing with the importance of charitable love, Paul expands the same figure: in this world, he says, "we see through a glass darkly, but then face to face: now I know in part; but then shall I know even as also I am known."[30]

Such a veil upon Milton's spiritual sight should lead us to anticipate the poet's inevitable disillusionment at the end of the sonnet: "But O, as to embrace me she inclin'd, / I wak'd, she fled, and day brought back my night." His Christian "trust" and his "fancied sight" have carried him as far as they can in this world. The final revelation, the lifting of the veil and the "face to face" confrontation that the "embrace" would entail, cannot take place yet. Up until now the sonnet has not really been about the loss of a beloved wife. It has been about the recovery of a progressively more glorious and ideal image of her. But, at the moment of greatest understanding and delight, when the dreamer seems to perceive that the true source of his delight in his wife must lie in her heavenly virtues, when he seems to realize that these virtues must be the source of her spiritual life, and when he feels that he is about to be reunited with her in her embrace, he suffers an abrupt awakening to his true condition. It is spiritual night in comparison with the bright, purified world of the dream.

The moment of the dreamer's unconsummated embrace drama-tizes what the veil symbolizes—the insufficiency of the dreamer himself. Tainted still by the inherited sin of which his wife is imagined to have been purified, he could neither see nor embrace his vision of her purity. She "fled" back to heaven, where she must be an object of quest. She was once Katherine almost certainly. He yearns for her. We cannot suppose that her individuality has disappeared into a luminous ideal. But personal details have fallen away. Perhaps what remains most personal is also most impersonal. The name Katherine, as Le Comte tells us (p. 246), derives from the Greek for "purity," the ideal that the saint strove for and achieved. Each of the three similes reveals more clearly that she cannot be just what she once was, certainly not his wife, for marriage does not last beyond death. Their relationship has changed. She is superior to him now. Though in dreaming he may temporarily create the illusion of the old relationship, even a "fancied" spiritual sight of her now, the truth is that he lives in darkness without her, still facing the task of purification that she has already accomplished.[31]

NOTES

1. See William R. Parker, "Milton's Last Sonnet," *RES*, XXI (1945), 235–38; Fitzroy Pyle, "Milton's Sonnet on his 'Late Espoused Saint,'" *RES*, XXV (1949), 57–60; Rolland Mushat Frye, "Milton's Sonnet 23 on his Late Espoused Saint," *N&Q*, XCIV (1949), 321; William R. Parker with a reply by Fitzroy Pyle, "Milton's Last Sonnet Again," *RES*, n.s. II (1951), 147–54; Edward S. Le Comte, "The Veiled Face of Milton's Wife," *N&Q*, XCIX (1954), 245–56; John T. Shawcross, "Milton's Sonnet 23," *N&Q*, n.s. III (1956), 202–04; E. A. J. Honigmann, *Milton's Sonnets* (New York, 1966), pp. 190–94; David R. Fabian, "Milton's 'Sonnet 23' and Leviticus XVIII.10," *Xavier University Studies*, V (1966), 83–88.

2. Merritt Hughes, ed., *John Milton: Complete Poems and Major Prose* (New York, 1957), pp. 170–71. All further quotations from the sonnet are from this edition.

3. "Milton's Last Sonnet," p. 237.

4. "Understanding Milton," *Hopkins Review*, IV (1951), 16–27.

5. "Milton's Twenty-Third Sonnet," *SP*, LVIII (1961), 510–15. The quotation is from p. 511.

6. *John Milton*, p. 170.

7. *Milton: A Biography* (Oxford, 1968), vol. II, p. 1045.

8. "The Theme and Imagery of Milton's Last Sonnet," *Archiv für das Studium der Neueren Sprachen und Literaturen*, CCI (1964), 267–71.

9. "Milton's 23rd Sonnet," *ELH*, XXXIV (1967), 468–79. The verdict (on p. 476) proved challenging and fruitful. Since this article was submitted, at least two other scholars have published articles on the sonnet: Marilyn L. Williamson, "A Reading of Milton's Twenty-Third Sonnet," in *Milton Studies*, IV, ed. James D. Simmonds (Pittsburgh, 1972), pp. 141–49, and John C. Ulreich, "Typological Symbolism in Milton's Sonnet XXIII," *Milton Quarterly*, VIII (1974), 7–10. The authors' findings correspond

to mine in several interesting respects, but we differ in our emphases, perspectives, and use of evidence.

10. "Milton's Last Sonnet Again," p. 150.

11. Ibid.

12. Pyle's reply to Parker, ibid., p. 153. See also Luke ii, 22.

13. *The Complete Prose Works of John Milton*, ed. Don M. Wolfe et al., vol. I (New Haven, 1953), pp. 830, 520, 939, 941. Le Comte ("The Veiled Face," p. 246) refers to the passage on p. 941, but makes nothing of it. The extreme dislike of ceremonies is, of course, a defining characteristic of Puritanism.

14. *The Works of John Milton*, ed. F. A. Patterson et al. (New York, 1931–38), vol. XVI, p. 103, hereafter cited as CM.

15. CM, XV, p. 329.

16. CM, XVI, p. 151.

17. XII, 287–306. See also Romans iii, 20.

18. See the *Institutes*, Book II, chap. vii.

19. *Mosis Reliqui Libri Quatuor in Formam Harmoniae Digesti*, in *Opera*, ed. Guilielmus Baum et al., vol. XXIV (Brunswick, 1882), col. 312.

20. See the influential medieval commentator Pierre Bersuire, *Ovidus Metta-phoroseos Moralizatus*, ed. Fausto Ghisalberti, in *Studj Romanzi*, vol. XXIII (Rome, 1933), p. 101. Chaucer seems to be using Bersuire's interpretation in the prologue to *The Legend of Good Women*. Boccaccio gives an interpretation emphasizing virtue more than grace in his *Genealogie Deorum Gentilium Librii*, ed. Vincenzo Romano (Bari, 1951), vol. II, p. 642. Alexander Ross (*Mystagogus Poeticas, or The Muses Interpreter* [London, 1648], pp. 7–8) gives Bersuire's interpretation.

21. See Edgar Wind, "Amor as the God of Death," in his *Pagan Mysteries in the Renaissance* (n.p., 1967), pp. 152–70. Wind cites interpretations by Leone Ebreo, Celio Calcagnini, Francesco Giorgio, Castiglione, Giordano Bruno, and Pico. Only Pico refers specifically to the Alcestis myth.

22. Giovanni Pico della Mirandola, *Commento . . . sopra una Canzone*, in *De hominis dignitate*, ed. Eugenio Garin (Florence, 1942), pp. 555, 558.

23. Cited in Wind, "Amor as the God of Death," p. 154.

24. "Milton and the Descent to Light," *JEGP*, LX (1961), 614–30.

25. See, for example, Milton's frequent condemnation of force in religion in two tracts written about the time that the sonnet was written: *A Treatise of Civil Power* (1659) and *The Ready and Easy Way* (1660).

26. CM, VI, p. 25.

27. The second simile can refer to Katherine, as Pyle explains. The evidence of the Trinity Manuscript supports a dating after Katherine's death and before Milton's remarriage on February 24, 1663. See Maurice Kelley, "Milton's Later Sonnets and the Cambridge Manuscript," *MP*, LIV (1956), 20–25, and my unpublished dissertation, "Milton's Sonnets" (Princeton, 1969, pp. 140–54). Add to this evidence the gross improbability that Milton would have idealized Mary as his saint. See the account of Milton's continuing difficulties with Mary, her relatives, and her children, in James H. Hanford, *John Milton, Englishman* (New York, 1949), pp. 131–32, 155–56, 323–38. On the other hand, consider the probability that Katherine's name, together with her death so shortly after the Feast of the Purification, would have powerfully suggested the same earnest play upon name and idea that Dante, Petrarch, and their followers make upon the names of their mistresses, as Le Comte suggests ("The Veiled Face," p. 246).

28. Mueller suggests the highly unlikely possibility that Milton means to contrast his veiled saint with an unveiled Alcestis and an unveiled mother under the old law ("Theme and Imagery of Milton's Last Sonnet," p. 268).

29. See the "Purgatorio," xxx, 3, 64 *et seq.*, and the "Paradiso," xxx, 46–51. In Petrarch's *Canzoniere*, ed. Gianfranco Contini and Daniele Ponchiroli (Torino, 1968), see especially CCLXXVII, and also CCCII, CCCXIII, CCCXIX, CCCXXIX, CCCLII, CCCLXII. See also the commentary on these sonnets by Bernardino Daniello (whose edition of Dante Milton quotes in his *Commonplace Book*), *Sonnetti e Triomphi di M. Francesco Petrarca* (Venice, 1549). In *The Faerie Queene*, see I, i, 5; I, iii, 4; VII, vii, 5–6. This tradition seems more important as an influence than the analogue pointed out by Thomas B. Stroup, "Aeneas's Vision of Creusa and Milton's Twenty-Third Sonnet," *PQ*, XXXIX (1960), 125–26.

30. Quotations are from the King James Version. Spitzer points to the second of these two passages ("Understanding Milton," p. 21).

31. Compare this interpretation with Adam's lament after his fall, *PL* IX, 1080–84.

THE DISSOLUTION OF SATAN IN *PARADISE LOST:* A STUDY OF MILTON'S HERETICAL ESCHATOLOGY

Leonora Leet Brodwin

The heretical eschatology of *Paradise Lost* has never before been recognized because it deviates from the orthodox position on eternal torment expressed in *De Doctrina Christiana.* Though masked by a consistent strategy of ambiguity and omission, the apocalyptic passages in the epic suggest the heretical belief in the final dissolution of Satan, of the men and angels he perverted, and of hell itself, as contrasted with the exclusive resurrection of the just to eternal life. Other passages which seem to support a belief in eternal torment are seen to embody two special strategies: the identification of this belief as a Satanic doctrine, or the suggestion of its questionable effectiveness as a deterrent to sin. A study of the Enoch reference (XI, 701-10) reveals scriptural and pseudepigraphal sources of this heresy, but a closer source is the eschatology of the Socinian sect and its Italian Anabaptist antecedents. Milton's knowledge of Socinian works and agreement with other Socinian heresies has long been established. His further agreement with Socinian eschatology in *Paradise Lost*, though covertly expressed·because of the peculiar social dangers thought to attend dissemination of this heresy, had many parallels in Interregnum England, including not only Hobbes, as previously recognized, but also Overton; and it illuminates the ethical contrast between Adam's reverent choice of life and Satan's "heroic" choice of death, an end which informs Milton's critique of conventional heroism.

THOUGH MILTON, in his theological treatise *De Doctrina Christiana,* supports the orthodox belief that "Satan . . . will be . . . condemned to everlasting punishment" and that the "eternal death, or

the punishment of the damned" consists in "eternal torment" in "Hell.
. . . as the place of the damned is the same as that prepared for
the devil and his angels,"[1] throughout *Paradise Lost* he appears to
profess a far more heretical view: the final dissolution of Satan, of
the men and angels he perverted, and of hell itself, as contrasted
with the exclusive resurrection of the just to eternal life.

That there should be such a discrepancy in theological views runs
counter to the general beliefs that there is no doctrinal difference
between the treatise and the epic and that Milton is more open in
stating his heretical convictions in his treatise. But if Milton avoids
this particular heresy in his treatise, he introduces it into his epic through
the same strategy of ambiguity and omission which marks his presentation of those heresies he does profess openly in the treatise, carefully
constructing each eschatological statement to appear orthodox on the
surface while admitting hidden heretical meaning.[2] The special caution he shows regarding this heresy in his formal theological treatise
was not unique in his age and becomes understandable in the context
of the time. As we shall later see, the practice of ambiguous profession
and explicit denial was standard among the heretics of Milton's day
who denied the doctrine of eternal torment. For of all heresies, this
alone was considered to be too socially dangerous to be openly
preached or even avowed, the deterrent of eternal torment being
thought necessary for maintaining social stability and mass morality
even by those who disbelieved in such post-mortem punishments.[3]

Before considering the few open confessions of this heresy during
the sixteenth and seventeenth centuries which exactly parallel Milton's
formulation and may have been its source, it will be necessary to
unravel Milton's heretical eschatology from the confusions of double
meaning which obscure it. Since it is the hope of this study not simply
to raise a speculative issue but to resolve it, an exhaustive analysis
of the semantic and syntactic equivocations in the eschatological passages and of additional strategies which qualify other seemingly unequivocal assertions of eternal torment is required to show how every
eschatological reference is susceptible to ambiguous readings and how
the consistent pattern of undermeanings formed by these readings
is not absolutely contested by any other textual evidence. Such precision and comprehensiveness are dictated as much by Milton's strategy
of expressing these meanings through the ambiguities of an apparently

orthodox presentation as by the importance of the findings which may be thus uncovered. For I hope in the process not only to demonstrate the existence of a new Miltonic heresy, hitherto unsuspected by students of Milton's theology because of its deviation from the position developed in *De Doctrina*, but also to show that both the characterization of Satan and the structure of values which informs *Paradise Lost* depend for their ultimate meaning upon Milton's heretical eschatology.

Milton reserves his clearest statement of the fate of Satan for his final depiction of the Last Judgment, a depiction which also illustrates the destinies of good and evil men:

> so shall the World go on,
> To good malignant, to bad men benign,
> Under her own weight groaning, till the day
> Appear of respiration to the just,
> And vengeance to the wicked, at return
> Of him so lately promis'd to thy aid
>
> . . . .
>
> Last in the Clouds from Heav'n to be reveal'd
> In glory of the Father, to dissolve
> *Satan* with his perverted World, then raise
> From the conflagrant mass, purg'd and refin'd,
> New Heav'ns, new Earth, Ages of endless date.
>
> (*PL* XII, 537–49)[4]

Though Milton leaves unspecified the nature of the promised "vengeance to the wicked," its syntactical opposition to the "respiration to the just" suggests that such resurrection is itself the reward of the just, in which case it could not be extended to the wicked dead, this exclusion from resurrection constituting their punishment. It is Milton's mortalist heresy, implicit throughout *Paradise Lost* and explicitly developed in *De Doctrina*—"as the whole man is uniformly said to consist of body, spirit, and soul . . . the whole man dies" (CM, XV, p. 219)—which elucidates the punishment involved in the simple denial of resurrection to the wicked dead at the Last Judgment, namely, that the death of "the whole man" is to last eternally. The "bad men" still among the living would presumably share the final doom of Satan when, after a long triumph on earth, God's justice arrives "to dissolve / *Satan* with his perverted World." This explicit statement of Satan's dissolution is not qualified by any suggestion of his continuing existence and torment following the Day of Judgment, and this omission of orthodox expectation is compounded by the ambiguous reference to "his perverted World." While the earth is clearly implied, the "perverted World" of Satan may equally apply to the "Perverse" (*PL* II, 625) "World" (II, 572) of hell. Just as there is no notice of any future existence of Satan, so there is no mention of hell after the conflagration but only of "New Heav'ns, new Earth." The implication is that Satan and hell, together with the wicked, both dead and still living, will all be consumed and perish with the final conflagration of the earth.

This conception of the Final Judgment also informs the briefer description immediately preceding it:

> and thence shall come,
> When this world's dissolution shall be ripe,
> With glory and power to judge both quick and dead,
> To judge th' unfaithful dead, but to reward
> His faithful, and receive them into bliss,
> Whether in Heav'n or Earth, for then the Earth
> Shall all be Paradise, far happier place
> Than this of *Eden,* and far happier days. (XII, 458–65)

As in the passage first discussed "respiration to the just" was understood to be a reward from its syntactical opposition to "vengeance to the wicked," so here the verb "to judge" must be equated with punishment from its syntactical contrast with "to reward." "To judge," then, signifies not a legalistic allotting of both rewards and punishments but rather the execution of punishments to the unfaithful, "both quick and dead." Michael has just explained to Adam that Christ's death "Annuls thy doom, the death thou shouldst have di'd, / In sin for ever lost from life" (XII, 428–29), and that this annulment of death is not general but reserved particularly for "as many as offer'd Life / Neglect not, and the benefit embrace / By Faith not void of works" (XII, 425–27). The antithesis is not between an eternity in hell or heaven but between "the death thou shouldst have di'd" and the "immortal Life" (XII, 435) reserved for the faithful when Christ returns "to reward / His faithful, and receive them into bliss." The final judgment of "th' unfaithful dead" is, then, the irrevocable decision that, for them, the doom of death is not to be annulled, the unfaithful among the living being consigned to perish with "this world's dissolution." There is no mention of the perpetuation of hell after the conflagration in these late eschatological passages or in the still briefer reference: "till fire purge all things new, / Both Heav'n and Earth, wherein the just shall dwell" (XI, 900-01).

Though the first description of the Final Judgment in *Paradise Lost* is far more detailed and apparently more orthodox, it will be seen that it does not differ significantly from the later versions:

> All knees to thee shall bow, of them that bide
> In Heaven, or Earth, or under Earth in Hell;
> When thou attended gloriously from Heav'n
> Shalt in the Sky appear, and from thee send
> The summoning Arch-Angels to proclaim
> Thy dread Tribunal: forthwith from all Winds
> The living, and forthwith the cited dead
> Of all past Ages to the general Doom
> Shall hast'n, such a peal shall rouse thir sleep.
> Then all thy Saints assembl'd, thou shalt judge
> Bad men and Angels, they arraign'd shall sink
> Beneath thy Sentence; Hell, her numbers full,
> Thenceforth shall be for ever shut. Meanwhile
> The World shall burn, and from her ashes spring
> New Heav'n and Earth, wherein the just shall dwell.
>
> (III, 321-35)

The first question that must be decided is the meaning of the ambiguous "cited dead," whether all or only the saintly dead are to be summoned. The possibility that the dead cited for resurrection are the elect of God is strengthened by the wind image, which also appears in a scriptural quotation on the Last Judgment in *De Doctrina*: "Matt. xxiv. 31. he shall send his angels with a great shout of a trumpet, and they shall gather together his elect from the four winds, from one end of heaven to the other'" (CM, XVI, p. 357). Another apocalyptic reference to the "four winds," indicative of the four cardinal directions on earth, occurs in Mark: "And then shall he send his angels, and shall gather together his elect from the four winds, from the uttermost part of the earth to the uttermost part of heaven" (xiii, 27). Given the eschatological context of the wind image in the Miltonic passage, it can only have been intended to recall the parallel Gospel quotations from the apocalypses of Mark and Matthew; and these refer specifically to the angelic summoning of the elect. From this it follows that only those among both the living and the dead are "cited" or summoned "from all Winds" or directions who are meant to constitute the assembly of the saints, "thy Saints assembl'd." But since it is only these "cited dead" who are roused from "thir sleep," there is no resurrection indicated for the wicked dead. Consequently, the "bad men" now to be judged can come only from those among the still living at the day of doom who have not been previously summoned to the assembly of the saints. The adjective "bad" is undoubtedly meant to apply also to the category of "Angels" who have already fallen and who now, with the bad men among the living, have been "arraign'd" to receive their final judgment. Since the Son is to "judge" only the bad, the word again signifies the immediate awarding of punishment alone.

The nature of this punitive Last Judgment is, however, stated with great ambiguity: "they arraign'd shall sink / Beneath thy Sentence; Hell, her numbers full, / Thenceforth shall be for ever shut. Meanwhile / The World shall burn." The orthodox suggestion of these lines is that the Judgment would involve the sinking of all the arraigned to hell, thus swelling its numbers to the "full" amount of all evil creatures, men as well as angels, and that the shutting of hell, an event coincident with the burning of the world, would consign them to an eternity of torment. The full numbers of hell need not imply an addition, however, but simply a complete in-gathering of all the fallen angels who, since Sin's opening of the gates of hell, "With easy intercourse pass to and fro" (*PL* II, 1031) between the bridged hell and earth. The final condemnation of the fallen angels would then be to a hell which "Thenceforth" would permit no egress, the shutting of hell's gates by the Son demonstrating the greater power of good to overcome the power of evil: "She [Sin] op'n'd, but to shut / Excell'd her power" (II, 883–84). But the duration of the condemned angels' confinement in hell is unclear despite the unalterable shutting of its gates. For the syntactical restriction of the words "for ever" to the single fact of the shutting of hell, rather than implying the perpetuation of hell, may be taken to signify no more than its permanent shutdown. The judgment regarding hell does not, then, specify either eternal torment or the punishment of men. A causal relationship between the sentencing of "Bad men and Angels" and the numbers of hell is suggested to the orthodox reader by the sequence of statements. But the "Sentence" is noncommittal on the nature and duration of punishment as well as on the question of whether the arraigned men and angels are to be punished in the same place. Moreover, the sequence has not two but three parts: the conjoined sentencing of bad men and bad angels; the shutting of hell; and the burning of the world. As the description of the judgment in the first part is confined to the ambiguous meaning of "sink," no more need be suggested by the term than that the judged would in some sense fall or falter at the sentence of their doom. The second and third parts of the sequence may then be viewed as defining the nature of the sentence pronounced against each category of the judged through its execution, for bad angels confinement in hell, for bad men dissolution in the conflagration of the earth.

Though hell, with its full census of confined angels, would thus seem to escape the conflagration of the world, this assumption is qualified by two circumstances. The first is that its doom of being "for ever shut" is mentioned before rather than after the conflagration and that no mention is made of the perpetuation of hell along with "New Heav'n and Earth." The second develops out of the possible implications of the opening paraphrase of Philippians ii, 10: "That at the name of Jesus every knee should bow, of things in heaven, and things in earth, and things under the earth." In his reference to the bowed knees of those "under Earth in Hell," Milton adopts the traditional equation of the Pauline phrase "things under the earth" with hell, an equation which follows from the conventional belief in a subterranean hell. But since Milton does not normally describe hell in these conventionally suggestive terms, and in *De Doctrina* clearly recognizes the inherent contradiction between the conventional placement of hell and a belief in its eternal duration—"hell, being situated in the center of the earth, must share the fate of the surrounding universe, and perish likewise" (CM, XVI, p. 375)—the natural suggestion of a subterranean connotation for the words "under Earth" seems calculated to allow for the very possibility Milton argues against in his treatise, namely, that hell would perish with the earth in the final conflagration. Such a possibility would explain how "for ever shut" might signify hell's shutdown of operations and would give new significance to the placement of the reference to the world's burning after the last mention of hell. The phrase "under Earth in Hell" is, of course, ambiguous, suggesting the conventional placement of hell under the surface of the earth while permitting a position beneath the whole "pendant world" (II, 1052) more consistent with the cosmic geography of *Paradise Lost* and with the corresponding analysis of the location of hell in *De Doctrina:* "Hell appears to be situated beyond the limits of this universe" (CM, XVI, p. 373). But while Milton's argument that only an extrauniversal hell could survive the earthly conflagration serves the orthodox eschatology of the treatise, the carefully depicted cosmic geography of the epic conflicts with its heretical eschatology, however useful it—like the Ptolemaic universe—may be dramatically; and in the ambiguous "under Earth" locution of Book III and the equally ambiguous "his perverted World" of Book XII, Milton provides subliminal suggestions of the dissolution of hell in the final conflagration.

A further resolution of this conflict is suggested by the allegorical apocalypse of Book X:

> I call'd and drew them [Sin and Death] thither
> My Hell-hounds, to lick up the draff and filth
> Which man's polluting Sin with taint hath shed
> On what was pure, till cramm'd and gorg'd, nigh burst
> With suckt and glutted offal, at one sling
> Of thy victorious Arm, well-pleasing Son,
> Both *Sin* and *Death*, and yawning *Grave* at last
> Through *Chaos* hurl'd, obstruct the mouth of Hell
> For ever, and seal up his ravenous Jaws.
> Then Heav'n and Earth renew'd shall be made pure
> To sanctity that shall receive no stain.   (X, 629–39)

The reference to "Heav'n and Earth renew'd" indicates that the event depicted by God is to take place on the Day of Judgment. Since the biblical apocalypses obviously make no reference to Milton's allegory of Sin and Death, Milton could not have intended this version of the apocalypse to be an objective representation of divine truth but must rather have meant it to be an allegorical interpretation of the final dissolution of the earth. It is, in fact, Milton's conception of "this world's dissolution" (XII, 459), rather than of its annihilation, which is most illuminated by investigation of this allegory of Judgment Day.

Most significant to the allegory is the introduction of "yawning *Grave*," with the assertion that it shall be "at last / Through *Chaos* hurl'd." Unlike Sin and Death, Grave would seem to personify a wholly physical reality, namely, earthly graves. To understand the implication of having earthly graves—with not only their mortal remains but the whole earth which contains them—hurled to chaos, we must relate this passage to Milton's earlier discussion of chaos:

>   this wild Abyss,
> The Womb of nature and perhaps her Grave,
> Of neither Sea, nor Shore, nor Air, nor Fire,
> But all these in thir pregnant causes mixt
> Confus'dly, and which thus must ever fight,
> Unless th' Almighty Maker them ordain
> His dark materials to create more Worlds.   (II, 910–16)

In addition to stating that chaos provided the basic material out of which God created the world of nature, Milton here offers two hypothetical possibilities: (1) that the destruction of nature might effect its return to the state of primordial chaos; and (2) that out of these materials God might "create more Worlds." Now both of these possibilities would seem to be affirmed if we accept the allegorical apocalypse as providing an interpretation of the apocalypses of Books III and XII. If the final hurling of "*Grave*" through "*Chaos*" means that the conflagration of the world will reduce it to its original "dark materials," then the statements concerning the renewal of heaven and earth—"The World shall burn, and from her ashes spring / New Heav'n and Earth" (III, 334–35); "then raise / From the conflagrant mass, purg'd and refin'd, / New Heav'ns, new Earth" (XII, 547–49)—can only mean that God will create these new heavens and earth from the same chaos to which the old polluted world had been reduced.

    Milton's analysis of the Creation in *De Doctrina* explains why the destruction of the world cannot involve its complete annihilation:

The world was framed out of matter of some kind or other. . . . Since . . . God did not produce everything out of nothing, but of himself, I proceed to consider the necessary consequence of this doctrine, namely, that if all things are not only from God, but of God, no created thing can be finally annihilated. (CM, XV, pp. 19, 27)

Milton's materialism thus causes his mortalist doctrine to be dissolutionist rather than annihilationist—"every constituent part [of 'the whole man'] returns at dissolution to its elementary principle" (CM, XV, p. 239)—though such dissolution has different eschatological implications in the treatise and the epic. The "matter" of *De Doctrina* is identifiable with the chaos of *Paradise Lost,* itself a part of God's infinite being: "Boundless the Deep, because I am who fill / Infinitude" (*PL* VII, 168-69). But since Milton, in his treatise, does not construe this "matter" to have a geographical area distinct from the world which was "framed" out of it, the discrete area attributed to chaos may be viewed as a symbolic translation of temporal into spatial terms. The allegorical hurling of "*Grave* at last / Through *Chaos*" may thus be taken to signify not a geographic dislocation of the earth but a figurative statement of the process of dissolution, the dissolved world providing the "matter" out of which "Heav'n and Earth" are "Then" to be "renew'd" in immutable purity.

But if the geographic separation of chaos and the burning world can be said to be allegorical, then the same can be said of hell. If the chaotic mass of Sin, Death, and Grave be viewed as the residue of the conflagration, then the "mouth of Hell" which it obstructs is also present at the chaotic site of the dissolved world. As this is the only eschatological context in the epic in which the separation of hell and earth is graphically depicted, its unique allegorical form permits a symbolic construction of their apparent geographic separation. Such a construction would resolve the earlier discussed conflict between the physical depiction of an extrauniversal hell and the covert sugges- tions of its ultimate dissolution, and resolve it without an absolute subscribing to the outmoded belief in a subterranean hell.

But an allegorical interpretation of the geographic position of hell is only possible if hell itself is viewed metaphorically. Milton had earlier suggested that hell is not a physical but a psychological state: "for within him Hell / He brings, and round about him, nor from Hell / One step no more than from himself can fly / By change of place" (IV, 20-23). Though *De Doctrina* is normally more orthodox on the subject of hell, Milton even there suggests such a view of hell when he refers to "that penal hardness of heart, which, after much long-suffering on the part of God, is generally the final punish- ment reserved for the more atrocious sins" (CM, XIV, p. 165). This conception is echoed in *Paradise Lost:* "This my long sufferance and my day of grace / They who neglect and scorn, shall never taste; / But hard be hard'n'd, blind be blinded more" (III, 198-200). Satan proceeds to "Heap on himself damnation" (I, 215) through that pro- gressive hardness of heart which constitutes the punishment of his internal hell: "myself am Hell; / And in the lowest deep a lower deep / Still threat'ning to devour me opens wide" (IV, 75-77). Milton's depiction of a physical hell can thus be viewed—in accordance with the analysis made popular in Reformation theology by Calvin[5]— as a metaphor for the psychological state of those alienated "from God and blessed vision" (V, 613), a state "where peace / And rest can never dwell" (I, 65-66). But in Milton's heretical eschatology, this hell of psychological alienation would be as mortal as the psyche it inhabits. The dissolution of "*Satan* with his perverted World" can be understood, in consequence, to include the destruction of hell, since "within him Hell / He brings."

This metaphorical conception of hell is not contradicted by the physical personification of hell in this allegorical apocalypse. For the reference to a personified hell, necessitated by the allegorical form, contains the same pattern of ambiguities that were observed in the Book III passage with regard to both its possible human inhabitants and futurity. We read that the chaotic residue of the grave will "obstruct the mouth of Hell / For ever, and seal up his ravenous Jaws." This might suggest that it is the "mouth of Hell" whose "Jaws" are "ravenous" for further food, which could come only from the wicked dead, and that having ingested this fare hell would continue "For ever," though no further passage through this entrance would be permitted. "For ever" does not, however, refer to hell's perpetuation but, as in the Book III apocalypse, is restricted to its closing and thus again may rather imply the permanence of its shutdown of operations because of its dissolution. It is, in fact, an external blockage, which would hinder the possibility of any passage beyond it, that is properly suggested by the verb "obstruct." The suggestion of a ravenous hell is derived from the seeming apposition of "and seal up his ravenous Jaws" to "obstruct the mouth of Hell." It is not hell, however, but Death, mentioned in the same syntactical construction, who has previously been identified with such ravenous hunger: "To mee, who with eternal Famine pine, / Alike is Hell, or Paradise, or Heaven, / There best, where most with ravin I may meet" (X, 597-99). And Death has been extensively and most graphically described as "cramm'd and gorg'd, nigh burst / With suckt and glutted offal." If Death, hurled through chaos with Sin and Grave, is in a position to "obstruct the mouth of Hell," then hell is likewise in a position "to seal up his [Death's] ravenous Jaws," and no passage from Death's sealed up jaws to hell's obstructed mouth is possible for the wicked dead.

In the apocalypses of Books III, X, and XII, there are, then, no unequivocal indications that wicked men are to be sentenced to an eternity of torment in hell and that either the fallen angels or hell is eternal. The primary aim of the foregoing analyses has been to demonstrate that Milton's presentation of the Last Judgment is ambiguous in every instance dealing with the doom of wicked men and angels, and that it either omits any mention of hell or refers only to the fact of its final shutting. The specific readings offered pinpoint these difficulties in the text and provide possible resolutions of each which mutually support an eschatology dooming evil men and angels to ultimate dissolution. While the argument regarding the dissolution of hell is not crucial to this larger eschatological issue, it is a logical correlative suggested by Milton's characteristic equivocations about hell in the apocalyptic passages and is consistent with the depiction of hell throughout the epic. For hell is objectified in the epic not as the place of man's eternal punishment but as the mortal abode of the fallen angels, a suggestion implied in the early definition of hell as "A Universe of death" (II, 622). The allegorical path which Sin and Death pave between hell and earth is not built for man's traversing but is an avenue "by which the Spirits perverse / With easy intercourse pass to and fro / To tempt or punish mortals" (II, 1030–32). The denial of eternal torment in hell, covertly suggested in the apocalypses, is stated with greater explicitness in other contexts.

The destiny of sinful men is made quite clear just before the allegorical apocalypse in an important comment on the departure of Sin and Death to earth after the Fall of Man: "This said, they both betook them several ways, / Both to destroy, or unimmortal make / All kinds, and for destruction to mature / Sooner or later" (X, 610–13). Here Milton explicitly states that the wages of sin are to become "unimmortal," that the sinful are to be denied even an eternity of torment; and, since the wicked are to be utterly destroyed when in the maturity of time the day of vengeance arrives, Sin and Death will also cease to function and will come to an end. Speeches by Adam and God give further evidence that there is no hell of postmortem torment reserved for the punishment of man.

That sinful man will become "unimmortal" and Death itself be destroyed is a conclusion Adam derives from his understanding of God's goodness:

> Can he make deathless Death? that were to make
> Strange contradiction, which to God himself
> Impossible is held, as Argument
> Of weakness, not of Power. Will he draw out,
> For anger's sake, finite to infinite
> In punisht Man, to satisfy his rigor
> Satisfi'd never; that were to extend
> His Sentence beyond dust and Nature's Law.   (X, 798–805)

Since this carefully reasoned argument, which demonstrates that God's nature precludes the possibility of eternal torment, occurs less than two hundred lines after the allegorical apocalypse with its prefatory remarks about the "unimmortal" destiny of sinful man, it can only be viewed as an explicit confirmation of the eschatological implications of this earlier section. The validity of the present argument against eternal punishment is underscored by the patent falsity of Adam's proof against it: "But say / That Death be not one stroke, as I suppos'd, / Bereaving sense, but endless misery / From this day onward . . . both Death and I / Am found Eternal" (X, 808–11, 815–16). Since Adam will, in fact, be subject to the "stroke" of death, and since he had earlier proven Milton's theological contention of the death of the "whole man"—"All of me then shall die" (X, 792)—the argument in favor of "endless misery" is invalid and the former proof of finite punishment of sinners must stand.

But the clearest proof that Adam's former analysis accords with God's nature and decrees is given by God himself:

> I at first with two fair gifts
> Created him endow'd, with Happiness
> And Immortality: that fondly lost,
> This other serv'd but to eternize woe;
> Till I provided Death; so Death becomes
> His final remedy, and after Life
> Tri'd in sharp tribulation, and refin'd
> By Faith and faithful works, to second Life,
> Wak't in the renovation of the just,
> Resigns him up with Heav'n and Earth renew'd.   (XI, 57–66)

Here Milton's God pointedly disclaims any intention "to eternize woe" but pledges that the faithful, after a life refined by trial, will be "wak't" from death to "second Life." After a life not so spent, and therefore unentitled to such "second Life," there is only death, the "dissolution wrought by Sin" (XI, 55).

God presents such mortality as the "final remedy" for pain. But though Moloch would embrace such mortality as "happier far / Than miserable to have eternal being" (II, 97–98), the voice of the fallen seems more accurately echoed in Belial's words:

> To be no more; sad cure; for who would lose,
> Though full of pain, this intellectual being,
> Those thoughts that wander through Eternity,
> To perish rather, swallow'd up and lost
> In the wide womb of uncreated night,
> Devoid of sense and motion?   (II, 146–51)

Such a remedy is a "sad cure" and the most terrible of punishments precisely because it dooms to extinction "those thoughts that wander through Eternity." To lose even a painful consciousness "in the wide womb of uncreated night," an accurate description of chaos, may be viewed by God, Adam, and Moloch as a desirable end to pain; for such as Belial, however, it is no sign of mercy, but rather the worst of punishments, and Belial's assessment is seconded by the remainder of the fallen angels when they applaud the supporting speech of Mammon.

But whether merciful or punitive (and Milton argues both cases), such final extinction of personal identity is recognized by both Moloch and Belial as a possible price of pursuing war against God. Though the fallen angels are persuaded that they can avoid such an end through a policy of "covert guile" (II, 41) against God's Creation, when Satan embarks for what he recognizes to be "the Coasts of dark destruction" (II, 464) his first encounter in furthering this policy is with Sin and Death, and his final end, dissolution. Milton's allegory of Sin and Death is normally viewed in its relation to man, but it is equally significant with regard to Satan and the fallen angels. Satan's successive encounters with Sin, Death, and Chaos are a clear allegory of his progress toward his stated dissolution in the final conflagration. Though he believes it is only the earth which his "revenge" (II, 987) will "reduce / To her original darkness" (II, 983–84) of chaos, the final punishment of his seeking "Evil to others" (I, 216) will be his conjoined dissolution "with his perverted World."

The disparity between Satan's beliefs and the larger perspective of divine truth is of the utmost importance to a discussion of Milton's eschatology. Satan draws the conclusion that "now we find this our Empyreal form / Incapable of mortal injury, / Imperishable" (VI, 433–35), from the healing of his wounds during the War in Heaven, though this conclusion is framed by the narrative assertions that spirits can "by annihilating die" (VI, 347) and that the Son has purposely preserved the existence of the rebelling angels: "Yet half his strength he put not forth, but check'd / His Thunder in mid Volley, for he meant / Not to destroy, but root them out of Heav'n" (VI, 853–55). Satan, however, maintains to the end, and despite all arguments directed toward him to the contrary, that "this Empyreal substance cannot fail" (I, 117), that he and his followers are "Eternal spirits" (I, 318). Beelzebub notes the corollary of this belief, "What can it then avail . . . eternal being / To undergo eternal punishment" (I, 153–55), a corollary understood by Satan when he first "views" (I, 59) hell and perceives it as a "dismal Situation" (I, 60) "where peace / And rest can never dwell, hope never comes / That comes to all; but torture without end / Still urges" (I, 65–68). This first statement of eternal torment in *Paradise Lost* is a masterful example of Miltonic ambiguity, for "urges" can suggest either the orthodox meaning that torture is driven onward without end or the heretical possibility that a belief in such endless torture is simply pressed strongly upon Satan's attention by his despairing hopelessness.

Significantly, Milton presents this first description of hell not objectively but in terms of Satan's perceptions; and its highly affective content, picturing the unremitting torture of a hopelessly restive state, marks it as an objectification of Satan's spiritual condition. As Satan views his own torture to be without end, so he beholds his followers to be "condemn'd / For ever now to have thir lot in pain" (I, 607–08). Satan's belief in his "endless pain" (II, 30) is echoed by Death when he recognizes Satan as one "condemn'd / To waste Eternal days in woe and pain" (II, 694–95). But this belief is countered by the description of their imminent conflict—"Each at the Head / Levell'd his deadly aim; thir fatal hands / No second stroke intend" (II, 711–13)—and by Sin's prescience of the divine "wrath which one day will destroy ye both" (II, 734); she further warns Satan to "shun / His [Death's] deadly arrow; neither vainly hope / To be invulnerable" (II, 810–12). Sin's foreknowledge of Satan's final end is supported by Abdiel's assertion to Satan, "Then who created thee lamenting learn, / When who can uncreate thee thou shalt know" (V, 894–95), and by the narrative reference to "his fatal bruise" (X, 191).

The limited perspective which "urges" Satan to adopt the belief in the eternal torment of damned spirits extends as well to his view of fallen man, and it is he who enunciates this doctrine in its only unequivocal form: "Hell shall unfold, / To entertain you two, her widest Gates, / And send forth all her Kings; there will be room, / Not like these narrow limits, to receive / Your numerous offspring" (IV, 381–85). Contrasted with this lack of equivocation is the sole reference to possible human punishment in hell unassociated with Satanic belief. The Miltonic narrator asserts that, were it not for the Son's offer to atone for man's sins, "without redemption all mankind / Must have been lost, adjudg'd to Death and Hell / By doom severe" (III, 222–24). This suggests the orthodox expectation that the atonement will redeem some from the doom of hell to which the remainder will still be adjudged. But the phrasing of this statement describes a hypothetical situation which no longer obtains and may equally suggest that this "doom severe" will be mitigated by the atonement for "all mankind" with the result that now no men will be adjudged to hell. Another example of equivocation occurs in Beelzebub's expression of Satanic belief. In pleading Satan's "devilish Counsel" (II, 379), Beelzebub looks forward to God's "darling Sons / Hurl'd headlong to partake with us" (II, 373–74), but the unspecified nature of Beelzebub's expectations allows for the heretical reading that unredeemed man will "partake" with the fallen angels not in eternal torment but in final dissolution. As the only unequivocal statements of eternal torment are those associated with the views of Satan, Milton would seem to be identifying such belief as a Satanic doctrine.[6]

There is a final reference to the eternal torment of man associated with Satan's views which suggests a second Miltonic strategy. This appears in Raphael's warning to Adam of Satan's intentions:

> Who now is plotting how he may seduce
> Thee also from obedience, that with him

Bereav'd of happiness thou mayst partake
His punishment, Eternal misery;

. . . .

       let it profit thee to have heard
By terrible Example the reward
Of disobedience; firm they might have stood,
Yet fell; remember, and fear to transgress.   (VI, 901–12)

It is again important to recognize that it is Satan's perception that seduced man would partake in the "Eternal misery" which he deems to be his own punishment which Raphael is presenting in his analysis of Satan's motivation. In his independent conclusion, Raphael goes no further in defining "the reward / Of disobedience" than to remind Adam of his just completed narration of Satan's fall from heaven, thus conforming to God's instructions to "warn him" that Satan "is plotting now / The fall of others from like state of bliss" (V, 237, 240–41). The deterrent to disobedience conveyed by Raphael from God is the specific danger of falling from bliss. If the deterrent of eternal torment is also suggested, it is only because Raphael has failed to comment on Satan's false perception of his "punishment."

A similar strategy may be discerned in what appears to be the most authoritative statement of the eternity of punishment in hell, God's warning to the still unfallen angels that any who disobey the Son in his exaltation "Mee disobeyes, breaks union, and that day / Cast out from God and blessed vision, falls / Into utter darkness, deep ingulft, his place / Ordain'd without redemption, without end" (V, 612–15). This warning is clearly intended by God as a deterrent to angelic disobedience, but its form is marked both by a serious question of credibility and by ambiguity. God states that the casting out from heaven will occur on "that day" in which such disobedience is shown. Yet God has also "ordain'd" (VI, 700) that the warfare will take three days, and this though he orders Michael on the first day to do what he is incapable of accomplishing, to "drive them out from God and bliss, / Into thir place of punishment, the Gulf / Of *Tartarus*, which ready opens wide / His fiery *Chaos* to receive their fall" (VI, 52–55). This further definition of "thir place of punishment" illuminates the central ambiguity in God's deterrent warning; for the place "without end" to which they are to be consigned is not specifically termed hell but simply one of "utter darkness." Though the first description of hell refers to its "utter darkness" (I, 72), Milton takes care to increase gradually the amount of light in hell until, by the end of Book I, hell is "Far round illumin'd" (I, 666) and, in Pandaemonium, "many a row / Of Starry Lamps and blazing Cressets fed / With *Naphtha* and *Asphaltus* yielded light / As from a sky" (II, 727–30). In the earlier discussion of the apocalyptic passages we saw that Satan, in the Final Judgment, would be returned by dissolution to chaos, and we now see that it is only his reduction to its "dark materials" (II, 916) which can insure his doom of "utter darkness" "without end." To underscore this meaning, God announces to Michael, though not to the now disobedient Satan, that it is, indeed, chaos which will "receive their fall." There is, further, no reference in God's deterrent warning to continuing torments but only to the loss of "blessed vision," a loss the fallen angels do not themselves recognize as a deprivation.

As the deterrent warnings of eternal torment, however qualified as to their objective validity, do not, in fact, deter either the angels or man from falling into disobedience to God, it would seem that Milton introduced these warnings to provide a critique of the prevailing view among his contemporary disbelievers in eternal torment that the fiction of such torment in hell needed to be maintained as a deterrent to sin. Yet however much he may question its deterrent value, he does follow their normal practice of making only covert suggestions of this heretical doctrine beneath a surface appearance of orthodox belief in hell.

There is, however, one circumstance in which Milton appears to employ the deterrent value of belief in eternal torment himself, in the question of suicide. When Moloch suggests renewed warfare as a way of achieving their cessation of being "On this side nothing" (II, 101), Belial begins by considering such extinction as possible though "doubtful" (II, 154) but concludes his answer to Moloch's suicidal project by asserting that God "so wise" (II, 155) will not "give his Enemies thir wish, and end / Them in his anger, whom his anger saves / To punish endless" (II, 157–59). And Adam answers Eve's suicidal intent by the similar assertion that "God / Hath wiselier arm'd his vengeful ire . . . rather such acts / Of contumacy will provoke the Highest / To make death in us live" (X, 1022–28). Though Belial's assertion may be viewed as simply another manifestation of disproved Satanic doctrine and Adam's as answered shortly by God's disclaimer of any intention "to eternize woe" (XI, 60), it may well be that Milton felt his doctrine of simple mortality for the unjust might make suicide too attractive a possibility for the weak and that he needed to maintain the appearance of eternal torment in this special instance as a specific deterrent against suicide.

In this last discussion of all the passages in *Paradise Lost* which appear to support the doctrine of eternal torment, we have seen, in addition to the already familiar use of ambiguity, two special strategies: (1) the identification of this belief as a Satanic doctrine; or (2) the suggestion of its questionable effectiveness as a deterrent to sin. To Milton the permanent loss of "blessed vision" in death was sufficient punishment and deterrent without the added specter of eternal torment; and though he allowed the deterrent value of future torments in the difficult case of suicide, from his perspective even such a willful choice of death was self-punishing. For the final judgments accorded in Milton's eschatology reveal the opposing values he placed upon the choice of life or death. As the choice of "Life / Tri'd in sharp tribulation, and refin'd / By Faith and faithful works" (XI, 62–64) leads to the reward of everlasting life, so the choice of death is reflected in the Satanic opposition to God's goodness and works which leads to the punishment of death.

There is one final eschatological passage in which this opposition between the choices of death and life is most forcibly expressed, the passage contrasting the nature and end of the giants with that of Enoch; and it is of special significance because it is the only eschatological context in which the opposition to the godly path of life is denoted not simply as wicked in some unspecified way, or at best as unfaithful, but as representing "Heroic Virtue":

> Such were those Giants, men of high renown;
> For in those days Might only shall be admir'd,
> And Valor and Heroic Virtue call'd;
> To overcome in Battle, and subdue
> Nations, and bring home spoils with infinite
> Man-slaughter, shall be held the highest pitch
> Of human Glory, and for Glory done
> Of triumph, to be styl'd great Conquerors,
> Patrons of Mankind, Gods, and Sons of Gods,
> Destroyers rightlier call'd and Plagues of men.
> Thus Fame shall be achiev'd, renown on Earth,

And what most merits fame in silence hid.
But hee the sev'nth from thee, whom thou beheld'st
The only righteous in a World perverse,
And therefore hated, therefore so beset
With Foes for daring single to be just,
And utter odious Truth, that God would come
To judge them with his Saints: Him the most High
Rapt in a balmy Cloud with winged Steeds
Did, as thou saw'st, receive, to walk with God
High in Salvation and the Climes of bliss,
Exempt from Death; to show thee what reward
Awaits the good, the rest what punishment.   (XI, 688–710)

In this discussion of heroic valor, Milton focuses upon the essential paradox that striving to achieve a godlike glory leads only to the infection and destruction of all human good. Opposed to this is the model of the godly man whose daring witness to the will of God even in the face of extreme hostility makes him "Exempt from Death." Michael presents Enoch's exemption from death as an indication of "what reward / Awaits the good, the rest what punishment." It follows that the punishment of the foes of God will be their lack of that exemption from death with which the good are to be rewarded, that death is the fate of the heroic pursuit of personal glory.

Since Michael presents these past examples of the rewarding of the righteous with eternal life and the punishing of the exponents of "Heroic Virtue" with death as a prefiguration of the Last Judgment which Enoch had prophesied, this passage is essentially eschatological; and it casts a most illuminating light on the relationship of Satan's character to his final end. For Milton also cast Satan in the heroic mold. In the giants passage, Milton makes his most devastating critique of the heroic code, showing that such heroism is the path to death; and this critique of heroism informs his heroic characterization of Satan. As John M. Steadman has demonstrated, "The so-called 'problem of Satan' tends to disappear, once one recognizes Milton's portrait for what it is—a conscious and consistent attempt to refute the conventional secular opinion of heroic virtue by assigning its principal attribute to the devil himself."[7] In recognizing the heroic quality of Satan, one no longer has to conclude either that Milton was "of the devil's party"[8] or that Satan's heroic posture is a spurious piece of "Nonsense,"[9] for the critical groundwork has been laid for viewing Milton's portrait of Satan as a " 'critique' . . . of the conventional heroic patterns established in epic tradition."[10] But we will fully understand Milton's critique of heroism and the honor code only when we recognize the larger context of values and eschatology in which he has placed it with its central issue of life against death.

The informing values of *Paradise Lost* uphold the Mosaic equation of "life and good, and death and evil" with the conclusion "therefore choose life . . . for he [God] is thy life" (Deuteronomy xxx, 15, 19-20). Since for Milton death is only the "Gate of Life" (*PL* XII, 571) to those who have reverently chosen life, it is otherwise a permanent and punishing evil. Thus Milton could not but see the evil implicit in the heroic quest for glory apart from God. For this involves a fundamental contradiction to the divine intention, a rejection of the limitations of dependent existence which God, in its Creation, said was "very good" (Genesis i, 31). As the virtue of the creature lies in that ultimate obedience to the divine will which is a grateful acceptance of the fact of Creation—"That rais'd us from the dust and plac't us here / In all this happiness, who at his hand / Have nothing merited" (*PL* IV, 416-18)—so the denial of this essential good engenders the principle of evil. Milton clearly recognized that the heroic endeavor to transcend the condition of creaturely limitation was "to Death devote" (IX, 901), that the condition of being "without restraint" was appropriate only to "God-head" and defined the "Death" of a creature (IX, 790-92). But if the death thus chosen is evil, that which not only leads to such an end but glamorizes it as well is most evil of all. Milton's eschatology, which postulated death rather than eternal torment as the punishment of sin, required a characterization of Satan which would illuminate the most culturally dangerous—because most attractive and pervasive—form of death-oriented values, and this was the heroic. In casting his Prince of Evil as the ultimate example of the heroic personality depicted in the epic literature of Greece, Britain, and France (I, 573-91), Milton was, then, making a critique of the valor "unmov'd / With dread of death to flight or foul retreat" (I, 554-55) which revealed the death-marked character and, therefore, fundamental evil of the heroic code.

Nowhere is this critique better epitomized than in the giants passage, which demonstrates the destructive nature of "Heroic Virtue" both to others and to the heroic personality. Intimately associated with Satan, this passage looks backward to the heroic characterization of Satan with its destructive effect both on man and on Satan's own character and forward to the final self-defeating result of Satan's heroic pursuit of personal glory, his ultimate dissolution. The final dissolution of Satan defines the fundamental thrust of Milton's critique of heroism, that it is "to Death devote"—both dedicated and consigned to death— even while it serves the theological purpose of indicating the ultimate destiny of the wicked. If the latter purpose is significant for what it reveals about Milton's heretical eschatology, the former shows how essential this eschatology is in determining both characterization and value in Milton's great epic.

The association of Satan's nature and end with those of the giants is not, however, an accidental product of Milton's heroic characterization of the giants but is derived from the same source which also details Enoch's prophecy of doom to the giants, the pseudepigraphical Book of Enoch. Associated with Satan in both theme and derivation, the Enoch-giants passage is especially important to a study of Milton's eschatology because it reveals Milton's use of his sources more clearly than any other eschatological portion of *Paradise Lost*. An investigation of the Jewish and early Christian sources of this passage will provide evidence both of scriptural authority for Milton's heretical eschatology and of the apocryphal source of his conception of hell.

As indicated, the primary source of the Enoch-giants passage is the Book of Enoch. Denis Saurat has demonstrated Milton's knowledge and use of the fragments of the Book of Enoch preserved in Georgius Syncellus' *Chronographia* (Paris, 1657).[11] But since the Syncellus fragments end with chapter 16[12] and I shall demonstrate Milton's close rendering of material from chapters 18 and 19 in *Paradise Lost*, it must be assumed that Milton had access to the complete Book of Enoch in manuscript form. R. H. Charles lists two manuscripts of the Book of Enoch which were in England during Milton's period as well as others then available at Paris and the Vatican.[13] And in his important comparative study, "The Book of Enoch and *Paradise Lost*," Grant McColley concludes: "It would seem probable that Milton and other interested scholars of the mid-seventeenth century knew more of the Book of Enoch than might be obtained from the often slender fragments of New Testament, patristic, and rabbinical writers, together with the passages preserved in Syncellus.[14]

In the portion of the Book of Enoch with which the Syncellus fragments begin, the genesis of the giants is ascribed to the angels who bound themselves together in their lust for the daughters of men: "And they have gone to the daughters of men upon the earth, and have slept with the women, and have defiled themselves, and revealed to them all kinds of sins. And the women have borne giants, and the whole earth has thereby been filled with blood and unrighteousness" (ix, 8-10). In punishment, God announces the imprisonment of the fallen angels and the destruction of the giants by the deluge (chap. x). In a dream-vision, the fallen angels appeal to Enoch to intercede with God on their behalf and that of their offspring; his petition is denied by God and he returns to prophesy their doom (chaps. xii–xvi). Uriel now takes Enoch on a cosmic journey to the place designed for the temporal punishment of the fallen angels prior to the Day of Judgment:

And beyond that abyss I saw a place which had no firmament of the heaven above, and no firmly founded earth beneath it: there was no water upon it, and no birds, but it was a waste and horrible place. I saw seven stars like great burning mountains, and to me, when I inquired regarding them, The angel said: 'This place is the end of heaven and earth: this has become a prison for the stars and the host of heaven. . . . Here shall stand the angels who have connected themselves with women, and their spirits assuming many different forms are defiling mankind and shall lead them astray into sacrificing to demons as gods, (here shall they stand,) till the day of the great judgment in which they shall be judged till they are made an end of.' (xviii, 12-14; xix, 1)

This passage is clearly Milton's source for his graphic depiction of hell as a "dismal Situation waste and wild, / A Dungeon horrible" (I, 60-61), for his inclusion of volcanic mountains in hell, and for his cosmic location of hell as separated from earth by an abyss. It would likewise seem to be the source of Milton's conception of the function of hell; for this "waste and horrible place" is both the temporary prison of the fallen angels and a launching station from which their spirits can go forth in various forms to lead men into the worship of "demons as gods." There they abide and work their evil will against mankind until the Final Judgment in which they shall be "made an end of." In the Book of Enoch, then, Enoch's prophecy of doom against the giants also includes the fate of the fallen angels, who, at the Final Judgment, will be utterly destroyed.

The final end of the fallen angels, and of Satan specifically, is also attested to in the Assumption of Moses: "And then His kingdom shall appear throughout all His creation, / And then Satan shall be no more" (x, 1).[15] Though it is unlikely that Milton knew the Assumption of Moses, both of these pseudepigraphical works are quoted in the Epistle of Jude,[16] which provides the only scriptural evidence for belief in the final destruction of Satan and the fallen angels:

> And the angels which kept not their first estate, but left their own habitation, he hath reserved in everlasting chains under darkness unto the judgment of the great day.
>   Even as Sodom and Gomorrha, and the cities about them in like manner, giving themselves over to fornication, and going after strange flesh, are set forth for an example, suffering the vengeance of eternal fire. (6-7)

Jude 6 derives directly from the Book of Enoch,[17] and the association of the punishment of the fallen angels with that of Sodom and Gomorrah (cf. Luke xvii, 29–30) indicates its finality; for the eternal fire which burned those cities cannot be viewed as eternal in duration but only in the supernatural origin of this judgment fire from the Eternal, God. The "everlasting" chains which bind the fallen angels prior to the Judgment Day would have been understood by Milton and other seventeenth-century heretical exegetes as signifying "ages of ages"[18] finite in duration.

Milton's use of Jude in his Enoch passage is indicated by his almost direction quotation from Jude on the punishment of sinners, "to whom is reserved the blackness of darkness for ever. And Enoch also, the seventh from Adam, prophesied of these, saying, Behold, the Lord cometh with ten thousands of his saints, To execute judgment upon all" (13–15). This Jude quoted almost verbatim from Enoch's opening prophecy in the Book of Enoch: "And behold! He cometh with ten thousands of His holy ones / To execute judgement [sic] upon all, / And to destroy all the ungodly" (i, 9). But though Jude takes from the Book of Enoch both Enoch's prophecy and the final extinction of the fallen angels, he connects neither with the giants of the pseudepigraph. Since Milton does make this connection and shows Enoch specifically prophesying doom against the giants (XI, 664–71, as well as XI, 701–05), it is clear that Milton made use not only of Jude but also of the Book of Enoch. Moreover, since the Syncellus fragments do not include Enoch's role as messenger of God's lengthy pronouncement of doom against the fallen angels and giants, it should be established that Milton's knowledge of the Book of Enoch was not confined to Syncellus, that he had access to the complete Book of Enoch, that he largely derived the location, form, and function of his hell from this Jewish apocalypse, and that it was one of the sources of his belief in the final destruction of Satan.[19]

This study of the relationship of the Book of Enoch to the Enoch-giants passage in *Paradise Lost* indicates that the fallen angels would have been intimately associated in Milton's mind with the giants; and it was probably this fact that led Milton to characterize the giants not simply as representative of bloodshed (as in Enoch ix, 10) but of "Heroic Virtue." Both the sources relating Enoch with the giants and the heroic characterization of the giants are, then, fundamentally associated with Satan and illuminate his corresponding "unexemption" from death.

I have developed Milton's use of the sources of this passage at such length because they are the only scriptural and apocryphal sources of his heretical eschatology for which there is clear evidence of his use in *Paradise Lost*. Another scriptural reference particularly close to Milton's language and thinking is 2 Peter:

The Lord knoweth how to deliver the godly out of temptations, and to reserve the unjust unto the day of judgment to be punished. . . . these, as natural brute beasts, made to be taken and destroyed . . . shall utterly perish. . . . all these things shall be dissolved. . . . Nevertheless we, according to his promise, look for new heavens and a new earth, wherein dwelleth righteousness. (ii, 9, 12; iii, 11, 13)

Similarly, the language of such Miltonic lines as "to second Life, / Wak't in the renovation of the just" (XI, 64-65) and "respiration to the just" (XII, 540) recalls the reference in the Luke Gospel to "the resurrection of the just" (xiv, 14).[20] Since in *De Doctrina* Milton did not develop the eschatological conceptions of special resurrection of the just and the complete destruction of wicked men and angels, we cannot be certain what scriptural sources beyond Jude he might have employed as supporting evidence for such a doctrine, though it is clear that there was some such eschatological tradition stretching from Isaiah xxvi, 19,[21] through the Epistles of Paul,[22] to the *Didache*.[23] Whatever other scriptural sources Milton may have used—and we may be sure that Milton would have developed no theological position without what he felt to be firm scriptural support—in Jude, as in *Paradise Lost,* we have epitomized in the person and prophecy of Enoch the essential eschatological message of Milton's epic: the salvation to eternal life of the saints and the judgment to the darkness of death of both wicked men and angels. Though Milton couches this heresy in a strategy of careful ambiguity and omission, it permeates every aspect of the epic and is an index to its meaning. As hints of his radical eschatology are numerous and pointed, as Milton would not be likely to toy with theology on such a vital point,[24] and as the heresy is developed with such astonishing consistency throughout *Paradise Lost,* it seems evident that Milton expressed his true eschatological belief, however covertly, in his epic rather than in his theological treatise. It will be instructive, nonetheless, to compare the eschatology of *Paradise Lost* with that of *De Doctrina* both to determine the relative quality of Milton's eschatological thought in the two works and to understand better Milton's strategy of omission to preserve the orthodox appearance of his epic.

Apart from the unorthodoxy of the epic and the orthodoxy of the treatise in this theological area, the most marked difference between the two is the matter of consistency. In opposition to the remarkable consistency of the epic treatment throughout its great length, within the few pages of the treatise which deal with the Final Judgment two different and contradictory eschatological time schemes are presented. The first would seem to involve an original analysis, though it is likely that, as with other apparently original positions, there are sources to be discovered:

Coincident, as appears, with the time of this last judgment—. . . as it is not easily imaginable that so many myriads of men and angels should be assembled and sentenced within a single day—beginning with its commencement, and extending a little beyond its conclusion, will take place that glorious reign of Christ on earth with his saints, so often promised in Scripture, even until all his enemies shall be subdued. (CM, XVI, p. 359)

Having argued that Christ's earthly reign with his saints and victory over his enemies is to be viewed as coincident with the time of judicial sentencing, Milton proceeds to take us point by point through the chronology of chapter xx of Revelation (CM, XVI, pp. 363–65) with no attempt to resolve the chronological contradictions. Milton's handling of Revelation, chapter xx, can be better gauged by reviewing this chapter of Scripture. There is to be a first resurrection of the just who participate in the millennial reign (Revelation xx, 4–6). Following the completion of this reign, Satan will be loosed from prison to deceive the nations then existing into battle against the resurrected saints, which will lead to the destruction by fire of these nations (Revelation xx, 7–9) and the punishment of Satan (Revelation xx, 10). Then will take place the general Resurrection and Final Judgment (Revelation xx, 11–15).[25]

Milton follows the Revelation account exactly, with one exception. He significantly alters the meaning of Revelation xx, 7–9, in his introductory summary to these verses when he includes Satan in the overthrow by fire of the rebel nations: "After the expiration of the thousand years Satan will rage again, and assail the church at the head of an immense confederacy of its enemies; but will be overthrown by fire from heaven, and condemned to everlasting punishment. Rev. xx. 7–9" (CM, XVI, p. 363). He does this by omitting any mention of Revelation xx, 10, in which Satan is explicitly separated from the conflagration which devours the wicked nations and reserved for special punishment which is specifically to involve eternal torment. It should be noted that such specific eternal torment is not explicitly affirmed of the rebel nations in Revelation xx, 9, or of the resurrected dead in Revelation xx, 15, both of which refer simply to fire, and that to identify the punishment of these wicked men with that of Satan, Milton has recourse to Matthew xxxv, 46. What Milton has done, then, is to include Satan in the destruction by fire of the existing rebel nations and then identify the eternal torment of the omitted verse (Revelation xx, 10) with the "fire" which "came down from God out of heaven, and devoured them [the nations]" (Revelation xx, 9).

There are, then, two elements in the Revelation apocalypse which accord with the final apocalypse of Book XII: the first particular resurrection of the saints and, through special Miltonic interpretation, the devouring by fire of Satan. As in *De Doctrina* this first resurrection is followed by a second general resurrection and Satan's being "overthrown by fire" does not preclude his being "condemned to everlasting punishment," it might be argued that Milton has simply omitted mention of these other understood events in the Revelation eschatology and is thus perfectly orthodox in *Paradise Lost*. But the omission is consistently maintained throughout the epic, and the resonances remain.

The last mention of Satan is his dissolution, and when Eve falls to his temptation of godhead, she also becomes "to Death devote." In turning back to the godly path, Adam and Eve are promised a second life; but no such promise is mentioned for the wicked, for whom the "final remedy" of death seems permanent, and this "remedy" provided against the deplorable alternative "to eternize woe" is one announced by no less an authoritative figure than God.

The eschatology of *De Doctrina* is developed with great speed, and the unresolved contradictions in this brief account would seem to indicate that Milton gave little attention to his presentation of the orthodox position on eternal torment. In contrast to this, each eschatological reference in *Paradise Lost* is composed with the utmost care to diction and syntactical construction; and the careful use of ambiguity and omission seems calculated as part of a consistent strategy of double meaning, the heresy hidden behind an appearance of orthodoxy. Even within this section of *De Doctrina* there is evidence of Milton's primary allegiance to the eschatology covertly expressed in his epic; for his forced interpretation of Revelation xx, 9, to include Satan in the conflagration which devours the enemies of God is required not by the eschatology of *De Doctrina* but by that of *Paradise Lost*. And there are other hints in *De Doctrina*, as we shall later see.

But if Milton largely suppressed his apparent disbelief in eternal torment in his treatise, there were other heretical positions, less socially dangerous, which he supported at length, and his statement in the preface to *De Doctrina* regarding the sources of these heresies would seem to apply as well to his heretical eschatology:

For my own part, I adhere to the Holy Scriptures alone; I follow no other heresy or sect. I had not even read any of the works of heretics, so called, when the mistakes of those who are reckoned for orthodox, and their incautious handling of Scripture, first taught me to agree with their opponents whenever those opponents agreed with Scripture. If this be heresy, I confess with St. Paul, Acts. xxiv. 14. "that after the way which they call heresy, so worship I the God of my fathers, believing all things which are written in the law and the prophets"; to which I add, whatever is written in the New Testament. (CM, XIV, p. 15)

Milton here admits that, though he does not "follow" any heresy or sect, he was led to the reading of heretical works by the ineptness with which they were refuted by the orthodox and had come to "agree" with such so-called heretics when his own analysis of Scripture confirmed their conclusions. I have already indicated some of the scriptural evidence Milton might have used in support of his heretical eschatology but have now to investigate the heretical sect and works which openly avowed this position and with whose scriptural exegesis Milton had come to agree.

This sect was that which has become known as the Socinians, a Polish Anabaptist group with Italian Anabaptist antecedents and members, the most prominent of the latter being Faustus Socinus, who stamped the sect with his theology and name. The Italian Anabaptist movement has been traced to the leadership of Camillo Renato,[26] a Sicilian scholar who escaped from imminent danger in Italy to settle in southern Switzerland and who, in the 1540s, held the position "that the soul of man is by nature mortal, and dies with the body, to be raised at the last day in another form, though the souls of the wicked will perish."[27] Though this was not the most important aspect of his theology, it provides the first clear evidence in the Renaissance of the position with which we are concerned. The influence of this teaching was felt in a most important Anabaptist council held in Venice in 1550.[28] It was attended by about sixty delegates from Italy and Switzerland. The sessions lasted for forty days, and ten points of doctrine were agreed upon, among which were the following four:

> The wicked do not rise at the last day, but only the elect, whose head is Christ.
> There is no hell but the grave.
> When the elect die, they sleep until the judgment day, when all will be raised.
> The souls of the wicked perish with the body, as do all other animals.[29]

With the exception of the death of Satan, whose very existence is denied along with that of the angels in two of the other ten points, these four points of Anabaptist doctrine sum up what I have deduced to be the eschatology of *Paradise Lost*: the exclusive resurrection of the elect at the Day of Judgment and the simple mortality of the wicked. There might be some question as to Milton's views on the interim sleep of the elect. In *De Doctrina* Milton states: "the lifeless body does not sleep, unless inanimate matter can b℉ aid to sleep" (CM, XV, p. 233), elsewhere referring to "the sleep of death" (CM,

XV, p. 235). In *Paradise Lost*, however, the "temporal death" (XII, 433) of the redeemed is explicitly defined as "a death like sleep, / A gentle wafting to immortal Life" (XII, 434–35), and this would seem to be the meaning of the few additional references to the waking of the just from "sleep" (III, 329). Since the mortalism of the treatise and the apparent psychopannychism of the epic are equally heretical, the contradiction between these works on the interim condition of the redeemed would seem to indicate some uncertainty in Milton's mind on this doctrine, unless it be argued that the "death like sleep" of the epic is to be construed simply as a manner of speaking by which "inanimate matter can be said to sleep." In both works, however, he employs at least the terminology of interim sleep. Milton would have been in essential agreement, then, with all four points of doctrine arrived at by the 1550 Venice council of Anabaptists.

Within a few years of this council the Inquisition succeeded in crushing the Anabaptist movement in Italy,[30] and the most notable of those who escaped moved first to Switzerland and then to Poland,[31] which, as a result of the Diet of 1555, enjoyed the greatest religious liberty to be found anywhere in Europe.[32] These Italian Anabaptists became part of the native Anabaptist movement in Poland,[33] and to them, in the following generation, came Faustus Socinus, whose thought had been influenced by that of his uncle, Laelius Socinus,[34] who, in turn, had been directly influenced by Camillo Renato.[35] In addition to the strong personal and doctrinal leadership of Socinus, what most distinguished the Socinians from other Anabaptist sects was the intellectual eminence of the university and press they established at Rakow. Socinian scholars and books of the highest order circulated widely through Europe to make their doctrines the most discussed and influential, though constantly refuted, of any heretical sect of their time.[36]

A famous refutation, which summarized Socinus' *De Officio hominis Christiani* and which Milton may well have known, was Cloppenburg's *Compendiolum Socinianismi Confutatum* (1652). D. P. Walker, in his valuable study of Socinian eschatology, presents the relevant portion of Cloppenburg's summary of Socinus' position:

The wicked will not resurrect. After the Last Judgment the wicked then alive, together with Satan and his angels, will be thrown into eternal fire, which will wholly consume them. Scriptural support is sought in passages such as

I Thessalonians IV, 14; I Corinthians XV, 23; John VI, 39-47; Luke XX, 35, where the resurrection is spoken of as if it were a privilege of the faithful, and of course in Revelations XX, 14. . . . The faithful sleep, or are virtually non-existent, until the Last Day. There will be no resurrection of the flesh, but they will be given celestial bodies like angels.[37]

Though agreeing with the Venice council in denying resurrection to the wicked, Socinus differs from the earlier confession in admitting the reality of Satan and the fallen angels who, together with the wicked then alive, will be wholly consumed in an eternal fire whose effects are temporally limited. Walker does not indicate Socinus' use of Jude in the informative list of supporting scriptural passages for this doctrine, but it is clearly implied in Socinus' interpretation of the "eternal fire" which wholly consumes the fallen angels. Whether Milton derived the scriptural support for his eschatology in *Paradise Lost* from Socinus or arrived at it independently, his doctrinal agreement with Socinus up to this point is exact. Milton would even seem to reflect Socinus' equivocation about the interim sleep of the faithful.

But Socinus' doctrine of resurrection in celestial bodies rather than in the flesh presents something of a problem. In *Paradise Lost* there is no mention whatever concerning the nature of the resurrection body, while in *De Doctrina* the evidence is confusing. In his first discussion of resurrection, Milton follows the reference to Job xix, 26-27, on fleshly resurrection with 1 Corinthians xv, 53, without indicating its clear association with the spiritual body of 1 Corinthians xv, 44, and concludes: "Otherwise we should not be conformed to Christ, who entered into glory with that identical body of flesh and blood, wherewith he had died and risen again" (CM, XVI, p. 353). The argument of conformity to Christ is particularly interesting with regard to another aspect of Milton's eschatology, the exclusive resurrection of the just. Socinus' Pauline references in support of such exclusive resurrection contain Paul's conception of resurrection in conformity to Christ. That these Pauline references had long been used in support of objections to universal resurrection is indicated by the third of five objections to resurrection of the wicked as well as the good which Aquinas states before undertaking its refutation:

Further, by the resurrection men are conformed to Christ rising again; wherefore the Apostle argues (I Cor. xv. 12, *seqq.*) that if Christ rose again, we also shall rise again. Now those alone should be conformed to Christ rising again who have borne His image, and this belongs to the good alone. Therefore they alone shall rise again.[38]

This is, then, a standard argument for exclusive resurrection, and Milton's discussion of the necessity of being "conformed to Christ" in the Resurrection would seem to indicate a hidden assent to this heretical doctrine within De Doctrina itself. As the argument of conformity to Christ was directed to the ethical nature of the resurrected rather than to the form of the resurrection body, the fleshly resurrection of Christ, assented to in Socinian doctrine,[39] need not imply man's resurrection in the flesh and did imply the exclusive resurrection of the good.

Though a surface reading of Milton's first discussion of resurrection does seem to assert resurrection in the flesh, in his second discussion (CM, XVI, p. 377), he quotes 1 Corinthians xv, 44, "it is sown a natural body, it is raised a spiritual body," at the end of a citation of 1 Corinthians xv, 42–43, and makes no reference to resurrection in the flesh. Since he does not resolve the apparent contradiction in the treatise and is noncommittal in the epic, we can conclude either that he was uncertain in his own mind, as may have been the case with his conception of interim sleep, or that he was being secretive about his agreement with Socinus on this point. The latter possibility is supported by Raphael's suggestion to Adam that, with proper obedience, "perhaps / Your bodies may at last turn all to spirit" (PL V, 496-97). There is, then, no clear disagreement between Socinus' eschatology and that of Paradise Lost and hidden suggestions as to the conformity of De Doctrina with both.

In the section of Smaltius' account of the Rakow Colloquy of 1601 which appears to have been dictated by Socinus,[40] the argument for the destruction of the wicked begins with an exposition of mortalism similar to that in De Doctrina,[41] from which state the faithful alone will be resurrected, and then disputes the supposed absurdity of denying eternal torment to the wicked:

But it should be considered much more absurd if the wicked were given immortality, which is a most special gift and blessing of God. Moreover, it seems to involve extreme injustice if God gave man, whom He created mortal by nature, immortality merely in order that he should be eternally tormented.[42]

The first argument of the denial of an immortality of torment as a deprivation for the wicked is similar to the position Milton has Belial express, while the second argument of the injustice of making torment eternal is reflected in the speeches of Adam and God.

Milton's close study of Smaltius' writings is indicated by the exact parallels which George Newton Conklin has drawn between Smaltius and *De Doctrina* in three instances of textual exegesis.[43] In addition, Conklin notes exact parallels between Milton's exegesis and that of Völkel,[44] who with Smaltius and Moscorovius composed the influential *Racovian Catechism*, as well as with Socinus himself.[45] In the latter passage, Milton refers to his exegetical sources as "interpreters of more sagacity" (CM, XIV, p. 129), and his whole discussion of those who "had shown themselves unworthy of everlasting life" (CM, XIV, 129) is clearly Socinian and again suggests Milton's hidden assent to Socinian eschatology within *De Doctrina*. Conklin further states: "Of all the religious groups of the period, the Socinians through their exegesis come closest to the specific heresies of Milton. . . . In rational criticism of Scripture, hermeneutics, sectarian tolerance, antitrinitarianism, materialism, and mortalism, the Socinians are not far from Milton."[46] Conklin does not discuss Milton's eschatology, but I believe we can now add this item to the Socinian heresies listed by Conklin for which there are Miltonic parallels.

At what point Milton first became acquainted with Socinian ideas cannot be clearly determined, though the spread of such ideas in England was great enough by 1640 to cause Archbishop Laud to issue a special Canon against "the damnable and cursed Heresie of Socinianism."[47] Milton's introduction to Socinian ideas and contacts may well have been furthered through Grotius, whom he visited in Paris in 1638. Grotius had met and been for some years in correspondence with the eminent Socinian scholar Martin Ruar, from whom he received many Socinian books at his request, and was then the center of a circle of Socinian Polish students in Paris.[48] By 1647, at any rate, Milton can definitely be associated with Socinian thought, for there is evidence that he owned and annotated a copy of Paul Best's *Mysteries Discovered* (London, 1647), the first English book to be burned for Socinianism.[49] It has been shown, moreover, that Milton may have been responsible for the printing of a Latin edition of the *Racovian Catechism* by William Duggard's London Press in 1650 and that he was examined by Parliament for his connection with this publication.[50] The high degree of religious tolerance in England during the Commonwealth led to a further growth of Socinian influence;[51] and Walker notes two examples in which the annihilation of the wicked is openly affirmed: John Biddle's *Twofold Catechism* (London, 1654) and Samuel Richardson's *A Discourse of the Torments of Hell. The foundation and pillars thereof discovered, searched, shaken and removed* (London, 1658).[52] Milton would certainly have been aware of these publications and the international currents of Socinian thought which had generated them, as he would probably have been aware of the latent Socinianism in the eschatology of the more significant mortalist writers Richard Overton and Thomas Hobbes.

The first major expression of mortalism in England, Overton's *Mans Mortallitie* (Amsterdam [London], 1643), states in its long title "*That at the Resurrection Is the Beginning of Our Immortallity, and Then Actuall Condemnation, and Salvation and Not Before*" and undertakes to discover "*the Multitude of Blasphemies, and Absurdities That Arise From the Fancie of the Soule.*" In this latter endeavor Overton includes "this Absurditie, that the *Soules* of the Damned shall not perish, but stand as well as the *Stative Angels*"[53] and "the most grand and blasphemous *Heresies* that are in the world, the *Mysterie of Iniquity* and Kingdome of Antichrist."[54] Though such "Absurdities" might be interpreted as applying only to the period before resurrection, since Overton believes "*Hell* and *Damnation* not yet,"[55] when he comes to discuss the place of hell he reveals his strong adherence to a Socinian-like doctrine of final dissolution for the wicked: "There is yet an other Opinion of the place of Hell, which is the best that ever I heard or read of, and that is (according to *Archers* judgment) the Earth reduced to its *prima materia* or *created matter*, which he saith cannot be consumed, and there shall the Damned be cast: But least I should dive further in the inquisition of the place then my Commission will reach, Ile leave it to the woefull experience of the *damned* at the day of Judgment."[56] As Overton nowhere argues that the condemnation of reprobates at the day of judgment is to involve either temporary or eternal torment, his present assertion, however tentatively expressed, clearly reveals his preferred analysis of the nature of "Condemnation in Hell,"[57] an analysis that approximates Milton's equivocating God on the place of punishment prepared for disobedient angels. Overton further asserts "that at the day of Judgment both Divels and Reprobate together shall be cast into the *Lake of Fire*,"[58] and though Milton would limit the number of those reprobates to those then living while Overton would resurrect the reprobate dead for this purpose, with this important exception the eschatology of Overton and of Milton in *Paradise Lost* is virtually identical.

The most significant philosophical work of its day, Hobbes' *Leviathan* (London, 1651), expresses the similar beliefs "that Christ's Passion is a discharge of sin to all that believe on him; and by consequence, a restitution of eternal life to all the faithful, and to them only,"[59] and "that that which is thus said concerning hell fire, is spoken metaphorically."[60] In chapters 38 and 44 of *Leviathan*, Hobbes develops a curious eschatology in which, after the general Resurrection, the good are to enjoy eternal life with Christ on earth while the wicked are to suffer punishment on earth during a second mortal existence in which they will breed an everlasting race of mortals individually subject to the second death of total extinction. But in *An Answer to Bishop Bramhall*, Hobbes claims that he had presented the resurrection of the wicked and their breeding of a new mortal race as simply a possibility, continuing: "But that they shall do so, is no assertion of mine. His Lordship knew I held, that after the resurrection there shall be at all no wicked men; but the elect (all that are, have been, and hereafter shall be) shall live on earth. But St. Peter (2 Epist. iii. 13) says, there shall then be *a new heaven and a new earth*."[61] With this retraction of his novel eschatology, Hobbes makes the latent Socinianism of *Leviathan* explicit, and his final assertion of belief in the particular resurrection of the elect was one with which the Milton of *Paradise Lost* would have wholly agreed.[62]

But if other Englishmen of Milton's day were openly espousing the Socinian position on the utter destruction of the wicked, Milton showed more caution in expressing his support of such a socially dangerous doctrine. In doing this, however, he was following the lead of the Socinians themselves. As Walker observes:

The Socinians were extremely cautious and secretive about their belief in the annihilation of the wicked. In the account of the Rakow Colloquy of 1601 the section expounding the annihilation of the wicked and the resurrection of only the just ends with this caution:

but this matter must be dealt with cautiously; indeed even Christ Himself and the Apostles adapted themselves to the understanding of the people, as the parable of Dives and Lazarus shows. It was not then the time to upset the Jews, as even now it is not the time, although now and then Christ spoke in such a way that it is quite evident that He is going to raise up only the faithful (John VI, 39-40). And Paul openly stated that he was striving to attain resurrection; in this way something may at times be said to give men a hint of this matter, until at length the age is ripe.[63]

The perfect example of such Socinian caution is the famous *Racovian Catechism* which nowhere discusses the fate of the wicked and yet hints of the matter in its opening statement: "The Christian Religion is the way of attaining eternall life, discovered by God."[64] A similar hint may even be discerned in the opening statement of *De Doctrina* which, indeed, seems to have been modeled upon this first profession of the *Racovian Catechism:* "The Christian Doctrine is that DIVINE REVELATION disclosed in various ages by CHRIST . . . for the promotion of the glory of God, and the salvation of mankind" (CM, XIV, p. 17). Though the eschatology of *De Doctrina*, despite various hints of exclusive resurrection, is explicitly orthodox, the silence of the *Racovian Catechism* on this matter has led most modern students of Socinianism to overlook this vital element of Socinian belief. Thus Earl Morse Wilbur's massive study of Socinianism betrays no awareness of Socinus' belief in the annihilation of the wicked and exclusive resurrection of the just or of the association of such a belief with that of the Italian Anabaptists.[65] Scholarship owes a great debt to Walker for his investigation of this aspect of Socinianism, for the textual evidence he has presented which fully demonstrates Socinus' personal belief in this regard, and for his analysis of the secretive practices by which this doctrine was generally concealed. Walker's discussion of such secretive practices explains the eschatological contradictions between *De Doctrina* and *Paradise Lost*, as well as the hidden form of this heresy in the latter:

Nearly all discussions of hell until well into the 18th century are veiled by a mist of secrecy and dishonesty.

The peculiar dangers attached to any discussion of the eternity of hell were such that they produced a theory of double truth: there is a private, esoteric doctrine, which must be confined to a few intellectuals, because its effect on the mass of people will be morally and socially disastrous, and a public, exoteric doctrine, which these same intellectuals must preach, although they do not believe it. . . . Poets and religious writers who concealed their meaning in symbols, fables and allegories could not be accused.[66]

Though Walker is unaware of Milton's conformity either with the Socinian position on hell or the practice of the double truth, Milton is clearly the greatest poet who practiced such concealment of this heretical doctrine. Walker's study of seventeenth-century Socinian eschatology enables us to fit the eschatology of *Paradise Lost* into the religious currents of Milton's day. If Saurat is, as I believe, correct in stating that Milton "expressed only ideas which were current before him, and around him in certain circles. . . . his originality lies in selection and not in invention,"[67] then the exact parallels between Socinian eschatology and that of *Paradise Lost* provide the greatest support for the validity of the critical analysis by which I was able to deduce the existence of such a heresy in Milton's epic.

In view of the "remarkable comparisons"[68] between the positions of Milton and Socinianism, it is hard not to apply the label of Socinian to him despite his disclaimer of following no heresy or sect. Though Milton sees a large distinction between following and agreeing with the doctrines of another man and his adherents, his independent confirmation of Socinian doctrines from Scripture is no more than would be expected of any theological scholar equipped as fully as Milton undoubtedly was to arrive at such independent agreement. Indeed, his adherence "to the Holy Scriptures alone" is itself a mark of Socinian theological method.[69]

And yet in one important respect his disclaimer may be valid: the divergent doctrines of Milton and Socinus on the nature of Christ. It is hardly credible that Milton would have expressed his heretical Arian views on the Son[70] so explicitly in *De Doctrina* and portrayed the Son of *Paradise Lost* in a manner so consistent with the treatise if, in fact, he secretly subscribed to the different Socinian heresy that Christ "is a true man by nature" though "conceived of the Holy Spirit."[71] Though the later Christ of *Paradise Regained* can support a consistent Socinian reading, which might suggest that Milton altered his Christology in final conformity with Socinus,[72] at the time he composed his treatise and epic Milton could claim that he did not "follow" Socinianism in the very doctrine which most distinguished it from the other sects of his day.[73] Nonetheless, if we accept Wilbur's view that "the controlling interest in Socinus's teaching is the attainment of eternal life,"[74] then the main thrust of Milton's theological concern may still be considered Socinian. Though church doctrine attached greater importance to Christology than to eschatology,[75] Milton's pervasive chiliasm invested his eschatology with great significance, and his views on this subject were unquestionably Socinian.

He revealed his essential agreement with Socinian eschatology in *Paradise Lost*,[76] but only in a form veiled "As when the Sun new ris'n / Looks through the Horizontal misty Air / Shorn of his Beams" (I, 594–96). It has been the attempt of this study to pierce the mist of ambiguity which almost obscures the heretical eschatology of *Paradise Lost*, to discover the sources and illuminate the implications of a vision of last things which contrasts the final reward to the just of eternal life with the judgment of wicked men and angels to death, a contrast which informs the ethical discriminations between good and evil throughout the epic and explains both the heroic characterization and final dissolution of Satan.

St. John's University

NOTES

1. *The Works of John Milton*, ed. Frank Allen Patterson et al. (New York, 1933), vol. XVI, pp. 363, 369, 371, and 373. Hereafter cited as CM.

2. See B. Rajan, *"Paradise Lost" and the Seventeenth-Century Reader* (1947; Ann Arbor, 1967), pp. 24–27, for an analysis of *Paradise Lost* which shows the same Miltonic strategy in the presentation of those heresies which do appear in *De Doctrina*.

3. See D. P. Walker, *The Decline of Hell: Seventeenth-Century Discussions of Eternal Torment* (Chicago, 1964), pp. 3–8, 76–78.

4. *John Milton: Complete Poems and Major Prose*, ed. Merritt Y. Hughes (New York, 1957). All further book and line references for *Paradise Lost* are to this edition as are the references in note 76.

5. See Roland Mushat Frye, *God, Man, and Satan* (Princeton, 1960), pp. 39–41, on Calvin's metaphorical view of hell and its influence in the Reformation. In the concluding pages of his discussion of *Paradise Lost*, Frye shows that "With the Final Judgment . . . the Son totally destroys evil" (p. 88); but though he is the only critic who has hitherto had such a perception of the meaning of the final eschatological passages, he does not recognize the heretical implications of his discerning analysis or the conflict it poses to his earlier analysis of hell (see pp. 40–41, 50).

6. For a similar identification of belief in the immortality of the soul with Satanic doctrine, see the early mortalist polemic of Martin Luther, "Defense and Explanation of All the Articles of Dr. Martin Luther Which Were Unjustly Condemned by the Roman Bull," in *Luther's Works*, ed. Jaroslav Pelikan and Helmut T. Lehmann, 55 vols. (St. Louis and Philadelphia, 1955–), vol. XXXII, pp. 77–78.

7. *Milton and the Renaissance Hero* (Oxford, 1967), p. 171.

8. William Blake, *The Marriage of Heaven and Hell,* in *The Complete Poetry and Selected Prose of John Donne & The Complete Poetry of William Blake,* ed. John Hayward and Geoffrey Keynes (New York, 1946), p. 652.

9. C. S. Lewis, *A Preface to "Paradise Lost"* (1942; New York, 1961), p. 97.

10. Steadman, *Milton and the Renaissance Hero,* p. vii.

11. *Milton, Man and Thinker* (New York, 1935), pp. 254–58.

12. R. H. Charles, in his monumental two-volume edition of *The Apocrypha and Pseudepigrapha of the Old Testament in English* (Oxford, 1913), gives the following chapters of the Book of Enoch as the portion preserved in the Syncellus fragments, which do not themselves note chapter and verse: "vi–ix.4; viii.4–x.14; xv.8–xvi.1 and another" (vol. II, p. 184). Grant McColley, in "The Book of Enoch and *Paradise Lost,*" *Harvard Theological Review,* XXXI (1938), 21–39, suggests that Charles' unspecified verse may be lxxii, 7 (pp. 36–37), but this comes much later than the section concerning the giants. The Charles translation and edition is used for all quotations from the Book of Enoch (vol. II, pp. 189–201).

13. Ibid., vol. II, pp. 165–66. See also Harris Francis Fletcher, *Milton's Rabbinical Readings* (1930; New York, 1967), p. 286, on the availability of Book of Enoch manuscripts. In his analysis of the Enoch material, however, Fletcher has unaccountably confused the much later version of the Enoch legend known as 3 Enoch with the portion of the Book of Enoch (1 Enoch) preserved by Syncellus (see pp. 272, 278), which is why McColley was "unable to verify" (p. 31) the Fletcher reference on p. 272.

14. Pp. 38–39.

15. Charles, *Apocrypha and Pseudepigrapha,* vol. II, p. 421.

16. Ibid., vol. II, pp. 180, 412.

17. See also Charles Cutler Torrey, *The Apocryphal Literature* (New Haven, 1953), p. 19.

18. Milton interprets many scriptural references translated by "for ever and ever," "everlasting," and of "no end" as signifying the "in saeculum saeculi" of Hebrews i, 8, translated in CM as "for ages of ages" (XVI, pp. 366–67), and Walker shows the currency of this translation of "everlasting" among seventeenth-century disbelievers in eternal torment; see p. 143 *et passim.*

19. My conclusions support and parallel those of McColley with regard to the correspondences between *Paradise Lost* and the Book of Enoch not contained in the Syncellus fragments, particularly with regard to Enoch's reprimanding of the giants and the location of hell (see "Book of Enoch," p. 38). The Book of Enoch contains two parallel passages on the final fate of the fallen angels: xix, 1, "in which they shall be judged till they are made an end of" (which I quoted); and xxi, 1, "This place is the prison of the angels, and here they will be imprisoned for ever" (quoted by McColley, p. 34). Though these contradictory verses both appear in the Book of Enoch, I suggest that it was the verse predicting the annihilation of the fallen angels, not hitherto recognized in modern scholarship, which influenced both Jude and Milton, since both betray "annihilationist" views.

20. See also Luke xx, 35–36, xxi, 16, 18, 36, for similar indications of Luke's conception of resurrection as the exclusive reward of the just.

21. D. S. Russell (*The method & message of Jewish Apocalyptic* [Philadelphia, 1964], pp. 368–71) views this Isaiah verse as the beginning of an apocalyptic belief in the exclusive resurrection of the righteous which reaches full development in such pseudepigraphal writings as the Psalms of Solomon and portions of the Book of Enoch. See also Joseph Bonsirven, S. J., *Palestinian Judaism in the Time of Jesus Christ* (New

York, 1964), pp. 227–51, for evidence of belief in the exclusive resurrection of the righteous in pseudepigraphal and rabbinical writings; and Charles, who states that the exclusive resurrection of "righteous Israelites . . . is the received Talmudic view" (Apocrypha and Pseudepigrapha, vol. II, p. 218).

22. George Eldon Ladd, in A Commentary on the Revelation of John (Grand Rapids, 1972), observes: "Paul nowhere in his epistles speaks of the resurrection of unbelievers" (p. 268). See 1 Thessalonians iv, 14–17; 1 Corinthians xv, 22–23; Romans vi, 22–23; Philippians iii, 8–11, 18–19. These references, which range from the earliest to the latest of the genuine Pauline Epistles, show a consistent understanding that resurrection to eternal life is the exclusive gift of God to those who believe in Christ, and have thus been redeemed from sin, and that the enemies of this belief will earn the wages of sin, death. The clearest proof that resurrection is intended only for the faithful is Paul's personal wish to "attain unto the resurrection of the dead" (Philippians iii, 11). From these earliest Christian documents to the latest documents of the New Testament, 2 Peter and Jude, there is no explicit reference in any of the canonical Epistles to the resurrection of the wicked or to eternal torment.

23. Though the discovery of the manuscript in 1873 precludes Milton's knowledge of the Didache, this "teaching" provides unequivocal proof that belief in the exclusive resurrection of the righteous was affirmed by a significant portion of the early Christian church. Written in Alexandria sometime prior to 150 A.D., it teaches "the rising of the dead—not of all the dead, but as it says, the Lord will come, and with him all his holy ones" (in Early Christian Writings: The Apostolic Fathers, trans. Maxwell Staniforth [Baltimore, 1968], p. 235).

24. One instance in which Milton does seem to play with his conception of the afterlife is the Limbo of Vanity section, which cannot be fitted into the eschatology of either Paradise Lost or De Doctrina. Perhaps it was included to reinforce the deterrent warnings against suicide, for to this limbo Milton briefly consigns all forms of life-denying ideologies from the heroic and neo-Platonic to Catholic hermits and friars. When, in what form, and for how long they are there consigned Milton does not specify, except to say that they, "Dissolv'd on Earth, fleet hither, and in vain, / Till final dissolution" (III, 457–58). Only their "final dissolution" is consistent with the eschatology of Paradise Lost.

25. The two separate resurrections in the Revelation text, first of the just alone and then of all the dead, might be viewed as an attempt by its author to synthesize these two different eschatologies which had developed during the intertestimental period and which would seem, on the basis of the evidence presented in notes 21–23, to have continued their separate lines of development during the early period of Christianity.

26. See Earl Morse Wilbur, A History of Unitarianism: Socinianism and its Antecedents (Cambridge, Mass., 1945), p. 104.

27. Ibid., p. 105. See also George Huntston Williams, The Radical Reformation (Philadelphia, 1962), pp. 24, 555–56.

28. See Wilbur, History of Unitarianism, p. 105, and Williams, Radical Reformation, p. 562.

29. Wilbur, History of Unitarianism, p. 85. Wilbur here lists all ten points of doctrine upon which this Anabaptist council agreed.

30. See Wilbur, History of Unitarianism, pp. 86–87, and Williams, Radical Reformation, pp. 563–64. Evidence for the 1550 Anabaptist council at Venice comes from the records of the Inquisition (see Wilbur, p. 84).

31. See Wilbur, *History of Unitarianism*, p. 282.

32. Ibid., pp. 275–76, 282, 393.

33. Ibid., p. 301.

34. Ibid., p. 247. See also Williams, *Radical Reformation*, pp. 631, 752.

35. See Wilbur, *History of Unitarianism*, p. 105, and Williams, *Radical Reformation*, pp. 569, 739.

36. See Wilbur, *History of Unitarianism*, pp. 556–57.

37. Walker, *Decline of Hell*, pp. 83–84.

38. *The "Summa Theologica" of St. Thomas Aquinas*, Third Part (Supplement), Q. 75, Art. 2, trans. Fathers of the English Dominican Province (London, 1920), vol. XX, p. 122.

39. See Wilbur, *History of Unitarianism*, p. 415.

40. See Walker, *Decline of Hell*, pp. 81–82.

41. "The dead are reduced to nothing: the body disappears, the spirit returns to Him who gave it, that is God. The soul feels neither pleasure nor pain. And thus, since the form of their life and their life has perished, they are all wholly non-existent" (Walker, *Decline of Hell*, p. 81). This exactly parallels and may well be the source of Milton's exegesis of Ecclesiastes xii, 7, in *De Doctrina* (CM, XV, pp. 237, 239).

42. Walker, *Decline of Hell*, p. 81.

43. *Biblical Criticism and Heresy in Milton* (1949; New York, 1972), pp. 81–83, 122. The reference on p. 122 is to another source of Smaltius' exegesis of Ecclesiastes xii, 7, to which I refer in note 41.

44. Ibid., p. 73.

45. Ibid., pp. 43–44.

46. *Biblical Criticism*, pp. 37, 87. Two of the items in Conklin's list require some comment. As I shall show in my conclusion, Milton's antitrinitarianism is not as close to that of the Socinians as Conklin seems to suggest. Conversely, Conklin argues that Milton is unique in asserting "the mortality of the soul (the whole man) rather than the sleep of the soul" (*Biblical Criticism*, p. 83) and differs in this from Smaltius and the Socinians; but his own reference to Smaltius' exegesis of Ecclesiastes xii, 7 (see note 43), as my quotation of it in note 41 should show, proves the invalidity of this argument. Moreover, as I have earlier shown, both Milton and Socinus hedge on the subject of soul sleep.

47. H. John McLachlan, *Socinianism in Seventeenth-Century England* (Oxford, 1951), p. 41.

48. See Wilbur, *History of Unitarianism*, pp. 527, 549.

49. See McLachlan, *Socinianism*, pp. 160–62.

50. Ibid., pp. 189–90.

51. See Walker, *Decline of Hell*, p. 104, and McLachlan, *Socinianism*, pp. 165, 198, 210.

52. See Walker, *Decline of Hell*, p. 93. For Milton's knowledge of Biddle, see H. McLachlan, *The Religious Opinions of Milton, Locke and Newton* (1941; New York, 1972), pp. 50–51.

53. R. O. [Richard Overton], *Mans Mortallitie* (Amsterdam, 1643), p. 47.

54. Ibid., p. 55.

55. Ibid., p. 26.

56. Ibid., p. 28.

57. Ibid., p. 5.

58. Ibid., p. 26.

59. Thomas Hobbes, *Leviathan*, ed. Michael Oakeshott (Oxford, 1960), p. 404.

60. Ibid., p. 298.

61. Thomas Hobbes, *An Answer to Bishop Bramhall's Book, called "The Catching of the Leviathan,"* in *The English Works of Thomas Hobbes*, ed. Sir William Molesworth (London, 1840), vol. IV, p. 359.

62. As Milton did not adopt any of the more idiosyncratic elements in the eschatologies of Hobbes and Overton but agreed with their positions only when they approximated prior Socinian analysis, the assertions of Overton and Hobbes on the ultimate fate of the wicked should probably be viewed as supportive analogues rather than sources of Milton's strictly Socinian eschatology, analogues which provide further evidence of the widespread dissemination and adaptation of Socinian eschatological beliefs at the time Milton composed *Paradise Lost*. Of these three major Interregnum mortalists, only Hobbes has been hitherto recognized as espousing the extinction of the wicked, for which see Walker, *Decline of Hell*, p. 51, and Norman T. Burns, *Christian Mortalism from Tyndale to Milton* (Cambridge, Mass., 1972), pp. 125, 186–87. Burns briefly notes the association of Hobbes' views in *Leviathan* (though not in *An Answer to Bishop Bramhall*) with the Anabaptist doctrine of particular resurrection as enunciated at the 1550 Venice council, a doctrine first and largely discussed only on p. 125 of his study. But he discounts other evidence for belief in the annihilation of the wicked suggested by his own evidence: the 1561 testimony of two members of the Family of Love (p. 61); the belief attributed to Samuel Gorton that he "taught a conditional immortality wholly dependent on the character of the individual" (p. 72); and the presence of the eighty-fourth heresy listed in Edward's *Gangraena* (1646) "That the souls of the faithful after death, do sleep till the day of judgement," a heresy which implies the doctrine of particular resurrection of the faithful—since it is only their souls which are said to sleep—and of which Edward specifically accused John Goodwin (p. 140). His conclusions—except in the case of Hobbes—are in essential accord with the earlier analysis of George Williamson, in "Milton and the Mortalist Heresy," *Seventeenth Century Contexts* (London, 1959), p. 162, that seventeenth-century mortalism appeared in only two forms, that of total annihilation or of universal resurrection (see Burns, pp. 13–18).

63. *Decline of Hell*, p. 76.

64. *The Racovian Catechisme* (Amsterledam, 1652), p. 1. This is the first English translation, and McLachlan provides impressive evidence that it was translated by Biddle and actually printed in London, these circumstances perhaps accounting for the curious misprinting of "Amsterledam" for "Amsterdam" (*Socinianism*, pp. 190–93).

65. McLachlan, similarly, though he mentions Biddle's denial of eternal torment in the *Twofold Catechism* (*Socinianism*, p. 201), nowhere indicates this to be a Socinian doctrine. Walker does connect this Socinian doctrine with the Venice Anabaptist council (*Decline of Hell*, pp. 73–74), and Williams shows the derivation of Socinus' eschatology from Camillo Renato (*Radical Reformation*, pp. 750–52). David Munroe Cory in an earlier work, *Faustus Socinus* (Boston, 1932), also recognized that for Socinus "immortality was the reward of right conduct" (p. 39).

66. *Decline of Hell*, pp. 5, 7.

67. *Milton, Man and Thinker*, pp. 247, 250.

68. Conklin, *Biblical Criticism*, p. 3.

69. See Wilbur, *History of Unitarianism*, p. 412, and Conklin, *Biblical Criticism*, pp. 37–38.

70. W. B. Hunter, in *Bright Essence: Studies in Milton's Theology* (Salt Lake City,

1971), suggests that "subordinationism" is a better term than Arian for Milton's position on the Son, since for Milton the Son was not created *ex nihilo* but *ex deo* (pp. 29–51 *passim*). It might be pointed out, however, that since for Milton all of the Creation is *ex deo* (*De Doctrina*, CM, XV, p. 26), the Son's creation from the substance of God does not accord the Son divine status, however subordinate, in and of itself. Milton's Christology parallels that of Servetus, which was considered to be Arian by the Calvinists (see Williams, *Radical Reformation*, pp. 610–11, 630).

71. *The Racovian Catechisme*, p. 27. For Socinus, man is saved not through the atonement of the Crucifixion but through the promise of the Resurrection for those who have followed the example of Christ's life (see Wilbur, *History of Unitarianism*, pp. 392, 413–14).

72. If this is so, it may have been Milton's reappraisal of the nature of salvation through Christ—of example rather than atonement—which led him to feel dissatisfied with his treatment of "Paradise Found" in his earlier work. See James Holly Hanford, *John Milton, Englishman* (New York, 1949), pp. 170–71, for the Ellwood anecdote. See also McLachlan, *Religious Opinions*, p. 18, for detection of Socinianism in *Paradise Regained* by T. Lindsey (1778) and S. T. Coleridge (1814).

73. The Socinian Samuel Crellius, who differed with Socinus' Christology, argued that "what distinguishes Socinianism" is "the erroneous view about our justification" (see note 71 and Wilbur, *History of Unitarianism*, p. 576).

74. *History of Unitarianism*, p. 412.

75. See S. G. F. Brandon, *The Judgment of the Dead* (New York, 1967), pp. 113–14.

76. Though my primary concern has been with the eschatology of *Paradise Lost*, I cannot close this study without noting evidence of Milton's disbelief in eternal torment extending back to his earliest poetry. *On the Morning of Christ's Nativity* (1629) contains Milton's first depiction of the Second Coming of Christ (125–50), at which time "Hell itself will pass away" (139). In *Comus* (1634) the final reduction of evil to a chaotic state is forcibly asserted: "But evil on itself shall back recoil, / And mix no more with goodness, when at last / Gather'd like scum, and settl'd to itself, / It shall be in eternal restless change, / Self-fed and self-consum'd; if this fail, / The pillar'd firmament is rott'nness, / And Earth's base built on stubble" (593–99). And in *Lycidas* (1637) the extended description of the eternal felicity of the good is contrasted with the total ambiguity of "that two-handed engine at the door" (130) which symbolizes the retribution awaiting the wicked. In *The Doctrine and Discipline of Divorce* (1643) Milton contrasts the various positions on hell, giving fullest emphasis to its identification with chaos, with the classical rejection of such punishment, which he seems here to favor: "To banish for ever into a locall hell, whether in the aire or in the center, or in that uttermost and bottomlesse gulph of *Chaos*, deeper from holy blisse then the worlds diameter multiply'd, they thought had not a punishing so proper and proportionat for God to inflict, as to punish sinne with sinne" (CM, III, 2, p. 442). As early as his Cambridge days and continuing consistently through his early poetry and into his prose writings, Milton would seem, then, to have rejected the doctrine of eternal torment. Whether this indicates that Milton had been introduced to Socinian thought while at Cambridge or that there were other classical sources for his original conviction in this matter which might have predisposed him to later agreement with Socinian eschatology, by the time he wrote *Paradise Lost* he was fully conversant with Socinian writings and the fuller development of his heretical eschatology in his epic exactly parallels and would appear to have been influenced by such works.

THE RHETOR AS CREATOR
IN *PARADISE LOST*

John T. Shawcross

In *Paradise Lost* Milton simulates the role of the creator by certain rhetorical aims and techniques: Milton's creation is to aid the replenishment of heaven with true, faithful, and loving spirits by asserting God's great love seen in his eternal providence and by countering the antiheroic element that sees God as unjust and tyrannic. The complexity of Milton's simulated creation of a world is seen in the poem's intricate structures; its philosophical technique is sustained by the literary device of opposites, each of which moves from one extreme to the other and which together create the vagueness of distinction between them which is characteristic of man's thought. His world, like God's, is ever changing: the techniques to emphasize this are the compounding of time, the "harassing" of the reader, the manipulation of language, the structure of the poem, alterations in style. But over all is a persistent threat of truth. The contrast between the first (in man's mind) and the second (in God's mind) is seen in Satan, who is a Steppenwolf wishing to become an Everyman. The world's problems owe much to Everyman's (Adam and Eve's) becoming Steppenwolf. Milton's thesis is: experience is fulfilled in living, not after death, if we accept life as it is.

A N UNDERLYING belief that I have about literature, and thus about *Paradise Lost*, is that it is a consciously contrived product of an author's mind, attitude, talents, planning, and execution. It deplores the attitude that seems to exist among some scholars that nothing much happens between the thought or emotion of the author and its presentation as art form. Obvious though this underlying belief seems to be, to me, a lack of realization of the full significance of it lies at the base of the antagonism one finds in criticism (particularly in Miltonic criticism) toward structural, numerological, mythic, and psychological studies.

The author is a creator and Milton's association of himself with the archetypal Creator, God, has been presented elsewhere.[1] The poem we read is Milton's creation, a similitude of God's Creation; and because of its subject matter he functions as a surrogate of God for man to "repair the ruins of our first parents by regaining to know God aright." The function describes the teacher, the minister, the prophet-priest. In *The Reason of Church-Government* Milton had equated the writer and the minister: "These abilities, wheresoever they be found, are the inspired guift of God rarely bestow'd . . . and are of power beside the office of a pulpit, to imbreed and cherish in a great people the seeds of vertue, and publick civility. . . . Whether this may not be not only in Pulpits, but after another persuasive method, at set and solemn Paneguries, in Theaters, porches, or what other place, or way may win most upon the people to receiv at once both recreation, & instruction, let them in autority consult" (London, 1641, pp. 39–40). The imagery of the ear as the entrance of God's Word to his earthly ministry is a commonplace, and one might compare the mutilation of the "false" minister's ears as a symbol of his inability to communicate God's Word. *Paradise Lost* is the work of a Milton who still conceived his function in life as that for which he had been schooled; the true minister he had epitomized in 1627 as one of those "whom provident God himself has sent to you [England], / and who bring joyous messages from heaven, and who / teach the way which leads beyond the grave to the stars" (*Elegia quarta*, 92–94). His creation becomes the surrogate Word of God, and like God he has had to accommodate his message to the comprehension of his readers. It has not always been an obvious accommodation, but then God's Creation is not an easily graphed or formulated product either. Indeed the work of Sir Isaac Newton was not only to reduce God's Creation to laws and formulas, but also to reassert, for the people, the reality of the God who had created so complex a world.

Like God's, Milton's creation is complex, built on structural principles and numerical organization; it is unified by elements ("ideas" accommodated as words) that are capable of adaptation and agglomeration of meaning, of destructive misuse and catalysis; it is a range of all manner of absolutes and aggregates from any one extreme to its opposite. It *is* a similitude of God's Creation. The world of man created by God is presented as if through a kaleidoscope, yielding a sense of its substance and its essence. The poem depicts "actual" events of man's history and the implied action which everyone in his life will undergo; it renders the thoughts of the past and present and the potentials of the future. The accumulated knowledge of the world is delineated in the poem through simile and suggestion (thus keeping time perspectives intact), and one can read what he wants, changing as twists of the instrument refocus the constituent parts or the angle of vision. The twists may predicate man's hopes and fears or man's psychological state, but throughout, the presence of the creator of the bits of glass can be discerned—whether he is the God whom Milton is trying to portray aright or the poet who has constructed the instrument. The prophet (or true minister) sees the world beyond toward which he leads his community, pointing out the paths that will end there and the paths that will detour, retrace, or pervert. The poet renders the vision, or accommodates it, by whatever means he can. The aims of the divine *vates,* or prophet-poet, are those of minister of God and few have denied Milton that post in *Paradise Lost.*

Yet such didactic aims demand three important considerations: the specific aim or intention of the *vates,* the means of achieving that aim, and the human medium through which such intention will be channeled. It is, of course, impossible to state with exact coincidence what anyone's intention is under any particular set of circumstances. Not only can the observer not make such statement, but neither can the person himself. He can give what seems to him to be his intention— whether conscious or unconscious—from authorial statement, from pragmatic evidence, from reader response, and from inferred significa- tion through psychological symbolization and analysis. But the fact remains that an author does write with a conscious intention and at the same time out of his individual being which colors that conscious intention as well as the execution. The rather recent hue and cry against the intentional fallacy has done a disservice to literary criticism by making it reprobatory to talk of authorial intention. For intention does exist, and it is the literary critic's duty to try to determine the contexts of that intention. Inevitably such analysis places the critic in a complex of experience and knowledge, and his own psychological being. That

this is so can be seen, as example, in the world of humor. The basis
of humor is encased in the foregoing remarks, for the comic plays
upon what he believes to be his audience's experience and knowledge
(most obvious is the topical joke) and attitudes. The audience will
not recognize, say, an obscene joke unless they previously have understood the meanings and application of the language implied. But this
in turn says that the comic knew these meanings and this substance,
and he assumed at least that some of his audience did, too. A fit
audience is always sought by the public communicator; he will adapt
to his expected hearers or try to manipulate them (the "warm-up")
to become receptive. The poet is not different. Of course, there are
unconscious jokes, ones in which the speaker has not realized what
he has said. Sometimes he becomes aware of what he has said; sometimes he must be told. And sometimes these unconscious jokes—like
psychological slips of the tongue—are the result of the unconscious.
"Intention," therefore, includes authorial statement and unconscious
meaning; it can be approached by analysis of pragmatic evidence,
by the reader's response (although at times this may say more about
the reader than about the writer), and by psychological analysis of
the author.

Milton's philosophical intention has been discussed in the past
in terms of thesis ("Eternal Providence can be asserted to Man, thereby
justifying God's ways") and theme (love).[2] His artistic intention is
to achieve an emulation of God's Creation.[3] The intentions are twins,
and the poem which they produce offers up Psyche's confused seeds
for man with incessant labor to cull out and sort asunder. God's Creation of the universe and man was intended, orthodoxly, to replenish
heaven with true, faithful, and loving spirits after the fall and expulsion
of the rebellious third of the original angelic host. Milton's creation
is to aid that replenishment positively by asserting God's great love
seen in his eternal providence and negatively by countering the antiheroic element that sees God as unjust and tyrannic. The didactic
aim of the prophet-poet is to teach how one knows which seed is
which. Direct statement will do it (God the Father's, God the Son's,
Raphael's) but few will ever heed direct statement. Accommodated
words will do it, like the meanings with which Milton imbues "stand"
and "sit,"[4] but one must listen and read, compare and contrast, and
remember and evaluate. Few do. The oneness of the intention through-

out the poem is scored by awareness of these elements of Milton's creation—by themselves, agglomerated, adapted. The minister must repeat himself, must give strong hints (not "tell," because the conceit of man makes only that which he "independently" determines acceptable to him), must offer the abstract by the tangible. In the sermon which is the epic *Paradise Lost,* the minister Milton gives such hints as when Belial argues that not making war will require "Hard liberty" whereas war will bring defeat and then "the easie yoke / Of servile Pomp" (II, 256-57). It is clear that Belial has exactly reversed the circumstances, for their liberty will be easy because they will "live to our selves, though in this vast recess, / Free, and to none accountable" (II, 254-55). The first hint which Milton provides for his reader in this instance is that such concepts as "hard" and "easy" (and "good /evil," "life/death," "love/hate," "obedience/disobedience") depend upon one's personal drives and id, not necessarily upon some inherent truth. And the second hint lies in the allusion to Matthew xi, 30: "For my yoke is easy, and my burden is light"; where God's truth is that only man's yoking of himself is hard. The dialectic and reversal of image and meaning is a major device used by Milton to establish his "message." The fit audience will realize the mirror image of argument, the twisting of truth, the paradox of the antidivine. Further, the minister of the poem repeatedly offers the abstract through a concrete image as typically in these lines:

> which having pass'd
> At length into the limits of the North
> They came, and *Satan* to his Royal seat
> High on a Hill, far blazing, as a Mount
> Rais'd on a Mount, with Pyramids and Towrs
> From Diamond Quarries hew'n, and Rocks of Gold,
> The Palace of great *Lucifer.*   (V, 754-60)

We recognize this description just prior to the opening of the War in Heaven as the first version of Pandemonium and Satan's throne as drawn in Book II, and the self-aggrandizement and psychological import of Satan are likewise clear. But the dialectic point is being made which similar iconographic representations yield: the ornate, resplendent, multifarious world is evil, and the contrastive "sacred Hill" of God is simple, unadorned, and only a kind of "flaming Mount" because the "Brightness" of God has made it "invisible" (V, 598-99).

Unfortunately, man is often given to material and tinsel values, and the plea of the psalmist, "Teach me thy way, O Lord, and lead me in a plain path, because of mine enemies" (xxvii, 11), or the admonition of Paul, "But I fear, lest by any means, as the serpent beguiled Eve through his subtilty, so your minds should be corrupted from the simplicity that is in Christ" (2 Corinthians xi, 3), is little heeded.

Pragmatic evidence of Milton's philosophical and artistic intentions can be seen in the structures of the poem; these structures exist to achieve the philosophical intention through the artistic execution.[5] If nothing else, the structure and numerological relationships indicate the complexity of creation; if nothing else, they evidence the existence of the creator behind the creation. Such examples of the pre-text for the poem manifest the nature of artistic work which lies between the thought of the author and the presentation in artistic form. In general the overall device is a philosophical one expressed in literary terms: the world of opposites, each of which moves from one extreme to the other and, for the most part, which both together create the vagueness of distinction characteristic of man's thought. That is, right reason and wrong reason, expressed in dialectic terms, are difficult to distinguish for man, who needs guidance in separating the essence of one from the essence of the other; the poem is itself structured to equate the potential confusion, although Milton points the way to truth by various means, and it is built with materials which man can confuse. But Milton has erected many signposts to point out the correct path to right reason, as articles cited in the notes attempt to describe. The ideological (and hence artistic) arguments over *Paradise Lost* that have repeatedly emerged from Dryden down to the present are a result of wrong reading by not being aware of such pragmatic evidence as structures. Milton's perspective concern for man in his everyday life, within his individual world and within his communal world, has been missed. But is the fault in Milton and his poem or in the reader (for example, the reader who sees only Sin and Death as allegoric figures)? Whether we view the poem as falling into the tragic mode or the comic mode really depends upon our angle of vision as we turn the kaleidoscope. Are the pieces of glass which constitute any view of life the "right" pieces of glass? Is a specific arrangement *only* a step toward a new—and "better" or more desirable—vision? Or is there a beauty in each specific arrangement, each to be cherished of itself and each change to be equally cherished without regret for the past and desire for further change in the future? Life is tragic, Milton says, if, like Satan, we lament the present because it is not the past, or if, like Eve, we lament the present because it is not what some future seems to hold. Adam, thus, partakes of the Satanic tragedy of life by an act which will purportedly maintain at least one aspect of the past as it was since he cannot accept what appears to be the new present without Eve, and he knows that his act will bring a changed and unknown future. While the comic mode suggests a kind of hope of the future through the maintenance of the present, it also understands that the present is not exactly maintainable. Change is thus desirable, and the final lines of the epic make clear this paradox of a moving present. The comic lies in accepting the present, but the present is ever changing.

The myths of return and of exodus exist together as complements, and Milton's intertwining of these mythic foundations makes that cogent.[6] While the present moves to the future and becomes the past, so too it moves in a directed line forward. Milton as Christian poet sees the end of that line as a reunification with the substance of God. But the line is composed of each individual generation (or rather, each individual life of each individual generation), who undergoes the cyclic movement of life. The tragic lies in the attempt to deter either of those movements: in the poem we see this in Satan, who wishes to return to a past which really did not exist, for the Son is and always was God; in Adam, who wishes to maintain a part of the present as if it were the whole; and in Eve, who wishes to change the present into a future which will never be a reality. Milton the creator has given us a similitude of God's Creation by offering up many views of the kaleidoscope. His urging for man is ultimately the moral one of acceptance of the paradox that the present is to be cherished though it changes with each moment of time. It is Joyce's "message" as well.

The technique of the author to make awareness of the present ever changing takes many forms: time is compounded and seemingly confused, though it moves in a straight line; the reader is harassed (to use Stanley Fish's term) to alter his way of thinking throughout the poem, and indeed again and again as he rereads and newly sees on the basis of the past readings; the language is manipulated to take

on the force of meaning of its current context and then to alter as
it is reused and remetaphored; the poem itself emerges as a structure,
but one which appears differently in different lights or from different
points of vantage or through altered emphases. As example of the
present ever changing, the poem is a shadow of God's Creation. But
what is to be especially remarked—and the various aspects of style
underscore this—is the persistence of a germ of truth which is unchanging throughout the poem and which is so because it is unchanging
in Milton's view of God. Concepts of change—time; past, present,
future; movement forward or back, as well as seeming nonmovement;
hope and fear—are in man's mind, not God's, whose omnipotence,
omnipresence, and omniscience are unadorned, always the same, unac-
commodated. The poem demonstrates the paradox in various ways
by time representation, by story lines, by characterizations, by the
underlying myths, by language usage, by style, and by a contrast
of the allegoric and realistic. Note that the most obvious example
in the poem of this contrast is the role of Satan, an allegoric figure
usually discussed as a realistic view of man. It is perhaps through
Satan that Milton's great achievement in *Paradise Lost* as a creation
emulating God's and as a rhetorical argument with a threefold basis
can most easily be seen. For while praise (employing the epideictic
stance of the rhetor) of God's providence is dependent upon recognition of the negativity of the Satanic which exists in life because of
the existence of free will, and while defense (employing the forensic
stance of the rhetor) of God's ways toward man is dependent upon
the factor of the Satanic in man, the primary intention of the poem
to guide man in this life (the deliberative stance of the rhetor) will
be achieved only if man is able to discharge the speciousness of the
Satanic appeals. Such specious appeals operate within concepts of
time, of meaning of life and action, and of the self, both alone and
in community.[7]

The romantic view of Satan has been that of the quester after
value and the rebel against a tyrannic God. He is a Steppenwolf,
in the terms that Hans Mayer discusses Hermann Hesse's novel,[8]
by being an outsider to the establishment and a troublemaker. Satan,
as has been repeatedly remarked, wishes to replace that which he
is outside by his own establishment, an imitation of the establishment
he rebels against. With the ascendancy of Satan in the world of men

the norm is replaced by the antinorm which in turn becomes the new norm. Whatever is eternal truth, such as God equates for Milton, is missing in such envisionable sallying backward and forward of political and social life. Without Adam's asides one can read Books XI and XII as this kind of oscillation. For Milton the eternal truth—the paradise within—will be realized only through Adam and Eve's (mankind's) acceptance of life as it is: as a present ever changing. It has been detrimental for an appreciation of *Paradise Lost* that literature has generally offered the outsider as some kind of hero against the abuses of society, largely, I suppose, because authors (and most politically radical thinkers) have taken the path of individual subjectivity (such as a Byron or a Paul Goodman) or the path of elitism (the Bloomsbury group). Apposed to the outsider is Everyman, who has too often been cast aside as bourgeois, and Adam and Eve both allegorically and intellectually can be so viewed. To reject Adam and Eve politically and socially is to superimpose a different kind of tyranny. The outsider may become part of the proletariat (Steppenwolf may become Everyman), but he has not balanced the rational and irrational in a given social system by doing so—although one must seriously question whether, say, an Engels ever truly was absorbed into this middle-class world.

As Mayer brilliantly demonstrates, our problems today are in great part a result of Everyman's becoming Steppenwolf—the defiance of establishment principles and values for the sake of defiance, with a resultant noncommunity and wallowing in individual subjectivity. Satan proposes becoming Everyman, and Adam and Eve presume in their fall to becoming Steppenwolfs. Milton rebuffs both courses of action resoundingly. For Milton, the revolutionist against the tyranny of monarchy, the answer lay in recognition that revolution is Everyman's concern, not just an intellectual elite's, not just his in some kind of ivory tower. He may not have quite rejected a disgust with the rabble because of their selfish predilections, but he did join in working toward a goal through functions contrary in various ways to his personal ambitions and denying an acknowledgment of his individual superiority. In his epic—and the reader, I trust, will have come to agree—he shows the way in which authentic values are pursued by Everyman and of what those authentic values consist. Sympathy for the oppressed and wronged is certainly maintained; but this depends upon definitions of oppression and injustice. And hate for the establishment depends upon the establishment. "As therefore the state of man now is," man must "sally out and see his adversary" (to paraphrase *Areopagitica*, and Satan in Hebrew means "adversary") or remain duped as to oppression, injustice, and establishment. The way to regain an unoppressed, just, nonestablished world is to achieve within men a change in themselves, and it is through the re-creation and instruction of his poem that Milton hopes his reader will be as Adam in Books XI and XII. One does not change man's social conditions or political institutions of and by themselves: these will change with man's education in good and truth and become lastingly changed *only* through such education. Nor does one simply cure man's immediate ills, or as Milton wrote in *Sonnet 15:* "For what can Warrs but endless warr still breed, / Till Truth, and Right from Violence be freed."

In talking of the path that the artist who is an outsider may take to aid in bringing about a successful world order, Mayer writes: "It is a combination of artistic individualism in the traditional bourgeois sense and a decision not for subjectivism but for revolution" (p. 319)— a true fusion of Steppenwolf and Everyman. *Paradise Lost*, built upon traditional forms and genre, employing some Latinate language and sublime style, dealing with material from which "any writer" would not have failed "to shrink back deterred,"[9] breaks all the rules and gives us a new form *sui generis*, employs a greater proportion of native language and syntax than any other comparable English work, and refashions the seemingly nonmalleable biblical legend into an excitingly unpredictable and iridescent poem, whose challenges lie in every line and image. What Milton has done is use a mold, as it were, which he has fractured into new form, and the unities of time, place, and action, which he has fractured into ostensible nonunities. While the narrator emerges as Milton the poem's creator, he often becomes the voice of collective conscience as well, offsetting material drives by moral behavior for a socially ethical world. Though much impels the reader to consider that death can become the gate of life, Milton, unlike his predecessors who stressed that life would not be fulfilled in life, leads us to discern that experience is fulfilled in living, not after death, if we accept life as it is. Not, I hasten to add, with an impassive attitude that things should be—*must be*—changed, but an acceptance of life as meaningful and wonderful, albeit imperfect. The poem in this light becomes one of the earliest statements of a political ethic common to the twentieth century: it is in daily life and in Everyman's being a hero (rather than through the heroics rejected in the proem to Book IX) that life has any true meaning and the worth of man can be meaningfully evaluated. The poem fuses the established values of man—artistic, human, ideological—with revolutionary values to forge a creation reasserting God's wisdom and presence. It is as much a political poem as a philosophical one, for its concern is man.

City University of New York

NOTES

1. See my "The Metaphor of Inspiration," in *Th' Upright Heart and Pure*, ed. Amadeus P. Fiore (Pittsburgh, 1967), pp. 75–85.

2. See my "The Son in His Ascendance: A Reading of *Paradise Lost*," in *MLQ*, XXVII (1966), 388–401.

3. Compare the structures discussed in my "Balanced Structure of *Paradise Lost*," in *SP*, LXII (1965), 696–718.

4. See my "Metaphoric Approach to Reading Milton" in *Ball State University Forum*, VIII (1967), 17–21.

5. See my "Balanced Structure of *Paradise Lost*."

6. See my "*Paradise Lost* and the Theme of Exodus," in *Milton Studies*, II, ed. James D. Simmonds (Pittsburgh, 1970), pp. 3–26.

7. Man is treated as male and female, since this discussion is concerned with mankind. But a careful study of Milton's view of male and female is needed. I discount as inadequate, prejudiced, apologetic, or not explicitly attentive to this problem the various discussions of the divorce tracts or Milton's Eve which have been published. For while many published items make very important and valid points, none has come to grips with the received notions of female inferiority and of sexual characteristics of worthiness and unworthiness which lie in the collective unconscious, or with Milton's own sexual orientation. These are matters too complex for investigation here, and indeed partially move away from literary concerns, although they help us understand the human medium through which the literary artifact has been pressed.

8. *Steppenwolf and Everyman*, trans. Jack D. Zipes (New York, 1971); see pp. 1–13 and 300–19.

9. The words are A. J. A. Waldock's in *"Paradise Lost" and Its Critics* (Cambridge, 1947), pp. 17–19.

"STAND" AND "FALL" AS IMAGES OF POSTURE IN *PARADISE LOST*

Nicholas R. Jones

Emphasis on the doctrines of *Paradise Lost* without constant reference to their narrative foundation obscures the clarity of Milton's
epic instruction. A major example of the unique conjunction of
physical and metaphysical action which characterizes *Paradise
Lost* is the multiple use of the verbs "stand" and "fall." These words
signify not only the moral aspect of the epic—obedience and
disobedience—but also, simultaneously, its physical adjuncts—
posture and position within the cosmos. Picturing the prelapsarian
unity of obedience and upright posture, Milton narrates theological
events in terms of concrete actions. Similarly, the wild infernal
oscillations of size and stance in Book I vividly present the inevitable fall of disobedient creatures. The metaphoric complex associated with "stand" and "fall" operates most fully in the events of
the temptation, where images of posture continually figure forth
the crucial moral decisions. After the Fall, mankind, bereft of the
image of God, learns of his promises to regenerate that image
through Christ: Milton demonstrates that man will again stand
upright in self-esteem.

R EADERS OF *Paradise Lost,* trying in retrospect to explain how Milton could possibly justify the ways of God to men, have often
turned to God's first speech, near the beginning of Book III. For most
of us, it is wonderfully convenient. Invited by the sudden ascent of
the poem out of the narrowly confined perspectives of the first two
books into the eternal mind which at once comprehends all places
and all times, we relax the vigilant distrust that hell demands, seizing
upon God's aphoristic phrases as explanations of human history. God,
to our relief, expresses with precision and authority the doctrines of
prescience and predestination, the nature of human obedience and

divine grace, and, most importantly, his own freedom from blame
for the events which Satan is now initiating:

> For Man will heark'n to his glozing lies,
> And easily transgress the sole Command,
> Sole pledge of his obedience: So will fall
> Hee and his faithless Progeny: whose fault?
> Whose but his own? ingrate, he had of mee
> All he could have; I made him just and right,
> Sufficient to have stood, though free to fall.
> Such I created all th' Ethereal Powers
> And Spirits, both them who stood and them who fail'd;
> Freely they stood who stood, and fell who fell.[1]

Although God's speech is knotty and paradoxical, the fragments are
at least memorable, and it is simple for us to believe that hearing
is understanding. In particular, the parallel structure and apparently
lucid diction of two phrases appeal to the ear:

> I made him just and right,
> Sufficient to have stood, though free to fall,

and

> Freely they stood who stood, and fell who fell.

By abstracting from these already abstracted formulas we may all
too conveniently argue about the freedom of the will, the apparently
arbitrary division of the good and reprobate in heaven, or the purpose
of such an ill-fated creation. We are not, however, likely to succeed
in clarifying these issues in our own minds, nor—as any teacher of
Paradise Lost can witness—in gaining any more than fatigued assent
from others. Like the devils, we are likely to find our high reasoning
"Vain wisdom all, and false Philosophie" (II, 565). The phrases, logically
extended, seem not to lead us to the expected fields of consistency.
As Northrop Frye has written, Milton invites "disastrous consequences"
when he causes God to speak.[2]

Nonetheless, we are right in ascribing significance to these phrases.
Unfortunately, their resemblance to points of abstract theology—their
similarity, for example, to Milton's own treatise, the *Christian Doctrine*
—blinds us to another, more uniquely poetic way in which they explain
the action. In emphasizing the figurative meanings of the prominent
verbs "stand" and "fall" we exclude their stronger, more literal mean-

ings. These concrete verbs of action, especially "fall," belong to a long tradition of theological uses, and in certain contexts this history undercuts their basic denotations of posture and position. "Stand" and "fall" are not at all obscure, and we should not allow them to become so merely because it is God who uses them. As concepts of a very familiar, physical nature, they and their interconnections and extensions in the rest of the poem give us a subtler focus than their theological correlatives. *Paradise Lost* is basically a narrative, not a theological poem. "They stood; they fell" is one of the simplest and most basic of narrative events, and, in the right context, one of the most powerful. I will outline in the rest of this article the context which *Paradise Lost* provides—the complex shape of events and ideas with which the poem surrounds these simple actions.[3]

I

At least three types of meaning come into play in God's aphorisms. The first and most obvious is the theological, figurative sense of the key words: "to stand" means "to remain obedient." God, by apposition, equates the verb form "will fall" with a specific action unrelated to the verb's literal sense: in this case, it means "will . . . transgress the sole Command, / Sole pledge of his obedience." In describing states of being, then, "stand" and "fall" represent two opposite conditions on a *moral* scale: obedience and disobedience. This meaning, though primary in this context, is nonetheless purely figurative. A second meaning moves closer to the literal. "To fall," in the traditional Christian cosmology, means to experience the transition between heaven and hell; "to stand" means simply not to undergo that change. This sense works toward the concrete by presenting not a moral state of being but a physically discernible effect: the good angels "stand" in heaven, the bad are fallen into hell. Throughout the first two books, of course, we are distinctly aware of this sense of "fall," as when Milton tells of the prison of the rebellious angels: "O how unlike the place from whence they fell!" (I, 75) The first description of the good angels, just before God's speech, introduces this sense of "stand":

> About him all the Sanctities of Heaven
> Stood thick as Stars, and from his sight receiv'd
> Beatitude past utterance. (III, 60–62)

This second meaning, representing the extremes of cosmic position, is applicable to human events and emotions only through a sort of anagogical reading. Thus, with the action of the poem centering on earth, we can hardly maintain a strong perception of this sense: only when the characters are angels, fallen or standing, does this cosmic meaning come to life. In the sections of vaster scope, Milton can draw upon these grand effects of obedience while establishing their connections (as I shall show later) with the third and literal sense, the posture of the human or angelic body. This is the level of action, dealing not with moral conditions or consequences but with physical stature—the erect and tall body of Adam, the radiant deportment of Raphael, the protean and diminishing changes of Satan. Raphael stands, Satan falls, and Adam, with Eve, falls and is again uplifted. In this myth, apparently trivial actions, repeated and varied, are not only important *signs* of crucial moral decisions: they are also, in an admittedly circular complex of language and ideas, the *means* by which those decisions are made.

The most vital and powerful idea linking the moral and physical ontologies is that stated in the first of the two Creation myths in Genesis: "And God said, Let us make man in our image, after our likeness: and let them have dominion . . . over all the earth. . . . So God created man in his *own* image, in the image of God created he him; male and female created he them."[4] The resemblance of man to God, stated four times in this text, became a stock tool of writers eager to stress man's stamp of favor and dominion.

The problem arises of how to interpret this "image of God." Writers of the Renaissance generally began by associating it with man's virtually unique ability to stand on two legs. C. A. Patrides, noting many appearances of the idea in the seventeenth century and earlier, remarks that the erect posture of man was the most significant aspect of the divine resemblance.[5] Man's stance not only symbolizes dominion over the beasts but also actively furthers God's plan by inducing man to look toward heaven: as Donne wrote, "*Man* in his *naturall forme*, is carried to the contemplation of that place, which is his *home, Heaven*."[6] For Donne, concerned with contemporary life, this upright form serves an essentially spiritual purpose, the reunion of God with man through contrition and repentance. For Milton in the early parts of *Paradise Lost*, the posture of yet unfallen man is more simply related to action, maintaining Adam and Eve in their dignified and easy relationship with the higher and lower orders of existence. As Raphael tells the story of Creation, he indicates that such a purpose informed God's act:

> There wanted yet the Master work, the end
> Of all yet done; a Creature who not prone
> And Brute as other Creatures, but endu'd
> With Sanctity of Reason, might erect
> His Stature, and upright with Front serene
> Govern the rest, self-knowing, and from thence
> Magnanimous to correspond with Heav'n,
> But grateful to acknowledge whence his good
> Descends, thither with heart and voice and eyes
> Directed in Devotion, to adore
> And worship God Supreme who made him chief
> Of all his works.   (VII, 505-16)

The diction of the verse ascends from "prone and brute" to "Supreme," by its very structure forming an image of the moral, physiological, and spatial scales of being. The position of man in these scales of God's universe is here imagined to be visible in his stance, which elevates him above other inhabitants of earth in sovereignty and directs his eyes toward heaven in devotion.

In Raphael's speculation, God's thought immediately takes shape in command:

> Let us make now Man in our image, Man
> In our similitude, and let them rule
> Over the Fish and Fowl of Sea and Air,
> Beast of the Field, and over all the Earth,
> And every creeping thing that creeps the ground.
>   (VII, 519-23)

Merritt Hughes notes, with reference to God's command, that biblical scholars had often interpreted "image" in a spiritual or figurative sense, meaning God's gift to man of a "reasonable and understanding nature."[7] So in Milton's verses on man the inner beauties are mingled with the outer: "endu'd / With Sanctity of Reason," "upright," "self-knowing," and so forth. Milton's attitude toward the question of the preferred meaning of "image" seems ambiguous. If at one point in the *Christian Doctrine* he seems to support the exterior likeness (p. 906), at another point he says, "it was not the body alone that was then made, but the soul of man also (in which our likeness to God principally consists)"

(p. 979). Most general statements in Milton's prose concentrate on associating God's image with all the virtues and endowments of a reasonable and obedient state.[8]

Milton's poetic use of the idea mingles the inner and outer aspects of similitude without logically restricting them. Perhaps the most resonant example is his first description of Adam and Eve:

> the Fiend
> Saw undelighted all delight, all kind
> Of living Creatures new to sight and strange:
> Two of far nobler shape erect and tall,
> Godlike erect, with native Honor clad
> In naked Majesty seem'd Lords of all,
> And worthy seem'd, for in thir looks Divine
> The image of thir glorious Maker shone,
> Truth, Wisdom, Sanctitude severe and pure,
> Severe, but in true filial freedom plac't;
> Whence true autority in men.   (IV, 285–95)

In this condensed description, we see a surprising variety of features in Adam and Eve—their unique posture, their responsible and ethical behavior, their reasonable obedience, and their sovereignty over the creatures of the earth. These qualities are united by a dependence upon man's creation in God's image, which is here interpreted as an imitation of more than merely physical attributes.

This first narrative expression of the multiple virtues of Adam and Eve uses four key repetitions as the syntactic markers of five sections. Each of the repeated words—"erect," "seem'd," "severe," and "true"—signals a thematic expansion of the material, tying man's physical and moral natures together in his resemblance to God. At first, the simple image of posture—"of far nobler shape erect and tall"—continues the literal sense of the transitional introduction ("the Fiend / Saw," "new to sight and strange"). We, fallen like Satan, tend at first to see only externals: we must be reeducated to this innocent equivalence of spirit and shape. What we see, then, is qualified by the repetition of a word of physical denotation, "erect." In its second use, that word leads us into a world of epic heroism: "Godlike erect, with native Honor clad / In naked Majesty seem'd Lords of all." The diction is that of descriptions of the all-sufficient heroes of Virgil and Homer. With the important exception of the nakedness, these phrases could as well apply to Aeneas, appearing from the mist in

Dido's court, or to Odysseus, radiantly prepared by Athena to approach the palace of Alcinous. Such allusions bring to mind not only the physical appearance of the epic heroes but also their social, political, and ethical dignity.

After two units of description, the second repeated word, "seem'd," establishes the special condition of Eden, the congruence of appearance and reality:

> And worthy seem'd, for in thir looks Divine
> The image of thir glorious Maker shone,
> Truth, Wisdom, Sanctitude severe and pure.

This central section of the passage reminds us that all man's qualities, physical and moral, are reflections of God; the image of God can both *seem* and *be* worthy. In this unfallen world, man's roles are all one. The intense negative connotation of "seeming," present in almost all seventeenth-century literature, is unavoidable even here: from our fallen perspective, we for a moment doubt this amazing unity of created man. But that initial hesitation on the repeated word makes the focal statement which follows all the more positive in its unambiguous equation of man's external and internal imitation of God.

The last sections of this passage balance the first two in symmetry about this central assertion. As the second introduced physical images of the epic hero, the fourth touches on the moral qualities which such a hero must embody—discipline, obedience, and reason: "Severe, but in true filial freedom plac't." Marked off by the repetition of "severe," this one line connects God's severity, his requirement of obedience, with man's self-control—a different sort of severity which in turn depends on man's "true filial freedom." Similarly, as the first section began the passage with reference to man's physical superiority on earth, so the fifth, signaled by a repetition of "true," ends the description with a reference to man's sovereignty: "whence true autority in men." Freedom and authority, two important abstract qualities in the ontology of *Paradise Lost*, are in this passage linked, through the concept of the image of God in man, with the concrete elements of man's posture and action. From the familiar we move to the remote and complex, and that movement is an important expansion of the statement which introduced this discussion: "I made him just and right, / Sufficient to have stood, though free to fall." From this first description of Adam and Eve standing in the garden, we gain a new perspective on the nontrivial importance of details of physical action in the mythological narrative.

Such is the power of the confident poise of Adam and Eve that even Satan recognizes the correspondence in them of virtue and appearance. His first sight of them reveals their favor with God to be even greater than his envy had supposed:

> O Hell! what do mine eyes with grief behold,
> Into our room of bliss thus high advanc't
> Creatures of other mould, earth-born perhaps,
> Not Spirits, yet to heav'nly Spirits bright
> Little inferior; whom my thoughts pursue
> With wonder, and could love, so lively shines
> In them Divine resemblance, and such grace
> The hand that form'd them on thir shape hath pour'd.
>
> (IV, 358–65)

Satan is no dull observer in a case that so nearly touches his own. Recognizing that man is made of dust, "earth-born perhaps," he gives by that perception greater glory to the miracle of Creation. Satan has the eye to appreciate beauty, though not the heart to love it; through his anguish we feel the extraordinary gap in man between matter and form, between dust and "naked Majesty." Such a creature as man is so naturally impossible that Satan immediately ascribes its radiance to its true source, the grace of God. This knowledge only increases his envy and wrath, so fully has he inverted God's order. Yet his perception allows the reader to see the beauty and dignity of mankind as a miraculous and tenuous elevation of the bestial to the rational, of a lower to a higher order. It is man's high stature which gives significance to the chance of his falling; yet his continued standing is also his only defense against that chance. Within his own high nature lie both his peril and his protection.

II

In the fallen world in which the poet and reader live, the actions literally denoted by the verbs "stand" and "fall" are usually devoid of moral qualities. A sense of posture and position as significant elements of moral imagery is a major contribution of the Satanic portions of *Paradise Lost*. If shape is to be a measure of grace, Satan's metamorphoses in the later books are the most obvious indicators of his damnation. We respond with full disgust to his voluntary assumptions of bestial shape and to his imposed transformation, when "supplanted down he fell / A monstrous Serpent on his Belly prone, / Reluctant, but in vain" (X, 513-15). Satan's close association with Sin and Death, whose bodies are the gross reflection of their godlessness, reminds us harshly that the fallen angel is the enemy of God's image. Book I, however, is particularly subtle in its involvement with shape and stance. Closer attention to its sequential ironies and its comic deflation of pride will establish Milton's practical use of the metaphoric complex associated with "stand" and "fall" and reveal one aspect of his preparation for the tragedy of man with the comedy of Satan.

When we first encounter Satan near the beginning of the poem, his situation incorporates all three senses of the word "fall"—moral, cosmological, and physical. The drama of his story involves his attempt to free the two literal meanings from the moral, a task at which he ultimately fails. The overriding, figurative sense of Satan's fall—the one that he is stuck with—is clearly stated: "He trusted to have equall'd the most High" (I, 40). Disobedience is for him irreversible. The spatial, cosmic sense of "fall" also applies to Satan; although the word itself is not at first used, the image is most dramatically present:

> Him the Almighty Power
> Hurl'd headlong flaming from th' Ethereal Sky
> With hideous ruin and combustion down
> To bottomless perdition.   (I, 44-47)

The third "fall," the fall from erect stature, strikes our mind's eye directly:

> Nine times the Space that measures Day and Night
> To mortal men, hee with his horrid crew
> Lay vanquisht, rolling in the fiery Gulf
> Confounded though immortal.   (I, 50-53)

Such is the context of Satan's memorable lines of confident and energetic hatred, beginning "What though the field be lost? / All is not lost; the unconquerable Will" (I, 105-06). From the perspective of a reader who knows Satan's starting point, this assertion of revenge at first sounds noble. Its logic is much like that of modern man: Satan is drawing a contrast, justifiable in postlapsarian thought, between exterior and interior conditions, between the fallen body and the indomitable spirit. But this logic fails in the eternal perspective. Milton constantly undercuts our tendency to agree with it, steadily reforming our thought. By the end of Book I, Satan, though apparently well on his way to intended victory, is just as apparently journeying to defeat.

Milton makes it clear by direct statement and comment that the devils' gradual reversal of their physical and cosmic "fall" is neither a reflection of an inner virtue nor a condition likely to last long: the "indomitable Will" has little to do with their actions. The failure of confidence and dissimulation of their leader is obvious: "So spake th' Apostate Angel, though in pain, / Vaunting aloud, but rackt with deep despair" (I, 125–26). In Satan's will there is no freedom, nor any real strength within his apparently heroic actions:

> So stretcht out huge in length the Arch-fiend lay
> Chain'd on the burning Lake, nor ever thence
> Had ris'n or heav'd his head, but that the will
> And high permission of all-ruling Heaven
> Left him at large to his own dark designs,
> That with reiterated crimes he might
> Heap on himself damnation.   (I, 209–15)

Satan's posture on the burning lake and his position in the cosmic topography are silent reminders of the futility of his vow to avoid any humble or contrite stance:

> To bow and sue for grace
> With suppliant knee, and deify his power
> Who from the terror of this Arm so late
> Doubted his Empire, that were low indeed,
> That were an ignominy and shame beneath
> This downfall; since by Fate the strength of Gods
> And this Empyreal substance cannot fail.   (I, 111–17)

In Satan's insistence on the separation between voluntary and enforced action, repeated to absurdity, lies much of his comedy of self-deception. He may raise "His mighty Stature" from the lake, with Beelzebub:

> Both glorying to have scap't the *Stygian* flood
> As Gods, and by thir own recover'd strength,
> Not by the sufferance of supernal Power.   (I, 239–41)

But their delusion is physically obvious in the horror of the burning land: "Such resting found the sole / Of unblest feet" (I, 237–38). Naturally enough, in surprise Satan immediately restates his doctrine that the will remains free: "The mind is its own place, and in itself / Can make a Heav'n of Hell, a Hell of Heav'n" (I, 254-55).

Again, Satan's renewed stature, emphasized by elaborate comparisons involving his spear and "ponderous shield" (I, 283-94), undergoes a half-comic, half-pathetic diminishment with the pain of walking:

> His Spear, to equal which the tallest Pine
> Hewn on *Norwegian* hills, to be the Mast
> Of some great Ammiral, were but a wand,
> He walkt with to support uneasy steps
> Over the burning Marl, not like those steps
> On Heaven's Azure, and the torrid Clime
> Smote on him sore besides, vaulted with Fire.   (I, 292-98)

So also the majestic awakening of the fallen legions—"as when men wont to watch / On duty, sleeping found by whom they dread, / Rouse and bestir themselves ere well awake"—qualifies heroism with fear and pain (I, 332-34).

The comedy of discomfiture is mixed with terror. At the moment of apparently full escape from torture, the devils are formidably strong and active:

> Forthwith from every Squadron and each Band
> The Heads and Leaders thither haste where stood
> Thir great Commander; Godlike shapes and forms
> Excelling human, Princely Dignities,
> And Powers that erst in Heaven sat on Thrones.   (I, 356-60)

Here the enemy is unqualifiedly noble in stature, and Satan himself stands with ease and dignity. These great adversaries, heroically loyal and fully capable of destroying God's image in man, are to be the cause of fallen mankind's continuing fall:

> For those the Race of *Israel* oft forsook
> Thir living strength, and unfrequented left
> His righteous Altar, bowing lowly down
> To bestial Gods; for which thir heads as low
> Bow'd down in Battle, sunk before the Spear
> Of despicable foes.   (I, 432-37)

Strangely, though, even in the long catalogue of their future successes, these "Princely Dignities" sound more and more like merely "despicable foes." There is a concentrated ridiculousness about their frauds and deceits, working by such monstrous transformations and disfigurements. These Middle Eastern idols seem to specialize in deforming themselves:

> First *Moloch*, horrid King besmear'd with blood
> Of human sacrifice, and parents' tears.
>
>   · · · · · · ·
>
>   Next came one
> Who mourn'd in earnest, when the Captive Ark
> Maim'd his brute Image, head and hands lopt off
> In his own Temple, on the grunsel edge,
> Where he fell flat, and sham'd his Worshippers:
> *Dagon* his Name, Sea Monster, upward Man
> And downward Fish.
>
>   · · · · · · ·
>
>   After these appear'd
> A crew who under Names of old Renown,
> *Osiris, Isis, Orus* and thir Train
> With monstrous shapes and sorceries abus'd
> Fanatic *Egypt* and her Priests, to seek
> Thir wand'ring Gods disguis'd in brutish forms
> Rather than human.   (I, 392–93, 457–63, 476–82)

After the interlude of these future degradations, the elevation of the devils' standard ("that proud honor claim'd / *Azazel* as his right, a Cherub tall" [I, 533–34]) signals an uplift of courage and morale, a new impulse wholly serious in nature. Now they are heroes, as with stoic acceptance they face no comic pain:

> Advanc't in view they stand, a horrid Front
> Of dreadful length and dazzling Arms, in guise
> Of Warriors old with order'd Spear and Shield,
>
>   · · · · · · ·
>
> Thir visages and stature as of Gods.   (I, 563–65, 570)

For one terrible moment, there is no question that they *stand* and that their stance reflects some inner strength. Satan, especially,

>   above the rest
> In shape and gesture proudly eminent
> Stood like a Tow'r; his form had not yet lost
> All her Original brightness, nor appear'd
> Less than Arch-Angel ruin'd, and th' excess
> Of Glory obscur'd.   (I, 589–94)

Yet once more the contradictions inherent in their position destroy the illusion that their stature is a meaningful sign. The author finds in Satan's countenance the scars of thunder and the darkened glory; in his oratory, again, will and condition are separated with logic more suited to earthly than cosmic affairs:

> For who can yet believe, though after loss,
> That all these puissant Legions, whose exíle
> Hath emptied Heav'n, shall fail to re-ascend
> Self-rais'd, and repossess thir native seat?   (I, 631–34)

The noise of the excited devils—"highly they rag'd / Against the Highest, and fierce with grasped Arms / Clash'd on thir sounding shields the din of war, / Hurling defiance toward the Vault of Heav'n"— resounds in fact only against the vault of hell (I, 666–69). The ingenuity of Mammon's gangs reduces the stature of the heroic devils by surrounding them with a gaudy and excessively magnificent hall. The reader's underlying emotions toward this architecture and toward the brief renaissance of strength in hell is figured in Milton's shift of tone as he tells of the architect, at first with Ovidian smoothness:

> from Morn
> To Noon he fell, from Noon to dewy Eve,
> A Summer's day; and with the setting Sun
> Dropt from the Zenith like a falling Star,
> On *Lemnos* th' *Aegaean* Isle.   (I, 742–46)

Then, with abrupt contempt, the poet denies the fairy-tale tone:

> thus they relate,
> Erring; for he with this rebellious rout
> Fell long before; nor aught avail'd him now
> To have built in Heav'n high Tow'rs; nor did he scape
> By all his Engines, but was headlong sent
> With his industrious crew to build in hell.   (I, 746–51)

This is a very real, harsh, and irreversible fall.

At the very end of the book, the stature of the chief devils appears once more firmly renewed as they prepare for the debate—"in thir own dimensions like themselves / The great Seraphic Lords and Cherubim" (I, 793–94). Milton certainly intended that at this point the stature of the devils be fully felt. Just before this scene of grandeur, however, is a series of comic actions and images which together present the eventual failure of "the great consult." First is the description of the crowding devils, surprising for its emphasis on their insectlike qualities:

> all access was throng'd, the Gates
> And Porches wide, but chief the spacious Hall
> . . . .
> Thick swarm'd, both on the ground and in the air,
> Brusht with the hiss of rustling wings. (I, 761-62, 767-68)

Having touched upon the ridiculous, Milton corroborates the grander aspect of the image by means of a simile:

> As Bees
> In spring time, when the Sun with *Taurus* rides,
> Pour forth thir populous youth about the Hive
> In clusters; they among fresh dews and flowers
> Fly to and fro, or on the smoothed Plank,
> The suburb of thir Straw-built Citadel,
> New rubb'd with Balm, expatiate and confer
> Thir State affairs. (I, 768-75)

The time-honored epic *topos* of the commonwealth of bees at first redeems the devils' stature with connotations of the ordered and diligent troops of Dido and Agamemnon. Subtly, however, the emphasis shifts toward incongruous comparison: the abrupt scorn of "Thir State affairs," with its hint of Restoration court manners; the hidden disapproval of "thir Straw-built Citadel," physically appropriate to bees, but only morally to the devils; and—comically mimicked by the sound of "New rubb'd with Balm"—the opprobrium of "suburb," which carries the contemptuous force of Milton's phrase from *Eikonoklastes*, "Dissolute swordsmen and Suburb roysters."[9]

The lines which follow in this rapid comic sequence complete the preparation for the "great Seraphic Lords and Cherubim" by emphasizing the details of physical size:

> So thick the aery crowd
> Swarm'd and were strait'n'd; till the Signal giv'n,
> Behold a wonder! they but now who seem'd
> In bigness to surpass Earth's Giant Sons
> Now less than smallest Dwarfs, in narrow room
> Throng numberless, like that Pigmean Race
> Beyond the *Indian* Mount, or Faery Elves. (I, 775-81)

Milton points to this mass "fall" with mock astonishment ("Behold a wonder!") to stress its absurdity and inevitability.

The stature of the devils, however, is significant only as it relates to human responses. Adam and Eve still stand obedient and, with reason intact, would only laugh at "the aery crowd." Modern, fallen man reacts less simply to the example of the "Faery Elves,"

> Whose midnight Revels, by a Forest side
> Or Fountain some belated Peasant sees,
> Or dreams he sees, while over-head the Moon
> Sits Arbitress, and nearer to the Earth
> Wheels her pale course; they on thir mirth and dance
> Intent, with jocund Music charm his ear;
> At once with joy and fear his heart rebounds.   (I, 781-88)

For fallen man, stature is no longer the key to moral values. This "belated Peasant"—and the reader shares many responses with him— cannot understand the complex emotions he feels in this mixture of beauty and danger. This is the same moonlight confusion, when only a moment earlier all things seemed clear, which Eve will experience when at noon she encounters the master of these "Revels."

III

The oscillations of Book I provide an example of Milton's preparation of the metaphoric complex associated with the words "stand" and "fall." Posture, behavior, cosmic position, countenance, reason, obedience, and morality are some of the abstract and concrete qualities connected by this network. I have outlined their interrelations in two extreme cases, that of the ideal man and that of the fallen devils. A more confusing situation is that of actual unfallen man—man no longer seen as a static creation but rather existing *in time,* subject to various passions and influences. In the everyday life of the garden, and ultimately in the special events of temptation, Adam and Eve must work not so much as gardeners but as continual guardians of that perfection in which they were created.

Man's effort to remain standing relies principally on a sense of self-esteem, which in turn depends on a firm subjective distinction between the self and the "other." Man finds in *himself* the image of God—reason, strength, love, and happiness—and in the security of that image he stands obedient. But in the beauty of the "other" there is a major distraction. As Adam reports to Raphael:

> here passion first I felt,
> Commotion strange, in all enjoyments else
> Superior and unmov'd, here only weak
> Against the charm of Beauty's powerful glance. (VIII, 530–33)

Adam wants to separate reason from appearance, intuitively subjecting himself to Eve even while he asserts that she is inferior to him in mind and in stature:

> For well I understand in the prime end
> Of Nature her th' inferior, in the mind
> And inward Faculties, which most excel,
> In outward also her resembling less
> His Image who made both, and less expressing
> The character of that Dominion giv'n
> O'er other Creatures; yet when I approach
> Her loveliness, so absolute she seems
> And in herself complete, so well to know
> Her own, that what she wills to do or say,
> Seems wisest, virtuousest, discreetest, best;
> All higher knowledge in her presence falls
> Degraded, Wisdom in discourse with her
> Loses discount'nanc't, and like folly shows;
> Authority and Reason on her wait,
> As one intended first, not after made
> Occasionally; and to consummate all,
> Greatness of mind and nobleness thir seat
> Build in her loveliest, and create an awe
> About her, as a guard Angelic plac't.   (VIII, 540–59)

For Adam in the presence of Eve, the "other" becomes a greater image of God than the self. The images of this long passage show how the metaphoric complex of the physical appearance especially describes Adam's passionate dependence on Eve: "knowledge . . . falls / Degraded, Wisdom . . . Loses discount'nanc't." Adam creates an imaginary court around Eve as a heavenly queen, attended by "Authority and Reason" and guarded and illuminated by "Greatness of mind and nobleness." How far he is from seeing in her a true reflection of God's image appears in his extraordinary tableau of Wisdom as the fool in the court of Eve.

Raphael's warning to Adam reasserts the power of the self to control its own thought and action: Eve is

> worthy well
> Thy cherishing, thy honoring, and thy love,
> Not thy subjection: weigh with her thyself;
> Then value: Oft-times nothing profits more
> Than self-esteem, grounded on just and right
> Well manag'd.   (VIII, 568-73)

Raphael replaces Adam's generalizations ("knowledge," "Wisdom," etc.) with specific instructions for action. "Self-esteem" is the key to the angel's counsel, for only in the full knowledge of God's attributes in the *self* can man retain his stance. I should note at this point that the situations of Adam and Eve are not reciprocal: while Adam is at fault in subjecting himself to Eve, she is at fault if she does *not* subject herself to him. Most of Milton's uses of the doctrine of self-esteem apply mainly to Adam's condition, for obvious reasons. Yet Eve has a parallel to Adam's passion: yearning for her reflection in the pond, she forgets that she is herself the image of God. She, like Adam, sacrifices her dignified and reasonable nobility in a misdirected search for another image. Most readers would agree that this search does not end with her acceptance of Adam as her mate. Eve's story of her own narcissistic passion corroborates Adam's problem: passion directs mankind toward weakness, while reason urges him toward strength.

The most explicit and moving statement of the sufficiency of the self comes in Raphael's parting benediction:

> Be strong, live happy, and love, but first of all
> Him whom to love is to obey, and keep
> His great command; take heed lest Passion sway
> Thy Judgment to do aught, which else free Will
> Would not admit; thine and of all thy Sons
> The weal or woe in thee is plac't: beware.
> I in thy persevering shall rejoice,
> And all the Blest: stand fast; to stand or fall
> Free in thine own Arbitrement it lies.
> Perfet within, no outward aid require;
> And all temptation to transgress repel.   (VIII, 633-43)

The central injunction is "stand fast," echoing the many previous uses of the word "stand." Raphael urges Adam to see himself as valuable and complete. He is a vessel of "weal or woe" whose only danger lies in heedlessness. His stature is both cause and effect in the angel's sequence: strength to stand firm leads to joy and love ("Be strong, live happy, and love"), and to love God is to remain obedient, to stand in God's favor and blessing. "Stand fast" is no vague warning; it is specifically directed to what Adam knows of his own virtue and appearance. The loss of that knowledge is the prelude to the Fall.

Man's posture has by this point become not only a sign of his innocence but the chief reminder to him of the means by which he may keep that innocence. In the elevation of reason, the strength of sufficiency, and the stature of dominion, man in his body openly displays the attributes of God. If the self is firm, the relationship with the "other"—be it Eve, or an image of the fancy, or the angel, or God—becomes not dependency but love. Raphael instructs Adam, "Perfet within, no outward aid require"; in Adam's nature is all his aid. Passion, the disastrous and unreasonable dependence upon an "other," cannot "sway" this conscious strength.

Adam has learned from Raphael that virtue consists in action, in a strenuous effort of the will: "Accuse not Nature, she hath done her part; / Do thou but thine" (VIII, 561–62). When Adam in turn warns Eve, he echoes Raphael's words: "God towards thee hath done his part, do thine" (IX, 375). The emphasis on action is an important element of the complex of images around the verbs "stand" and "fall." Here Adam and Eve are each about to experience actively the test of their obedience. To match their situation the reader has in mind the example of Abdiel, who in the test of angels acted with the energy of a single being conscious of his sufficient strength. Abdiel's stance and movement reflect the image of God as it appears later in Christ, victorious in heaven:

> *Abdiel*, than whom none with more zeal ador'd
> The Deity, and divine commands obey'd,
> Stood up, and in a flame of zeal severe
> The current of his fury thus oppos'd.
>
> . . . .
>
> From amidst them forth he pass'd,
> Long way through hostile scorn, which he sustain'd
> Superior, nor of violence fear'd aught;
> And with retorted scorn his back he turn'd
> On those proud Tow'rs to swift destruction doom'd.
>
> (V, 805–08, 903–07)

This vibrant, energetic posture contrasts sharply with the moral wavering of the rebellious angels. As the reader already knows from Book

I and as Adam is about to learn from Raphael, this Satanic fall from obedience implies the swift humiliation of a literal fall. Abdiel's moral and physical stance—"Among innumerable false, unmov'd, / Unshak'n" (V, 898–99)—invests the active search for virtue in temptation with a memorable precedent of success.

That precedent, however, is forgotten. The lengthy debate between Adam and Eve which precedes their separation just before the Fall (IX, 204–384) allows the reader to watch the process by which sin grows out of inaction. Remembering Abdiel's zeal in a similar situation, we cannot read these polite, even loving speeches without a reaction of horror. This drama is based on a graceful wavering which grows ever more obvious until it includes the fall of each participant and at last the wild dislodging of the cosmic orbits. There is no idea in the debate which is itself sinful: each response seems to reflect some virtue or some example of success in the poem. The whole, however, leads to a separation which is important not only as a device of plot but also as a seal on the passions of the debate. It ensures that Eve's discontent and Adam's subjection continue to sway them from their proper self-esteem. Adam's laxity appears in his sudden reversal ("Go; for thy stay, not free, absents thee more" [IX, 372]) and his failure to correct Eve's last words:

> The willinger I go, nor much expect
> A Foe so proud will first the weaker seek;
> So bent, the more shall shame him his repulse.   (IX, 382–84)

Adam's reason submits to his passion, even though he has brought to mind again the injunctions of Raphael. He applies them only to Eve, not to himself, telling her that the image of God, the stamp of her creation, is sufficient to preserve her:

> O Woman, best are all things as the will
> Of God ordain'd them, his creating hand
> Nothing imperfet or deficient left
> Of all that he Created, much less Man,
> Or aught that might his happy State secure,
> Secure from outward force; within himself
> The danger lies, yet lies within his power:
> Against his will he can receive no harm.   (IX, 343–50)

Security will be found only in a conscious and active posture of strength and self-confidence.

The two human beings, separated, are made frail by passion—Adam's desire to please Eve (which later surfaces ironically as the "glorious trial of exceeding Love" [IX, 961]) and Eve's sensation of triumph and of perils safely past. Her frailty is brought home to us in the explicit poetic leap from her environment to her moral state, as we see her through Satan's eyes,

> oft stooping to support
> Each Flow'r of slender stalk, whose head though gay
> Carnation, Purple, Azure, or speckt with Gold,
> Hung drooping unsustain'd, them she upstays
> Gently with Myrtle band, mindless the while,
> Herself, though fairest unsupported Flow'r,
> From her best prop so far, and storm so nigh.   (IX, 427–33)

This metaphoric glimpse of Eve's failure to stand fast is the more ironic when Satan soon after successfully appeals to her posture, the sign of her dominion over the beasts, telling his lies about the forbidden tree:

> About the mossy Trunk I wound me soon,
> For high from ground the branches would require
> Thy utmost reach or *Adam's:* Round the Tree
> All other Beasts that saw, with like desire
> Longing and envying stood, but could not reach.   (IX, 589–93)

Again, ironically, her beauty briefly conquers the evil in Satan:

> her Heav'nly form
> Angelic, but more soft, and Feminine,
> Her graceful Innocence, her every Air
> Of gesture or least action overaw'd
> His Malice, and with rapine sweet bereav'd
> His fierceness of the fierce intent it brought.   (IX, 457–62)

If she were only conscious of it, her countenance and posture would be the key to her obedience, the outward image of him "whom to love is to obey, and keep / His great command." Yet she is so resolutely proud of her adventure that Satan can distort that same image to his evil purpose: "Fairest resemblance of thy Maker fair, / Thee all things living gaze on" (IX, 538–39). Forgetting her true creation "erect and tall," Eve falls.

Milton's expression of Adam's frailty as he perceives Eve's fall is the climax of the complex associations developed between the moral and physical conditions. Adam's passion is at once more intense and more obvious than Eve's. Here Adam loses his freedom of action as he loses his strength:

> On th' other side, *Adam*, soon as he heard
> The fatal Trespass done by *Eve*, amaz'd,
> Astonied stood and Blank, while horror chill
> Ran through his veins, and all his joints relax'd;
> From his slack hand the Garland wreath'd for *Eve*
> Down dropp'd, and all the faded Roses shed:
> Speechless he stood and pale. (IX, 888–94)

Milton stresses that Adam, at the point of fall, still knows the right but will not act upon it:

> he scrupl'd not to eat
> Against his better knowledge, not deceiv'd,
> But fondly overcome with Female charm. (IX, 997–99)

His reason, though it seems still to perceive and understand, has lost its connection with the will.

The rapid degradation of God's image in man after the Fall creates a new theme: the shamefulness of the body. Though many correspondences in the terrestrial order are broken with the Fall, that between body and spirit remains for a while longer; no more, however, can either soul or flesh reflect the image of God or generate that self-esteem which was their ornament and protection. Milton describes the loss of moral qualities as if it were physical:

> innocence, that as a veil
> Had shadow'd them from knowing ill, was gone,
> Just confidence, and native righteousness,
> And honor from about them, naked left
> To guilty shame. (IX, 1054–58)

As in the case of Satan, the poet leaves unspecified the details of metamorphosis, the marks of the encroachment of Sin and Death. They are, nonetheless, real erosions of the image of God:

> Bad Fruit of Knowledge, if this be to know,
> Which leaves us naked thus, of Honor void,
> Of Innocence, of Faith, of Purity,
> Our wonted Ornaments now soil'd and stain'd,
> And in our Faces evident the signs
> Of foul concupiscence. (IX, 1073–78)

Uselessly, pathetically, Adam and Eve try to disguise the effects and the instruments of passion:

> Those Leaves
> They gather'd, broad as *Amazonian* Targe,
> And with what skill they had, together sew'd,
> To gird thir waist, vain Covering if to hide
> Thir guilt and dreaded shame; O how unlike
> To that first naked Glory.   (IX, 1110–15)

The task is "vain" because the body, formerly the source and sign of strength, has become the instigator and reminder of sin.

IV

The first solace Adam and Eve obtain will continue to be the major solace of their children: the knowledge of Christ, whether in promise or in presence. The Son's role in providing consolation and reordering begins on a simple, physical level—clothing the naked, disguising the corrupted image of God:

> As Father of his Family he clad
> Thir nakedness with Skins of Beasts, or slain,
> Or as the Snake with youthful Coat repaid.   (X, 216–18)

But some continuing grace is more sorely needed. That gift comes also through Christ, who renews in each repentant man the image of God. Christ himself is that image—

> The radiant image of his Glory
> . . . .
> Begotten Son, Divine Similitude,
> In whose conspicuous count'nance, without cloud
> Made visible, th' Almighty Father shines.   (III, 63, 384–86)

Through Christ's continuing gift, unjust man, guilty of sin, can rediscover his self-esteem and stand once more justified before God.

The struggle of history—the long stretch of time between the Fall and the last day—demands of us a constant wariness, a posture far more diligently kept than Adam's. As before the Fall, our knowledge of the image of God in us is both the cause and the effect of our standing in the face of repeated temptations and assaults. The difference is that now the image of God is no longer born in us but imputed to us through Christ's free gift.

The doctrine of the historical struggle of man is naturally more explicit in Milton's lesser works than in *Paradise Lost*. Particularly in the prose, Milton refers again and again to the revived dignity of the human form and its role in salvation. In *The Reason of Church Government*, he links it both to Creation and to redemption:

> But there is yet a more ingenuous and noble degree of honest shame, or call it, if you will, an esteem, whereby men bear an inward reverence toward their own persons. . . . [H]e that holds himself in reverence and due esteem, both for the dignity of God's image upon him and for the price of his redemption, which he thinks is visibly marked upon his forehead, accounts himself both a fit person to do the noblest and godliest deeds, and much better worth than to deject and defile with such a debasement and such a pollution as sin is, himself so highly ransomed and ennobled to a new friendship and filial relation with God. (p. 680)

The idea of the rediscovery of self-esteem is crucial to Milton's belief in Christian liberty. In a long passage from the same treatise, his images of posture and countenance, used both for the individual and for the church, reflect in physical terms the moral sufficiency which only Christ gives to the faithful:

> But when every good Christian . . . shall be restored to his right in the church, . . . this and nothing sooner will open his eyes to a wise and true valuation of himself, which is so requisite and high a point of Christianity, and will stir him up to walk worthy the honorable and grave employment wherewith God and the church hath dignified him; not fearing lest he should meet with some outward holy thing in religion which his lay touch or presence might profane, but lest something unholy from within his own heart should dishonor and profane in himself that priestly unction and clergy-right whereto Christ hath entitled him. Then would the congregation of the Lord soon recover the true likeness and visage of what she is indeed, a holy generation, a royal priesthood, a saintly communion, the household and city of God. (p. 681)

The individual and the church must stand firm, independent of external props and controls. In regeneration, both man and society assume once more the posture of self-esteem and the image of God.

The same images and themes recur in Milton's autobiographical writings. There is in his strong passages of self-consolation that same sense of a full but patient use of one's given being. His rejoinders in *The Second Defense of the People of England* concentrate with particular force on his opponent's charges of physical deformity. He replies, "how can that be called diminutive which is great enough for every virtuous achievement?" (p. 824). In defending his blindness, Milton anticipates the easy transition between physical and spiritual strength which he develops in *Paradise Lost:*

There is, as the apostle has remarked, a way to strength through weakness. Let me then be the most feeble creature alive, as long as that feebleness serves to invigorate the energies of my rational and immortal spirit; as long as in that obscurity, in which I am enveloped, the light of the divine presence more clearly shines; then, in proportion as I am weak, I shall be invincibly strong, and in proportion as I am blind, I shall more clearly see. (p. 826)

Such confident assertions of self-esteem are, of course, part of the public image necessary to an international apologist. Milton more privately expresses his doubts about uselessness and physical disability in the sonnet, "When I consider how my light is spent." He presents a state of confusion between the eagerness to act in God's behalf and the annoyance that his means of action are so severely curtailed through blindness:

> "Doth God exact day-labor, light denied,"
> I fondly ask; But patience to prevent
> That murmur, soon replies, "God doth not need
> Either man's work or his own gifts; who best
> Bear his mild yoke, they serve him best; his State
> Is Kingly. Thousands at his bidding speed
> And post o'er Land and Ocean without rest:
> They also serve who only stand and wait."

Both action, which he seeks, and patience, which he finds, are redefined in his self-consolation. Action, because God does not *need* it, is important mainly as a test of obedience; patience meets action in the key word, "stand." The final image of the sonnet pictures a far more active, strenuous engagement than may at first appear. He who can *stand* fulfills that crucial condition which was hoped of Adam—obedience; for that, he must employ the whole sufficiency of nature and grace, maintaining the image of God by means of and in behalf of his creation and redemption.

Man's life after the Fall is both active and patient: standing in the knowlege of his strength and in preparedness for trial, walking in the restless labor of procuring physical and spiritual nourishment and shelter. The easy tasks of Eden are transformed, in the final books of *Paradise Lost,* into the nearly impossible demands of Michael's histories and of the harsh settlement of the world. The consolation for this harsh change appears, in part, in those pictures of Adam and Eve which physically illustrate the sustaining covenant of grace. Adam says to Michael,

> Ascend, I follow thee, safe Guide, the path
> Thou lead'st me, and to the hand of Heav'n submit,
> However chast'ning, to the evil turn
> My obvious breast, arming to overcome
> By suffering, and earn rest from labor won,
> If so I may attain.   (XI, 371-76)

Adam's apparent literal dependence on the guidance of heaven, which supports his own natural but fallen strength, is an image of the militant Christian soul upheld in virtue by faith and reason.

The "ingenuous and noble degree of honest shame, or . . . esteem," which Milton describes as an essential quality of Christian liberty, is a major element in Adam's new stature of dependent dignity:

> Henceforth I learn, that to obey is best,
> And love with fear the only God, to walk
> As in his presence, ever to observe
> His providence, and on him sole depend.   (XII, 561-64)

We are to remember how Adam, earlier in the poem, walked with confidence in the presence of God.

At the very end, in the midst of a vast landscape, the tiny figures of Adam and Eve maintain by means of God's support that sufficiency and freedom in which they were created:

> The World was all before them, where to choose
> Thir place of rest, and Providence thir guide:
> They hand in hand with wand'ring steps and slow,
> Through *Eden* took thir solitary way.   (XII, 646-49)

They have fallen, yet they stand. Providence now guides them, whereas previously reason was enough; their dependence—on God and on each other—is now undoubted. Much is desolate in their future and in the future of their children—grief, sin, damnation—and many will fall along this "solitary way." Yet implicit in this ending is the hopeful and developed knowledge, poetically secure in the image in which it is expressed, that whoever walks in the consciousness of his created and sustained capacity to serve God shall finally stand the test.

Kent State University

NOTES

1. *PL* III, 93–102. All quotations from Milton are from *John Milton: Complete Poems and Major Prose,* ed. Merritt Y. Hughes (New York, 1957), unless otherwise indicated.

2. *The Return of Eden: Five Essays on Milton's Epics* (Toronto, 1965), p. 99.

3. Throughout this paper, I am indebted to the work of Stanley E. Fish, particularly to "Standing Only: Christian Heroism," the fourth chapter of his *Surprised by Sin: The Reader in Paradise Lost* (New York, 1967).

4. Genesis i, 26–27 (Authorized Version).

5. "Renaissance Ideas on Man's Upright Form," *JHI,* XIX (1958), 256–58.

6. *Devotions upon Emergent Occasions,* quoted in Patrides, "Renaissance Ideas," p. 256.

7. *John Milton,* p. 359 n.

8. See C. A. Patrides, *Milton and the Christian Tradition* (Oxford, 1966), pp. 49–51.

9. See *OED,* s.v. "suburb," 4 b.

SPEECH IN *PARADISE LOST*

Beverley Sherry

In the sixteenth and seventeenth centuries several treatises (religious, philosophical, and rhetorical) discussed the Fall of Man as involving a corruption of mankind's speech. In *Paradise Lost* we witness a dramatization of that corruption. Adam and Eve lose what Thomas Wilson, in his *Arte of Rhetorique* (1560), calls the "Eloquence first giuen by God"; their speech is confounded in the way Godfrey Goodman describes fallen man's speech in *The Fall of Man* (1616). This confounding of their utterance is particularly noticeable in Adam and Eve's speech rhythms, which in the context of *Paradise Lost* are transformed from a celestial to an infernal resemblance. Adam and Eve's conversation also suffers an impairment, so that by the close of the poem they have inaugurated what Richard Allestree in *The Government of the Tongue* (1675) calls "our rusty drossy Converse." Their conversation with each other has been changed and limited, their converse with God and the angels virtually lost. The poem itself, however, curiously makes up for this fall in Adam and Eve's speech. The poet projects himself as a fallen man, a son of Adam and Eve, but as a man conversing freely with God and graced with an eloquence given by God. The poem itself is in fact the result of the poet's converse with God.

"SPEECH," WROTE Ben Jonson, "is the only benefit man hath to express his excellency of mind above other creatures";[1] Godfrey Goodman, in his treatise on *The Fall of Man* (London, 1616), calls speech "the only companion, and witnesse of reason" (p. 295). This was a commonplace Renaissance belief, and it is also one of the first things Milton's Adam discerns about himself; surveying the animals of paradise, Adam complains to his Creator, "I by conversing cannot these erect / From prone, nor in thir wayes complacence find" (VIII, 432–33).[2] So he asks God for a mate to converse with. His request is granted and Adam has his Eve—"With thee conversing I forget all time," says Eve to Adam (IV, 639), and Adam to Eve, "How can I live without thee, how forgoe / Thy sweet Converse?" (IX, 908–09). John Halkett warns us that by "conversation" Milton meant essentially "association, living with, companionship, society."[3] Milton did use the word in this sense, but he used it in our sense too;[4] in *Paradise Lost* "converse" generally means at once companionship and speech, and both meanings are essential.

Speech, a gift peculiar to man and the poet's special gift, has an important role in Milton's story of the Fall of Man. This has been recognized by critics, notably by Anne Davidson Ferry in *Milton and the Miltonic Dryden* and also in her *Milton's Epic Voice*. It is now commonly agreed that there is a decorous change in Adam and Eve's speech with the Fall, a transition from a stylized to a more natural manner. Furthermore, several critics feel that the Fall results in a deterioration in clarity and a Satanic influence invading mankind's speech.[5] The present essay looks again at the subject of speech in *Paradise Lost*, speech considered as utterance itself and also as conversation, and attempts to throw more light on the subject by doing two things. First, I relate speech in *Paradise Lost* specifically to several sixteenth- and seventeenth-century treatises which discuss speech and the Fall of Man; second, in my analysis of particular passages from the poem I concentrate on one element of speech, rhythm.

I

In the sixteenth and seventeenth centuries all arts and wisdom, including eloquence, were thought to have originated in Adam and to have been corrupted by the Fall. So Thomas Wilson, in his *Arte of Rhetorique*, writes that eloquence was "first giuen by God, and after lost by man, and last repayred by God againe"; after "the fall of our first Father," men degenerated into savages and lost the gift of rational speech until God "gaue his appointed Ministers knowledge both to see the natures of men, and also graunted them the gift of vtteraunce, that they might with ease win folke at their will, and frame them by reason to all good order."[6] The ideas here—the original excellence of man's speech, its corruption with the Fall, its subsequent repair, and the regenerative power of eloquence upon fallen mankind—all recur, often expanded, in other sixteenth- and seventeenth-century writings, religious, philosophical, and rhetorical.

The original excellence of Adam and Eve's speech and its corruption are interpreted quite literally by some commentators on Genesis: God spoke Hebrew, so did Adam, and this language was lost at Babel.[7] Milton, in *The Art of Logic*, refers to the language "which Adam spoke in Eden" as distinct from the languages "which the builders of the tower of Babel suddenly received" (CM, XI, p. 221), and in *Paradise Lost* the confusion of tongues (XII, 48–62) is manifest evidence of the Fall, in the world of the poem a kind of second hissing episode. A more interesting interpretation of the confusion of tongues, however, and one also relevant to *Paradise Lost*, is offered by Godfrey Goodman in *The Fall of Man*. Rather than emphasizing the corruption of a pristine Hebrew, Goodman connects the confusion of tongues with a general obscurity and ineloquence in our speech; as a fallen man himself he feels bound to make this rather quaint apology:

> Here rather I wil now snatch at the present occasion, so fitly offered: if I haue spoken any thing, or shall hereafter speake in this Pamphlet, vnadvisedly, illiterately, without good order or methode; acknowledge (I beseech Thee) the generall punishment of whole mankind, which more especially discouers it selfe in my weakenesse, the confusion of tongues. I am confounded, I am confounded, poore silly wretch that I am, I am confounded, my minde is distracted, my tongue is confounded, and my whole nature corrupted. (p. 310)

According to Goodman, the angels speak with a kind of miraculous directness and clarity (pp. 299, 304), as did Adam before his fall: "It were to bee wished, that we might speake the language of *Adam*, where names were imposed according to the nature of things" (p. 302). This is that "first *rectitude of words*" noted by Theophilus Gale.[8] Several other seventeenth-century writers discuss man's unfallen speech and its deterioration. A typical view is that of John Weemse, who, in *The Pourtraiture of the Image of God in Man* (London, 1627), writes that "before the fall, the *Tongue* of man was like *the pen of a swift writer*," but that this eloquence was lost (pp. 22–23). In *The Gift of Prayer* (London, 1655) John Wilkins writes that the tongue, "which should be *our glory, the best member that we have,* is by this Original corruption, become the worst, defiling all the rest" (p. 80). In a lengthy treatise entitled *The Government of the Tongue* (Oxford, 1675), Richard Allestree makes the distinction that when Eve entered into conversation with the serpent, "Original sin came first out of the mouth by speaking, before it entred in by eating"

(p. 7), and he laments the loss of mankind's "pristine integrity" of speech (p. 10); after ten chapters which analyze the various defects of fallen speech, Allestree concludes that "those who would turn this Iron Age into Gold, that would convert our rusty drossy Converse into a purer strein, must be perfectly clean themselves" (p. 218).

Such a repairing of man's defective speech was believed possible through the grace of God, and this recovered eloquence was thought to work a kind of cure for the Fall. We see the theme of the healing power of eloquence in Book VI of Spenser's *Faerie Queene*, where Calidore, whose gracious speech "did steale mens hearts away," opposes the monstrous abuser of speech, the Blatant Beast, and throughout the Book the power of true eloquence, as distinct from the sophistry of a Blandina's "pleasing tongue," wins people over to goodness.[9] The most powerful eloquence of all in the sixteenth and seventeenth centuries was God's own Word, which could effect a man's regeneration and was held to be incomparably more eloquent, because more truthful, than human eloquence.[10] The idea that God's eloquence (embodied in the Bible or breathed into "appointed Ministers") could restore savage mankind is parallel to another Renaissance idea, derived from Horace, the theme of the civilizing power of poetry: "While men still roamed the woods, Orpheus, the holy prophet of the gods, made them shrink from bloodshed and brutal living; whence the fable that he tamed tigers and ravening lions."[11] This in turn is related to the idea of Mercury as a tamer of men because he introduced speech to them and speech is the instrument that links man to man and man to God; Ben Jonson writes that Mercury, "who is the president of language, is called *Deorum hominumque interpres*."[12]

Before relating these ideas to *Paradise Lost*, I want to point out that Milton's own ideas on eloquence, expressed mainly in his prose works, form part of this body of Renaissance thought on speech and the Fall of Man. Even for a humanist Milton had an unusually strong belief in the oneness of eloquence and virtue. He held that whenever there is a fall from virtue there is a decay of eloquence, that a lack of truth is betrayed by ineptitude in words.[13] Like Thomas Wilson, he believed in the civilizing power of some solitary Orpheus, a chosen man of God: "When men were first scattered asunder and straying about, some wise and eloquent man brought them over into civil life"; Moses was such a man who charmed the multitude with "true eloquence."[14] In Milton's writings one can trace a pattern of statements which amounts to an identifying of true eloquence with virtue, wisdom, truth, and God;[15] Milton distinguishes, as do all the humanists, between true eloquence and sophistry. For him true eloquence *is* truth, and God is its source: God cannot but speak truth, hence the absolute eloquence of the Bible. These ideas are close to the usual sixteenth- and seventeenth-century thinking on speech and the Fall of Man, and they are part of *Paradise Lost*.

A deterioration in Adam and Eve's paradisal eloquence, like that described by Thomas Wilson, Godfrey Goodman, or Richard Alles- tree, actually occurs in *Paradise Lost* at Book IX—that is, at the time of the Fall itself and long before the Babylonian confusion de- scribed in Book XII. To begin with, this corruption is hinted at by the narrator. The poet comments on what Thomas Wilson would have called the "Eloquence first giuen by God":

> neither various style
> Nor holy rapture wanted they to praise
> Thir Maker, in fit strains pronounc't or sung
> Unmeditated, such prompt eloquence
> Flowd from thir lips, in Prose or numerous Verse.   (V, 146–50)

Equally instinctive is the "first *rectitude of words*," the ability to name things: God praises Adam for "rightly" naming the animals (VIII, 437– 40), and Eve names the flowers (XI, 273–77). That most eloquent of angels, Raphael, who is likened to Mercury (V, 285), "the president of language," praises Adam's eloquence (VIII, 218–19, 247–48). But at the Fall, what Richard Allestree calls "the pristine integrity" of speech declines as Eve (like Spenser's false Blandina) speaks "bland words at will" (IX, 855), "bland" in the Latin sense of "fawning." With the Fall, Adam and Eve become for a time like the inarticulate savages described by Thomas Wilson: "silent, and in face / Confounded long they sate, as struck'n mute" (IX, 1063–64), until Adam, now a wild man of the woods, "estrang'd in look and alterd stile" (IX, 1132), recovers speech. Sin's plan to infect man's very words (X, 608) ma- terializes, and Adam himself begins to feel what "farr other Song" was his before the Fall (X, 860–62). God the Son reports that Adam and Eve are now "Unskilful with what words to pray" and asks the Father to hear their sighs, "though mute" (X, 31–32), and these are the pair who once lacked no words to use in prayer, "such prompt eloquence / Flowd from thir lips." These hints of a loss of paradisal eloquence are actualized in Adam and Eve's speeches and confirmed by the wider context of dramatic styles in the poem.

That context is a pattern of "fallen" and "unfallen" speech.[16] Before Adam and Eve utter a word, a structure of dramatic styles has been set up, celestial against infernal, like the two forms of speech—from heaven and hell—into which Richard Allestree says man must choose to mold his own speech (*The Government of the Tongue*, p. 223). In the world of the poem, as the poem interprets itself, God's voice emerges as absolute eloquence, and this parallels Renaissance thought: celestial speech in *Paradise Lost*, like the "true eloquence" defined in Milton's prose works or the divine eloquence praised by seventeenth-century rhetoricians, is characterized chiefly by its bare truth, though also by measured, composed rhythms; infernal speech is recognized mainly by untruth (conscious or unconscious), but also by aggressive and often irregular rhythms. Measured against this yardstick of "good" and "bad" eloquence, the change in Adam and Eve's speech at Book IX appears indeed as a "confounding" of an originally godlike speech. In *Paradise Lost* we witness a dramatization of that depravation of speech discussed in the treatises of Wilson, Goodman, Allestree, Wilkins, Weemse, and others.

One of the surest signs of the loss of the "Eloquence first giuen by God" is the disappearance of Adam and Eve's vocal prayers, earthly shadows of the angels' biblical hymns.[17] In Milton's myth Adam and Eve are literally the first poets: their "psalms" (IV, 724–35; V, 153–208) are really the originals of David's, as their love songs (IV, 635–56; V, 17–25) are prototypes of Solomon's Song. In a century which regarded the Bible as true eloquence, such psalms and canticles must have seemed man's prime vocal accomplishment, and they vanish with the Fall, to be replaced by an idolatrous hymn (IX, 795 ff.), uncannily like Satan's (IX, 679 ff.), and by a silent morning prayer described at the close of Book X and the beginning of Book XI. Adam and Eve are not damned, since they *can* pray, but their loss of paradise is total and is reflected partly in the loss of their God-given poetry.

When we scrutinize their speeches, the Fall seems to corrode Adam and Eve's godlike eloquence in every detail. All the defects of fallen speech which Godfrey Goodman lists, "fallacies and sophistrie, through Tautologies, ambiguous words, darke sentences" (*The Fall *of Man*, p. 294), infest their speeches in Books IX and X. But *Paradise Lost* is a poem, we listen to it, we hear it creating special effects of different voices, different rhythms; and within its own scheme of dramatic styles, a single element of speech very audibly confounded at the time of the Fall is rhythm. Before the Fall human speech has the measured rhythms and steady grace of celestial speech; after the Fall it moves in the restless rhythms of infernal speech. In reply to Albert Cook, who claims that "one can seldom find in *Paradise Lost* a line where only three of the accents stand out over the other two, and never, I believe, a line in which one can distinguish a single major accent alone,"[18] I would point to:

> That we were fórmd then saist thou? and the work
> Of sécondarie hands.   (V, 853–54)

> Hast thou not wónderd, *Adam*, at my stáy?   (IX, 856)

> Would thou hadst héark'nd to my words, and stái'd
> With me, as I besóught thee.   (IX, 1134–35)

> O voice once heard
> Delightfully, *Encrease and multiply*,
> Now déath to heare! for what can Í encrease
> Or multiplie, but cúrses on my head?   (X, 729–32)

Among the speeches of the fallen characters one does not have to look far to find lines with three or two or even one major accent. There is a rhythmic reorientation of Adam and Eve's speech at Book IX which is actually a transition from the kind of "abstract music" that Albert Cook hears everywhere in *Paradise Lost* to uneven, individualized speech rhythms.

To hear this rhythmic shift one might compare Adam's consolation of Eve (V, 95–128) with his speech beginning "Out of my sight, thou Serpent" (X, 867–908). The first speech moves in these rhythms:

> Best Ímage òf my sélf and déarer hálf   (V, 95)

which has the rhythmic serenity of:

> O Són, in whóm my Sóul hath chíef delíght   (III, 168)

Likewise, these rhythms:

> But knów that ín the Sóule
> Are mány lésser Fácultíes that sérve
> Réason as chíef   (V, 100–02)

resemble Raphael's,

> For knów, whatéver wàs creáted, néeds
> To bé sustáind and féd; of Éleménts
> The grósser féeds the púrer, Eárth the Séa   (V, 414-16)

or Michael's,

>   yet knów witháll,
> Since thý original lápse, true Líbertìe
> Is lóst.   (XII, 82-84)

In his consolation of Eve, as in his discourses on the stars and free
will (IV, 660-88; IX, 343-75), Adam indeed has the voice of an instructing angel. But in Book IX the controlled, calm rhythms have given
place to assertive, uneven rhythms:

>   But for thée
> I had persisted háppie, . . .
>
>   .   .   .   .
>   O whý did Gód,
> Creator wíse, that people'd highest Heav'n
> With Spirits Másculine, create at last
> This nóveltie on Earth, this fair deféct
> Of Nature, and not fill the World at once
> With Mén as Ángels withóut Feminine,
> Or find some óther way to generate
> Mankind? this mischief had not then befáll'n
> And more that sháll befall.   (X, 873-96)

Here the iambic pentameter is subordinate to a thrusting, uneven
rhythm which traces out the emotional emphases of the speaker. It
is, to our ears, the natural, animated movement of a human voice.
At the same time, in the context of *Paradise Lost* it betrays itself
as Satanic:

> O had his powerful Destiny ordaind
> Me some infériour Angel, I had stood
> Then háppie.   (IV, 58-60)

> Know ye not mée? ye knew me ónce no mate
> For you, there sítting where ye durst not sóare;
> Not to know mée argues your sélves unknown.   (IV, 828-30)

Here, as in Adam's fallen speech, the iambic pattern is in abeyance,
composure is gone, the rhythms twist and turn nervously, tracing out

emotional thought rather than reason. The infernal dislocating of
rhythm in Adam's voice and Satan's echoes the dislocating of the godlike faculty of reason by passion. Reason in us was once God's word,
says Thomas Blount, in *The Academie of Eloquence* (London, 1654),
"and would be so, if it were the same he gave; But it is now fallen" (pp.
21–22), and with it is fallen speech itself. The rhythmic confounding of
Adam's speech shows that fall, as do other qualities of his utterance. In
diction and tone, for example, his tirade against Eve approaches the
low talk of Satan or Belial ("then whom a Spirit more lewd / Fell not
from Heav'n"). With sardonic wit Adam refers to Eve as "a Rib /
Crooked by nature, bent, as now appears, / More to the part sinister
from me drawn" (X, 884–86); the double meanings continue as Adam
accuses his Maker of not devising "some other way to generate / Mankind" apart from "straight conjunction with this Sex" (X, 888–98). This
is an example of the "Ribaldrie, and luxurious speech" which Godfrey
Goodman sees as marks of fallen speech (*The Fall of Man*, pp. 293–94);
and it is on the same level as the sarcastic punning of Belial and Satan in
the War in Heaven (VI, 558–67, 609–27). The essential corruption, of
course, is Adam's weakened grasp on truth: the speech is full of what
Goodman calls fallacies, and Adam has now become one of those
many men and women whom Goodman regards as dumb beasts because they make a lot of noise but little sense (*The Fall of Man*, p. 300).

The corruption of speech is just as drastic with Eve's fall. The
flowing rhythms of such beautiful lines as these:

> but fóllow mé
> And Í will bríng thee whére no shádow stáies
> Thy cóming   (IV, 469–71)

are quite broken by the time we hear Eve's soliloquy:

> But to Ádam in what sort
> Shall I appeer? shall I to him make knówn
> As yet my change, and give him to partake
> Full happiness wíth mee, or rather nót,
> But kéep the odds of Knowledge.   (IX, 816–20)

The irregular rhythms of the voice of someone thinking aloud immediately brand this speech as fallen in the context of *Paradise Lost*
and recall another voice:

> all is not théirs it seems:
> One fatal Tree there stands of Knówledge call'd,
> Forbidden them to táste: Knowledge forbídd'n?
> Suspícious, réasonless.   (IV, 513-16)

Eve's soliloquy after eating the fruit is her most Satanic speech, from the idolatrous hymn, "O Sovran, vertuous, precious of all Trees" (IX, 795 ff.), to the sophistic rhetorical question, "for inferior who is free?" (IX, 825), to the theatrical exit flourish:

> So dear I love him, that with him all deaths
> I could endure, without him live no life.
> So saying, from the Tree her step she turnd.   (IX, 832-34)

—a little less histrionic than but similar to some of Satan's exit lines.[19] When Adam is furthest from Milton's God, "author both of purity and eloquence," he too soliloquizes in the Satanic style (X, 720-844).[20] The strident rhythms of Adam and Eve's accusing speeches at the close of Book IX, moreover, recall the individual, assertive rhythms of the egocentric speeches in Pandemonium. At the depths of their fall, surrounded in spiritual darkness, a kind of hell, both Adam and Eve take on an infernal eloquence.

This diabolical confounding of their speech is most violent in Books IX and X. At the close of Book X a new peace enters their speech, the Satanic accents fade. For there is, of course, a difference between man's fall and Satan's, and although Adam and Eve lose their pristine eloquence, they do recover some kind of speech. It is not insignificant that Satan, father of lies and therefore the most monstrous abuser of speech, finally loses his power of utterance; having desecrated speech by causing an animal to speak and to speak lies, he plays his final scene in the poem speechless ("he would have spoke, / But hiss for hiss returnd with forked tongue" [X, 517-18]). Satan's departure from God is now complete: in *Paradise Lost* God is preeminently a *voice*, a bare voice speaking truth; Satan has now become a mere brute body without a speaking voice. Reason, God's stamp in man, and speech, "the only companion, and witnesse of reason," are not thus erased in Adam and Eve. From their reconciliation to the end of the poem their speech is a mixture: vestiges of "good" and "bad" eloquence remain. The aggressive Satanic rhythms recur, for example, in: "Why is life gív'n / To be thus wrésted from us? rather why / Obtrúded on us thus?" (XI, 502-04), and the gulf between

Michael's voice and Adam's reminds us that Adam no longer sounds like an angel. Near the end of the poem, though, there is also this style:

> Whénce thou retúrnst, and whíther wéntst, I knów;
>
> . . . .
>   but nów lead ón;
> In mée is nó deláy; with thée to góe,
> Is to stáy hére; withóut thee hére to stáy,
> Is to gó hénce unwílling; thóu to mée
> Art áll things únder Héav'n, all pláces thóu.   (XII, 610-18)

The composed rhythms and biblical echoes are shades of celestial speech. And yet, placed beside Eve's canticle on the same theme before the Fall (IV, 635-56), this speech in Book XII appears as a poetically impoverished version of that first love poem. The "Eloquence first giuen by God" is lost, and with it is lost, as we shall see next, the converse given by God.

II

Conversation changes and deteriorates with the Fall. Again, this is something discussed by seventeenth-century writers and dramatized in *Paradise Lost*. Speech was first ordained for two things: for what Samuel Purchas calls man's "blessed familiarity with God, societie of Angels" (*Purchas his Pilgrimage* [London, 1626], p. 18), and for Adam and Eve's "mutual conference and conversation amongst themselves" (Gale, *The Court of the Gentiles*, I, i, 55). With the Fall, man lost his "great happinesse" of conversing with the angels (Weemse, *The Pourtraiture of the Image of God in Man*, p. 299). At the same time, speech, "the fittest instrument to manage a commerce between the rational yet invisible powers of human souls cloathed in flesh" (Allestree, *The Government of the Tongue*, p. 3), degenerated into "our rusty drossy Converse," became an embodiment of our fallen condition, "this Iron Age" (p. 218). Godfrey Goodman writes that the Fall resulted in men's no longer being able to speak to each other's understanding, and he looks forward to a "higher state" when men will be "like the Angels of heauen, who speake to each other, by directing the edge of their understanding to each other, as it were opening the glasses, and casting foorth a light to each other" (*The Fall of Man*, pp. 299-300, 304).

In Milton's poem, conversation is part of the joy and glory and fulfillment which is paradise. Before the Fall, Adam and Eve's marriage is like that ideal marriage described in *The Doctrine and Discipline of Divorce*, in which conversation plays its ideal role as a remedy for loneliness: Adam's desire for a mate was a desire "to put off an unkindly solitarines" and for this purpose man needs "an intimate and speaking help," no "mute and spiritles mate" (CM, III, pt. 2, pp. 396–97). Indeed there is one line which typifies Milton's unfallen Adam and Eve: "Thus talking hand in hand alone they pass'd" (IV, 689). Speech, like a golden chain of concord, is "the instrument of society," as Ben Jonson would say, in an ideal society of man, woman, angels, and God. So loneliness is an impossibility. Conversation is not just utilitarian, it is delighted in for its own sake. Eve says to Adam, "With thee conversing I forget all time" (IV, 639), and Adam cannot bear the thought of forgoing "sweet Converse" with Eve (IX, 909). Adam also enjoys "celestial Colloquie sublime" with his Maker (VIII, 455), and converse with Raphael charms his soul (V, 544-48; VIII, 1-3, 210-16, 252-53). The prospect of not being able to speak with God torments him after the Fall (XI, 315-22) and, although Michael says that God will be in the lower world, the vision of history shows little actual converse between God and man.

The dramatization of the decay in Adam and Eve's conversation, like the dramatization of the decay in their "Eloquence first giuen by God," is bound up with the pattern of celestial and infernal speech. The early conversations of Adam and Eve, those in Book IV particularly, are stylized dialogues similar to the dialogue in heaven. They are not real conversations in our sense, but approximate more to emblems, emblems of harmony. Like the speeches of the Father and Son, these early speeches are complementary: a speech of Adam will find its continuation and other half in a following speech by Eve, thus forming a *duologue*. This strange confluence is hardly real to us and suggests a complete intimacy of two beings in "blisful solitude." Perhaps the overtones of Solomon's Song in these early speeches makes for the sense of two-in-oneness, for the voices of Bride and Bridegroom intermingle in a binary fashion. But the sense of harmony is strengthened most by the shape of the heavenly dialogue behind Adam and Eve's and also by the following pattern of phrases: "O Son, in whom my Soul hath chief delight, / Son of my bosom, Son who art alone

/ My Word, my wisdom" (III, 168-70); "Sole partner and sole part of all these joyes, / Dearer they self then all" (IV, 411-12); "O thou / My sole complacence!" (III, 275-76); "O Sole in whom my thoughts find all repose, / My Glorie, my Perfection" (V, 28-29); "Best Image of my self and dearer half" (V, 95); "Son, thou in whom my glory I behold / In full resplendence, Heir of all my might" (V, 719-20); "Effulgence of my Glorie, Son belov'd" (VI, 680); "Sole *Eve*, Associate sole" (IX, 227). It is an incantation celebrating union: before the Fall, Adam and Eve are one as the Father and Son are one, as the rays of light and its center, the stream and its source in Milton's hymn to light are one (III, 1-8), and their shapely duologues shadow forth this harmony. With the Fall, they are never one in that more than mortal way again.

A sign of separation is the disintegration of their converse as duologue gives place to monologue, a characteristically fallen mode of utterance in *Paradise Lost*. The only occasion when Adam and Eve soliloquize before the Fall interestingly illustrates Richard Allestree's comment that "Original sin came first out of the mouth by speaking, before it entred in by eating" (*The Government of the Tongue*, p. 7). Just prior to the eating of the fruit, evil comes into Adam's and Eve's minds and is expressed in soliloquy (IX, 745-79, 896-916); they make their choice to approve that evil by eating the fruit. Thereupon the Satanic tendency to soliloquize grows stronger, Adam and Eve turn away from each other and from God into themselves, and the chain of converse is broken. With it is destroyed that ideal society of paradise, and Milton's allusions (IX, 1115-18) suggest the descent into savagery which Thomas Wilson describes as the aftermath of the Fall. Adam degenerates into a wild man of the woods, and the nadir in the fall from duologue to monologue is the longest speech in the poem, his soliloquy (X, 720-844), "one of the loneliest scenes in literature."[21] Converse with God and his angels was once sweeter to Adam than "Fruits of Palm-tree" (VIII, 212); now the voice of God seems like thunder in his ears (X, 779-80), as it will seem to his descendants (XII, 227-36).

The deterioration in Adam and Eve's converse emerges more subtly in the different qualities of their arguments preceding and following the Fall. The argument about gardening (IX, 205-384) has sometimes been taken as a sign that Adam and Eve are virtually fallen. I do not hold this view. As yet there is no false eloquence because there is no untruth. The argument is eminently reasonable: each person listens to the other, then proffers alternative arguments; Adam and Eve are well intentioned, both speak truth. Eve is rightly aware of the difficulty of controlling the garden; Adam himself sees that (IV, 623–29), as the narrator does (IX, 202–03). Adam rightly fears Satan's strength and wishes to protect Eve. Eve rightly believes that God gave her strength to stand alone and not unreasonably feels that goodness is not worth much if it cannot stand alone. She wants to tie up some roses with myrtle and, once Adam agrees, goes directly and does that (IX, 424–31). Neither Adam nor Eve is fallen: passion has not overthrown reason— Eve speaks with "sweet austeer composure," Adam replies fervently but in "reasoning words." Neither is disobeying God: Eve is free to debate with Adam, as Adam is free to debate with his superiors; she was not forbidden to leave his side, he was not commanded to force her obedience. There is a tension and a give and take, particularly at the conclusion, with Adam respecting Eve's free will ("Go; for thy stay, not free. . .") and Eve respecting his wisdom ("With thy permission then, and thus forewarnd / Chiefly by what thy own last reasoning words / Touchd."). It is a debate between two unfallen creatures, true eloquence versus true eloquence, unlike the confrontations of true and false eloquence in *Comus* or the debate between Abdiel and Satan, where Comus and Satan do not hear, or do not want to hear, their opponents' points. The debate in paradise resolves itself with difficulty but with honesty after Adam and Eve have communicated rationally, honestly. They are still a little lower than the angels, "who speake to each other, by directing the edge of their understanding to each other" (Goodman, *The Fall of Man*, p. 304). After the Fall, the "vain contest" which appears to have "no end" (IX, 1134–90) is far removed from such reasoned discourse. Adam is now "estrang'd in look and alterd stile"; so is Eve ("Was I to have never parted from thy síde? / As good have grown there still a liveless Ríb"). There is no communing, no refining of thought, enlarging of the heart, as Raphael would have wished. The gist of the quarrel is:

ADAM: Why didn't you listen to me?
EVE: What do you mean? Why did you let me go?
ADAM: Is this the thanks I get for choosing to fall with you?

—a lonely and manifestly fallen conversation, always focusing on the self. Adam and Eve have inaugurated once and for all "our rusty drossy Converse." Here is none of the dovetailing of the earliest speeches nor any of the rational rapport of the argument about gardening; Eve is blinded by her own selfish emotion, Adam by his, and the speeches consequently rebound upon contact. This is the origin of all such "Harangues" and "factious opposition" as typify discourse in our world (XI, 663-64) and the origin of the ultimate confusion, that "hideous gabble" when "each to other calls / Not understood" (XII, 56-58). How ironic now is Adam's cry, "How can I live without thee, how forgoe / Thy sweet Converse?"

Adam and Eve reestablish communication; reason and love revive. Their reconciliation speeches at the close of Book X are moving in their bareness, reticence; here is a new converse, not made out of paired speeches, neither stylized nor celestial, and wholly utilitarian. The sheer joy in conversing, so powerfully sensed in Books IV and V, is gone. Gone too is "celestial Colloquie sublime." The difference between the two archangels' visits is an index of this: with Raphael Adam converses ("Go," says the Father, "half this day as friend with friend / Converse with *Adam*" V, 229-30)—Raphael, that Miltonic Mercury, is indeed *Deorum hominumque interpres;* but with the Fall there can be no more "Venial discourse unblam'd" between angels and men (IX, 5), and so Adam does not really converse with the archangel Michael. In the last line of the poem man is indeed "solitarie" as he never was before the Fall: his converse with his own kind has been impaired, his converse with God and the angels virtually lost. This accounts partly for the sense of desolation as Adam and Eve leave paradise and silence descends upon them and the alienated angels behind them. But the sense of loss is offset somewhat by the very fact of the poem's existence: we sense strongly a man speaking this poem and speaking with God; we feel the poet's presence, a fallen man, one of Adam's sons, and we see him attaining converse with God again, receiving speech from God, and undertaking the task of taming fallen mankind with his gift of utterance.

III

I would like to suggest finally, then, how the character of the poet relates to what I have been saying about speech in *Paradise Lost*.[22] Eloquence, as Thomas Wilson wrote, was "first giuen by God, and after lost by man, and last repayred by God againe"; a few sons of Adam recover the gift of divine utterance and, as a cure for the

Fall, use the gift to "win folke at their will, and frame them by
reason to all good order." With these men Milton would have placed
the few who produce works "doctrinal and exemplary to a Nation,"
whose Orphean abilities, "wheresoever they be found, are the inspired
guift of God rarely bestow'd, but yet to some (though most abuse)
in every Nation: and are of power beside the office of a pulpit, to
imbreed and cherish in a great people the seeds of vertu, and publick
civility, to allay the perturbations of the mind, and set the affections
in right tune."[23] The Christian poet who has such abilities can and
must *converse* with God. Milton himself hoped to produce a work
not with the aid of the nine muses, "but by devout prayer to that
eternall Spirit who can enrich with all utterance and knowledge, and
sends out his Seraphim with the hallow'd fire of his Altar to touch
and purify the lips of whom he pleases."[24] Such chosen men are Ezekiel
and Isaiah and also the Apostles, whose gift "To speak all Tongues"
(XII, 501) was traditionally regarded as the reverse of the confusion
of tongues. If we should believe Milton's third wife, Milton himself
spoke his poem exactly as the Holy Spirit had dictated it to him.[25]
The bard of *Paradise Lost* certainly portrays himself, in the way the
seventeenth century saw the writers of Scripture, as the amanuensis
of the Holy Spirit, and he aspires to be one of the few eloquent
men of the fallen world, associating himself with Moses (I, 1–5), David
and Solomon (I, 10–13; III, 29–32); St. John the Divine (IV, 1–5),
as well as with Homer (III, 32–35), Orpheus (VII, 32–37), and also
the soothsayer Tiresias (III, 36), who (like Abdiel, Enoch, and Noah)
was truly eloquent because he spoke truth. The poet projects himself
as a man speaking to God and receiving speech from God.

The whole of *Paradise Lost* could be regarded as a mortal man's
conversation with God—the poet asks and God in the form of the
heavenly muse replies. But more particularly, it is in the prologues
to Books I, III, and VII that we overhear converse with God, not
unlike what Richard Baxter describes in *The Christians Converse with
God* (London, 1693). And the poet's converse with God is analogous
to Adam's converse, which he lost, with God and the angels. Indeed
quite a noticeable parallel exists, I believe, between the poet's address
to Urania and Adam's speeches to Raphael—"Descend from Heav'n
Urania" (VII, 1), for example, is echoed in "Deign to descend now
lower" (VII, 84), which in turn anticipates "who deignes / Her nightly
visitation" (IX, 21–22). It is in Book VII that the blind bard's converse
with his heavenly muse reaches its greatest intimacy; by this stage

the poet clings to his Urania, his only solace in a world which is fallen and still haunted by a Blatant Beast:

> Standing on Earth, not rapt above the Pole,
> More safe I Sing with mortal voice, unchang'd
> To hoarce or mute, though fall'n on evil dayes,
> On evil days though fall'n, and evil tongues;
> In darkness, and with dangers compast round,
> And solitude; yet not alone, while thou
> Visit'st my slumbers Nightly, or when Morn
> Purples the East: still govern thou my Song,
> Urania.   (VII, 23-31)

This is the kind of solace Richard Baxter derives from converse with God ("Come home then, O my Soul, to God: Converse in Heaven; Turn away thine eyes from beholding Vanity," "O speak to him that teacheth thee to speak" [*The Christians Converse with God*, pp. 132, 139]). And here in the converse with Urania is a definite claim that the muse visits the poet in sleep. His muse is like a combination of God, angel, and lover; his converse with her is a remedy for loneliness and analogous to Adam's sweet converse before the Fall with God, Raphael, and Eve. The poet has recovered in fact something of what seventeenth-century writers regarded as "mans great happinesse before the fall, that he conuersed with the angels, and they loued him" (Weemse, *The Pourtraiture of the Image of God in Man*, p. 299).

The poet has also recovered something of the peculiar "Eloquence first giuen by God" to Adam and Eve. In Book IX he speaks of the "answerable" or fit style he hopes to obtain from his "celestial Patroness, who deignes / Her nightly visitation unimplor'd, / And dictates to me slumbring, or inspires / Easie my unpremeditated Verse" (IX, 20-24). The words curiously recall the description of Adam and Eve's prefallen orisons,

> each morning duly paid
> In various style, for neither various style
> Nor holy rapture wanted they to praise
> Thir Maker, in fit strains pronounc't or sung
> Unmeditated, such prompt eloquence
> Flowd from thir lips, in Prose or numerous Verse.   (V, 145-50)

Adam and Eve lost their God-given eloquence, but the blind bard has recovered something like that "Eloquence first giuen by God, and after lost by man," for the easy flow of "unpremeditated Verse" which God gives him nightly is like the "Unmeditated" strains of Adam and Eve's "prompt eloquence." The poet's recovery of man's unfallen

eloquence is emphasized by an actual stylistic parallel between the
poet's own voice and the unfallen voices of *Paradise Lost*. In particular,
the verse rhythms in the poet's prayers and invocations are characteristically serene; Albert Cook singles out these passages for their
"abstract music."[26] The entire hymn to light (III, 1–55) exemplifies
the rhythmic composure we perceived in Adam and Eve's prefallen
speeches, and it is also close, in rhythms, images, and diction, to the
angels' hymn to God as light (III, 372–82). In several hymns, too,
the poet's voice intermingles with the voices of the unfallen angels
and Adam and Eve, and the voices become indistinguishable.[27] The
poet has certainly recovered a gift of prayer to make up for Adam
and Eve's lost vocal prayers. Further, the narrative voices of blind
bard, Raphael, and Michael are alike and all "with Grace Divine /
Imbu'd"; in the world of *Paradise Lost* Adam loses but the blind
bard finds again an angelic voice. Finally, the poet's voice is constantly
close to the Word of God and therefore truly eloquent.[28] All these
details strengthen the persona of the poet as the inspired bard of
God.

   The poet is a son of Adam, very conscious of that, but he is
graced with a "prompt eloquence" with which he tries to repair Adam's
sin by explaining God's ways to fallen men. All his ability for this
task arises out of converse with God. The poet and his heavenly muse
are like two separate characters and their converse an inner action
of the epic. The flowering of their converse is the making of the
poem. This counterbalances the loss of paradisal eloquence and paradisal converse by the poet's first parents. Although Adam and Eve
lose those gifts, become for a while even Satanic in speech, and breed
Satanic speech for the rest of mankind, some few of their descendants
are able to converse with God again and are granted the gift of divine
eloquence as an instrument to soften savage mankind. The poet in
Paradise Lost is one of those descendants.

University of Queensland

NOTES

   1. *Timber or Discoveries*, ed. Ralph S. Walker (Syracuse, 1953), p. 45.
   2. Quotations from Milton are from *The Works of John Milton*, ed. Frank Allen
Patterson et al. (New York, 1931–38), hereafter referred to as CM.

3. *Milton and the Idea of Matrimony* (New Haven and New York, 1970), p. 58.

4. In the seventeenth century "converse" had the general meaning "to associate with" and the particular meaning "to speak with." Milton sometimes uses the word strictly to mean "speak," for example: "Our Saviour, who had all gifts in him, was Lord to expresse his indoctrinating power in what sort him best seem'd; sometimes with mild and familiar converse, sometimes with plain and impartiall home-speaking" (*An Apology for Smectymnuus*, CM, III, pt. 1, pp. 312–13). He also uses the word to signify simultaneously speech and association, as in *The Doctrine and Discipline of Divorce:* "Who knowes not that the bashful mutenes of a virgin may oft-times hide all the unliveliness and natural sloth which is really unfit for conversation" (CM, III, pt. 2, p. 394).

5. See particularly *Milton's Epic Voice* (Cambridge, Mass., 1962), pp. 116–19, and *Milton and the Miltonic Dryden* (Cambridge, Mass., 1968), pp. 69–76, but also the following: Arnold Stein, *Answerable Style* (Minneapolis, 1953), pp. 66–67, 130, 138; Frank Kermode, "Adam Unparadised," in *The Living Milton*, ed. Frank Kermode (London, 1960), p. 95; Christopher Ricks, *Milton's Grand Style* (Oxford, 1963), pp. 109–17; Harold E. Toliver, "Complicity of Voice in *Paradise Lost*," *MLQ*, XXV (1964), 153–70; Stanley Eugene Fish, *Surprised by Sin* (New York, 1967), pp. 107–30, 139–40.

6. *Wilson's Arte of Rhetorique, 1560*, ed. G. H. Mair (Oxford, 1909), preface.

7. See Arnold Williams, *The Common Expositor* (Chapel Hill, 1948), pp. 162–63, 228–29; D. C. Allen, "Some Theories of the Growth and Origin of Language in Milton's Age," *PQ*, XXVIII (1949), 5–16. Cf. Patrick Hume, *Annotations on Milton's "Paradise Lost"* (London, 1695), p. 311.

8. *The Court of the Gentiles* (Oxford, 1672), vol. I, pt. i, p. 52.

9. *The Poetical Works of Edmund Spenser*, ed. J. C. Smith and E. De Selincourt (London, 1912), pp. 337, 364.

10. See William Whately, *The New Birth* (London, 1618), pp. 110–11; John Barton, *The Art of Rhetorick* (London, 1634), sig. A3; Thomas Blount, *The Academie of Eloquence* (London, 1654), pp. 21–22; William Nicholson, *David's Harp Strung and Tuned* (London, 1662), preface; Rene Rapin, *Reflections upon the Eloquence of these Times* (London, 1672), pp. 91–93; *The Art of Speaking* (London, 1676), pp. 76–77; James Durham, *Clavis Cantici* (Glasgow, 1688), pp. 1–2.

11. *The Art of Poetry*, 391–93, in *Horace, Satires, Epistles, Ars Poetica*, trans. H. Rushton Fairclough, Loeb Classical Library ed. (London, 1926), p. 483.

12. *Timber*, p. 41. On Mercury as the god of speech, see Gale, *The Court of the Gentiles*, vol. I, pt. ii, p. 45, and Weemse, *The Pourtraiture of the Image of God in Man*, p. 23.

13. See *The History of Britain*, CM, X, pp. 32–33, 101; *Colasterion*, CM, IV, pp. 235–73; *The First Defence*, CM, VII, p. 9.

14. *The First Defence*, CM, VII, pp. 395, 397; *The Reason of Church Government*, CM, III, pt. 1, pp. 181–82. Milton would have known Wilson's *Arte of Rhetorique*, since it was widely used in the schools and universities of his day. See George P. Rice, Jr., "Early Stuart Rhetorical Education," *Quarterly Journal of Speech*, XXIX (1943), 433–34.

15. See particularly *An Apology for Smectymnuus*, CM, III, pt. 1, pp. 287, 316, 362.

16. On the two extremes of rhetoric in all Milton's longer poems see: J. B. Broadbent, "Milton's Rhetoric," *MP*, LVI (1958–59), 224–42; John M. Major, "Milton's View of Rhetoric," *SP*, LXIV (1967), 685–711; John M. Steadman, "*Ethos* and *Dianoia*: Character and Rhetoric in *Paradise Lost*," in *Language and Style in Milton*, ed. Ronald David Emma and John T. Shawcross (New York, 1967), pp. 210–14; John M. Steadman,

"Milton's Rhetoric: Satan and the 'Unjust Discourse,'" in *Milton Studies*, I, ed. James D. Simmonds (Pittsburgh, 1969), pp. 88-91.

17. For a detailed discussion of Adam and Eve's morning hymn see Joseph Summers, *The Muse's Method* (London, 1962), chap. III.

18. "Milton's Abstract Music," *UTQ*, XXIX (1959-60), reprinted in *Milton: Modern Essays in Criticism*, ed. Arthur E. Barker (New York, 1965), p. 399.

19. For example, IV, 533-35; IX, 174-78; IX, 490-93.

20. On the similarity between Adam's soliloquy and Satan's soliloquy on Mount Niphates, see James Holly Hanford's comment in "The Dramatic Element in *Paradise Lost*," *SP*, XIV (1917), 191.

21. Kester Svendsen, "Adam's Soliloquy in Book X of *Paradise Lost*," *College English*, X (1949), reprinted in *Milton: Modern Essays in Criticism*, ed. Arthur E. Barker (New York, 1965), p. 329.

22. The ideas of this section are basically in accord with Anne Davidson Ferry's *Milton's Epic Voice* and *Milton and the Miltonic Dryden*, but my emphasis differs from Ferry's in that I am particularly concerned with the connection between *Paradise Lost* and other Renaissance writings on the Fall.

23. *The Reason of Church Government*, CM, III, pt. 1, pp. 237, 238.

24. Ibid., p. 241.

25. Newton, in his "Life of Milton," writes that Milton's third wife confirmed several things which others had reported, namely, "that her husband used to compose his poetry chiefly in winter, and on his waking in the morning would make her write down sometimes twenty or thirty verses. . . . that he stole from nobody but the Muse who inspired him; and being asked by a lady present who the Muse was, replied it was God's grace, and the Holy Spirit that visited him nightly" (*Paradise Lost*, ed. Thomas Newton et al., 3d ed. [London, 1754], vol. I, p. lxv).

26. "Milton's Abstract Music," p. 400.

27. See III, 372-415; IV, 720-25; V, 202-03.

28. For evidence of this see James H. Sims, *The Bible in Milton's Epics* (Gainesville, Fla., 1962), particularly chap. I. See also Anne Davidson Ferry's excellent discussion of the language of sacred metaphor which the narrator shares with the unfallen Adam and Eve (*Milton's Epic Voice*, chaps. IV and V).

RECALCITRANCE, DAMNATION, AND THE JUSTICE OF GOD IN *PARADISE LOST*

Desmond M. Hamlet

The persistent notion of a dichotomy in *Paradise Lost* between the narrative idea and the affective dimension of the poetry—based on Milton's supposed subconscious repudiation of basic Christian doctrine—misrepresents both the poet's understanding of the nonsentimental character of the divine love and his complex portrayal of the essentially creative and restorative nature of divine justice. In *Paradise Lost*, God's justice is an indispensable instrument of the divine restorative processes of the poem's world, whose continuous aim is to induce from the creature a truly creative response to the divine ways. It is the dramatic fulfillment of precisely this objective which is enacted, throughout the poem, in the dynamic relationship between the merciful Father and the creatively responsive Son. Satan, through the willful perversion of his God-given capacities for creative conduct, functions parodically—and so, indirectly—to confirm the poem's total, positive, moral pattern. Through his increasingly distorted career in the poem, Satan effectively exemplifies both the crippling inadequacies of all recalcitrant behavior and the inevitable process of a self-imposed damnation which accompanies an obdurate and tyrannical abuse of others.

IN HIS well-known study of Milton's Satan,[1] Sir Rostrevor Hamilton, with a cogency characteristic of the age-old debate, objected vigorously to Milton's portrait of God in *Paradise Lost* in terms which, even after William Empson's equally forceful condemnation of Milton's God,[2] are still being energetically argued today. The most recent objection to the God of *Paradise Lost* comes from Lawrence Hyman in his study of art and morality in Milton's poetry, *The Quarrel Within*.[3]

In terms reminiscent of Hamilton's argument, Hyman suggests that the main conflict in *Paradise Lost* arises from the fact that "the universe which God has created and which He governs cannot be reconciled with human standards of reason and justice" but that "this contradiction between God's ways and our human values is not a weakness in the poem but the source of its dramatic power."[4] In his essay, Hamilton, observing "a notable division between Milton the sensuous and passionate, and Milton the moralist," insists that the cleavage does not amount to a split personality, "for, short of complete harmony, the two sides can and do work together, and then only do we have in a full sense Milton the poet."[5]

However, both Hamilton and Hyman, in spite of their ostensibly positive view of Milton's art, find it more than a little difficult to accept either Milton's idea of God or the concept and function of divine justice in the poem. Instead, they cast their critical vote for the obduracy and recalcitrance of human experience in the face of "the inexplicability of God's justice."[6]

Objecting to the fact that "Milton's imagination creates an Almighty who is not first and foremost a King of Love,"[7] Hamilton argues that it is difficult not to rebel against such a God, or to sympathize with rebellion against him. The conflict between love and self-love, he suggests, is indeed "human and contemporary" and has "a great deal of interest for us." He insists, however, that

the intended lesson, so far as it is to be drawn from the contrast between Satan and the Divine Hierarchy, is spoilt and confused in the telling, because the Heaven whose harmony we are to admire is a Heaven of "judicious" Reason, whose love does not warm the heart, and whose anger therefore repels the imagination.[8]

In a similar vein, Hyman insists that "by giving full and unqualified expression to his feeling that God's actions are irrational and cruel and to his equally strong feeling that God is just and merciful, Milton is satisfying impulses that are deeply rooted in all men."[9]

Endorsing the application of a viable contextualist aesthetics to *Paradise Lost,* Hyman forcefully argues in favor of a proper appreciation of the imaginative experience of the poem in terms of the dramatic tension created by both Milton's doubts and his certainties. This is the source of the poem's strength, argues Hyman, since "it is not Milton's doctrine but his strong doubts about the doctrine that provide the emotional center of the poem."[10] Although our moral feelings are engaged, as were Milton's, "if we accept this duality in the rhythmic pattern as central to the action, we can respond to the poem without reference to our moral presuppositions," since those presuppositions will have been absorbed "in the poetic experience, in the tragic irony of the action, just as Milton's religious feelings were absorbed by the intractable myth."[11]

Clearly, Hyman's own theory of poetry is perceptive and essentially liberating, and he is correct to insist that "both the writing and the reading of great literature does involve a capacity for *going beyond our personal feelings in order to enter into another kind of experience*."[12] But surely such an aesthetic experience must, to be valid, be true for us all and would seem, most logically, to preclude preconceptions about "the stubborn intractability of experience," the need to fit God's ways "into our own concepts of justice," and the "inexplicability of God's justice,"[13] as well as the distinctly religious feelings of both the writer and the reader. For, even if we assume the possibility of such an objectivity for writer or reader, it should be clear that such a premise requires a capacity for going beyond personal feelings of every sort (including even a predisposition to avoid making moral responses of any kind) in order to enter into the *total* aesthetic experience through our involvement with a work of art. Despite his commitment to contextualist criticism, Hyman fails, I suggest, to do just that.

Admittedly, the greatness of a poem does not necessarily lie "in its power to inculcate a moral feeling."[14] Yet it is equally true that the "level of experience" which emerges from a great work of art may be indispensably informed by what Rajan calls "a certain awareness of tradition, a certain 'given' structure of values and responses [which] are taken for granted by the movement of the poem,"[15] and which—it is not unreasonable to suggest—should at least be respected in terms of the significance of those very contextual postulates. Moreover, when such a work of art happens to be *Paradise Lost*, for example, it is more than likely that a narrowly pedantic, impressionistic approach "may be more provincial than the narrow historicism it tries to overcome."[16] As Seaman correctly suggests, it is possible that the modern reader will enlarge his experience more "by the difficult process of adjusting his view to Milton's than by having Milton retailored."[17]

Milton's poetry, precisely because of its fusion of content and form (of dogma and drama), is constantly working away from the accidental and the contingent in human affairs, from an obdurate individuation (a recalcitrance of experience, if you will), toward an extraordinary apprehension of reality, a transcendent level of experience. Stanley Fish is quite right when, in his recent comment on Russell Fraser's assessment of Milton's poetry, he insists that

> Fraser assumes that Milton loses sight of a great truth about the way poetry works, but it is Milton's insight into what the working of poetry means, that is, of what it is a symptom, which underlies his aesthetic and dictates his strategy. . . . The appeal of the poetry of particulars is an appeal to something in us that Milton would have us transcend; his poetry, by working against its own best interests (in a narrow sense), works against that something and so becomes a vehicle for the raising of the reader's mind to the point where reality discloses itself. . . . Poetry is merely an inevitable casualty of this deliverance, because like all earthly forms—physical, linguistic, perceptual— it falls away when the aspiring mind embraces, and so becomes indistinguishable from, the object of its search. To be free of poetry is to be free of the self, of its uniqueness and therefore of its partiality, and this, I would argue, is the impulse behind Milton's art—to lose the self in a union with God, to exchange our (human) values for his, so that it can be truly said, "In him we live and move and have our being."[18]

Fish's insight here is instructive in two important ways. First, it clearly repudiates all notions of the validity or desirability of an intractable and recalcitrant human experience seriously involved with Milton's poetry, since to be so involved is to become free of the uniqueness of self and, thus, of its partiality—in an upward, transcendent movement, along with the essentially ego-destroying vehicle of Milton's poetry. Second, the so-called "inexplicability of God's justice" simultaneously begins to define itself, through the upward-tending poetry, in terms which are increasingly comprehensible, even if transcendent. For it, too, moves upward toward an unveiling of what, from an existentialist perspective, is a mystery, but of what progressively is thrown into sharper relief as the finite questing mind pursues the goal of union with infinite reality at the highest level of transcendental experience. The successful result is that the recalcitrant self is transformed into a malleable character, and the seemingly incomprehensible divine justice is now clearly understood for what, in fact, it always was: an instrument of the divine creative purpose.

Thus, if the moral beliefs in Milton's poetry, both explicit and implicit, are seen as being subjected to an experience within the poem which contradicts them in some essential way, it is only because we persist in driving a wedge, however surreptitiously, between Miltonic dogma and drama—evidently for the convenience and comfort of the "modern" reader. Moreover, to begin with such a premise is almost inevitably to end with the irreconcilable dichotomy between "the need to find justice in His ways and the full portrayal of His arbitrary nature" instead of with the organic union of the medium and the message which logically resolves itself into "the poet's success in justifying God's ways to man."[19]

II

One fundamental reason for our failure to appreciate Milton's fusion of dogma and drama in *Paradise Lost* and for our insistence on the "inexplicability of God's justice" in the poem is the evidently desperately felt need to fit God's ways "into our own concepts of justice."[20] For however frank a recognition we may bring to our reading of *Paradise Lost* that God's ways are not our ways, we will hardly be able to appreciate the nature and function of divine justice in the poem if we insist on approaching the world of *Paradise Lost* with intractable attitudes which are tightly controlled by our extra-contextual notions of what the justice of Milton's God ought to be or to do. It would seem to be equally reasonable, in this regard, that our reading of *Paradise Lost* should "involve a capacity for going beyond our personal feelings in order to enter into another kind of experience."[21]

Much of the confusion about Milton's God would be considerably reduced if only we would remember that Milton's treatment of God in *Paradise Lost* is "So told as earthly notion can receive" (VII, 179). Dame Helen Gardner is quite right when she argues that Milton "can no more have thought the Father of his poem to be God as He is than Michelangelo can have thought his mighty Ancient creating Adam to be anything but a faint image of the Author of all being."[22] Yet the theory of accommodation, a commonplace throughout the history of Christian thought,[23] is only a first step in any effort to understand Milton's treatment of God in *Paradise Lost*. Much more important is the recognition that for Milton, God's unchangeable eternal purpose for all his creatures is continuously and invariably motivated by the divine love. This, in turn, is so because the ultimate objective of that divine purpose, motivated by that divine love, is the growth of the creature in the divine image—a growth which depends on, more than anything else, the freely creative use of God's gifts to his creatures. For the poet of *Paradise Lost*, God's ways are designed precisely to induce such a creative response to the wide variety of challenges and opportunities represented in the epic—challenges and opportunities which may often cause those ways to appear harsh or capricious or tyrannical, but which are, in fact, only ironically so.

It is only in the context of Milton's perception and portrayal of this particular insight that we can ever hope to understand his treatment of God in *Paradise Lost*. For it is this complex of motive, process, and result which we see at work in the poem, and everything else (including all the divine attributes as well as all human and angelic response) must lead ultimately to this, or will lead erroneously to a narrow, sentimentalized view of God—in which God's love is seen as rescuing even obstinate and recalcitrant creatures from their continued state of perversity; in which atonement becomes a kind of sentimentally loving ransom imposed on the creature despite his own intentions and desires; and in which the Fall is understood to be a rather fortunate paradox because it enables God's "love" to transcend his "justice." Such sentimental notions, however, will not do, for they grossly misrepresent not only the character of the divine love as Milton understands it and its purposes for God's creatures, but also the complex methods by which, precisely because of its character, that love operates for God's creatures in God's apparently harsh ways.

It is especially in this context that justice, which J. S. Lawry correctly calls "the sharp right profile of Mercy,"[24] must be understood: as an indispensable instrument of the divine creative purpose, which is continuously seeking, from beginning to end, only the creative response of the creature to the divine ways. Consequently also, it is the response of the creature which becomes the key to his growth in the present, as it was to his growth in the past, and as it will be to his growth in the future.

Thus understood, *Paradise Lost* resists the suggestion either that it is "a monument to dead ideas"[25] or that its only future must be "as a majestic derelict, a great white elephant of poetry without real use or function."[26] For the suggested conflict, for example, between Milton's intention and the reader's response turns out to be, upon careful examination, more imagined than real, since, as has been effectively argued,[27] the response of the reader proves, more often than not, to be precisely what Milton intended that response should be. This, in fact, is the clearest evidence of the poetic interaction of Miltonic dogma and drama in *Paradise Lost*. It is because Miltonic dogma and drama demand, at the crux of their interaction in *Paradise Lost*, a creative response from the reader to "another kind of experience" which goes "beyond our personal feelings" that Milton's execution is able to guide the reader's response—much less with forced contrivance than with poetic complexity.

III

It is such complexity which we see at work, for instance, in the closing lines of the poem (XII, 641–49). Adam and Eve obviously regret that they must leave paradise, "so late thir happy seat" (642), but they do leave with confident faith, for now they are able to appreciate the virtue of freely fulfilling the divine purpose. "Some natural tears they dropp'd" (645), a perfectly normal reaction to the loss of a cherished gift; yet, just as normally, they "wip'd them soon" (645), for they know that they can once again entrust themselves to their Creator's mercy.

Despite their confidence in that mercy, however, Adam and Eve must face the new circumstances with which God's justice now confronts them. We can sense, imbedded in these final lines of the poem, the implicit thought that even this inevitable departure from paradise is not simply a matter of punishment for the Fall but another in a continuing series of trials—tests of their freedom and personal dignity in their relation with each other, but more significantly, in their relation with God. When we see them for the last time, they are poignantly human, but also basically at peace. And we can sense that their future motto will be Adam's answer to Michael's penultimate speech (XII, 557–66). Clearly, the process of regeneration, with its fundamental effects of repentance and saving faith, is well in progress.[28]

Milton shows us the unique relation between divine justice and divine mercy on a number of occasions and in a variety of ways. It is evident, for instance, in the instructions which God the Father gives to Michael at the beginning of Book XI (104–17), after the Son, interceding for the penitent Adam and Eve, has presented their prayers to the Father. That Adam and Eve, "th' unholy" (106), must leave the "hallow'd ground" (106) of Eden is irrevocable. However, Michael is instructed to drive them out "Without remorse" (105) and to "Dismiss them not disconsolate" (113). Moreover, not only is he to hide all terror from them, but he is to reveal to Adam the future, including God's promise of a new covenant with men. Yet, because Adam and Eve have sinned (and despite their penitence), Michael is instructed to "denounce / To them and to thir Progeny from thence / Perpetual banishment" (106–08). At the same time, he is to "send them forth, though sorrowing, yet in peace" (117). Adam and Eve must feel the justice of God in sorrow, yet recognize his mercy in peace.

Michael proves, of course, to be an excellent teacher, compassionately reassuring Adam of God's mercy (XI, 349–53). However, lest Adam should become forgetful of God's justice in his relief and joy, Michael is equally careful to remind him of that justice and of its practical purpose in his continuing education (XI, 355–66).

It is in the opening scenes of Book X, however, where Milton describes the actual judgment by the Son, that we witness the virtual epitome of the complex harmony of divine justice and divine mercy. From the Father's commissioning of the Son to judge the two transgressors, because

> Easy it may be seen that I intend
> Mercy colleague with Justice, sending thee
> Man's Friend, his Mediator, his design'd
> Both Ransom and Redeemer voluntary,
> And destin'd Man himself to judge Man fall'n,   (X, 58–62)

to the compassionate action of the Son when he

>   disdain'd not to begin
> Thenceforth the form of servant to assume,
> As when he wash'd his servants' feet, so now
> As Father of his Family he clad
> Thir nakedness with Skins of Beasts
>
>   .   .   .   .
>
>   but inward nakedness, much more
> Opprobrious, with his Robe of righteousness,   (X, 213–22)

the whole presentation is a graphic illustration of the practical way in which a loving God employs his justice, within the framework of his mercy, to induce in man the right response to his creative purpose. In the action of the Son, God reaches out not only to destroy the demonic in man, but especially to renovate man's impaired faculties of reason and will in preparation for a gradual and progressive regeneration.

In connection with the destruction of the demonic in man, Milton begins by describing the decisive, future overthrow of the demonic principalities and powers by the Son as the rising Christ (X, 182-91). However, Milton is careful to point out (through Michael's explanation to Adam in Book XII) that the triumph of the Son (as Christ) over the demonic forces is best effected in the gradual and practical destruction of Satan's works in man (XII, 386-95). Regarding the process of renovation and regeneration, Milton carefully demonstrates the fact that God's judgment of man is no mere pretense of justice. Not only is the Son perfectly aware of the sacrifice necessary to effect man's redemption (X, 71-77), but Adam becomes increasingly aware (through an excruciating process of self-justification, then confusion, then despair, then remorse and penitence) of his desperate need for renovation and regeneration.

At the end of Adam's soliloquy, for instance, not only does Adam admit that the responsibility for his fall was solely his, not God's (X, 832-33), but he expresses the wish that, just as "all the blame lights due" (X, 833) on him for his own corruption, "So might the wrath" (X, 834). And Adam can express such a wish only because he has been judged earlier by the Son, who did so judge Adam that Adam has come to realize, as he clearly admits, "in mee all / Posterity stands curst" (X, 817-18).

In one of his most dramatically powerful descriptions, Milton portrays, through Adam's painful experiences, the sobering reality of divine justice. Not only does Adam cry out painfully to his conscience (X, 842-44), but he literally writhes upon the ground in despair, cursing his very creation, accusing death and truth and divine justice of "tardy execution" (X, 852), and shamelessly abusing Eve, belligerently spurning her effort to console him with her soft words (X, 850-908). Eve, for her part, is no less distraught, as her physical appearance and her pitiful remarks make clear (X, 910-36).

Significantly, all of this is effected initially, as Milton makes clear, through the person and action of the Son, to whom the Father has transferred "All Judgment, whether in Heav'n, or Earth, or Hell" (X,

57), and upon whom "the worst . . . must light" (X, 73), in order
that he "may mitigate thir doom" (X, 76). As the Son puts it, "I shall
temper so / Justice with Mercy, as may illustrate most / Them fully
satisfied, and thee appease" (X, 77–79). The Son is concerned to make
Adam and Eve "fully satisfied," through the tempering of justice with
mercy, because he knows himself to be not merely their judge, but
especially "Man's Friend" (X, 60) and "Redeemer voluntary" (X, 61),
whose office includes the essential function of inducing in the fallen
Adam and Eve (through his use of tempered justice) the penitence
and faith which we begin to see at work in the closing scenes of
Book X. As the poet is careful to depict for us (first through the
despair of the fallen pair, and then through their repentance and faith),
neither justice nor mercy loses its essential quality because of its dependence on the coexistent attribute. Justice is no less justice because
it is tempered with mercy. Similarly, mercy is no less mercy because
it uses the instrument of justice to implement itself in a way that
"may illustrate most" its practical application and effect.

IV

It is especially in his portrayal of the council in heaven in Book
III that Milton characterizes the practical application and effect of
God's justice in his delineation of the developing stages of the Son's
exemplary response to the Father's inducing ways. It is neither possible
nor necessary to deny the contention that God "seems to be playing
to the gallery of his auditors, the Son and the unfallen angels,"[29] in
this scene. Impossible, because that is the effect we get from Milton's
presentation of the Father; and unnecessary, because that is precisely
the effect Milton wishes us to get. However, to go on to regard the
Father's role in this scene as "little better than celestial hypocrisy"[30]
is to fail to ask a very basic question about that role: Why such a
role?—both in terms of what actually happens in the scene and in
terms of the Father's ironic (even if anthropomorphic) pose.[31]

Significantly, there is nothing in the "Argument" to Book III, for
example, to suggest that Milton conceived of his God as anything
but a God of love, whose ways include justice and wrath, as well
as mercy—all of which are, however, motivated by his gracious purpose
toward man. Admittedly, we ought not to ignore the subtleties and

nuances of the language of poetry, nor should we overlook the brevity and conciseness of the prose statement. It is not likely, however, that Milton would have stated in his prose "Argument" what he did not intend to develop in his poetic presentation. The fact is that Milton's idea of God is precisely the same in both the prose "Argument" and the poetry which follows.

Milton explains in the "Argument" that God clears himself of all responsibility for man's Fall, "having created Man free and able enough to have withstood his Tempter: yet declares his purpose of grace towards him."[32] Exactly the same point is made in the corresponding lines of the poetry that follows (III, 98-99; 116-19; 130-34). Moreover, it is most significant that what the Son actually does in his first speech is to praise the Father for his promise of grace toward man. Milton tells us in the "Argument" that "the Son of God renders praises to his Father for the manifestation of his gracious purpose towards Man."[33] And the poetic parallel is no less interesting (III, 144-49). Obviously, the Son would hardly have used such words unless the Father had, in fact, so manifested his gracious purpose toward man.

Milton confirms this fact toward the end of the scene, for it is as "Father of Mercy and Grace" (III, 401) that the angels hail the Father. Moreover, what the angels go on to sing of the Father, as well as the manner in which this is expressed by the poet, is quite significant:

> Father of Mercy and Grace, thou didst not doom
> So strictly, but much more to pity incline:
> No sooner did thy dear and only Son
> Perceive thee purpos'd not to doom frail Man
> So strictly, but much more to pity inclin'd.   (III, 401-05)

We should note here not only the use of the past tense ("didst not doom," "[didst] incline," "did . . . / Perceive thee purpos'd not to doom," and "inclin'd") and the adverbial phrase "So strictly" (together with the negative "not"), but also the obvious emphatic repetition of the thought: not to doom so strictly, but much more to pity inclined. Furthermore, however promptly the Son responded to the Father's inclination to be merciful, he did, after all, respond. Clearly, the angels have absolutely no doubt either about the appropriateness of the title they are ascribing to the Father, or about the initial indication, by the Father, to be merciful, and the consequent response, by the Son, to the Father's declared intention.

At the same time, neither the true nature of Milton's God nor the fact that he initiates the whole process of the Atonement should encourage us to lose sight of the unstated purpose or of the dramatic significance of the scene. Milton did not do so, and neither should we. The fact is that the burden of the scene of the council in heaven rests on the Son's exemplary response to the Father's inducing ways, and everything else in the scene is intended to contribute to "the dramatic role which the Father purposely adopts in order to challenge the Son and to induce from him a loving and sacrificial response."[34]

It is only from this perspective, for instance, that the section of Book III which deals with the crux of Milton's meaning (210–16)— and which has evidently caused some readers the greatest difficulty[35]— becomes intelligible as an important part of the Father's conscious effort to challenge the Son and to induce from him a response that is sufficiently creative and exemplary. Most significantly, Milton presents the Father as recognizing a decisive relation between the two great issues: "rigid satisfaction" and "charity so dear"—itself an indication of the extent to which the Father's inducing ways can themselves appear *rigid* and *dear*.

Isabel MacCaffrey's point is well taken that the great question with which the Father's second speech concludes "leads from theory to practice, from the 'great idea' to history."[36] This, in fact, is the point of the entire episode. Far from being a theological blunder, the great question which the Father poses (III, 213–16) is entirely consistent with his essential purpose of inducing from the Son a loving and sacrificial response. No less consistent with the Father's adopted role of a merely harsh, demanding Deity is the rigid satisfaction of his justice (III, 210–12). Further, by associating the great question with the rigid demand that his justice be satisfied, the Father is able to demonstrate, through the Son's creative response, the essentially instrumental nature of even such an apparently harsh and unconscionable demand. Thus, both the Father's apparently unreasonable demand and his seemingly incredible question are, in terms of his adopted role, just as logical an instrument of his larger creative purpose for the Son as his justice (in Books X, XI, and XII) will later be a similar instrument of his larger creative purpose for Adam and Eve.

Moreover, the appropriateness of both the Father's adopted role and his seemingly insoluble question (based on his apparently harsh demand) is clearly confirmed by the obvious success of what, in fact, takes place: first, through the great angelic silence (which sets off and heightens the Son's sacrificial offer), and second, by the Son's second speech (in which he dutifully and lovingly offers to make the necessary sacrifice for man). Thus can the Father hail the Son "My sole complacence" (III, 276), proclaim his exaltation because he has been found "By Merit more than Birthright Son of God" (III, 309), and advise the angelic host to "Adore the Son, and honor him as mee" (III, 343); and thus the angelic choir can acclaim the Son: "O unexampl'd love . . . nowhere to be found less than Divine!" (III, 410–11).

V

Totally different from the creative response of the Son is the attitude of Satan, whose entire career in the poem is a glaring example of recalcitrance and incorrigibility. Consistently refusing to respond positively to all opportunities for redemption, Satan blindly confuses repentance with lame submission (IV, 79–82) and commits himself to a gross perversion of his heaven-permitted opportunities for any kind of genuine creative response (IV, 110–13). Even when, on Niphates' top, he is prompted by his conscience (IV, 23–26) to consider the possibility of repentance (IV, 93–94), he bluntly recommits himself to an incorrigible perversity: "Evil be thou my Good" (IV, 110).

If, for the sake of argument, we grant Empson's famous condemnation of Milton's God,[37] then it would be only fair to applaud Satan's obduracy, and at least to respect, with Helen Gardner, the heroic dimensions of this cosmic Macbeth.[38] Two facts argue against such a conclusion, however: first, Milton's God, as we have seen, is anything but a harsh tyrant and is, as a matter of fact, "first and foremost a King of Love";[39] second, Satan's rebellion, however energetic and recalcitrant, is (despite Werblowsky's essentially enlightening discussion)[40] that of "a hero darkened and perverted,"[41] or, to put the responsibility where it rightly belongs, a hero who darkens and perverts himself. As Hamilton correctly observes, "sin is terrible because it is the revolt against love, not because it is the revolt against sheer power."[42] Applied to Satan, this insight pinpoints the crux of Satan's problem in *Paradise Lost*, which Hamilton partly perceives when he argues in favor of

the rebellion . . . of a Prometheus, not of a Satan: a rebellion founded on
the principle of love, not of self-seeking and personal ambition. There was
room in Milton's Heaven for a wholly splendid rebel. . . . Such a figure,
fighting in a hopeless cause, would be worthy of unstinted admiration, and
we may be inclined to transfer it undiminished to Satan, who showed some
of the proper heroic qualities. But Satan, though a hero, is a hero darkened
and perverted; admiration cannot blind us to the selfishness of his pride.[43]

One wonders what Sir Rostrevor's conclusions would have been had
he been able to recognize the fundamentally creative purposes of
"Milton's Almighty."[44]

The fact is that Satan's commitment to evil, at the end of his
soliloquy on Niphates' top, for instance (IV, 110–13), despite the agonies
of his awakened conscience, underscores the enormity of his perversion
and calls attention also to Milton's sophisticated sense of the complexity
of Satanic evil. Looked at from this perspective, all notions about
Satan as the hero of *Paradise Lost*, or as the consummate fool of
Milton's epic, ought to be closely reexamined in terms of the poet's
keen awareness of such perversity. Correspondingly, the source of
such perversion and evil ought to be understood not merely in terms
of pride or ambition or self-assertion or disobedience or any number
of partial Satanic failings, but essentially in terms of the whole complex
of Satanic aberrations which only together can properly define the
primary Satanic culpability: the obdurate and incorrigible distortion
of his God-given powers and opportunities.

Hyman agrees, to some extent, with Sir Rostrevor Hamilton's
understanding of Satan's character, at least in terms of "the heroic
energy of Satan."[45] However, Hyman would probably seriously question Hamilton's differentiation between "the outward appearance and
inner reality."[46] For Hyman,

everything in a poem is real. The actions of Satan do not then have to be
explained away, but accepted as being just as much a part of Milton's universe
as the actions of God. In such an interpretation, since we are concerned with
the myth rather than the theology of Christianity, we can see Hell and Heaven,
evil and good, not only as polar opposites but as interdependent forces.[47]

In fact, Hyman argues the exciting thesis that "from the literary perspective the tragic stature of Satan is not a problem but is consistent with
the pattern of the entire poem."[48] Consequently, Hyman is evidently
far from bothered by what Hamilton finds "a dark and repellent idea."
As Hamilton puts it,

we cannot be reconciled to 'permissive' evil, which must remain a mystery, unless we are satisfied that behind it is a more than human mercy. In *Paradise Lost* Satan is permitted to have power, only in order that he may 'heap on himself damnation'; it is a dark and repellent idea.[49]

Despite his misreading of the basic character of Milton's God,[50] Hamilton's comment pinpoints a crucial issue in any consideration of the recalcitrance of Milton's Satan: the whole question of the reality of Satan's power. Despite his insistence on what amounts to a virtual Manichean struggle between God and Satan in *Paradise Lost*, Hyman is, in fact, deeply concerned about this issue, as his comment on Northrop Frye's thesis regarding the parodic nature of the typical demonic "act" would seem to indicate.[51] Significantly, Hyman, unlike either Hamilton or Frye, does not analyze this crucial issue in Satan's relationship to the God of *Paradise Lost*—either from the perspective of the issue of "permissive evil" or from the viewpoint of Satan's possible parodic posture in the poem.

As a matter of fact, the question of the reality of Satan's actions is vital to "the pattern of the entire poem." Admittedly, "everything in a poem is real," including the actions of Satan in *Paradise Lost*. Precisely because of this, however, it would seem reasonable to ask whether—especially from the contextualist perspective—Satan's actions (indeed, Satan's entire character) serve the pattern of the entire poem in terms of "the amazing similarity and interdependence"— "in the struggle between Satan and God"—and despite the fact that "we are told, of course, by the narrator that God and Satan are completely opposed."[52] My argument is that they do not, essentially because, though capable of self-fulfillment (in terms of the pattern of the entire poem), Satan chooses instead to pervert his God-given powers (of reason and will) and his heaven-permitted opportunities (for positive, creative response).

Satan's distortion of his God-given powers and his heaven-permitted opportunities is portrayed by the poet especially in terms of Satan's falsehood. And that falsehood expresses itself in *Paradise Lost* not only in his perpetual cunning and treachery throughout his entire career in the poem,[53] but especially in his virtually unavoidable use of empty rhetoric and bombast, as well as in the essentially parodic mode through which his evil schemes are represented by the poet. Moreover, to recognize the remarkable affinity between Satan's themes and his most effective style of actualizing them is, in fact, to recognize Satan's basically parodic posture throughout *Paradise Lost*.

Despite his elaborate and dynamic characteristics, as they are portrayed by the poet in Books I and II (and elsewhere in the poem), Satan, though contributing indeed to the total imaginative experience, nevertheless fails to confirm the fundamental pattern of the entire poem. And he so fails simply because he is false to the imagistic, linguistic, tonal, thematic, and structural patterns which together define the total frame of reference (essentially characterized by the divine creative purposes) against which all the major characters of the poem must be measured and analyzed. Ultimately, it is not Satan (or for that matter, any single character in the poem) that determines the poetic structure, theme, tone, language, and imagery (which only together can determine the total imaginative experience) of the work, but all of these elements, integrally fused, which must portray and define each of the characters of *Paradise Lost*.

Seen from this perspective, the character of Satan does indeed contribute to the total imaginative experience of the poem. However, this is so not because that character embodies or represents the poet's "strong doubts about the doctrine,"[54] or because he best exemplifies the so-called intractable Christian myth, but because the character of Satan (in terms of the total thematic and stylistic scheme of the work) confirms the poet's vision only indirectly. The character of Satan succeeds precisely because it "fails," and it "fails" because it is essentially incapable of surmounting or escaping what MacCaffrey has called the "larger design" (or the "moral pattern," if you will)[55]— itself characterized by a thematic and stylistic harmony which, in its turn, is informed from beginning to end by the total poetic vision.

Unquestionably "moral" in its total structural pattern, as well as in its total poetic vision, *Paradise Lost* nevertheless, I am arguing, does exactly what Hyman understands it basically to do—that is, to accommodate its "contradictions" and to unite its polarities within a complex artistic structure which is characterized by a viable emotional center and a dynamic dramatic intensity. The difference between his point of view and mine, as I understand it, however, is that whereas Hyman insists on assessing the worth of Milton's poetry in terms of its ability "to make us aware of the limitations of the moral categories when they are confronted by the complexities of human experience,"[56]

I am suggesting that in the world of Milton's poems (that is to say, in the context of their own existence), the imaginative experience is undeniably permeated by a moral significance, based on a total moral pattern, which is just as capable of enveloping and transforming notions of intractable human experience as it is of challenging and expanding limited moral categories. In short, I completely agree that "the imaginative experience of the poem is indeed permeated by a morality, but it is not a morality bound up with any set of doctrines."[57] Indeed, it is a morality which transcends and transforms doctrines and theories of practically every sort.

As a matter of fact, the reader is not being asked by the poet to reconcile the characteristics of rebellion and submission in the work. Rather, the reader is being guided by the poet's complex execution to recognize that such a reconciliation, in fact, already exists within the "larger design" of *Paradise Lost,* and to the extent that he is capable of "unveiling the mystery,"[58] to respond to that larger (even if complex) harmony.

VI

St. Augustine makes a significant comment on the question of antitheses which is pertinent, to some extent, to the present point. In discussing "the beauty of the universe, which becomes, by God's ordinance, more brilliant by the opposition of contraries," Augustine declares:

For God would never have created any, I do not say angel, but even man, whose future wickedness He foreknew, unless He had equally known to what uses *in behalf of the good* He could turn him, thus embellishing the course of the ages, as it were an exquisite poem set off with antitheses.[59]

Augustine appears here not only to recognize the beauty of "an exquisite poem set off with antitheses," but also to applaud such a process of artistic effort in the context, and for the purpose, of enhancing the fundamental objective (in this case of God's Creation, "in behalf of the good") by utilizing even the antithetical.

But Augustine's point here is far from incidental, as is clear from his discussion, in the preceding paragraph, of "the flaw of wickedness." To Augustine, "the flaw of wickedness is not nature, but contrary to nature, and has its origin, not in the Creator, but in the will."[60] Augustine is insistent on this point, vigorously arguing a few chapters later that "the angels who, though created good, are yet evil now, became so by their own will. And this will was not made evil by their good nature, unless by its voluntary defection from good; for good is not the cause of evil, but a defection from good is."[61] Moreover, Augustine not only pinpoints the origin of evil but also attempts to establish the purpose of the Creator's particular response to, and use of, that evil. As he puts it, "God, as He is the supremely good Creator of good natures, so is He of evil wills the most just Ruler; so that, while they make an ill use of good natures, He makes a good use even of evil wills."[62] Finally, in discussing the natural gradations of being, especially regarding their free will and their response to the divine goodness, Augustine clearly shows a keen sense of the enormity of the Satanic perversion when he asserts that "of such consequence in rational creatures is the weight, so to speak, of will and of love, that though in the order of nature angels rank above men, yet, by the scale of justice, good men are of greater value than bad angels."[63]

These salient points in Augustine's understanding of the Creator's permission of, and response to, the evil in the universe are clearly supported by Milton in *De Doctrina Christiana* (Book I, chaps. VIII and IX). For example, Milton explains, in commenting on Isaiah xlv, 7, "I make peace and create evil": "that is, what afterwards became evil, and now remains so; for whatever God created was originally good, as he himself testifies, Gen. i."[64] "Nor does God make that will evil which was before good," Milton further explains, "but the will being already in a state of perversion, he influences it in such a manner, that out of its own wickedness it either operates good for others, or punishment for itself."[65] Regarding the difficult question of God's "hardening the heart" or "blinding the understanding," Milton asserts that

as God's instigating the sinner does not render him the author of sin, so neither does his hardening the heart or blinding the understanding involve that consequence; inasmuch as he does not produce these effects by infusing an evil disposition, but on the contrary by employing such just and kind methods, *as ought rather to soften the hearts of sinners than harden them.* First, by his long-suffering. . . . Secondly, by urging his own good and reasonable commands in opposition to the obstinacy of the wicked.[66]

Finally, concerning the fallen angels and Satan, Milton explains that "the evil angels are reserved for punishment." Although they are permitted to wander throughout the whole earth, the air, and even heaven itself to execute God's judgments, their proper abode is hell, from which they cannot escape without the command of God. Though their knowledge is great, it "tends rather to aggravate than diminish their misery; so that they utterly despair of their salvation."[67]

These fundamental points in Milton's understanding of evil and its operation in the universe are at the center of the integrity of divine justice as it is represented by the poet in *Paradise Lost*. For example, not only does the father, contemplating the perversity of the fallen angels, declare in Book III:

> The first sort by thir own suggestion fell
> Self-tempted, self-deprav'd; Man falls deceiv'd
> By th' other first: Man therefore shall find grace,
> The other none,   (III, 129–32)

but the poet makes abundantly clear, at several places throughout the epic,[68] the inescapable consequences of angelic apostasy, precisely because, as the Father tells the Son during his first speech in Book III,

> Such I created all th' Ethereal Powers
> And Spirits, both them who stood and them who fail'd;
> Freely they stood who stood, and fell who fell.   (III, 100–02)

And not much later, in the same speech:

> I form'd them free, and free they must remain,
> Till they enthrall themselves: I else must change
> Thir nature, and revoke the high Decree
> Unchangeable, Eternal, which ordain'd
> Thir freedom: they themselves ordain'd thir fall.
>
> (III, 124–28)

This is exactly Satan's point during his soliloquy on Mount Niphates (IV, 63–67), and despite his attempted rationalization (IV, 67–70), he does admit that "against his thy will / Chose freely what it now so justly rues" (IV, 71–72). Satan is absolutely right also about "what it now so justly rues," as he painfully, but accurately, makes clear (IV, 73–102). In fact, Satan's entire soliloquy on Niphates' top, as Merritt Hughes correctly suggests, not only reviews "his private experience on the way to the tyrant's fall into the trap of leadership," but is also "simply the obverse of the public experience of the society

which Michael describes to Adam as doomed to servitude 'When upstart
Passions catch the Government / From Reason' [XII, 88–89]."[69] Hughes'
point is well taken that in the world of *Paradise Lost*, Satan is "the
archetypal tyrant."[70]

Understandably disturbed by "the great losses" to the human race
outlined by Michael in Books XI and XII, W. J. Grace suggests that
it would appear that "any experiment in freedom entails big losses,"
and that "God must then have thought that freedom was worth such
a price."[71] Apart from the fact that in the world of the poem, God's
creating all his creatures with "Rational Liberty" (XII, 82) is no "experiment" or gamble, as the poet makes clear throughout the epic
(for example, III, 100–16; IV, 66–67; 71–72; V, 233–37; 529–40, and
IX, 1173–74, to cite some of the more significant references), the answer
to Grace's query is unequivocally affirmative. However, two observations are of crucial importance here. First, the reader, it would appear,
is not intended by the poet to accept such losses "calmly." On the
contrary, he ought indeed to react with an abhorrence comparable
to Adam's, but also with a twofold recognition of the reprehensible
nature of evil and of the possibility of still exercising one's rational
liberty for good in a situation in which, most realistically, "so shall
the World go on, / To good malignant, to bad men benign, / Under
her own weight groaning" (XII, 537–39). Second, the poet appears
indeed to be suggesting that it is only such a recognition on the part
of the reader (as is finally true for Adam in the imaginative experience
of the poem) that will correctly define the heinousness of evil, egoism,
and injustice and simultaneously, the desirability of good, altruism,
and true liberty in the inevitable relationships which all men are required to establish and vigilantly to pursue.

Nor can we justifiably read into the total pattern of the poem
the mistaken notion, so frequently attributed to Milton, that the exercise of such rational liberty requires an existential situation in which
evil is as necessary as good, egoism as requisite as altruism, and injustice
as indispensable as liberty either for right human choice or, as is sometimes vigorously argued, for the most creative structure and vision
of all significant poetic execution. For Milton, as Irene Samuel suggests,
it is finally a question of "the 'ratio' of virtue," in connection with
the complex issue of the existence of evil in the world,

as virtue is tested, brought to light, or exercised by evil. . . . He [Milton]
did not hold that virtue needs evil—the doctrine sometimes misread into *Areo-*

pagitica—and he did not condone the evils of willed injustice. Satan is the fit target of just anger in *Paradise Lost* as in himself and his policies he sums up every evil detail in the human panorama of Books XI and XII.[72]

Significantly, during his painful experience of misery and despair, prompted by his accusing conscience, Adam readily likens his situation to Satan's—both in motive and in result, both in terms of his misuse of his God-given opportunities and in terms of the harsh reality of divine justice (X, 837–44). Few readers will miss the echo here of the Father's decree during his second speech in Book III regarding the obstinately perverted misuse of God-given powers and opportunities (198–202) or of Satan's admission on Mount Niphates (IV, 93–109). Satan is the "fit target" of damnation in *Paradise Lost* precisely because, as he so accurately confesses, "never can true reconcilement grow / Where wounds of deadly hate have pierc'd so deep" (IV, 98–99), especially when such "deadly hate" actualizes itself in an incorrigible and tyrannical abuse of others.

Fortunately for Adam, he—after an excruciating process (comparable to Satan's on Mount Niphates) of wrestling with the stark reality of the instrumental divine justice—changes his developing perversion of his opportunities for redemption into a positive, creative response that is consonant with the larger divine creative purposes for all of God's creatures. Satan, on the other hand, is quite right when he observes "all Good to me is lost" (IV, 109), after he has dismissed all chances for redemption, with his perverted "Farewell Remorse" (IV, 109). Later, as he prepares to implement his evil strategy against man, Satan is right again when he declares:

> all good to me becomes
> Bane, and in Heav'n much worse would be my state.
> But neither here seek I, no nor in Heav'n
> To dwell, unless by Maistring Heav'n's Supreme;
> Nor hope to be myself less miserable
> By what I seek, but others to make such
> As I, though thereby worse to me redound.   (IX, 122–28)

As Death so appropriately asserts in Book II, Satan is—we, too, realize —"Hell-doom'd" (697). For unlike Adam, who makes a positive and *re*-creative about-face (X, 1097–1104), Satan never does.

State University of New York, Buffalo

NOTES

1. *Hero or Fool?* (1944; reprint ed., Folcroft, Pa., 1969).
2. *Milton's God* (London, 1961).
3. (Port Washington, N.Y., 1972).
4. Ibid., p. 56.
5. *Hero or Fool?*, pp. 37–38.
6. Hyman, *Quarrel Within*, p. 71.
7. *Hero or Fool?*, p. 35.
8. Ibid., p. 41.
9. *Quarrel Within*, p. 56.
10. Ibid., pp. 36–37.
11. Ibid., p. 73.
12. Ibid.; italics added.
13. Ibid., pp. 73, 71.
14. Ibid., p. 116.
15. *Milton's "Paradise Lost": Books I and II* (New York, 1964), p. xxii.
16. John E. Seaman, *The Moral Paradox of "Paradise Lost"* (The Hague, 1971), p. 10.
17. Ibid.
18. "Inaction and Silence: The Reader in *Paradise Regained*," in *Calm of Mind: Tercentenary Essays on "Paradise Regained" and "Samson Agonistes" in honor of John S. Diekhoff*, ed. Joseph Anthony Wittreich, Jr. (Cleveland, 1971), pp. 26–27.
19. Hyman, *Quarrel Within*, p. 115.
20. See n. 13.
21. See n. 12.
22. *A Reading of "Paradise Lost"* (London, 1965), p. 28.
23. See, for example, C. A. Patrides, "*Paradise Lost* and the Theory of Accommodation," in *Bright Essence: Studies in Milton's Theology*, ed. W. B. Hunter, C. A. Patrides, and J. H. Adamson (Salt Lake City, Utah, 1971), pp. 159–63; and Patrides, *Milton and the Christian Tradition* (Oxford, 1966), pp. 9 ff., 24, 94, 210, and 283. See Milton's own statement on the question in *De Doctrina Christiana*, Book I, chap. II (*John Milton: Complete Poems and Major Prose*, ed. Merritt Y. Hughes [New York, 1957], pp. 905–07).
24. *The Shadow of Heaven: Matter and Stance in Milton's Poetry* (Ithaca, 1968), p. 160.
25. Sir Walter Raleigh, *Milton* (London, 1900), p. 88.
26. A. J. A. Waldock, *"Paradise Lost" and Its Critics* (Cambridge, 1947), p. 8.
27. See Stanley E. Fish, " 'Not so much a teaching as an intangling': Milton's Method in *Paradise Lost*," in *Milton: Modern Judgements*, ed. Alan Rudrum (London, 1968), pp. 104–35. Cf. chap. I of Fish's *Surprised by Sin: the Reader in "Paradise Lost"* (New York, 1967). See also his "Discovery as Form in *Paradise Lost*," in *New Essays on "Paradise Lost*," ed. Thomas Kranidas (Berkeley and Los Angeles, 1969), pp. 1–14, where his understanding of the reader's response to the poem is reiterated and expanded in terms of the poem's "form."
28. See *De Doctrina Christiana*, Book I, chap. XIX (*The Student's Milton*, ed. Frank Allen Patterson [New York, 1961], p. 1015).
29. John Peter, *A Critique of "Paradise Lost"* (New York, 1960), p. 12.
30. Ibid.

31. See Arthur E. Barker, *"Paradise Lost:* The Relevance of Regeneration," in *"Paradise Lost": A Tercentenary Tribute,* ed. Balachandra Rajan (Toronto, 1969), p. 69. See also Michael Wilding, *Milton's "Paradise Lost"* (Sydney, 1969), pp. 64–65.

32. *John Milton: Complete Poems and Major Prose,* ed. Merritt Y. Hughes (New York, 1957), p. 257. All references to *Paradise Lost* are to this edition of Milton's poem.

33. Ibid.

34. Barker, "Relevance of Regeneration," p. 68. See also Stella P. Revard, "The Dramatic Function of the Son in *Paradise Lost:* A Commentary on Milton's 'Trinitarianism,'" *JEGP,* LXVI (1967), 45–58. Revard's understanding of the Son's exercise of his free will is especially instructive and reinforces her thesis that "the Son's career in *Paradise Lost* is a progress from good to better; he is constantly in the process of proving himself by assuming and exercising more power" (p. 50).

35. See, for example, Peter, *A Critique,* pp. 13–14, and Patrides, *Milton and the Christian Tradition,* p. 158.

36. "The Theme of *Paradise Lost,* Book III," in *New Essays on "Paradise Lost,"* ed. Thomas Kranidas (Berkeley and Los Angeles, 1969), p. 74.

37. *Milton's God;* see especially chaps. 2 and 3, pp. 36–146. I must express my partial agreement with Kitty Cohen's recent comments on Empson's inadequate criticism of *Paradise Lost* ("Milton's God in Council and War," in *Milton Studies,* III, ed. James D. Simmonds [Pittsburgh, 1971], pp. 159 and 181). Cohen is quite right that Empson's thesis "is not substantiated by the text." On the other hand, Empson may well claim validity for his thesis on the basis of his own reading of the history of Christianity (or even of Milton's theology and religious attitudes), as is implied indeed both by the inclusion of chapter 7, "Christianity" (pp. 229–77), and by the particular emphases in that section of Empson's work. A far better approach to a reasonably accurate analysis of *Paradise Lost* would seem to lie with a perspective whose emphasis is less on particular readings of Christian history as a basis for one's analysis of Milton's poem than on the text of *Paradise Lost.* Indeed, Cohen's own understanding of Milton's God, even based as it is on the text, does not completely avoid the impression of a dangerous and unnecessary dichotomy between Hebraic and Christian thought in the biblical background of *Paradise Lost* and implies precisely the sentimentalized view of Christianity with which my own discussion sharply disagrees.

38. "Milton's Satan and the Theme of Damnation in Elizabethan Tragedy," *English Studies,* I (1948), 46–66, reprinted in *Milton: Modern Essays in Criticism,* ed. Arthur E. Barker (New York, Oxford, and London, 1965), pp. 205–17.

39. See n. 7.

40. R. J. Zwi Werblowsky, *Lucifer and Prometheus: A Study of Milton's Satan* (London, 1952).

41. Hamilton, *Hero or Fool?,* p. 37.

42. Ibid., p. 35.

43. Ibid., p. 37.

44. Ibid.

45. Hyman, *Quarrel Within,* p. 38.

46. Ibid. The words are Hyman's, but the thought would seem to lie at the heart of Hamilton's distinction between Prometheus and Satan. See n. 42. See also Werblowsky, *Lucifer and Prometheus,* pp. 47–48.

47. *Quarrel Within,* p. 38.

48. Ibid., p. 41.

49. Hamilton, *Hero or Fool?*, p. 35.

50. Although Hamilton correctly observes that "terror is not confined to the Old Testament, and there are stern and terrible sayings of Christ in the New, which cannot be disregarded without producing a false and diluted Christianity" (*Hero or Fool?*, p. 35), he fails to understand the nature and function of the instrumental divine justice in *Paradise Lost;* the "heinous wickedness and abysmal evil of Satan" (by what Werblowsky correctly calls "a very dangerous *sous-entendu,* a critical shift of emphasis" [*Lucifer and Prometheus,* p. 48]); and the complexities (including the skillful use of irony by Milton) of the poetic structure of *Paradise Lost.* The inevitable result is, in fact, Hamilton's false, "diluted," and oversimplified notion of what the God of *Paradise Lost ought* to be and to do.

51. *Quarrel Within*, p. 38.

52. Ibid., p. 40.

53. For some of the more pointed references to Satan's falsehood, guile, and deception, see, for example, I, 33–35, 120–22, 528–29, 645–47; II, 815–16; III, 639, 681; IV, 83–88, 115–16, 121–22; V, 243, 709–10; VI, 120–21, 901–02; IX, 733–34, 904–05; and X, 485.

54. Hyman, *Quarrel Within*, pp. 36–37.

55. *"Paradise Lost" as "Myth"* (Cambridge, Mass., 1959), p. 208. See Hyman, *Quarrel Within*, p. 37.

56. Hyman, *Quarrel Within*, p. 116.

57. Ibid., p. v.

58. See p. 270.

59. *The City of God*, Book XI, chap. 18, trans. Marcus Dods, in *Great Books of the Western World*, ed. Robert Maynard Hutchins (Chicago, Ill., 1952), vol. XVIII, p. 331, italics added.

60. Ibid., Book XI, chap. 17.

61. Ibid., Book XII, chap. 9, p. 347.

62. Ibid., Book XI, chap. 17, p. 331.

63. Ibid., Book XI, chap. 16.

64. In *John Milton: Complete Poems and Major Prose*, ed. Hughes, p. 984. This would seem also to be the most satisfactory interpretation of that otherwise inscrutable section in Book II of *Paradise Lost* where the poet tells us that "God by curse / Created evil" a universe of death (II, 622–23):

> for evil only good,
> Where all life dies, death lives, and Nature breeds,
> Perverse, all monstrous, all prodigious things,
> Abominable, inutterable, and worse
> Than Fables yet have feign'd, or fear conceiv'd,
> *Gorgons* and *Hydras*, and *Chimeras* dire.   (II, 623–28)

Cf. the ironic lines in Book IV, 194–204, with their subtle interplay on death, life, and the perversion of the good. See also IV, 423–26.

65. *Complete Poems and Major Prose*, p. 986.

66. Ibid., p. 987; italics added.

67. Ibid., p. 992.

68. For example, in the words of the poet (I, 44–48, 53–54, 70–72, 209–20, 607–08; IV, 15–23, 846–50; IX, 467–70; and X, 509–17); the Father (III, 84–86; and V, 611–15); the Son (VI, 736–39); the unfallen angels (IV, 570–71, 823–24, 835–40; V, 541–43, 883–85;

and VI, 172-73, 181); the fallen angels (I, 141-42; and II, 85-89, 158-59, 197-99, 315-31, 377-78); Satan himself (II, 29-30; IV, 73-78, 86-92, 375, 508-11; and IV, 889-90); and even Death (II, 693-97, 699-700).

69. "Satan and the 'Myth' of the Tyrant," in his *Ten Perspectives on Milton* (New Haven, 1965), p. 195.

70. Ibid., p. 166.

71. *Ideas in Milton* (Notre Dame, Ind., 1968), p. 99.

72. *Dante and Milton: "The Commedia" and "Paradise Lost"* (Ithaca, 1966), p. 182. See also Thomas H. Blackburn's excellent essay, " 'Uncloister'd Virtue': Adam and Eve in Milton's Paradise," in *Milton Studies*, III, ed. James D. Simmonds (Pittsburgh, 1971), pp. 119-37.